The … Succession

IN SOUTH AFRICA

PRIVATE LAW

JUANITA JAMNECK (Editor)
CHRISTA RAUTENBACH (Editor)
MOHAMED PALEKER | ANTON VAN DER LINDE
MICHAEL WOOD-BODLEY

OXFORD
UNIVERSITY PRESS
SOUTHERN AFRICA

OXFORD
UNIVERSITY PRESS
Southern Africa

Oxford University Press Southern Africa (Pty) Ltd

Vasco Boulevard, Goodwood, Cape Town, Republic of South Africa
P O Box 12119, N1 City, 7463, Cape Town, Republic of South Africa

Oxford University Press Southern Africa (Pty) Ltd is a subsidiary of
Oxford University Press, Great Clarendon Street, Oxford OX2 6DP.

The Press, a department of the University of Oxford, furthers the University's objective of excellence in research, scholarship, and education by publishing worldwide in

Oxford New York

Auckland Cape Town Dar es Salaam Hong Kong Karachi
Kuala Lumpur Madrid Melbourne Mexico City Nairobi
New Delhi Shanghai Taipei Toronto

With offices in

Argentina Austria Brazil Chile Czech Republic France Greece
Guatemala Hungary Italy Japan Poland Portugal Singapore South Korea
Switzerland Turkey Ukraine Vietnam

Published in South Africa
by Oxford University Press Southern Africa (Pty) Ltd, Cape Town

The law of succession in South Africa

ISBN 978 0 19 598643 3

First published 2009
Second impression 2010

Publisher: Penny Lane
Development editor: Mark Townsend
Editors: Tammin Barker, Jeannie van den Heever
Designer: Christopher Davies
Cover design: Oswald Kurtin/Schalk Burger
Indexer: Adrienne Pretorius
Set in Utopia Std 9.5 pt on 12 pt by Orchard Publishing
Printed and bound by ABC Press, Cape Town
114545

Acknowledgements
LexisNexis Butterworths has granted permission to reproduce the Wills Act No. 7 of 1953 (p. 257), the Intestate Succession Act No. 81 of 1987 (p. 266) and the Reform of Customary Law of Succession and Regulation of Related Matters Act No., 11 of 2009 (p. 270).
The authors and publisher gratefully acknowledge permission to reproduce copyright material in this book. Every effort has been made to trace copyright holders, but if any copyright infringements have been made, the publisher would be grateful for information that would enable any omissions or errors to be corrected in subsequent impressions.

Table of contents

List of authors x
Preface xi
Acknowledgements xii
About the book xiii

CHAPTER 1: INTRODUCTION (CHRISTA RAUTENBACH) 1
1.1 General background to the law of succession 1
1.2 Law of succession in the legal system 2
1.3 Dual character of the law of succession 2
1.4 Conflict of laws 4
1.4.1 The problem of conflicting rights and obligations 4
1.4.2 Testate law of succession 4
1.4.3 Intestate law of succession 5
1.4.4 Administration of estates 6
1.5 Succession terminology 6
1.6 Ground rules of succession 12
1.6.1 Person must have died 12
1.6.2 Transfer of rights and/or duties with regard to assets and/or the status of the deceased 15
1.6.3 Beneficiary should at the time of *dies cedit* be alive or have been conceived 15
1.6.4 Beneficiary must be competent to inherit 16
This chapter in essence 16

CHAPTER 2: INTESTATE SUCCESSION (MOHAMED PALEKER) 17
2.1 Introduction 17
2.2 When does a person die intestate? 20
2.3 Vesting of an intestate inheritance 20
2.4 Capacity to inherit intestate 22
2.4.1 Only natural persons may inherit 22
2.4.2 Extramarital, adulterine, and incestuous children 22
2.4.3 Children born as a result of artificial fertilisation 22
2.4.4 Children born as a result of surrogacy arrangements 22
2.4.5 Adopted children 23
2.4.6 Unborn children 23
2.5 Constitutional challenges 23
2.5.1 *Bhe v Magistrate, Khayelitsha; Shibi v Sithole; South African Human Rights Commission v President of the Republic of South Africa (Bhe v Magistrate, Khayelitsha)* 23
2.5.2 *Daniels v Campbell, Hassam v Jacobs* and *Govender v Ragavayah* 25
2.5.3 *Gory v Kolver* 25
2.6 Order of succession 27
2.6.1 Rule 1 (S 1(1)(a)) 27
2.6.2 Rule 2 (S 1(1)(b)) 28
2.6.3 Rule 3 (S 1(1)(c)) 29
2.6.4 Rule 4 (S 1(1)(d)(i)) 32
2.6.5 Rule 5 (S 1(1)(d)(ii)) 32

2.6.6 Rule 6 (S 1(1)(e)(i)(aa)-(cc)) 33
2.6.7 Rule 7 (S 1(1)(e)(ii)) 34
2.6.8 Rule 8 (S 1(1)(f)) 35
2.7 Disqualification and repudiation 35
2.8 Reform of the Customary Law of Succession Act (RCLSA) 37
2.8.1 Contents of the RCLSA 37
2.8.1.1 Definitions 38
2.8.1.2 Interpretation 39
2.8.1.3 Freedom of testation 39
2.8.1.4 Disputes 39
2.8.1.5 Traditional leaders 39
2.8.1.6 Property rights 39
2.8.2 Order of succession in former customary law estates 40
2.8.2.1 Succession in monogamous households 41
2.8.2.2 Succession in polygynous households 42
2.8.2.3 Practical applications of the customary succession rules 42
This chapter in essence 45

CHAPTER 3: TESTATE SUCCESSION – GENERAL RULES (JUANITA JAMNECK) 47
3.1 Introduction 47
3.2 Wills, codicils and testamentary writing 48
3.2.1 Definition of a will 48
3.2.2. Basic requirements for a valid will 49
3.2.2.1 *Animus testandi* 49
3.2.2.2 Volition (or choice) 50
3.2.3 Codicil and testamentary writing 51
3.3 Joint and mutual wills 53
3.4 Adiation and repudiation 54
3.5 Doctrine of election 56
3.6 Customary law of succession 57
This chapter in essence 57

CHAPTER 4: TESTAMENTARY CAPACITY (JUANITA JAMNECK) 59
4.1 Introduction 59
4.2 Testamentary capacity 59
4.2.1 What is testamentary capacity? 59
4.2.2 Prescribed age 59
4.2.3 Mental capabilities 60
4.2.4 *Animus testandi*, volition, testamentary capacity and freedom of testation 63
4.3 Customary law of succession 63
This chapter in essence 64

CHAPTER 5: FORMALITIES FOR A WILL (MICHAEL WOOD-BODLEY) 65
5.1 Introduction 65
5.2 Formalities in terms of s 2(1)(a) of the Wills Act 66
5.2.1 Requirement of a written document 66
5.2.2 Meaning of 'sign' and 'signature' and the concept of a 'mark' 67
5.2.3 Where must the testator sign? 68
5.2.4 Signature by an amanuensis 70

5.2.5	Who is required to witness a will?	70
5.2.6	The meaning of witnessing	71
5.2.7	Acknowledging a signature	72
5.2.8	Must a will be dated or have an attestation clause?	72
5.2.9	Additional formalities associated with a mark or an amanuensis	72
5.3	**Formalities for the amendment of wills**	**77**
5.4	**Section 2(3) of the Wills Act**	**78**
5.4.1	Executing a will	81
5.4.2	Intention requirement of section 2(3)	82
5.5	**Customary law of succession**	**84**
This chapter in essence		**84**
CHAPTER 6: REVOCATION AND REVIVAL OF WILLS (MICHAEL WOOD-BODLEY)		**85**
6.1	**Introduction**	**85**
6.2	**Methods of revoking a will**	**86**
6.2.1	Revocation by destruction of the whole will	86
6.2.2	Destruction of part of a will	87
6.2.3	Express revocation (including informal revocation)	87
6.2.4	Implied revocation	88
6.2.4.1	Execution of a later conflicting will	88
6.2.4.2	Ademption	89
6.3	**Presumptions concerning the revocation of wills**	**89**
6.4	**Doctrine of dependent relative revocation**	**91**
6.5	**Revival of wills**	**92**
6.6	**Revocation by the court: section 2A**	**93**
6.7	**Customary law of succession**	**98**
This chapter in essence		**98**
CHAPTER 7: CAPACITY TO INHERIT (MOHAMED PALEKER)		**99**
7.1.	**Introduction**	**99**
7.2.	**Persons capable of inheriting: Natural persons**	**99**
7.2.1	Major beneficiary of sound mind with legal standing	100
7.2.2	Minor beneficiary	100
7.2.3	*Nasciturus* (or unborn)	101
7.2.4	Illegitimate children	103
7.2.5	Persons of unsound mind	103
7.2.6	Insolvents	103
7.3.	**Persons capable of inheriting: Juristic persons**	**104**
7.4.	**Persons disqualified from inheriting**	**105**
7.4.1	Beneficiary who caused the death of the deceased or the *coniunctissimi* of the deceased	105
7.4.1.1	Onus and evidence	106
7.4.1.2	Tricky questions relating to causation	107
7.4.1.3	Extension of the *bloedige hand* maxim	108
7.4.2	*Indignus* (unworthy person)	109
7.4.3	Persons involved in the execution process	111
7.4.4	Consequences of disqualification	112
7.5	**Customary law of succession**	**113**
This chapter in essence		**113**

CHAPTER 8: FREEDOM OF TESTATION (JUANITA JAMNECK) **115**
8.1 Introduction **115**
8.2 Limitations on freedom of testation **116**
8.2.1 Statutory limitations 116
8.2.2 Common law limitations 117
8.2.2.1 Conditions that interfere with a beneficiary's marital relationship 118
8.2.2.2 Conditions limiting a beneficiary's freedom of movement 121
8.2.3 Constitutional limitations 122
8.2.4 Indirect limitations 122
8.2.4.1 Maintenance of children 122
8.2.4.2 Maintenance of the surviving spouse 123
8.2.4.2.1 The meaning of 'spouse' 123
8.2.4.2.2 The Civil Union Act and the meaning of 'spouse' 126
8.3 Power of appointment **126**
8.4 Customary law of succession **129**
This chapter in essence **130**

CHAPTER 9: CONTENT OF WILLS – ABSOLUTE BEQUESTS, CONDITIONS, THE MODUS AND ESTATE MASSING (JUANITA JAMNECK) **131**
9.1 Introduction **131**
9.2 Vesting of rights **132**
9.3 Bequests **134**
9.3.1 Absolute bequests 135
9.3.1.1 When does a legacy lapse? 137
9.3.1.2 Time clauses 138
9.3.2 Conditional bequests 139
9.3.2.1 Resolutive (or terminative) conditions 139
9.3.2.2 Suspensive conditions 139
9.4 *Nudum praeceptum* **140**
9.5 Modus or obligation **141**
9.5.1 Types of modus 141
9.5.2 Difference between a modus and a condition 143
9.6 Estate massing **143**
9.6.1 How can estate massing be effected? 144
9.6.2 Section 37 of the Administration of Estates Act 145
9.6.3 Consequences of estate massing 146
9.6.3.1 Consequences of adiation 146
9.6.3.2 Consequences of repudiation 147
9.7 Customary law of succession **147**
This chapter in essence **149**

CHAPTER 10: CONTENT OF WILLS – SUBSTITUTION, USUFRUCT AND ACCRUAL (ANTON VAN DER LINDE) **151**
10.1 Introduction **151**
10.2 Substitution **151**
10.3 Direct substitution **152**
10.3.1 Express direct substitution by the testator 152
10.3.2 Direct substitution implied by law (*ex lege*): Section 2C 153

10.4 Fideicommissary substitution (fideicommissum) 156
10.4.1 Various forms of the fideicommissum 157
10.4.1.1 Fideicommissum expressly created 157
10.4.1.1.1 Conditional fideicommissum 157
10.4.1.1.2 Special power of appointment 157
10.4.1.1.3 Fideicommissum *residui* 157
10.4.1.2 Fideicommissum created impliedly 158
10.4.1.2.1 *Si sine liberis decesserit* clause 158
10.4.1.2.2 Other forms 159
10.5 Statutory restriction on the fideicommissum 159
10.6 Legal position of the parties to a fideicommissum 159
10.7 Presumption against a fideicommissum 162
10.8 Usufruct 162
10.8.1 Influence on *dies cedit* and *dies venit* 162
10.8.2 Difference between usufruct and fideicommissum 163
10.9 Accrual 163
10.9.1 What is the intention of the testator? 164
10.9.2 Where the testator's intention is not clear 165
10.10 Customary law of succession 167
This chapter in essence 167

CHAPTER 11: CONTENT OF WILLS - TRUSTS (ANTON VAN DER LINDE) 169
11.1 Introduction 169
11.2 Brief historical perspective 171
11.3 Defining a trust 171
11.4 Legal nature of the testamentary trust 174
11.5 Requirements for the creation of a valid trust 176
11.5.1 Intention to create a trust 176
11.5.2 Create a binding obligation 176
11.5.3 Testamentary formalities 176
11.5.4 Determined or determinable trust property 176
11.5.5 Clear trust object 177
11.5.6 Lawful trust object 178
11.6 Core elements of a trust 179
11.7 Trustees 180
11.7.1 Appointment and authorisation 180
11.7.2 Duties of a trustee 180
11.7.3 Breach of fiduciary duty 182
11.7.4 Powers of a trustee 183
11.7.5 Termination of trusteeship 184
11.8 Beneficiaries 185
11.8.1 Nomination and qualifications 185
11.8.2 Rights of beneficiaries 185
11.8.2.1 Income beneficiary 186
11.8.2.1.1 Non-discretionary trusts 186
11.8.2.1.2 Discretionary trusts 187
11.8.2.2 Capital beneficiaries 187

11.8.2.2.1 *Bewind* trusts 187
11.8.2.2.2 Ownership trusts 187
11.9 Amendment of trust provisions 188
11.9.1 Common law 188
11.9.2 Section 13 of the Trust Property Control Act 189
11.9.3 Validity of power to amend given to a trustee 189
11.10 Termination of a trust 189
11.11 Customary law of succession 190
This chapter in essence 190

CHAPTER 12: COLLATION (MICHAEL WOOD-BODLEY) 191
12.1 Introduction 191
12.2 Who participates in collation? 193
12.3 What benefits are collatable? 196
12.4 Valuation of collatible benefits 198
12.5 Customary law of succession 200
This chapter in essence 201

CHAPTER 13: INTERPRETATION OF WILLS (MOHAMED PALEKER) 203
13.1 Introduction 203
13.2 Golden rule 203
13.3 Statutory rules of interpretation 204
13.3.1 Ex-spouses 204
13.3.2 The terms 'child' or 'children' 205
13.4 Common law rules of interpretation 207
13.4.1 Ordinary and plain meaning 207
13.4.2 Construction of the will as a whole 209
13.4.3 Armchair and extrinsic evidence 210
13.4.4 Implied provisions 212
13.4.5 Legal presumptions 213
13.4.5.1 Writing or typing prevails over standard form wills 213
13.4.5.2 Presumption against intestacy 213
13.4.5.3 Ambulatory nature of a will 213
13.4.5.4 Immediate vesting, acceleration of benefits, finality of institution, maximum benefit and minimum burden 214
13.4.5.5 Presumption against disinherison 215
13.5 Variation of wills 217
13.6 Rectification of wills 219
13.7 Customary law of succession 221
This chapter in essence 221

CHAPTER 14: SUCCESSION BY CONTRACT (*PACTUM SUCCESSORIUM*) (CHRISTA RAUTENBACH) 223
14.1 Introduction 223
14.2 Origin of the prohibition of the *pactum successorium* 224
14.3 What is a *pactum successorium*? 225
14.3.1 Identifying the *pactum successorium* 225
14.3.2 Valid forms of the *pactum successorium* 229
14.3.2.1 *Donatio mortis causa* 229
14.3.2.2 Antenuptial contract 230

14.4 Customary law of succession 231
This chapter in essence 231

CHAPTER 15: ADMINISTRATION OF ESTATES (Christa Rautenbach) 233
15.1 Introduction 233
15.2 Legal reform of the administration of intestate estates of black persons 234
15.2.1 Black persons who died before 6 December 2000 235
15.2.2 Black persons who died between 6 December 2000 and 15 October 2004 237
15.2.3 Black persons who died on or after 15 October 2004 239
15.3 Uniform rules for the administration of deceased estates 241
15.3.1 Basic concepts of administration of estates 241
15.3.1.1 Estate 241
15.3.1.2 Executor 242
15.3.1.3 Master 243
15.3.2 The administration process 244
15.3.2.1 Phase 1 244
15.3.2.2 Phase 2 245
15.3.2.2.1 Awarding and handing over of specific assets 245
15.3.2.2.2 Partial sale 246
15.3.2.2.3 Total sale 246
15.3.2.2.4 Taking over by surviving spouse 246
15.3.2.2.5 Redistribution agreement 246
15.3.2.3 Phase 3 248
15.3.3 Liquidation and distribution account 249
15.3.3.1 Heading 249
15.3.3.2 Money column 249
15.3.3.3 Liquidation account 249
15.3.3.4 Recapitulation statement 250
15.3.3.5 Distribution account 250
15.3.3.6 Income and expenditure account 251
15.3.3.7 Fiduciary assets account 251
15.3.3.8 Estate duty addendum 251
15.3.3.9 Certificate 251
15.3.3.10 Example of a simple liquidation and distribution account 251
This chapter in essence 255

Appendix A: Wills Act No. 7 of 1953 257
Appendix B: Intestate Succession Act No. 81 of 1987 266
Appendix C: Reform of Customary Law of Succession and Regulation of Related Matters Act, No. 11 of 2009 270
Bibliography 277
Table of cases 283
Table of legislation 292
Index 296

List of authors

Juanita Jamneck (Editor)
BLC LLB LLD (University of Pretoria)
Juanita Jamneck is a Professor in the Department of Private Law at the University of South Africa, where she teaches the law of succession. She also teaches Wills and Succession for the Distance Learning School for Legal Practice, as well as the Certificate Course in Deceased Estates for the Law Society of South Africa (Legal Education and Development).

Christa Rautenbach (Editor)
BIuris LLB LLM LLD (Potchefstroom University for Christian Higher Education, now the North-West University)
Christa Rautenbach is a Professor in the Faculty of Law at the North-West University, where she teaches the law of succession and legal pluralism, as well as postgraduate courses in the law of succession and child law. She is a co-editor of the Potchefstroom Electronic Law Journal. She is also an Advocate of the High Court of South Africa and a Commissioner of the Small Claims Court of Potchefstroom.

Mohamed Paleker
BA LLB LLM (University of Cape Town)
Mohamed Paleker is a Senior Lecturer in the Department of Private Law at the University of Cape Town, where he teaches the law of succession and civil procedure. He is also an Attorney of the High Court of South Africa.

Anton van der Linde
LLB LLM LLD (University of Pretoria)
Anton van der Linde is a Professor in the Department of Private Law at the University of Pretoria, where he teaches the law of succession and the law of trusts and estates, as well as the Certificate Program in Advanced Trust Law through Continuing Education at the University of Pretoria. He is also an Attorney of the High Court of South Africa.

Michael Wood-Bodley
BCom LLB LLM (University of Natal, now the University of KwaZulu-Natal)
Michael Wood-Bodley is a Senior Lecturer in the Faculty of Law at the University of KwaZulu-Natal, where he teaches the law of succession and an introductory law course, as well as being an adjudicator in the school's Moot Court Program. He is also an Attorney and Conveyancer of the High Court of South Africa.

Preface

The Constitution places an obligation on the courts to promote the values enshrined in the Bill of Rights when developing the common and the customary law. To this end, the Constitutional Court has progressively developed both the common and the customary law of succession, most notably in the cases of *Bhe v Magistrate, Khayelitsha*, *Gory v Kolver*, and *Hassam v Jacobs*. Furthermore, Parliament has recently enacted the Reform of Customary Law of Succession and Regulation of Related Matters Act 11 of 2009, which has as its object the modification and clarification of aspects of the customary law of succession.

However, the common and the customary law of succession have traditionally been taught separately at most tertiary institutions in South Africa – the common law of succession as forming a division of private law, and the customary law of succession as forming a subdivision of customary law. This book, however, covers both the common and the customary law of succession together, explaining their respective principles as they relate to each other.

The book has been written to cover the core content of undergraduate courses in the law of succession as taught at South African universities. To a large extent, it follows the established conceptual subdivisions of the law of succession, but it also includes chapters on trusts and the administration of estates. The content covered in these chapters has often been taught separately to the standard course content, but its inclusion is important for obtaining a holistic perspective of the subject. These two chapters, however, serve as an introduction to the specialised areas of law they cover, and they are therefore not comprehensive and all-encompassing.

As the book has been written primarily for undergraduate students of law, its focus is to establish a sound theoretical foundation, rather than to offer intricate and technical discussions. Simple, everyday language is used to make the subject more accessible to students, while standard legal terminology is retained. Special features are included to encourage students to think independently, reflectively and critically about the subject and the law in general, and to broaden their understanding and perspectives. These skills should enhance the performance of students while at university, and they are important for the development of good lawyers. Voluminous referencing has been avoided, and we have included only what we regard as the most important cases and academic writings. The comprehensive bibliography will serve as a useful reference for further study.

Juanita Jamneck
Christa Rautenbach

Acknowledgements

We wish to specifically thank the following people for their assistance in the preparation of this book:

The authors, for their hard work in writing their contributions, and their patience through the editing process;

Tanya du Plessis, for checking the references contained in the book;

Johan Scott, for translating the English manuscript into Afrikaans;

Penny Lane and Mark Townsend from Oxford University Press, for initiating the project and supporting the writing process.

Juanita Jamneck
Christa Rautenbach

About the book

The Law of Succession in South Africa is a pedagogically rich learning resource. This book is designed to form a strong foundation of understanding, to develop the skills to engage independently and judiciously with legal principles, and to create skilled and proficient lawyers.

Brief description of features:

Pause for Reflection boxes: These boxes may consider the policy ramifications of the law; how it works in practice; its logic and consistency with other principles; possible alternatives; and other key issues.

This feature instils a broader and deeper understanding of the subject matter. It stimulates discussion, supports independent thinking, and develops the ability to engage meaningfully with relevant issues.

Counterpoint boxes: These boxes highlight specific criticisms of the law just described and identify reform options. They identify areas of controversy, problems with current law, and possible alternatives.

This feature supports the ability to think critically and flexibly. It assists students to conceptualise legal issues from various perspectives, develops skills in formulating legal argument, and builds an awareness of various opinions about a particular principle.

Legal Thinking boxes: These boxes demonstrate how legal principles are applied to solve legal problems, coaching students to follow a logical, systematic thought process.

These features illustrate, in a generic and step-by-step manner, how to work through problems conceptually in order to identify the relevant issues and to reach a rational and legally acceptable conclusion.

Diagrams: These provide overviews and explain key concepts visually. This feature reinforces understanding, helps to clarify key concepts, and shows more clearly the interrelationship between distinct legal concepts and processes.

Tables: These are used to distinguish content, and to aid conceptualisation.

Example font style: This font style distinguishes illustrative examples from the core text.

This subtle design feature ensures that any discussion of examples and cases is not confusing or distracting, and allows students to retain conceptual focus when comprehending core principles which are introduced in the text. It allows students to refocus their attention when they are ready to access further detail and clarity, without interrupting the essential explanation of the principles.

This chapter in essence: This section summarises the key areas and core topics covered in the chapter in a succinct list of essential points.

Table of concepts (in chapter 1): This contains explanations of the words and phrases that constitute the jargon or terms of art that are particular to the area of study covered in the book. Latin phrases and many others are explained and contextualised.

Chapter 1

Introduction

What is the nature, scope and application of the law of succession in South Africa?

1.1	General background to the law of succession	1
1.2	Law of succession in the legal system	2
1.3	Dual character of the law of succession	2
1.4	Conflict of laws	4
1.5	Succession terminology	6
1.6	Ground rules of succession	12
This chapter in essence		16

1.1 General background to the law of succession

The law of succession forms part of private law. It prescribes legal rules that determine what should happen to a person's estate after his or her death. The rules of succession identify the persons entitled to succeed the deceased (the beneficiaries) and the extent of the benefits (inheritances or legacies) they are to receive. They also determine the rights and duties that persons, for example beneficiaries and creditors, may have in the deceased's estate.

Succession may take place in three ways:

1. In accordance with a valid will (testamentary succession or *successio ex testamento*). Testamentary succession is discussed from Chapter 3 onwards.
2. Through the operation of the law of intestate succession in the absence of a valid will (*successio ab intestato* or *successio legitima*). Intestate succession is discussed in Chapter 2.
3. In terms of a contract or agreement (*successio ex contractu* or *pactum successorium*). This form of succession is discussed in Chapter 14.

A number of Acts are of importance for the law of succession and will be referred to throughout the book. They include the following:

1. Administration of Estates Act 66 of 1965 (hereinafter referred to as the Administration of Estates Act)
2. Black Administration Act 38 of 1927 (hereinafter referred to as the Black Administration Act)
3. Children's Act 38 of 2005 (hereinafter referred to as the Children's Act)
4. Children's Status Act 82 of 1987 (hereinafter referred to as the Children's Status Act)

5. Civil Union Act 17 of 2006 (hereinafter referred to as the Civil Union Act)
6. Constitution of the Republic of South Africa 200 of 1993 (hereinafter referred to as the Interim Constitution)
7. Constitution of the Republic of South Africa, 1996 (hereinafter referred to as the Constitution)
8. Immovable Property (Removal or Modification of Restrictions) Act 94 of 1965 (hereinafter referred to as the Immovable Property Removal or Modification of Restrictions Act)
9. Intestate Succession Act 81 of 1987 (hereinafter referred to as the Intestate Succession Act). A copy of this Act is included at the end of the book.
10. Law of Evidence Amendment Act 45 of 1988 (hereinafter referred to as the Law of Evidence Amendment Act)
11. Maintenance of Surviving Spouses Act 27 of 1990 (hereinafter referred to as the Maintenance of Surviving Spouses Act)
12. Marriage Act 25 of 1961 (hereinafter referred to as the Marriage Act)
13. Recognition of Customary Marriages Act 120 of 1998 (hereinafter referred to as the Recognition of Customary Marriages Act)
14. Reform of Customary Law of Succession and Regulation of Related Matters Act 11 of 2009 (hereinafter referred to as the Reform of Customary Law of Succession Act and abbreviated as RCLSA). A copy of this Act is included at the end of the book.
15. Trust Property Control Act 57 of 1988 (hereinafter referred to as the Trust Property Control Act)
16. Wills Act 7 of 1953 (hereinafter referred to as the Wills Act). A copy of this Act is included at the end of the book.

1.2 Law of succession in the legal system

The law of succession forms part of Private law. It prescribes what becomes of a person's estate after death, who the beneficiaries are and what they will inherit. It also determines the different rights and duties that persons, for example beneficiaries, may have in a deceased's estate.

1.3 Dual character of the law of succession

Colonialism in its various forms had a considerable impact on the development of law in South Africa. Modern South African law is based on Roman-Dutch law, as influenced by English common law, and indigenous laws or customary law. In terms of the Recognition of Customary Marriages Act,[1] customary law is defined as the 'customs and usages traditionally observed among the indigenous African people' and in terms of the partly repealed Black Administration Act,[2] the term 'black' included 'any person who is a member of any aboriginal race or tribe of Africa.' The Law of Evidence Amendment Act[3] defines indigenous law as 'the law or custom as applied by the Black tribes in the Republic,' and the South African Law Reform Commission[4] defines customary law as the 'customs and usages traditionally observed among indigenous African peoples of South Africa and which form part of the

1 Section 1.
2 Section 35.
3 Section 1(4).
4 *Report on Project 90: Customary Law of Succession* (2004) 77.

culture of those people'. Although the terms customary law and indigenous law are used synonymously in South African law, customary law is the expression used in the Constitution of the Republic of South Africa.

Traditional textbooks on the law of succession distinguish between the common and customary laws of succession. Legal literature has yet to recognise fully that both common law and customary law form part of modern South African law and that the law of succession is a dual system of law comprising two main branches, namely the common law and the customary law.

However, while customary law and the common law have equal status,[5] there are four issues that must be considered when looking at the two branches of succession law:

1. Customary law is subject to two provisos, namely it must be compatible with the Constitution and it may be amended by means of legislation.[6]
2. The decision as to which law (common or customary) is applicable to a particular deceased estate is made by applying choice of law rules that can be derived from statute or judicial precedent. The choice of law rules for the law of succession are discussed at para 1.4.
3. Because customary law is not a single, unified system of law but is comprised of the different customary laws of the various traditional communities in South Africa, s 1(3) of the Law of Evidence Amendment Act provides certain rules for dealing with conflict between the different customary laws. Section 1(3) reads:

   In any suit or proceedings between Blacks who do not belong to the same tribe, the court shall not in the absence of any agreement between them with regard to the particular system of indigenous law to be applied in such suit or proceedings, apply any system of indigenous law other than that which is in operation at the place where the defendant or respondent resides or carries on business or is employed, or if two or more different systems are in operation at that place (not being within a tribal area), the court shall not apply any such system unless it is the law of the tribe (if any) to which the defendant or respondent belongs.

   Although a discussion of these rules is beyond the scope of this book, the differences between the various customary laws must be kept in mind when deciding which customary laws will be applicable to a relevant deceased estate.
4. The differences between the common and customary laws of succession are mostly based on societal and economic considerations. For example, the main purpose of the customary law of succession is the preservation of the family unit and the community after the death of the deceased. For this reason, the heir steps into the shoes of the deceased and acquires all the deceased's rights and obligations. On the other hand, the common law of succession rules are designed to regulate the transfer of the wealth of the deceased, and they allow the deceased more freedom to dispose of his or her property as he or she pleases. The differences between the common and customary laws of succession based on societal and economic considerations will become more evident when the various rules are discussed in later chapters.

5 *Alexkor Ltd v Richtersveld Community* 2003 (12) BCLR 1301 (CC) at para 51.

6 Section 211 of the Constitution. Note that the common law may also be developed by means of legislation or the judiciary.

1.4 Conflict of laws

1.4.1 The problem of conflicting rights and obligations

The duality of the South African legal system inevitably leads to situations where persons are subject to overlapping or conflicting rights and obligations. Whenever this happens, the courts have to apply choice of law rules to determine which law is applicable. This process forms part of the legal discipline known as the conflict of laws or interpersonal conflict of laws. The relevant choice of law rules can be derived from statute and judicial precedent, the application of which is, unfortunately, not always without difficulty.

PAUSE FOR REFLECTION

Common and customary systems of succession

In the past, particularly prior to 1994, the common and customary systems of succession were kept strictly separate in South Africa. There were specific statutes regulating the succession of the property of black people and the administration of their estates. Section 23 of the Black Administration Act prohibited black persons from disposing of certain property (movable house property and quitrent land) by means of a will. House property had to devolve according to customary law and quitrent land had to devolve according to special statutory tables of succession similar to customary law. The only property that black persons could dispose of by means of a will, was family property and other immovable property not qualifying as house property. In the case of property bequeathed by means of a will, the common law of succession applied.

As for intestate succession, the Intestate Succession Act expressly laid down that estates subject to s 23 of the Black Administration Act fell outside the provisions of the Act.[7] The result was that the intestate estates of black persons were excluded from the Intestate Succession Act. These intestate estates had to devolve according to rules laid down in special regulations promulgated under the Black Administration Act. In general terms, the regulations linked the relevant succession laws to the deceased's form of marriage or matrimonial property system. For example, if a deceased had concluded a civil marriage in community of property, his or her estate had to devolve according to the common law rules of succession. If, however, he or she had concluded a customary marriage, the customary succession laws would be applicable. In a similar vein, a distinction was drawn between the administration of estates of black persons and other persons. These differences and subsequent developments will be discussed in Chapters 2 and 15.

1.4.2 Testate law of succession

The concept of a will is not found in the customary law of succession and, in the absence of a direct provision indicating which law should be applicable, the common law of succession should apply, especially with regard to questions of capacity and validity. A testator could, of course, indicate in his or her will which law should apply by using the well-known common law notion of freedom of testation discussed in Chapter 8.

7 See repealed section 1(4)(b) of the Black Administration Act.

PAUSE FOR REFLECTION

Common or customary laws of succession?

It is not always obvious whether the common or customary law of succession is applicable to a particular deceased estate. For example, although the concept of a will is thought to be unknown in customary law, it is accepted that a family head can make certain allocations of property to houses and individuals, and that his deathbed wishes must be respected. It could prove difficult to decide which law is applicable if a deathbed wish, which is also a phenomenon of the common law, appears in a will.

Another example is a conflict situation that may develop when a vague clause in a will has to be interpreted. A usually clear-cut reference to 'my children' can be problematic if the deceased lived under a system of customary law. Although 'my children' usually refers to the descendants of a testator in terms of the common law, 'my children' could also include any person who was a dependant of the deceased in terms of the customary law.

It is an elementary principle of the common law that every document (including a will) must be read in the light of the circumstances that existed at the time of the drafting of the document. This principle is referred to as the armchair evidence rule and is applied when the court places itself in the position of the testator to determine what the intention was when the will was drafted. The customs or culture of the testator will obviously be one of the factors that the court takes into consideration and it could be that customary law principles would influence the interpretation of the will.

1.4.3 Intestate law of succession

In the past statutory choice of law rules determined the law of succession applicable to persons: s 23 of the Black Administration Act prohibited black persons from making wills regarding certain property, whilst s 1(4)(b) of the Intestate Succession Act confirmed that estates falling under s 23 fell outside the scope of the Intestate Succession Act. In addition, regulations promulgated under the Black Administration Act laid down certain choice of law rules if a person living under a system of customary law died without a valid will.

In the landmark case *Bhe v Magistrate, Khayelitsha (Commission for Gender Equality as Amicus Curiae); Shibi v Sithole; South African Human Rights Commission v President of the Republic of South Africa*[8] (hereinafter referred to as *Bhe v Magistrate, Khayelitsha* unless indicated otherwise), the Constitutional Court made major changes to the choice of law rules to be applied to the intestate estates of persons living under a system of customary law. The Court declared s 1(4)(b) of the Intestate Succession Act, s 23 of the Black Administration Act, and the regulations promulgated under the latter Act unconstitutional and invalid. Consequently, the Court ordered that, as from 15 October 2004, the Intestate Succession Act had to be applied to all intestate estates, irrespective of the cultural affiliation of the deceased. The customary law of succession can now only be applied if so chosen by means of freedom of testation; in other words, by means of a clause in a will.

8 2005 (1) SA 580 (CC).

In line with these developments, the Reform of Customary Law of Succession Act has been drafted to modify the customary law of succession. The President assented to the Act on 19 April 2009, but its date of operation has not yet been published. The Act contains an important choice of law rule, namely that the estate of any person who is subject to customary law that does not devolve in terms of a will, must devolve according to the Intestate Succession Act.[9] Although the Act applies the Intestate Succession Act to customary law estates, there are important differences between the devolution of these estates and ordinary common law estates.[10] The Department of Justice and Constitutional Development foresaw that there might be disputes or uncertainty with regard to the question of whether customary law is applicable or not. To resolve this, there is a provision in the Act giving jurisdiction to the Master of the High Court regarding disputes or uncertainties in connection with the devolution of family property.[11] The Master may also refer a matter to a magistrate who must hold an enquiry and make recommendations. However, laying down these rules in the Reform of Customary Law of Succession Act, does not necessarily mean that it is going to be applied in practice. It is customary for a family to informally distribute the estate of a deceased living under customary law. Normally, authorities, such as the Master of the High Court or a magistrates' court official appointed as a designated officer of the Master, are only consulted if there is a serious disagreement between the family members of the deceased. Thus it is almost impossible to speculate on the extent to which the rules of intestate succession contained in the Intestate Succession Act will actually be applied, without conducting empirical research in this regard.

1.4.4 Administration of estates

Prior to December 2000, a separate system existed for administering intestate estates. Black persons' estates were administered by a magistrate. The estates of all other race groups, and the testate estates of black persons were administered by the Master of the High Court. *Moseneke v The Master*[12] brought these differences to the fore when the Constitutional Court declared any legislation that creates different systems of administration on the grounds of race to be unconstitutional. The Court did not, however, change the circumstances pertaining to the administration of estates having to devolve in accordance with the customary law of succession. Various other legislative measures have since been enacted, but they have been applicable to all estates except those having to devolve in terms of customary law. On 15 October 2004, the Constitutional Court in *Bhe v Magistrate, Khayelitsha*, amended the position even further by declaring that South Africa should have a unified and unbiased system of administration of estates. The Court ordered that all new estates were to be administered under the Master's supervision according to the Administration of Estates Act.

1.5 Succession terminology

This section comprises an easy-to-use reference list of concepts, inherent in the law of succession, that are used in this textbook.

---

9 Section 2.
10 See Chapter 2 where these differences are discussed.
11 Section 5 of the Intestate Succession Act.
12 2001 (2) SA 18 (CC).

Table 1.1 List of concepts inherent in the law of succession

Concept	Meaning
absolute bequest	a bequest that does not contain any conditions. It is the simplest way of making a bequest and the effect of such a bequest is that vesting normally takes place upon the testator's death
accrual or *ius accrescendi*	the right of a testator's beneficiaries, under specific circumstances, to inherit an asset or assets which another beneficiary is not capable of inheriting or might not want to inherit
ademption	a form of tacit revocation of a legacy when a testator voluntarily alienates the object of a legacy during his or her lifetime causing the legacy to fail
adiation	the acceptance of a benefit from the estate of a testator
administration of estates	the process, including all administrative actions to initiate and complete the process, by which a deceased estate is liquidated by an executor under the supervision of the Master of the High Court and is divided amongst the beneficiaries
amendment	deletion, addition, alteration or interlineation by the testator. An amendment is distinguished from rectification, which takes place when a court adds, deletes or changes something in a will because the testator made a mistake
animus testandi	the intention of the testator to make a will
armchair evidence	evidence used by the court to place itself in the position in which the testator was at the time of the making of the will
ascendants	ancestors of the deceased; anybody in the ascending (upwards) line of relationship
attestation clause	a clause that appears at the end of the will in which it is declared that all the parties were present and signed in one another's presence. It may also record the place and date of signature
beneficiary/ beneficiaries	the person or persons to whom a testator's estate is transferred. Beneficiaries are called heirs when they receive an inheritance and legatees when they receive a legacy. See also heir and legatee
bequeath	to dispose of assets by means of a will
capacity to act	a person's capacity to enter into legal acts. The required age is 18. This capacity must be distinguished from testamentary capacity. See also testamentary capacity
collation or *collatio bonorum*	under certain circumstances, a descendant who receives property (including money) from a testator during the testator's lifetime has to collate (bring in) such property (or its value) before he or she may inherit from the estate of the testator to ensure a fair distribution of the deceased estate amongst all the descendants
commorientes	people who die simultaneously in a disaster
competent witness	with regard to a will, any person over the age of 14 years who is competent to give evidence in a court of law
compos mentis	of sound mind
conditional bequest	a bequest that depends on a future event which is uncertain, in the sense that it may or may not occur
coniunctissimae personae	the persons closest to the deceased namely the surviving spouse, parents and children

Concept	Meaning
contractual succession or *pactum successorium*	a contract in which the parties attempt to regulate the devolution of the entire or part of the assets of one or both parties
curator	a person who has been legally appointed to take care of the interests of someone who is unable to manage his or her affairs, for example someone who is a minor or mentally ill. A *curator ad litem* is a person appointed to assist someone to litigate in court, and a *curator bonis* is a person appointed to administer property or an estate
customary house	in customary law, the word 'house' refers to the family, property, rights and status connected to the customary marriage of a man and a woman. Since polygyny is still practised amongst certain traditional communities, one family head may have more than one wife and thus more than one house because each wife constitutes a house with certain property, rights and status
customary law property	there are three categories of customary law property, namely family property, house property and personal property. Family property is property that has neither been allotted nor has accrued to a specific house. Family property is controlled by the head of the family, although the property is owned by all the family members together. It includes property that the family head inherited from his mother's house, property he acquired by his own labour and land allotted by the traditional authority to the family group, but not to a particular house. House property is property that accrues to a specific house in terms of customary law or is allocated by the family head to a particular house and must be used for the benefit of that house. It includes the earnings of the members of the house, livestock allocated to the house and its increase, property given to a wife at the time of her marriage, lobolo received for daughters of the house on their marriage, compensation for delicts against members of the house, agricultural products produced by the wife of the house, and other products produced by other members of the house. Personal property belongs to the person who acquired it and includes items of a personal nature such as a walking stick, a snuff box, clothing and jewellery
customary marriage	a marriage concluded in terms of customary law
deceased estate	consists of the assets and liabilities of a deceased person at the time of his or her death. The estate therefore consists not only of property, but also of any debts that the deceased incurred before his or her death. The **residue of the estate** refers to that part of the deceased's estate which remains after the payment of funeral expenses, administration costs, tax (if any), the testator's debts, and the legacies
descendants	common law descendants include the lineal descendants (persons in the downwards line) of the deceased. The customary law concept of descendants generally includes a wider circle of descendants. According to s 1 of the Reform of Customary Law of Succession Act, the following categories of persons qualify as descendants: 1. a person who is a descendant in terms of the Intestate Succession Act (thus common law descendants) 2. a person who, during the lifetime of the deceased person, was accepted by the deceased person in accordance with customary law as his or her own child 3. a woman who was involved in a substitute marriage or a woman to woman marriage.

Concept	Meaning
dies cedit	the day will come. The time when a beneficiary obtains a vested right to claim delivery of bequeathed property unconditionally (whether or not the exercise of this right is delayed until some future date which is certain to arrive)
dies venit	the day has come. The time at which a beneficiary's right to claim delivery of bequeathed property becomes enforceable or the day when delivery of the property has to take place
direct substitution	occurs where a testator names a substitute or a series of substitutes who are to inherit if the heir or legatee named to benefit in a will does not inherit. Direct substitution is substitution in the alternative
estate massing	when two or more testators (usually two spouses) mass the whole or parts of their estates into one consolidated economic unit for the purpose of testamentary disposal and the disposal becomes effective upon the death of the first-dying spouse
execution of a will	the process whereby the testator and other parties comply with all the formalities required to bring a valid will into existence
executor	the person who is charged with the administration of a deceased estate; the person who winds up the estate. An executor in a deceased estate is distinguished from a curator of an insolvent estate and from a trustee or administrator of a trust
extrinsic evidence	evidence outside the will itself; evidence of facts that do not appear from the will itself
fideicommissary substitution or fideicommissum	occurs where a testator directs that a series of beneficiaries are to own his or her whole estate or part of it, or specific assets one after the other. The first heir is known as the fiduciary and the succeeding beneficiary as the fideicommissary
fideicommissum *residui*	where property is left to a fiduciary subject to the condition that as much of it as may be left at the time of his or her death is to devolve upon another person (the fideicommissary)
formalities	the formal legal requirements with which a will must comply to be valid
freedom of testation	the freedom of a person to dispose of his or her estate as he or she pleases
heir	a beneficiary who inherits a testator's entire estate, a portion thereof, or the residue thereof. An heir is distinguished from a legatee, who is a beneficiary who inherits a specific asset. See also legatee
inter vivos	between the living
intestate law of succession or *successio ab intestato*	the legal rules or legal norms that determine how succession should take place in cases where a testator fails to regulate succession on death by way of a valid will or a *pactum successorium* contained in an antenuptial contract
joint will	where two or more testators have set out their respective wills in the same document. Such a will differs from a mutual will in that the parties do not necessarily appoint each other as beneficiaries
juristic act	an act that is intended to create or alter rights and obligations; an act to which the law attaches at least some of the consequences envisaged by the acting party or parties. Such an act may be multilateral, in other words, an act performed through the cooperation of two or more persons, for example to conclude a contract, or unilateral, in other words, an act performed by one person, for example the making of a will

Concept	Meaning
law of succession	comprises legal rules that control the transfer of those assets of a deceased that are eligible for distribution to beneficiaries, or those assets of another person over which the deceased has the power of disposal
legatee	a person who inherits a specific asset or a specific amount of money from a testator. The inheritance is known as a legacy (plural: legacies)
living customary law	the actual version of customary law as applied by the people living under a system of customary law which may differ from the official version. See also official customary law
lobolo	the property in cash or in kind that a prospective husband or the head of his family undertakes to give to the head of the prospective wife's family in consideration of a customary marriage
male primogeniture	under customary law the heirs of the deceased are usually male and are identified by their relationship to the deceased through the male line. The firstborn son in a monogamous household is normally the deceased's heir; in a polygynous household, it is normally the firstborn son of the main house. In the absence of a firstborn son or his descendant, succession passes to the second son or his descendants, and keeps on passing to the male descendants until one is found. If the deceased had no male descendants, his father will be the heir. If the father is already deceased, the deceased's eldest brother will be next in line. Failing him, his male descendants in order of seniority will succeed, and so the order continues to the other brothers, then the grandfather, paternal uncles, or their descendants in order of seniority and keeps passing on until a male heir in the specific line is found
modus or obligation	a qualification added to a gift or testamentary disposition, whereby the beneficiary is required to devote the property received (or the value thereof) in whole or in part to a specific purpose
mortis causa	in contemplation of death
mutual will	where two or more testators draw up a joint will and confer benefits on each other in the same will
official customary law	the version of customary law as applied by the courts and entrenched in legislation
polygyny and polygynous	polygyny is a form of polygamy where a man has more than one wife
posthumous	something that occurs or continues after someone's death. For example, a posthumous child means a child born after the death of the father of the child
power of appointment	the power to appoint certain beneficiaries as heirs or legatees given to someone else by the testator
prodigal	a spendthrift; someone who is characterised by excessive or imprudent spending
quid pro quo	something for something; mutual consideration
quitrent land (the Afrikaans term is *erfpag*)	the owner of land held under a quitrent title does not have full ownership of the land but only the right to loan the property from the government for a certain period of time and against payment of a certain amount of money
rectification	takes place when a court adds, deletes or changes something in a will because the testator made a mistake when making the will and the will does not reflect his or her intention correctly
repudiation	the rejection of a benefit or refusal to inherit a benefit from the estate of a testator

Concept	Meaning
resolutive (terminative) condition	a bequest is subject to a resolutive condition when the bequest is made to terminate if a particular uncertain future event takes place
resolutive (terminative) time clause or resolutive term	a bequest subject to a terminative (resolutive) time clause is one in which the beneficiary's rights are terminated when a certain time arrives
***si sine liberis decesserit* clause**	a clause that stipulates that if a beneficiary dies without children after the testator, the benefit must pass to a third party
spes	hope or expectation
stipulatio alteri	a contract in favour of a third person
stipulation or provision	general terms used for clauses in a will where the testator has made his or her intentions known
stirps or *stirpes*	a line of descendants of common ancestry
substitution	occurs when a testator appoints a beneficiary to inherit a benefit and, at the same time, appoints another beneficiary to take the place of the first-mentioned beneficiary. Substitution may take place either in the alternative (direct substitution) or one beneficiary after another (fideicommissary substitution). See also direct substitution and fideicommissary substitution
succession to status	in the customary law of succession, the successor steps into the shoes of the deceased and gains control over the property and people that the deceased controlled. In other words, the successor succeeds to the status of the deceased as well as to both the assets and liabilities of the estate
survivor or surviving spouse	the spouse who is still alive after the death of his or her spouse. In terms of the common law, the term 'spouse' normally refers to someone with whom the deceased had a valid civil marriage. However, in modern South African law, the following categories qualify as surviving spouses: 1. a spouse in a marriage in terms of South African law, namely a marriage concluded under the Marriage Act, the Recognition of Customary Marriages Act or the Civil Union Act 2. a spouse in a customary marriage that does not fall within the ambit of the Recognition of Customary Marriages Act 3. a spouse in a marriage concluded in accordance with a system of Muslim or Hindu law. Special circumstances exist in the case of customary marriages, especially in the context of succession. Section 2 of the Reform of Customary Law of Succession Act recognises two additional categories of spouses, namely a woman with whom the deceased entered into a union in accordance with customary law with the purpose of providing children for the spouse's house (substitute marriage), and any woman who was married to a deceased woman under customary law for the purpose of providing children for the house of the deceased (woman to woman marriages)
suspensive condition	if a bequest is made subject to a suspensive condition, the beneficiary does not obtain a vested, finally established right to the benefit unless and until a particular uncertain future event takes place
suspensive time clause or suspensive term	a bequest subject to a suspensive time clause is a bequest from which the beneficiary will receive the benefit only at a certain future time

Concept	Meaning
testamentary capacity	capacity to make a will. Every person aged 16 years or more may make a will unless at the time of making the will, he or she is mentally incapable of appreciating the nature and effect of the act. This capacity must be distinguished from capacity to act. See also capacity to act
testamentary writing	a document that defines any one of the three essential elements of a bequest: (a) the property bequeathed; (b) the extent of the interest bequeathed; or (c) the beneficiary
testate law of succession or *successio ex testamento*	comprises those legal rules or norms that regulate the devolution of a deceased person's estate upon one or more persons according to the testator's wishes as expressed in a will
testator	a natural person who makes a will in which he or she bequeaths an estate in the form of bequeathable assets
trust	the arrangement through which the property of a person is by virtue of a trust instrument bequeathed: (a) to another person, the trustee, in whole or in part, to be administered or disposed of according to the provisions of the trust instrument for the benefit of the person or class of persons designated in the trust instrument or for the achievement of the object stated in the trust instrument; or (b) to the beneficiaries designated in the trust instrument, which property is placed under the control of another person, the trustee, to be administered or disposed of according to the provisions of the trust instrument to the benefit of the person or class of persons designated in the trust instrument or for the achievement of the object stated in the trust instrument, but does not include the case where the property of another is to be administered by any person as executor, tutor or curator in terms of the provisions of the Administration of Estates Act. In other words, in a trust the testator entrusts the ownership and control of his or her property to a third party (the trustee) to manage the property in the interests of a beneficiary/ies
trust instrument	a written agreement, a testamentary writing, or a court order in terms of which a trust is created
usufruct, *ususfructus* or life interest	occurs when ownership is bequeathed to one person but the right to use, enjoy and take the fruits of the property bequeathed to another. The latter is called the usufructuary and the owner is called the *dominus*, remainderman or nude owner
vest	to confer legal ownership of property or legal rights on someone
will or testament	a unilateral, voluntary juristic act contained in a document which complies with formalities required by law, and in which the testator gives instructions pertaining to what must happen to his or her estate after his or her death

1.6 Ground rules of succession

There are a few requirements (basic ground rules) that must be fulfilled before the rules of succession can come into operation.

1.6.1 Person must have died

In both the common and customary law of succession (in the case of property), a prerequisite for succession is that the owner of the estate must have died. In customary law, succession to status positions takes place only on the death of a family head, while the deaths of another family member does not give rise to succession to his or her status.

The application of the rule is illustrated in *Estate Orpen v Estate Atkinson*[13] where the testators, the Atkinsons, massed their estates in a joint will. They had only one child, a daughter. According to the stipulations of the will, the massed estate would, upon the death of Mr Atkinson, should he die first, be handed over to the executors of the estate and they would act as trustees (a trust was, in other words, created). From the moment of death of the testator, Mrs Atkinson, also a testator, and the daughter would receive the income of the trust in equal parts (in other words, they would be income beneficiaries). Should one of them die, the survivor would receive the whole of the trust income for the rest of her life. Should the daughter die, the whole trust (corpus) would go to her children in equal shares, subject to the usufruct of Mrs Atkinson should she still be alive. The will also stipulated that if the daughter should upon death have no children, 20% of the trust capital (corpus) would go to such person as the daughter might designate in her will. She therefore obtained a 'power of appointment' in her parents' will with regard to 20% of the corpus of the trust. The destination of the other 80% was arranged for in the parents' will and is not of concern for purposes of this discussion. On 5 March 1963, while her father was still alive, the daughter (Mrs Orpen) made a will in which, with reference to her 'power of appointment', she bequeathed the 20% trust capital to her husband, Mr Orpen. She thus exercised her 'power of appointment' in favour of her spouse. Mrs Orpen died on 23 March 1963 without children. Her father, Mr Atkinson, the creator of the 'power of appointment', died after his daughter on 9 November 1963. Mr Orpen died on 23 December 1964.

The legal question was whether the exercise of Mrs Orpen's 'power of appointment' in favour of Mr Orpen in terms of her father's will, was valid, and whether her spouse's deceased estate had obtained vested rights with regard to the 20% trust capital that she bequeathed to him, regardless of the fact that she died before her father. Her father was therefore still alive when her will, in which she exercised her 'power of appointment', came into operation. The Court held that Mr Orpen's estate had no right to 20% of the trust capital. Mrs Orpen obtained her 'power' from her father and she could not exercise it unless she survived her father. Because he was still alive when she died, she could not exercise rights left to her in his will. She could only validly exercise her rights if she survived him.

Although the requirement of the death of the testator seems so obvious, it is not always a simple matter and there are various examples of situations where the application of the rule has been problematic or deviated from.

The first exception to the rule that a person must be dead before succession can occur, is where a court pronounces a presumption of death and makes an order for the division of the estate. Those who allege that a person is dead have to prove it. Where the body is present and can be identified, death can easily be proved. However, where a person has disappeared and a body has not been found, death is difficult to prove. Only when a court makes a presumption of death order, can the disappeared person's estate be administered. Because it is possible that the deceased might still be alive, this case constitutes an exception to the rule that he or she must be dead before succession can occur. For this reason it is also customary for a court to order that the estate of the person presumed to be dead should be distributed amongst his heirs subject to the provision of security that the estate can be returned to him should

13 1966 (4) SA 589 (A).

he reappear. Factors which a court may take into consideration in making such an order include the length of time that the person has been missing, the age, health and position in society of the missing person as well as the circumstances of the disappearance. The principles applicable to judicial presumption of death have been reviewed in detail by the higher courts, for example in *Re Beaglehole,*[14] *Ex parte Engelbrecht,*[15] *Ex parte Rungsamy,*[16] *Ex parte Govender,*[17] *Ex parte Pieters*[18] and *Ex parte Stoter.*[19]

A second exception to the rule that a person must be dead can be found in the case of estate massing. When estates are massed, the entire estates or parts of the estates of various testators are consolidated into a single economic unit for the purpose of testamentary disposal. The effect of estate massing is that the surviving testator's estate dissolves according to the will of the first-dying whilst he or she is still alive.[20]

Another aspect worth mentioning, occurs when a number of people are killed in the same disaster (*commorientes*) and it is difficult to determine who died first. It might be important to be able to determine who died first in order to choose the beneficiaries, especially if the victims are family members. It could happen that the estate of the victims are devolved as if they died simultaneously whilst in actual fact one or more of them died at a later time.

Consider the following example: Xavier and Brenda die in a plane crash in which there are no survivors. In terms of Xavier's will, Claire is his only heir. Xavier's estate is only worth R100. In terms of Brenda's will, Xavier is her only heir, and Brenda was wealthy. If Xavier died after Brenda and could first inherit from her, Claire, who inherits from Xavier, is in a favourable position. Claire would want to prove that Brenda died before Xavier. If Xavier and Brenda died simultaneously and on impact, Xavier cannot inherit anything from Brenda, as he was not alive at *dies cedit* (that is, upon Brenda's death).

PAUSE FOR REFLECTION

No presumption of simultaneous death

In Roman-Dutch law, certain presumptions existed when members of the same family died in circumstances where it was difficult to determine who died first. The South African courts, however, did not apply these presumptions and the general rule is that there is no presumption of simultaneous death. In *Greyling v Greyling,*[21] a husband and wife were killed in a car accident. According to the evidence, the husband probably lived longer than his wife. In their joint will the spouses had a provision to the effect that if they died simultaneously, their estate had to devolve in a certain way. The Court held that the words 'gelyktydig te sterwe kom' (to die simultaneously) meant the death of the testators as the result of a single incident, irrespective of the fact that there was a difference in the exact time at which they died.

---

14 1908 TS 49.
15 1956 (1) SA 408 (E).
16 1958 (4) SA 688 (N).
17 1993 (3) SA 721 (D).
18 1993 (3) SA 379 (D).
19 1996 (4) SA 1299 (E).
20 See Chapter 9 for a discussion of estate massing.
21 1978 (2) SA 114 (T).

1.6.2 Transfer of rights and/or duties with regard to assets and/or the status of the deceased

This ground rule is linked to the issue of *dies cedit* and *dies venit* discussed in Chapter 9. The fact that there has to be a transfer of rights and/or duties with regard to the bequest and/or status of the deceased can also be regarded as a ground rule of the law of succession. Somebody must take the place of the deceased testator with regard to ownership of his assets, or in the case of customary law, with regard to status. In the case of the common law of succession, there is a transfer of rights (and sometimes also responsibilities) which belonged to the deceased. In the case of the customary law of succession, the situation is more complicated and depends on the type of property and the status of the deceased. In general, it can be said that succession to status positions takes place only after the death of a family head. Distinction is made between general succession (succession to the general status of the deceased) and special succession (succession to the position of the head of the various houses of the deceased). Although there have been exceptions to the rule, succession to status is mainly limited to males and succession follows the rule of male primogeniture, which means that a family head is succeeded by his firstborn son of a particular house.

1.6.3 Beneficiary should at the time of *dies cedit* be alive or have been conceived

The transfer of rights (and occasionally also responsibilities) is a prerequisite for succession - there must be somebody on whom the rights (or responsibilities) can devolve. Where a beneficiary has already died (is predeceased) when the bequeathed benefit vests, there can be no succession except if the deceased made provision in his or her will or antenuptial contract for the predecease of the beneficiary or in circumstances where *ex lege* substitution applies.[22]

An exceptional situation is where a beneficiary has been conceived but not yet born when the bequeathed benefit vests. Since an unborn child is incapable of bearing rights and cannot inherit, the vesting of the bequest is held over until the child is born alive. This situation is referred to as the *nasciturus* fiction (a common law concept) in terms of which a child who survives birth is regarded as having obtained rights from the moment of conception, provided that conception took place before the death of the testator.

Customary law does not have a similar fiction, but some communities have customs that are meant to produce heirs for a husband after his death. *Ukungena*, for example, is a custom which expects a widow to marry one of her husband's brothers after his death. If a man dies childless, the custom of *ukungena* allows for the continuation of his family line. Another custom, *ukuvusa*, allows for the natural heir of the deceased (for example, his brother) to take the deceased's property and then to take a wife who will be regarded as the deceased's wife and whose children will be known as the deceased's children. It is, however, difficult to determine to what extent these customs are still followed by indigenous communities. In addition, the *nasciturus* fiction has been codified in the testate law of succession by s 2D(1)(c) of the Wills Act, which provides that any benefit allocated to the children of a deceased shall vest in such children who are alive at the time of the devolution of the benefit, or who have already been conceived at the time of the devolution of the benefit and who are later born alive.

22 See Chapter 10.

1.6.4 Beneficiary must be competent to inherit

The mere fact that somebody has been named as heir or legatee in a will or in terms of the rules of intestate succession does not necessarily mean that the person has the right to the relevant benefit. Although most persons are competent to inherit, there are some who do not have the competence to take up a benefit in terms of a specific will. There are also certain persons who are not competent to benefit intestate from a specific deceased. All these cases will be dealt with in Chapters 2 and 7.

In customary law, the competence of the beneficiary is often linked to the rule of male primogeniture. The customary rule of male primogeniture was declared unconstitutional by the Constitutional Court in *Bhe v Magistrate, Khayelitsha*. This case brought about fundamental changes to the customary law of succession and the administration of estates, and will be discussed in more detail in Chapters 2 and 15.

THIS CHAPTER IN ESSENCE

1. The law of succession prescribes rules that determine what should happen to a person's estate after his or her death. The rules of succession identify the persons (the beneficiaries) entitled to succeed to the deceased's estate and the extent of the benefits they are to receive.
2. The law of succession determines the different rights and duties that persons, for example, beneficiaries and creditors, may have in a deceased's estate and forms part of private law.
3. The law of succession comprises two branches, namely the common law of succession and the customary law of succession. These two branches enjoy equal status and are subject to the Constitution and other legislation. The common law of succession is divided into the testate law of succession and the intestate law of succession, whilst the customary law of succession only operates intestate.
4. There are various rules to determine whether the common law rules or the customary law rules are applicable:
   - The common law of succession applies to testate succession except if a testator, living under customary law prescribed otherwise in his or her will or if a court decides otherwise.
   - The Intestate Succession Act applies to all intestate estates irrespective of the cultural affiliations of the deceased.
5. Succession may take place in three ways:
   - in accordance with a valid will (testamentary succession)
   - through the operation of intestate succession (without a valid will)
   - in terms of a contract (*pactum successorium*) contained in a duly registered antenuptial contract or a *donatio mortis causa*.
6. There are a few requirements (with exceptions) that must be fulfilled before the rules of succession can come into operation:
   - The testator must have died.
   - There has to be a transfer of rights and/or duties with regard to the estate and/or the status of the deceased depending on the nature of the succession rules (common law or customary law).
   - At the time of *dies cedit*, the beneficiary has to be alive or have been conceived.
   - The beneficiary must be competent to inherit.

Chapter 2

Intestate succession

What are the rules for intestate succession?

2.1	**Introduction**	17
2.2	**When does a person die intestate?**	20
2.3	**Vesting of an intestate inheritance**	20
2.4	**Capacity to inherit intestate**	22
2.5	**Constitutional challenges**	23
2.6	**Order of succession**	27
2.7	**Disqualification and repudiation**	35
2.8	**Reform of the Customary Law of Succession Act (RCLSA)**	37
This chapter in essence		45

2.1 Introduction

The law of intestate succession comprises the legal rules or norms that determine how succession should take place in cases where a testator fails to regulate succession on death by way of a valid will or a *pactum successorium* contained in an antenuptial contract.[1]

The intestate law of succession used to be a dual system of law: the common and customary law of succession. The common law of succession is governed by the Intestate Succession Act[2] and Roman-Dutch law principles, whilst the customary law component was governed by the Black Administration Act and customary law principles.

PAUSE FOR REFLECTION

Official or living?

There is a difference between the official and living versions of customary law. Living customary law is the law that is actually applied by indigenous South African people. This law often conflicts with the official customary law that is applied by the state courts or is entrenched in legislation. Nevertheless, the courts increasingly take cognisance of living customary law, as happened for example in *Bhe v Magistrate, Khayelitsha*[3] and

1 The *pactum successorium* is discussed in Chapter 14.

2 The Intestate Succession Act came into operation on 18 March 1988, was amended by the Law of Succession Amendment Act 43 of 1992, and has been the subject of several constitutional challenges.

3 2005 (1) SA 580 (CC). See the discussion in this chapter and in Chapter 15.

> *Alexkor Ltd v Richtersveld Community*.[4] It is not easy to determine exactly what the living customary law is; it is usually based on research done by legal anthropologists or the evidence of an elder living in the particular community. This chapter focuses on the official version of customary law, in other words, as found in the legislation and court decisions.

In a number of cases, such as *Daniels v Campbell*,[5] *Hassam v Jacobs*[6] and *Govender v Ragavayah*,[7] the Courts extended the application of the Intestate Succession Act to spouses in Muslim and Hindu marriages. As regards persons in same-sex life partnerships, the Constitutional Court in *Gory v Kolver*[8] held that a surviving partner of a same-sex relationship should be entitled to inherit intestate from his or her deceased partner, provided it can be shown that the couple owed each other a reciprocal duty of support. The Constitutional Court ordered that the Intestate Succession Act should be read in such a way so as to make allowance for this. Regrettably, the Constitutional Court has been less inclined to recognise rights for persons in cohabitive heterosexual relationships.[9]

To understand the way that the law of intestate succession works, it is important to understand a few basic concepts:

- **Descendant:** see definition on page 8.
- **Ascendant:** see definition on page 7.
- **Collateral:** refers to a person who is related to the deceased because he or she has the same ancestor as the deceased, for example a full brother, a half-brother, full sister, half-sister, niece, nephew, cousin, uncle or aunt. A full brother or sister of the deceased is a brother or sister descended from both parents of the deceased. A half-brother or half-sister is a brother or sister descended from one parent of the deceased.
- **Stirps:** means a line of descendants of common ancestry. A stirps includes every descendant of the deceased who *survives* the deceased, or a predeceased descendant of the deceased who leaves *living* decendants. In other words, a stirps is a surviving child of the deceased, and the descendants of a predeceased child.

  In Figure 2.1, Anne, Ben and Dan are predeceased children of Thomas and Sally. Fred is the surviving son of Anne, and Gina and Hank are the surviving children of Dan. In Figure 2.1, Thomas has three stirps, namely:
  1. Anne and Fred form one stirps;
  2. Candy forms one stirps; and
  3. Dan, Gina and Hank form one stirps.

4 2003 (12) BCLR 1301 (CC).
5 2004 (5) SA 331 (CC).
6 Case CCT 83/08 [2009] ZACC 19.
7 [2009] 1 All SA 371 (D); 2009 (3) SA 178 (D).
8 2007 (4) SA 97 (CC).
9 See in this regard *Volks v Robinson* 2005 (5) BCLR 446 (CC) and the discussion in Chapter 8.

Figure 2.1 Stirps include surviving children and descendants of predeceased children

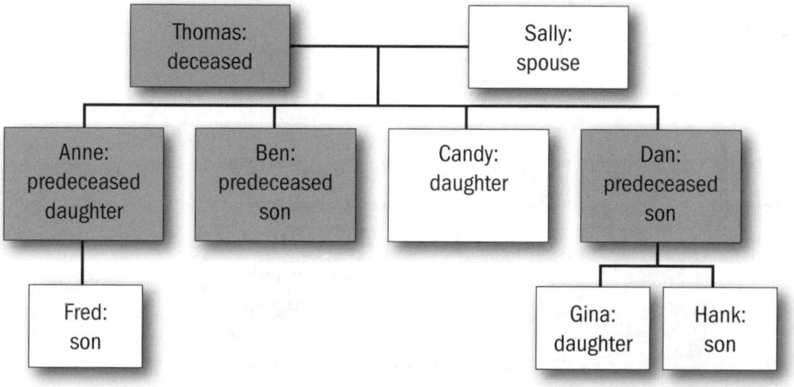

All the children of a predeceased heir together form a stirps and they inherit any part of the deceased's intestate estate jointly. Within the stirps, all blood relations who are related to the deceased in the same degree will inherit equally. Should one of the children (descendants) of a predeceased heir also have died before the deceased, the descendants of that predeceased heir, in their turn, constitute a stirps and they move up into the place of that predeceased heir to inherit intestate from the deceased.

- **Succession by representation (*per stirpes*)** Succession by representation occurs when an heir is called to inherit on the basis of his or her blood relationship with a predeceased heir of the deceased whose place he or she fills. In other words, in succession by representation, a descendant of a predeceased heir 'moves up' into the place of the predeceased heir.

  Per capita succession occurs when an intestate heir is called to inherit on the basis of the blood relationship (degree of consanguinity) which he or she has with the deceased. More than one blood relation of the same degree to the deceased will inherit equally.[10]

  In Figure 2.2 on page 20, John, Sam and Jane each form a stirps. Sam and Jane inherit equally from the deceased, because they are blood relations (the children) of the deceased. The grandchildren (Tim and Tod) inherit **by representation**, because they move up into the place of their predeceased father, John. In other words, Sam and Jane inherit one-third of the deceased estate each, and Tim and Tod share the one-third that their father, John, would have inherited if he were alive, in equal shares (or *per capita*). Each grandchild thus receives one-sixth of the estate.

10 Section 1(f) of the Intestate Succession Act.

Figure 2.2 How stirps inherit per capita *and by representation*

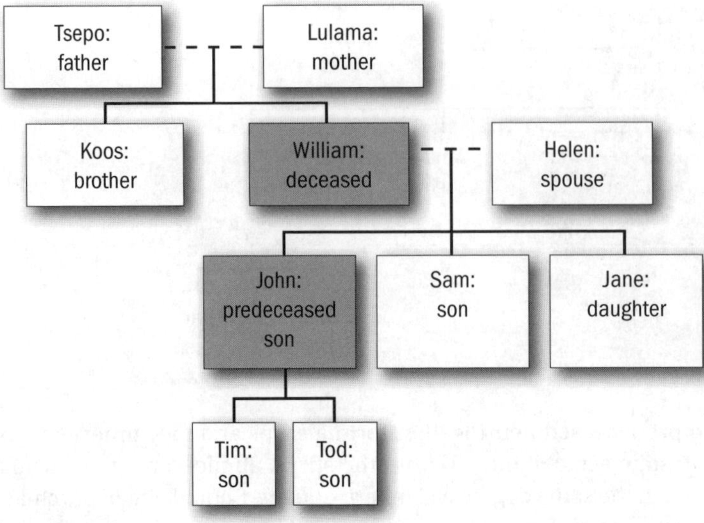

2.2 When does a person die intestate?

In South African law, it is possible for a deceased to die wholly intestate, wholly testate, or partly testate and partly intestate. Intestate succession applies if a deceased dies:

- without leaving a will at all
- having executed a valid will which has subsequently become wholly or partly inoperative for some or other reason
- with a valid will that fails to dispose of all the deceased's assets
- leaving a document purporting to be a will, but which does not comply with the formalities for wills and is not condoned in terms of s 2(3) of the Wills Act.

2.3 Vesting of an intestate inheritance

The question of vesting of rights in the context of intestate succession is best illustrated by referring to the leading case on the subject *Harris v Assumed Administrator, Estate MacGregor*.[11]

In *Harris v Assumed Administrator, Estate MacGregor*, the deceased executed a valid will in 1941 and died in 1943. He stipulated that on his death, his entire estate was to go into a testamentary trust of which his wife, the appellant, was to be the income beneficiary. He provided that on her death, the trust capital was to be paid to the children born of their marriage. In the event of their dying without surviving children and on the death of the appellant, the capital of the trust was to go to the deceased's brother. If his brother predeceased the appellant, the capital of the trust was to pass to his brother's children, if any.[12] The deceased died leaving no children born of his marriage to the appellant. Furthermore, in 1979, while the appellant was still alive, the brother

11 1987 (3) SA 563 (A).
12 *Harris v Assumed Administrator, Estate MacGregor* 1987 (3) SA 563 (A) at 571G–J.

died leaving no children of his own. There was no provision made in the will for this contingency, and the result of this was that there was intestacy as regards the devolution of the trust capital. Whilst the appellant and the respondent (the administrator of the trust) agreed that intestacy had occurred as regards the trust capital, they differed about the date when this occurred - was it when the deceased died (1943) or did it occur when it was first determined that the will had failed (the date when the brother died in 1979)? This decision was vital because if it was determined that the intestate estate vested in 1943, then in terms of the then prevailing Intestate Succession Act of 1934, the deceased's mother, who only died in 1960, would have been an intestate heir and her estate would have been a recipient of the benefit. However, if it was determined that vesting of the deceased's intestate estate occurred in 1979, the appellant would have been the only heir as she would have been his only surviving intestate relation at that date.

After a careful analysis of the common law, Joubert JA decided the following:

1. Where a deceased dies without having made a will at all, or without leaving a valid will, his or her intestate estate vests on the date of his or her death when his or her intestate heirs have to be determined.
2. Where a testator dies leaving a valid will which took effect on his or her death but which subsequently became inoperative, either in total or in part, his or her intestate estate vests on the date when it first became factually certain that his or her will had become inoperative. Any intestate heirs would have to be determined, not at his or her death, but when the intestacy occurred.

PAUSE FOR REFLECTION

Vesting of an intestate inheritance

Applying the ***Harris v Assumed Administrator, Estate MacGregor***[13] ruling to the four instances of intestacy listed on page 20 will have the following results:

- **without leaving a will at all:** In theory, vesting of the intestate inheritance occurs the moment the testator dies, but in practice it will take place when the liquidation and distribution account is lodged with the Master without objection.
- **having executed a valid will which has subsequently become wholly or partly inoperative for some or other reason:** Vesting of the intestate inheritance occurs when it is first factually determined that the will, or parts thereof, has failed. As regards the parts of a will that have not failed, vesting of those parts is determined according to the rules of vesting for testate succession.
- **with a valid will that is executed but fails to dispose of all of the deceased's assets:** The assets which have not been dealt with in the will, will devolve according to the rules of intestate succession. In theory, vesting of the intestate inheritance occurs the moment the deceased dies, but in practice, it takes place when the liquidation and distribution account is lodged with the Master without objection.
- **leaving a document purporting to be a will, but which does not comply with the formalities for wills and is not condoned in terms of s 2(3) of the Wills Act:** In theory, vesting of the intestate inheritance occurs the moment the deceased dies, but in practice, it takes place when the liquidation and distribution account is lodged with the Master without objection.

13 1987 (3) SA 563 (A).

2.4 Capacity to inherit intestate

2.4.1 Only natural persons may inherit

A juristic person or a commercial entity may not inherit intestate. This means that a company, close corporation, firm, association, trust, syndicate, body corporate, or any such entity cannot inherit intestate. In terms of the Intestate Succession Act, only natural persons, irrespective of their age, can inherit intestate.

2.4.2 Extramarital, adulterine, and incestuous children

In terms of the common law, an extramarital child (that is, a child born out of wedlock) can inherit intestate from the mother and her relations only, and not from the father and his relations. This rule found impetus in the rather tactless common law maxim, *een moeder maakt geen bastaard* (a woman cannot have an illegitimate child).

The aforementioned position was altered by s 1(2) of the Intestate Succession Act, which provides that 'illegitimacy shall not affect the capacity of one blood relation to inherit the intestate estate of another blood relation.' Thus, irrespective of the circumstances under which a child is conceived, any child has capacity to inherit intestate from both parents and their relations.

2.4.3 Children born as a result of artificial fertilisation

Section 1(2) of the Intestate Succession Act was subject to the provisions of s 5(2) of the Children's Status Act which was repealed by s 40 of the Children's Act.[14] Section 40 deals with artificial fertilisation, otherwise known as artificial insemination. If a child is determined to be extramarital after applying the provisions of s 40 of the Children's Act, he or she will only inherit from the birth mother and her relations. However, if the child is determined to be legitimate, the child will inherit from his or her birth mother, including from her spouse at the time of the artificial insemination, and their respective relations. The resurgence of the common law position in the case of artificial insemination is a consequence of the special conditions under which artificial insemination occurs.

2.4.4 Children born as a result of surrogacy arrangements

Historically, surrogacy arrangements (surrogate motherhood) were regarded as contrary to public policy. However, on the recommendation of the South African Law Commission,[15] surrogacy arrangements are now recognised in Chapter 19 of the Children's Act. If the relevant parties entered into a valid surrogacy arrangement, the child will be considered to be the legitimate child of his or her commissioning parent or parents and will thus inherit intestate from them and their relations. If, however, the agreement is defective or rescinded by a court, the child born will be considered the child of the surrogate mother only and will thus inherit intestate from her and her relations.[16]

---

14 Section 40 came into operation on 1 July 2007.

15 South African Law Commission *Report on Surrogate Motherhood* Project 65 (1992), paras 4.7.3 & 4.9.

16 Section 297(2) of the Children's Act 38 of 2005.

2.4.5 Adopted children

In terms of s 1(4)(e) of the Intestate Succession Act, an adopted child shall be deemed a descendant of his or her adoptive parent(s) and not a descendant of his or her natural parent(s), except in the case of a natural parent who is also the adoptive parent of that child or was at the time of the adoption married to the child's adoptive parent. In the same vein, s 1(5) provides that the adoptive parent(s) shall be deemed to be the ancestors of the adoptive child.

This means that the effect of an adoption is that it terminates all rights and obligations that may have existed between the child's natural parents and the child placed for adoption. For the purposes of intestate succession, once a child is adopted, he or she is regarded as the child of the adoptive parents and will inherit from them as if he or she were their biological descendant. Where applicable, the child will also inherit from the relations of his or her adoptive parents as if he or she were their biological relation.

2.4.6 Unborn children

There is a detailed discussion of the capacity of unborn (but already conceived) children to inherit intestate in Chapter 7.

2.5 Constitutional challenges

The law of intestate succession is more than a series of legal rules; it has a far-reaching socio-economic impact. The constitutionality of the Intestate Succession Act, as well as certain other intestate succession rules and their application, has been tested numerous times in court.

2.5.1 *Bhe v Magistrate, Khayelitsha; Shibi v Sithole; South African Human Rights Commission v President of the Republic of South Africa (Bhe v Magistrate, Khayelitsha)*

In *Bhe v Magistrate, Khayelitsha,*[17] the Constitutional Court declared s 23 of the Black Administration Act and the customary rule of male primogeniture unconstitutional, and extended the Intestate Succession Act to the customary law of intestate succession.

The Constitutional Court decided to join three cases because they turned on similar issues. The only differences were:

- in *Bhe v Magistrate, Khayelitsha*, the deceased's two daughters were excluded from inheriting from the intestate estate of their father on account of the principle of male primogeniture
- in *Shibi v Sithole*, the deceased's sister was excluded from inheriting intestate from her brother on account of the principle of male primogeniture
- in *South African Human Rights Commission v President of the Republic of South Africa* (and with them the Women's Legal Centre), the applicants applied for direct access to the Court as *amici curiae* (friends of the courts), arguing that s 23 of the Black Administration Act and the regulations promulgated thereunder were unconstitutional on the grounds that its provisions infringed the rights of equality, dignity, and those of children.

17 2005 (1) SA 580 (CC).

According to the traditional African customary law of succession, succession is not concerned so much with the distribution of a person's estate on death, but with the preservation and perpetuation of the family unit. The family head (usually a male) holds all property as a nominal owner for the benefit of his family. When the family head dies, the heir does not simply succeed to the assets of the deceased, but steps into the shoes (as it were) of the deceased. He acquires not only the rights of the deceased, but also incurs all the deceased's obligations. Persons who were formerly under the guardianship of the deceased would fall under the guardianship of the heir. It would be the latter's responsibility to maintain and support all the family members.

It was on this understanding of the African customary law of succession that the rule of male primogeniture came to be entrenched in s 23 of the Black Administration Act and its regulations. For women, the consequence of male primogeniture was not only that they were disqualified from inheriting, but that it perpetuated a system 'dominated by a deeply embedded patriarchy which reserved for women a position of subservience and subordination and in which they were regarded as perpetual minors under the tutelage of the fathers, husbands, or the head of the extended family.'[18] There was, perhaps, a time when male primogeniture might have been defensible, but, by the time that *Bhe v Magistrate, Khayelitsha* was decided, there was considerable evidence to suggest that the very basis for having the rule had been eroded. On account of changed social and economic circumstances, male heirs were not living up to their customary roles and this translated into considerable hardship for women and children. In *Bhe v Magistrate, Khayelitsha*, Langa DCJ noted that because customary law was officially captured in legislation, in textbooks, in the writings of experts, and in court decisions, it did not have the space to adapt and to keep pace with changing social conditions. When viewed in its entirety, the rule of male primogeniture not only discriminated against women, it discriminated against men too. Younger men were, by and large, excluded from inheriting intestate. Furthermore, since the rule favoured heirs who were legitimately born, extramarital male children suffered discrimination when it came to inheriting.

Against this background the Constitutional Court held that s 23 of the Black Administration Act, its regulations, and the rule of male primogeniture amounted to unfair discrimination in terms of s 9(3) of the Constitution. The Court also held that the principle of male primogeniture violated the right of women to human dignity as guaranteed in s 10 of the Constitution, because it implied that women were not fit or competent to own and administer property. Its effect was also to subject women to a status of perpetual minority, placing them automatically under the control of male heirs, simply by virtue of their sex and gender.[19] The male primogeniture rule also discriminated against male extramarital children as it prevented them from inheriting.

The Court held that women and children are particularly vulnerable groups and it is a constitutional duty to ensure their well-being. Denying females the ability and opportunity to inherit from their deceased fathers, spouses and other male relations was clearly unconstitutional.

The Court decided to modify the Intestate Succession Act to take into account polygynous African customary marriages with retroactive effect, namely from 27 April 1994 (when the Interim Constitution came into operation). However, where a completed transfer of ownership has taken place, the order of the Court will not apply unless it can be shown that the heir was in bad faith (*mala fide*) in the sense that he was aware that the constitutionality of the African customary

---

18 At paras 76–78. See also the discussion at para 9 where the effect of the rule of male primogeniture is explained.

19 Gender refers to the societal and cultural differences between females and males. Sex refers to the physical or biological differences.

law of succession was being challenged and still insisted on taking transfer of ownership to the property.[20]

2.5.2 *Daniels v Campbell, Hassam v Jacobs* and *Govender v Ragavayah*

In *Daniels v Campbell*,[21] the Constitutional Court extended the meaning of the term 'spouse' in the Intestate Succession Act and the meaning of 'survivor' in the Maintenance of Surviving Spouses Act[22] to the parties involved in a monogamous Muslim marriage. In *Hassam v Jacobs*,[23] the Court further extended this principle to include a situation where a woman in a polygynous Muslim marriage claimed the right to receive an intestate share from her deceased husband's estate. The Constitutional Court, having regard to the case of *Bhe v Magistrate, Khayelitsha*, concluded that there was no reason to preclude the applicant from claiming her intestate succession share[24] and modified the provisions of the Intestate Succession Act accordingly.[25]

In *Govender v Ragavayah*,[26] the question before the Court was whether a spouse in a monogamous Hindu marriage would be a spouse for the purposes of s 1 of the Intestate Succession Act. The Court (referring to *Daniels v Campbell*,[27] *Hassam v Jacobs*,[28] and *Gory v Kolver*[29]) held that not recognising the rights of a spouse in a Hindu marriage would amount to unjustifiable unfair discrimination. Consequently, the Court ruled that the word 'spouse', as used in s 1 of the Intestate Succession Act, includes the surviving partner in a monogamous Hindu marriage.[30]

2.5.3 *Gory v Kolver*

Before the Civil Union Act,[31] same-sex couples could neither marry, nor formalise their relationships in any other state-sanctioned manner. In intestate succession, this meant that when a gay person died, his or her life partner had no right to inherit from him or her. Even if the deceased and the survivor had been in a relationship for an extended period of time, and it could be shown that they supported each other financially as well as emotionally, the law simply disregarded the relationship.

It was within this context that the case of *Gory v Kolver*[32] came before the Constitutional Court. The applicant, Mr Gory, and a Mr Brooks (the deceased) were, at the time of the latter's death, partners in a permanent same-sex life partnership in which they had undertaken reciprocal duties of support. They lived together and wanted to have an agreement drawn up to record the applicant's half-share in their common home which was registered in the name of the deceased but, at the time of the deceased's death, they had not yet done so. The Master of the High Court and the deceased's family took the position that Mr Gory was not to be regarded as the intestate heir of the deceased as he was not the spouse of the deceased in terms of the Intestate

20 At paras 101–124 and see the Court's order at para 136.
21 2004 (5) SA 331 (CC); see also the discussion in Chapter 8.
22 27 of 1990.
23 [2008] 4 All SA 350 (C).
24 Case CCT 83/08 [2009] ZACC 19.
25 Case CCT 83/08 [2009] ZACC 19.
26 [2009] 1 All SA 371 (D); 2009 (3) SA 178 (D).
27 2004 (5) SA 331 (CC).
28 [2008] 4 All SA 350 (C).
29 2007 (4) SA 97 (CC).
30 *Govender v Ragavayah* 2009 (3) SA 178 (D).
31 The Act commenced on 30 November 2006.
32 2007 (4) SA 97 (CC).

Succession Act. When the matter came before the Constitutional Court, the Court held that on a literal interpretation of the Intestate Succession Act, s 1(1) of the Act conferred rights of intestate succession on heterosexual spouses but not on permanent same-sex life partners. As these partners were not legally entitled to marry, this amounted to discrimination on the listed ground of sexual orientation in terms of the equality clause of the Constitution.[33]

The Court went on to state that the failure of s 1(1) to include within its ambit surviving partners to permanent same-sex life partnerships in which the partners have undertaken reciprocal duties of support, was inconsistent with Mr Gory's rights to equality and dignity in terms of ss 9 and 10 of the Constitution. The Court ruled that with effect from 27 April 1994, s 1(1) of the Intestate Succession Act was to be read as though the following words appear after the word 'spouse', wherever it appears in the section: 'or partner in a permanent same-sex life partnership in which the partners have undertaken reciprocal duties of support'. Just as in *Bhe v Magistrate, Khayelitsha*, the Court decided to make its order retrospective to when the Interim Constitution came into operation, but held that its order would not invalidate any transfer of ownership that had already taken place.

PAUSE FOR REFLECTION

What happens if you don't say 'I do'?

An interesting question is whether the Court's original order in *Gory v Kolver* must still be applied in light of the Civil Union Act which commenced after this judgment was handed down. The Court's decision in *Gory v Kolver* was based on the fact that same-sex couples could not marry at the time. The Civil Union Act subsequently provides that same-sex couples can either marry or enter into a civil union to formalise their relationship. If these couples do not take steps to formalise their relationship, should they endure the harsh consequences following from their decision not to formalise their relationship?

This question is particularly pertinent in light of the Constitutional Court's decision in *Volks v Robinson*[34] where it refused to extend the meaning of the word 'survivor' in terms of the Maintenance of Surviving Spouses Act. Although this Court was willing to concede that the applicant who had been involved in a heterosexual life partnership with the deceased may have suffered some form of discrimination, the Court thought that the discrimination was justified. The Court held that since heterosexuals had capacity to marry, the consequences of their decision not to marry had to be borne by them. The Court, therefore, held that the Maintenance of Surviving Spouses Act was not unconstitutional.[35]

The question is, of course, whether the line of reasoning in *Volks v Robinson* will or should apply to the Intestate Succession Act as well? It may be argued that if heterosexual cohabitants were to challenge the Intestate Succession Act for not accommodating the survivor to a heterosexual permanent life relationship, the court would in all likelihood dismiss such a challenge for precisely the reasons stated in *Volks v Robinson*, namely that they should bear the brunt of their decision not to marry. Secondly, if marriage (where marriage is possible) is a precondition for inheriting, persons in same-sex unions who have not solemnised their relationship after the coming into force of the Civil Union Act on 30 November 2006 may be precluded from inheriting intestate from each other.

33 *Gory v Kolver* 2007 (4) SA 97 (CC) at para 19.
34 2005 (5) BCLR 446 (CC). See Chapter 8 for a discussion of the facts of the case.
35 *Volks v Robinson* 2005 (5) BCLR 446 (CC) at paras 56 & 70.

2.6 Order of succession

The developments over the last few years in both the common and customary law of succession have important implications for the future application of intestate succession rules. The position at present is as follows: if a black person died intestate before 27 April 1994, his or her estate would devolve according to the Black Administration Act and the relevant regulations (the customary law). As regards a person of any other racial group, whether he or she died before or after 27 April 1994, his or her estate would devolve according to the Intestate Succession Act. The following discussion of the order of intestate succession in terms of the Intestate Succession Act now applies where someone (irrespective of the deceased's race or lifestyle) died on or after 27 April 1994.

2.6.1 Rule 1 (S 1(1)(a))

This rule may apply in two possible scenarios:

1. Where the deceased is survived by **one spouse**, but not by a descendant, the spouse inherits the entire intestate estate. This means that even if the deceased is survived by parents, or brothers and sisters, they are excluded.

   Romeo dies intestate. His son, Drew, and father, Murray, predeceased him. Romeo is survived by his wife, Juliet, his mother, Ophelia and his brother, Terence. Juliet will inherit the whole of Romeo's estate.

   Figure 2.3 When there are no descendants, the surviving spouse inherits the entire estate

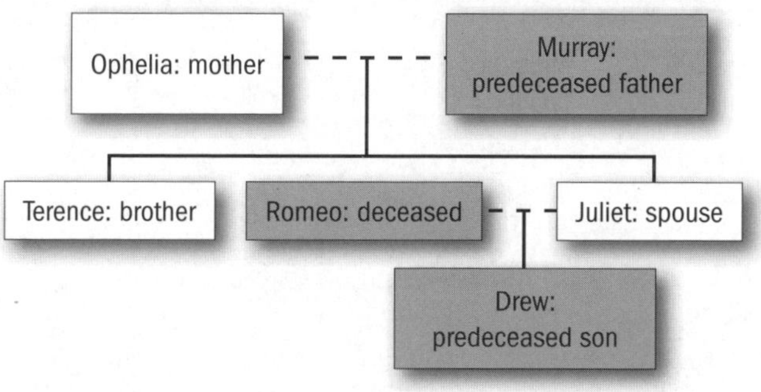

2. Where the deceased is survived by **more than one spouse** and no descendants, the intestate estate must be divided equally between all the spouses.[36]

   Emily, Anna and Sophie are the wives of the deceased. Since there are no descendants, Romeo's intestate estate is divided equally amongst his three wives - each wife inherits a third of Romeo's intestate estate.

   Figure 2.4 When there are no descendants, the surviving spouses share the estate equally

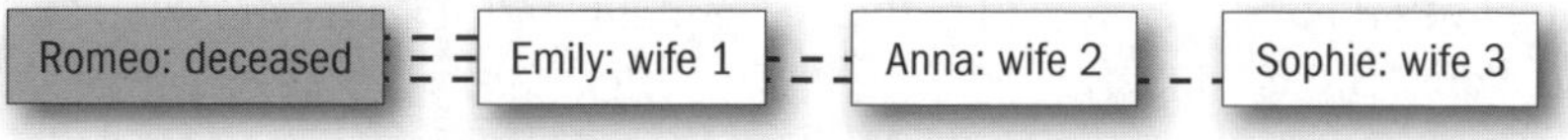

36 *Bhe v Magistrate, Khayelitsha* at para 136 and s 3(2)(iii) of the Reform of Customary Law of Succession Act; *Hassam v Jacobs* unreported case CCT 83/08 [2009] ZACC 19.

2.6.2 Rule 2 (S 1(1)(b))

Where the deceased is survived by a descendant or descendants, but not by a spouse or spouses, the descendant or descendants inherit the entire intestate estate equally and representation is possible.

Rodney dies intestate. His wife, Juliet, and his son, Bert, have predeceased him, and he is survived by his son, Oliver, and his daughter, Miranda, and also by two granddaughters, Winnie and Lisa (the daughters of his predeceased son, Bert).

Rodney's estate is divided into three equal parts and each stirp of the deceased will inherit equally. This means that Oliver and Miranda will inherit one-third each and as Bert is predeceased, his share will be divided equally between his descendants, Winnie and Lisa, who will each receive one-sixth of Rodney's estate.

The same would be true if Winnie had been born as a result of artificial insemination or a surrogacy arrangement. A posthumous child (a child born after the death of a parent) of the deceased will also inherit along with any other living child of the deceased, provided that he or she was conceived at the time of the deceased's death and is subsequently born alive.[37]

Figure 2.5 The descendants inherit the intestate estate equally and representation is possible

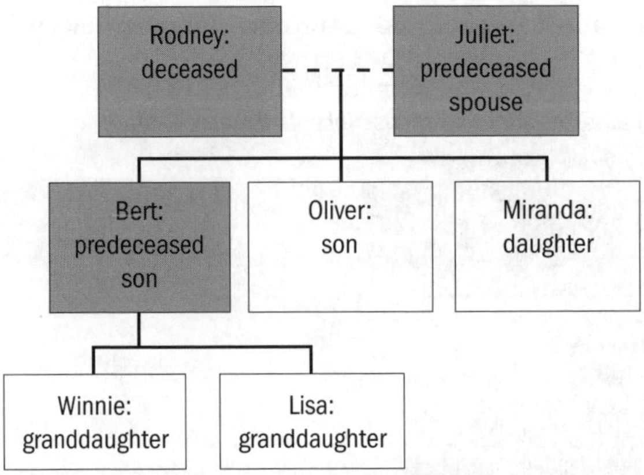

In terms of s 1(6) of the Intestate Succession Act, if a child of the deceased has predeceased the deceased, or is disqualified from inheriting, or renounces the inheritance, then the share (which that child would have received) passes equally to descendants of that child. This process is known as representation *ex lege* (by operation of law) and continues ad infinitum.[38]

If Oliver (see Figure 2.5) had two children, William and Harriet, and was disqualified from inheriting because he had murdered Rodney, his children would inherit his third of the estate in terms of s 1(6) – in other words, one-sixth share each. If Winnie was an adopted child, she would still share equally with Lisa as she would be regarded as a descendant of Bert.

37 *Ex Parte Boedel Steenkamp* 1962 (3) SA 954 (O).
38 Section 1(4)(a) and (f) of the Intestate Succession Act.

PAUSE FOR REFLECTION

Property regimes recognised by South African law

South African law recognises three property regimes:

(a) marriage in community of property

(b) marriage out of community of property with accrual

(c) marriage out of community of property with no accrual.

The determination of the consequences of the different property regimes and how to calculate what a spouse is to receive on dissolution of a marriage (whether by death of a spouse or divorce) is governed by the Matrimonial Property Act 88 of 1984.

2.6.3 Rule 3 (S 1(1)(c))

There are two possible scenarios for this rule depending on the number of spouses surviving the deceased. It may also be further divided according to the matrimonial property regime applicable:

1. Where the deceased is survived by **one spouse** as well as a descendant or descendants, the surviving spouse inherits whichever is the greater of either a child's portion (also called a child's share) or an amount fixed from time to time by the Minister for Justice and Constitutional Development (the amount is presently R125 000).[39] The descendants of the deceased will inherit the residue (if any) of the intestate estate.

   To calculate a child's portion, the value of the estate is divided by the number of children who either survive the deceased, or who predeceased the deceased but are survived by their descendants (i.e. the number of stirps), plus the number of spouses left by the deceased.[40]

   The share inherited by a surviving spouse is unaffected by any amount to which he or she might be entitled in terms of the matrimonial property laws. Where the spouses were married in community of property or under the accrual system, the surviving spouse's share of the joint estate or accrual share does not form part of the intestate estate of the deceased. The amount that the surviving spouse is entitled to in terms of the applicable matrimonial property regime is deducted first and the balance of the intestate estate after all liabilities are paid is then distributed to the surviving spouse and descendants (if any). The same would happen if the spouses had an antenuptial contract containing testamentary provisions.

   Anthony dies intestate. He is survived by his wife, Patience, his son, Marco, and his daughter, Cleo. He is also survived by his two granddaughters, Emma and Claire (the daughters of his predeceased son, Thabo).

39 GN 483 *GG* 11188 of 18 March 1988.

40 See the definition of a child's portion in s 1(4)(f) as amended by the Courts in *Bhe v Magistrate, Khayelitsha* and *Hassam v Jacobs* CCT 83/08 [2009] ZACC 19. The situation will be exactly the same under the Reform of Customary Law of Succession Act.

Figure 2.6 Dividing an intestate estate amongst a spouse and descendants

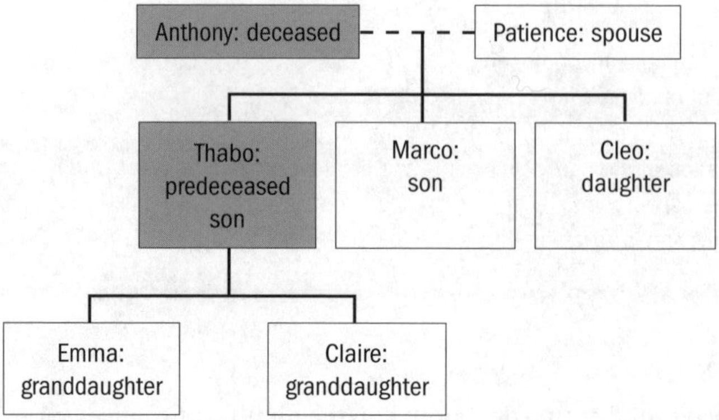

Example 1

Anthony and Patience were married in community of property and the joint estate amounts to R400 000. His estate will be divided as follows:

- Patience receives her half-share (R200 000) of the joint estate in terms of the matrimonial property rules.
- Anthony's intestate estate is worth R200 000 and this must be divided between Patience and the children as follows:
  - The child's portion is R200 000 ÷ 4 (i.e. the number of stirps plus number of surviving spouses) = R50 000; Patience will thus inherit R125 000 (as it is greater than a child's portion).
  - This R125 000 must be subtracted from the amount available in the intestate estate (R200 000 – R125 000) and the remaining R75 000 will be shared equally between Thabo, Marco and Cleo (each inherits R25 000). However, since Thabo is predeceased, his portion will be inherited by his two children, Emma and Claire, in equal shares by representation (each inherits R12 500).

Example 2

Anthony and Patience were married out of community of property with the inclusion of the accrual system and his estate amounts to R450 000. Patience is entitled to R50 000 as accrual. Anthony's estate will be divided as follows:

- The R50 000 accrual due to Patience in terms of the matrimonial property regime must be deducted from Anthony's intestate estate before it is divided.
- Anthony's remaining intestate estate (R400 000) must be divided as follows:
  - The child's portion will be R400 000 ÷ 4 = R100 000 and Patience will thus inherit R125 000 (as it is greater than a child's portion).
  - The remaining R275 000 (R400 000 – R125 000) will be divided equally between Thabo, Marco and Cleo (each inherits R91 666,66), but since Thabo is predeceased, his portion will be inherited by his two children, Emma and Claire, in equal shares by representation (each inherits R45 833,33).

Example 3
Anthony and Patience were married out of community of property with the inclusion of the accrual system. Anthony's estate amounts to R650 000 but his estate is also entitled to R150 000 as accrual from Patience.

Remember, the spouse inherits a child's portion or R125 000 (whichever of the two is the greater), and the residue is divided between the descendants. In this case, the deceased estate is also entitled to the accrual and therefore the accrual must first be added to the estate before it can be divided. In this example, Anthony's estate will be divided as follows:

- Anthony's estate is R800 000 (R650 000 plus R150 000 to which the deceased estate is entitled in terms of the accrual system).
- Patience will inherit the child's portion (R200 000) as it is greater than R125 000.
- The remaining R600 000 (R800 000 – R200 000) will be divided equally between Thabo, Marco and Cleo (each inherits R200 000), but since Thabo is predeceased, his portion will be inherited by his two children, Emma and Claire, in equal shares by representation (each inherits R100 000).

Example 4
Anthony and Patience were married out of community of property with the exclusion of the accrual system and his estate amounts to R600 000. Anthony's estate will be divided as follows:

- Patience will inherit a child's portion of R150 000 as it is greater than R125 000.
- The remaining R450 000 will be divided equally between Thabo, Marco and Cleo (each inherits R150 000), but since Thabo is predeceased, his portion will be inherited by his two children, Emma and Claire, in equal shares (each inherits R75 000).

2. Where the deceased is survived by **more than one spouse**, each surviving spouse inherits whichever is the greater of a child's portion or an amount fixed from time to time by the Minister (the amount is presently R125 000). The descendants will inherit the residue (if any) of the intestate estate. Where the assets of the deceased are not sufficient to provide each spouse with the amount fixed by the Minister, the estate is divided equally between the surviving spouses and the descendants receive nothing.[41]

   See Figure 2.7 – Thabo (the deceased) was married to Emily, Anna and Sophie in chronological order in terms of the Recognition of Customary Marriages Act. He is survived by his three wives and four children.
   - If Thabo's intestate estate amounts to R75 000, Emily, Anna, and Sophie will each inherit R25 000 from the estate and the children will inherit nothing.
   - If Thabo's intestate estate amounts to R500 000, Emily, Anna and Sophie will each inherit R125 000, and the residue of R125 000 will be divided equally amongst the children (Andries, Ben, Charles, and Dina), and each will inherit R31 250.

41 *Bhe v Magistrate, Khayelitsha* at para 136, and s 3(3) of the Reform of Customary Law of Succession Act; *Hassam v Jacobs* unreported case CCT 83/08 [2009] ZACC 19.

- If Thabo's intestate estate amounts to R1 400 000, Emily, Anna, and Sophie (the wives), and also Andries, Ben, Charles and Dina (the children) will each inherit R200 000.

Figure 2.7 *Dividing an intestate estate amongst spouses and descendants*

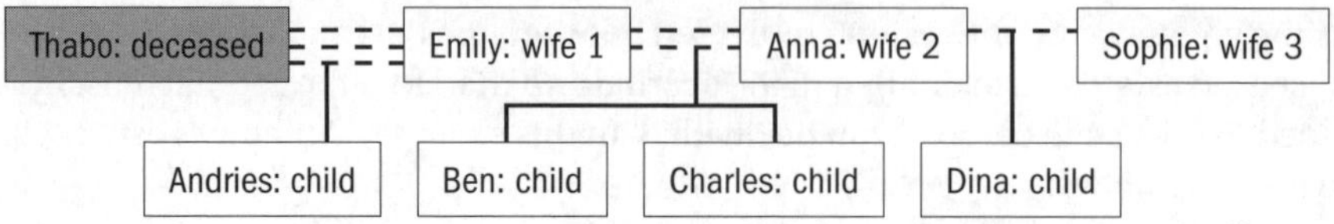

2.6.4 Rule 4 (S 1(1)(d)(i))

Where the deceased leaves no spouse or descendant, but is survived by both parents, they inherit the intestate estate in equal shares. Parents include the biological, adoptive and the commissioning parents (in the case of surrogacy)[42] of the deceased but not a step-parent. If both parents of the deceased are alive, all other collaterals of the deceased related to him or her are excluded from inheriting.

Figure 2.8 *Where there is no spouse or descendant, then the parents inherit*

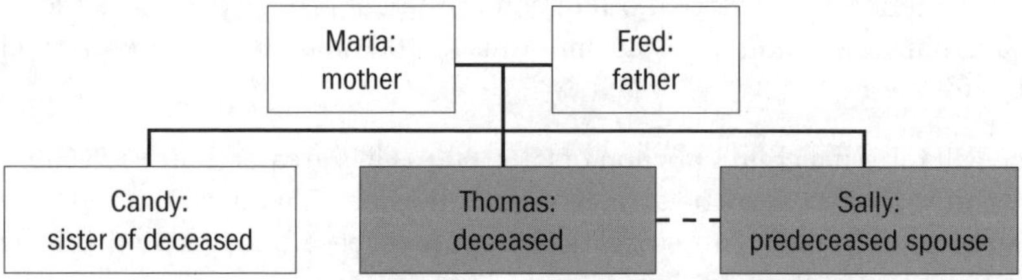

Thomas is survived by his mother, Maria, father, Fred, and sister, Candy. Maria and Fred will inherit Thomas' estate in equal shares because he is not survived by a spouse or spouses, and/or any descendants.

2.6.5 Rule 5 (S 1(1)(d)(ii))

Where the deceased is survived by one of his parents but no spouse or descendant, the surviving parent inherits one half of the intestate estate and the descendants of the deceased parent the other half. If the deceased parent has no descendants, the surviving parent inherits the entire estate. Division between the descendants of a predeceased parent of the deceased takes place by representation (*per stirpes*).[43]

In Figure 2.9, Thomas is survived by his mother, Maria, sister, Candy and half-brother, Dan. Thomas' estate is cloven into two halves. Maria inherits one half of Thomas' estate. The other half that would have devolved to Fred, is divided equally between Fred's descendants (Dan and Candy).

42 See paragraph 2.4.4 on page 22.
43 Section 1(4)(a).

Figure 2.9 Where there is only one surviving parent, the estate is cloven into two halves

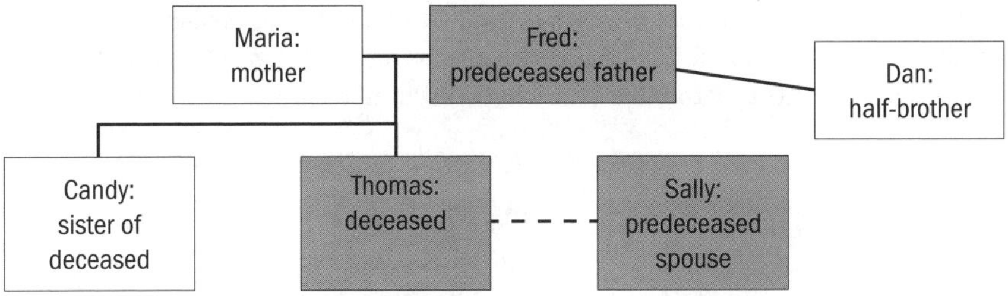

2.6.6 Rule 6 (S 1(1)(e)(i)(aa)–(cc))

Where the deceased is not survived by a spouse, a descendant, or a parent, but is survived by descendants of his or her parents (for example, by a brother or sister, whether of full or half blood), the intestate estate is divided into halves. It is said that the estate is cloven into two equal shares with each share going to the side of one of the deceased's parents. From there, one half goes to the descendants of the deceased father by representation *per stirpes*, and the other half to the descendants of the deceased mother by representation *per stirpes*.[44] The full brothers and sisters of the deceased will take a share from both halves. However, half-brothers and half-sisters take a share from the half of the estate of the parent through which they are related to the deceased.

Xavier dies intestate, and is survived by Ben and Carl, the children of his predeceased half-brother, Hank, on his mother, Mona's, side. He is also survived by Susan, his half-sister on his father, Fred's, side. Xavier's intestate estate amounts to R100 000 and will be divided as follows:

Figure 2.10 (a) Dividing an estate per stirpes *amongst descendants of the parents (example 1)*

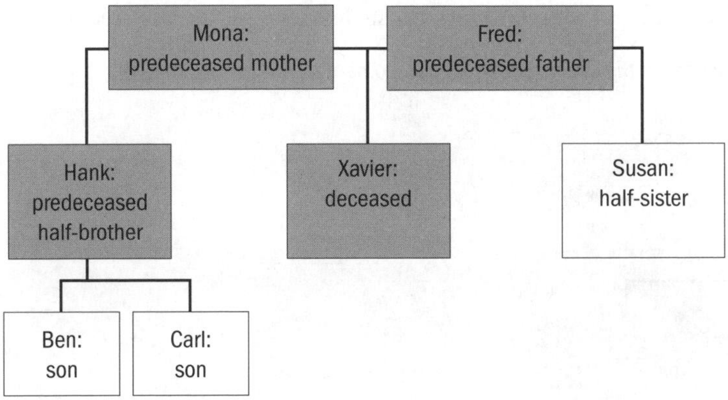

See Figure 2.10:
Since both parents have predeceased Xavier, his estate is cloven or divided into two halves. Susan will inherit R50 000 on the father's side by representation *per stirpes*, and on the mother's side, Ben and Carl will each inherit R25 000 by representing Hank.

44 Section 1(1)(e)(i), read with s 1(4)(a).

Rupert dies intestate and is survived by Drew and Ashleigh, the children of his predeceased half-brother, Mercutio, on his mother, Gina's, side. He is also survived by a full brother, Tibault, and a half-sister, Ariala, on his father, Edward's, side. Rupert's intestate estate amounts to R100 000 and will be divided as follows:

***Figure 2.10** (b) Dividing an estate amongst descendants of the parents (example 2)*

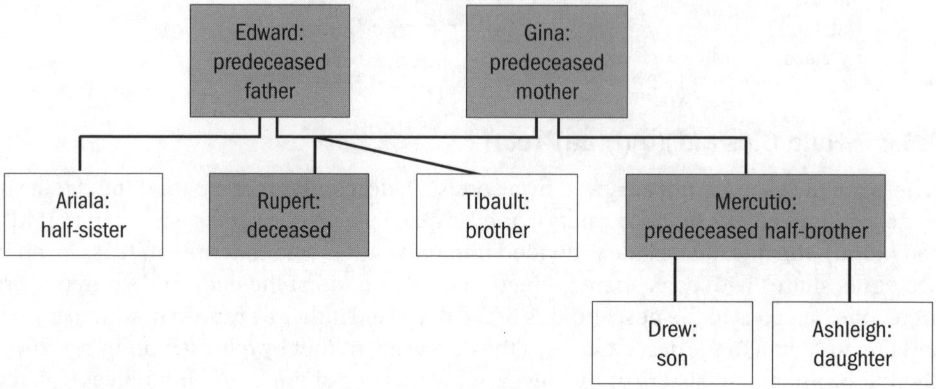

Since both parents have predeceased Rupert, his estate is divided into two halves. Tibault will receive R50 000 since he inherits through both Gina and Edward, the parents of the deceased. Ariala will inherit R25 000 on the father's side by representation (*per stirpes*), and on the mother's side Drew and Ashleigh will inherit R12 500 each by representing Mercutio.

2.6.7 Rule 7 (S 1(1)(e)(ii))

If the deceased is not survived by a spouse or spouses, descendants or parents, and only one of his predeceased parents has left descendants, those descendants are the sole heirs.

***Figure 2.11** Where only one of the deceased's predeceased parents has decendants, they are the sole heirs*

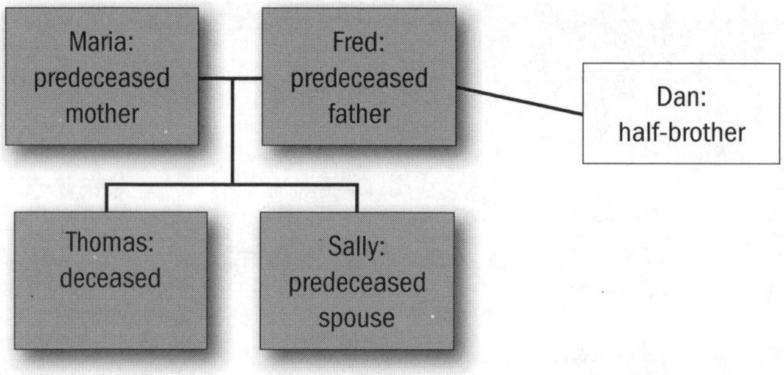

Thomas dies intestate. He is survived by his half-brother, Dan, from his father's side. Dan will inherit Thomas' entire estate.

2.6.8 Rule 8 (S 1(1)(f))

Where the deceased is not survived by a spouse, descendant, parent, or a descendant of a parent, the nearest blood relation inherits.

> In Figure 2.12, Aunt Anne, being the closest blood relation to the deceased Thomas, will inherit Thomas' entire estate.

Figure 2.12 *When the nearest blood relation inherits*

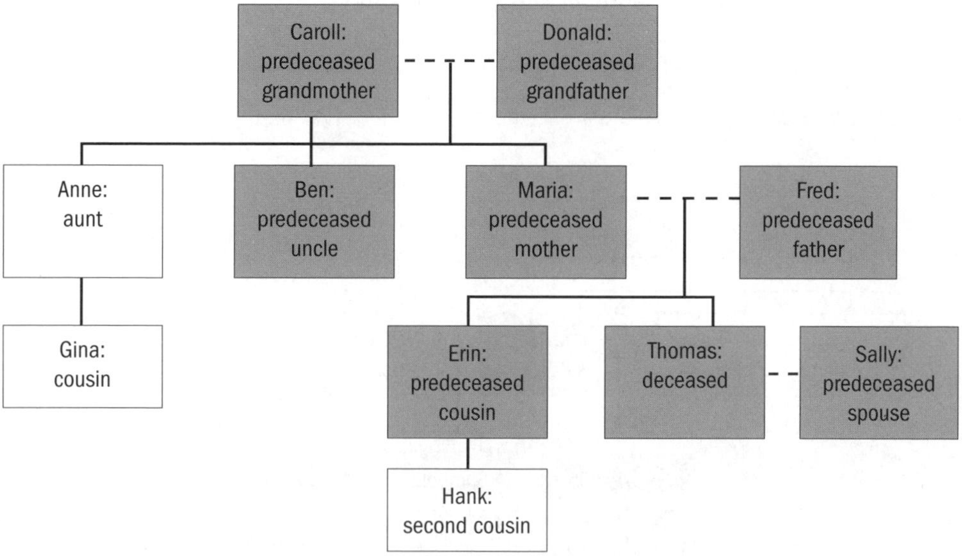

2.7 Disqualification and repudiation

In terms of s 1(7) of the Intestate Succession Act, if a person is disqualified[45] from being an intestate heir of the deceased, the benefit which that heir would have received devolves as if the heir had died immediately before the death of the deceased, and as if the heir had not been disqualified from inheriting. What this means, is that the disqualified heir is deemed to have predeceased the deceased. If the disqualified heir has descendants of his or her own, those descendants will inherit by representation (*per stirpes*) the inheritance which the disqualified heir would have inherited. If the disqualified heir has no descendants, then the share which the disqualified heir would have received will go to the other heirs of the deceased according to the normal principles of intestate succession.

Aside from disqualification, s 1(7) also deals with the issue of repudiation. Section 1(7) is subject to s 1(6) of the Act. Applying the two sections together the following is the position: If an intestate heir of the deceased repudiates an inheritance and the deceased is survived by a surviving spouse, the surviving spouse, will inherit the repudiating heir's share. However, if the deceased is not survived by a surviving spouse then the repudiating heir will be deemed to have predeceased the deceased and his or her descendants will inherit by representation (*per stirpes*). In the latter scenario, should it turn out that the repudiating heir has no descendants, the inheritance will pass to the intestate heirs of the deceased according to the normal rules of intestate succession.

45 Disqualification of an heir is dealt with in Chapter 7, and also under the heading 'substitution' in Chapter 10.

In May 2007, John and William entered into a civil union (in terms of the Civil Union Act) subject to the accrual system. In January 2008, John died intestate and left the following relatives as shown in Figure 2.13:

- William, who is entitled to R100 000 as accrual
- Samuel and Dina, the adopted children of John and William (when the estate is liquidated, Dina refuses to inherit any part of John's estate)
- Frans, the grandson of John (Frans is the son of John's predeceased son, Gerald, who was born from John's first marriage to Kathy)
- Mary, John's mother
- Ben, John's brother.

Figure 2.13 John's relatives

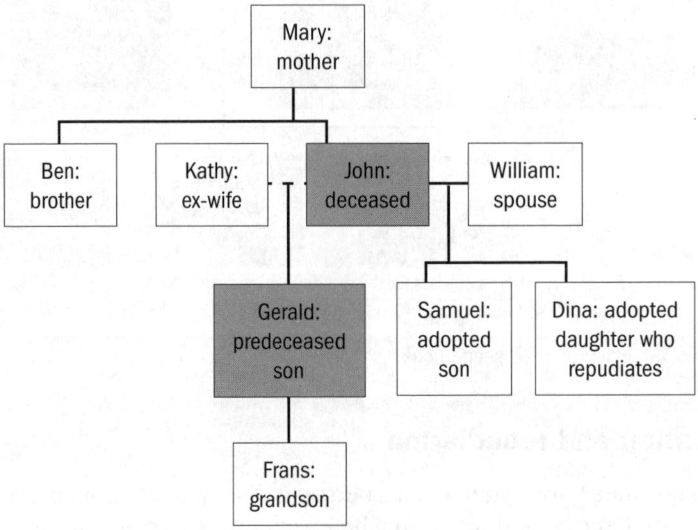

The total value of John's estate is R900 000. John's estate will devolve as follows:

- William is entitled to R100 000 accrual in terms of matrimonial property law. The R100 000 is subtracted from John's estate: R900 000 – R100 000 = R800 000. This means that the total value of John's estate to be divided in terms of intestate succession rules is R800 000.
- William is entitled to inherit a child's portion or R125 000, whichever is the greater. A child's portion = R800 000 ÷ 4 (Samuel, Dina, Gerald + 1) = R200 000, which is greater than R125 000 and therefore William inherits R200 000.
- The remaining R600 000 (R800 000 – R200 000) has to be divided equally amongst the children, Samuel, Dina and Gerald (R200 000 each) but, because Gerald is predeceased, his share of R200 000 will go to William's grandson, Frans, by way of representation.
- Dina repudiates the inheritance and therefore her share of R200 000 must go to William in terms of s 1(6) of the Intestate Succession Act which provides that if a descendant refuses to inherit, his or her share goes to the surviving spouse.

- Mary, John's mother, and Ben, John's brother, inherit nothing because Mary is an ascendant and Ben is a relative in the collateral line; there are closer relatives who exclude them.

PAUSE FOR REFLECTION

The surviving spouse

Section 1(6) of the Intestate Succession Act refers only to the 'surviving spouse' of the deceased in the singular. It is not clear what the situation is going to be if the deceased had more than one spouse. The Reform of Customary Law of Succession and Regulation of Related Matters Bill[46] contained a clause that regulated the situation where a descendant renounces his or her right to a benefit from the deceased's intestate estate. This was especially important in the case where a deceased had more than one wife who bore him children. According to this clause, the renounced benefit vested in the surviving spouse who was the parent of the said descendant. However, this clause was not included in the Reform of Customary Law of Succession Act and, as a result, the situation is uncertain where a descendant in a polygynous marriage renounces his or her right to a benefit from the intestate estate.

2.8 Reform of the Customary Law of Succession Act (RCLSA)

The RCLSA was assented to on 19 April 2009. The Act is not yet in operation but all indications are that the commencement date will soon be published. At this stage it is important to consider the provisions of the Act from the point of view of intestate succession, especially with regard to the customary law of succession.

The RCLSA not only harmonises the common and customary law of intestate succession, but also provides for differences depending on a person's cultural affiliations. For example, if a person lives under a system of customary law and dies without a valid will, his or her estate must devolve in terms of the Intestate Succession Act, but with certain modifications typical to customary law (such as polygyny, a wider circle of relations and other marriage forms).[47]

2.8.1 Contents of the RCLSA

The RCLSA reaffirms that the Intestate Succession Act will be applicable to all estates, for it provides in s 2(1) that the estate or part of the estate of any person who is subject to customary law and whose estate does not devolve by means of a valid will, must devolve in accordance with the law of intestate succession as regulated by the Intestate Succession Act. What this means is that the Intestate Succession Act is applicable to all intestate estates in South Africa irrespective of the race or Western or African lifestyle of a deceased. However, in the application of the Intestate Succession Act, s 2 of the RCLSA makes special provision for situations usually encountered in customary law only. Its contents in relation to the Intestate Succession Act are summarised below.

46 Bill 10B-2008, clause 4(e).

47 See Chapter 1 for a discussion of the rules of conflict.

2.8.1.1 Definitions

Section 1 of the RCLSA defines the terms 'customary law', 'descendant', 'house', 'Intestate Succession Act', 'spouse',[48] 'traditional leader', and 'will'. None of these definitions are contained in the Intestate Succession Act, but some of them have been interpreted by the courts to mean something specific.

The term 'descendant' is defined by the RCLSA to include:

> *... a person who is a descendant in terms of the Intestate Succession Act, and includes:*
> *(a) a person who is not a descendant in terms of the Intestate Succession Act, but who, during the lifetime of the deceased person, was accepted by the deceased person in accordance with customary law as his or her own child; and*
> *(b) a woman referred to in section 2(2)(b) or (c).*

A woman in terms of these two sections could include a spouse in terms of a substitute marriage or a woman to woman marriage.

PAUSE FOR REFLECTION

Dealing with definitions

The fact that the RCLSA refers back to the customary law to determine the legal position in various instances is not an unfamiliar phenomenon. Because the customary law is in essence an uncodified legal system, it would be necessary to refer back to customary law principles to find out what the specific legal position would be. This also makes it possible to determine the living version instead of the official version of customary law.

The common law understanding of the word 'descendant' usually means blood relations in the descending line (for example, children, grandchildren or great-grandchildren). The extended meaning of descendants in the context of customary law is thus quite a deviation - see Chapter 1 for the definition.

In customary law, a woman might conclude a substitute marriage to procreate male offspring for her deceased husband. Although the deceased is not the biological father of the child, he is responsible for the maintenance of the child and therefore the child will be regarded as a descendant who should succeed to the property of the deceased. In certain communities, the husband of a wife who died young or who proved to be barren could demand that the wife's family provide her sister as a replacement. While these types of marriages are not common today, they potentially still exist. For this reason, the legislature decided to recognise the inheritance rights of the new 'wife' by declaring her a descendant of the deceased. In the case of woman to woman marriages the purpose of the marriage is also to provide offspring for the deceased on behalf of his wife. In some communities an older woman of wealth and status is able to acquire another woman as her 'wife'. The 'wife' is expected to have sexual relations with a selected male (usually the son or the brother of the older women's husband) so that she can produce children for the older woman's husband's house. In terms of the Act, the new 'wife' is considered to be the descendant of the older woman on the death of the older woman.

48 The common law meaning of 'spouse' is extended to include other unions. See Chapter 1 for a definition of a spouse.

2.8.1.2 Interpretation

Section 3 of the RCLSA introduces special rules to interpret certain provisions of the Intestate Succession Act. These rules include, firstly, a wider meaning which must be given to the term 'spouse' when dealing with customary marriages to include all the 'spouses' of the deceased. Secondly, a special circumstance prevails where the fixed amount is not enough to provide for all the 'spouses' of the deceased.

2.8.1.3 Freedom of testation

Section 4 of the RCLSA allows for freedom of testation, a concept unfamiliar to the customary law of succession, by giving women living under customary law the right to dispose of house property by means of a will. In addition, s 2 of the Act makes it clear that a customary law estate can devolve in terms of a will, thus introducing the concept of freedom of testation into the customary law of succession.

2.8.1.4 Disputes

In the case of customary law disputes regarding the status of persons, the nature and content of assets, or devolution of family property, s 5 of the RCLSA lays down that the Master of the High Court has jurisdiction to resolve these matters. This section is in accordance with the jurisdiction of the Master in connection with the administration of estates.[49] However, when dealing with customary estates, the matter may be referred to a magistrate to make an enquiry into the matter in order to provide the Master with a recommendation. When making a determination, both the Master and the magistrate must have due regard to the best interests of the family members and the equality of spouses.

PAUSE FOR REFLECTION

The Master or the magistrate

Keeping in mind the fact that it used to be magistrates who were involved in the administration of customary estates, this provision comes as no surprise. Magistrates might be in a better position than the Master to hold an enquiry into the customary law issues. For example, there are fewer Master's offices (usually only in the bigger centres and not in smaller towns or rural areas), whilst there are magistrates' offices in almost all the districts of South Africa.

2.8.1.5 Traditional leaders

Property held by a traditional leader in his official capacity in terms of the Traditional Leadership and Governance Framework Act[50] is excluded from his estate by s 6 of the RCLSA. This is a special provision to ensure that the Intestate Succession Act does not interfere with such property held by a deceased traditional leader.

2.8.1.6 Property rights

The purpose of s 7 of the RCLSA is to protect spouses involved in certain customary marriages. Until 2 December 1988 a man involved in a customary marriage could enter into a civil marriage with another woman, thereby dissolving his customary marriage. Section 7(1) is

49 See Chapter 15 for a discussion of the functions of the Master.
50 41 of 2003.

meant to protect the rights of those 'discarded' customary law wives by providing that the proprietary rights of customary spouses and children will not be affected by a civil marriage if the latter was entered into on or after 1 January 1929,[51] but before 2 December 1988.[52] Section 7(2) also affords equal rights in the deceased estate to the spouses and children of both the civil and customary marriages.

2.8.2 Order of succession in former customary law estates

Customary succession rules are mostly uncodified,[53] but the legal rules indicating when the customary law of succession should be applied and when not, were contained in s 23 of the Black Administration Act and the regulations issued in terms of that Act.[54] These two pieces of legislation were found to be unconstitutional and were invalidated with retrospective effect to 27 April 1994 in *Bhe v Magistrate, Khayelitsha*.

Nevertheless, there is currently no legal prohibition that forbids a testator to execute a will in which he or she stipulates that his or her estate must devolve according to the customary law of succession. For this reason, it is important that legal practitioners still have a basic knowledge of what these rules entail.

The customary law of succession reflects the polygynous marriage system as well as the broad family context. The customary law of succession is concerned not merely with the inheritance of property, but also with succession to the status of the deceased – the successor steps into the shoes of the deceased and gains control over the property and people over which the deceased had control. Thus, the successor succeeds not only to the assets of the estate, but also to its liabilities.

The concept 'house' as explained in Chapter 1 and the various categories of property in terms of customary law are in line with the polygynous family system. Although there are tangible differences between the various indigenous groups in South Africa, the following general principles may be identified:

- Similar to the common law rule, the family head must be dead before succession to his status position can take place; there can be no question of succession where the family head is still alive. However, the deaths of other members of the family do not give rise to succession to their statuses.
- A distinction is made between general succession (that is, succession to the general status of the deceased), and special succession (that is, succession to the position of head of the various houses of the deceased in a polygynous household).
- Succession to status is limited largely to males, especially those of the patrilineage, the line of descent traced through the paternal side of the family, and, as a general principle, a man cannot be succeeded by a woman.
- Succession follows the rule of male primogeniture, which means that a man is succeeded by his firstborn son in a particular house.
- Succession is a duty that cannot be relinquished or ceded, and a son is obliged to take up all the responsibilities associated with the status position to which he succeeds. The general successor, in particular, has the duty to care for all members of the family, and

51 The date of commencement of ss 22 and 23 of the Black Administration Act.

52 The date of commencement of the Marriage and Matrimonial Property Law Amendment Act 3 of 1988.

53 An exception is the succession rules in KwaZulu-Natal which have been codified in the Code of Zulu Law (KwaZulu Act on the Code of Zulu Law 16 of 1985 and the Natal Code of Zulu Law contained in Proc R151 of 1987).

54 Regulations for the Administration and Distribution of the Estates of Deceased Blacks in *GG* 10601 of 6 February 1987 (hereinafter GN R200 of 1987).

has to perform rituals on behalf of the family to maintain the blessing and goodwill of the family ancestors.

- As with the common law of succession, descendants enjoy preference over ascendants and ascendants over collaterals. However, the preference is only applicable to male descendants, male ascendants and male collaterals.
- A successor may, on good grounds, be removed from the line of succession. Such a step has serious consequences since the person who is disinherited is ousted not only from the financial and emotional support of the family, but also from the spiritual bond with the family ancestors.
- Originally, succession was universal – the successor succeeded to the status of the deceased in respect of his control over people, and the assets and liabilities of the family. Presently, the position is not uniform and variations exist amongst different groups. For example, in KwaZulu-Natal, a successor is only liable for debts in respect of the estate and only to the extent of the assets to which he succeeds. Outside KwaZulu-Natal, a successor succeeds to the assets and debts of the deceased, and among the Pondo, the successor is not liable for the delicts committed by the deceased.
- The order of succession depends largely on the structure of the deceased's household, in other words, whether he was the head of a monogamous or polygynous household.

2.8.2.1 Succession in monogamous households

The order of succession in a monogamous household is described in the following example.

Thabo Monchusi from the Nguni group is married in terms of customary law to Sophie Sekgotho. Together they have three children: Petrus (the firstborn son), Jonna (the secondborn son), and Tembi (the youngest daughter). See Figure 2.14. Thabo and Sophie constitute a house. When Thabo dies the following general succession rules will be applicable:

- The principle of male primogeniture is applicable. This means that the eldest son, Petrus, succeeds to the deceased, and if Petrus is predeceased, Thabo's male descendants in order of birth will inherit.
- If Petrus is predeceased and has no male descendants, the second son, Jonna, or, if predeceased, Jonna's male descendants in order of birth will inherit.
- If Thabo dies without male descendants, his father will inherit.
- If Thabo dies without male descendants and without a father, his eldest brother or, if predeceased, the eldest brother's male descendants in order of birth will inherit.
- If Thabo's elder brother and male descendants are predeceased, all Thabo's brothers will be considered according to their order of birth.
- If Thabo dies without male descendants, a father and brothers, the grandfather of the deceased or one of his male descendants according to seniority will succeed.
- If Thabo dies without male descendants, a father, brothers and a grandfather, the next successor in line is the paternal great-grandfather and his male descendants in the order of seniority.
- If Thabo dies without a male successor, and no other sons were 'conceived' on his behalf, his estate will go to the traditional leader of the particular community.

Figure 2.14 *John's relatives*

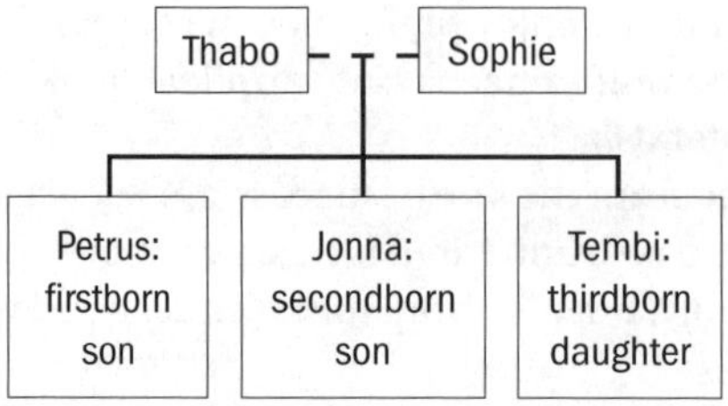

2.8.2.2 Succession in polygynous households

When a man marries more than one wife, a polygynous marriage is formed where each wife constitutes a household with house property. The status of each household, and that of the wives associated with each house, differs according to the rules of each group. For example, in the Nguni group the man's first wife is his left-hand wife and his second wife is his right-hand wife. All other wives are affiliated to these two houses in the order of marriage. In the case of Zulus (part of the Nguni group), the man can usually decide which wife will be his left-hand wife and which one will be his right-hand wife, and also which wife will be affiliated to which house. For the Tswana, the status is usually seated in the order of marriage. The following example is based on the customs of the Nguni group:

Over the years, Thabo marries four wives in terms of the customary law and thus has a polygynous household. He has various children (sons and daughters) with each wife. The following general succession rules are applicable when Thabo dies:

- The eldest son of the great house (left-hand wife) in the male lineage is the successor to the family property and to the status of the deceased Thabo or, if the eldest son is predeceased, his eldest living son will be the successor.
- The eldest son of each house, or if he is predeceased, the eldest son's eldest living son, inherits the house property.
- If there is no son in the house who could inherit the house property, the property is transferred to the eldest son of another house which is next in rank.

2.8.2.3 Practical applications of the customary succession rules

Monogamous family with descendants

Keeping the general rules in mind, the following situations may prevail in Figure 2.15:

- Frans is excluded because he descends through a female, namely Anna.
- Ben was the eldest male in the family, but is now deceased, and his eldest child, Hanna, is a daughter, and therefore her son, Lamos, is also excluded.
- Hanna's daughter, Martie, cannot inherit and Ben's second son, John, is also deceased. But John has a son, Nel, who will inherit according to the rules.
- Nel excludes all other potential beneficiaries, even Ben's younger brother, Charles.
- If Nel was also deceased, then Keliboge will inherit, and if Keliboge were also deceased, Charles would inherit because if the firstborn male lineal descendancy

of the deceased family head are exhausted, the inheritance will go to the second eldest son and, failing him, his male descendants.

- Remember that the principle is that the eldest son or his descendants inherit and, if they are deceased, the second son and his descendants (always through the male line) inherit, and then the third and so on.

Figure 2.15 How an estate devolves in a monogamous family with descendants

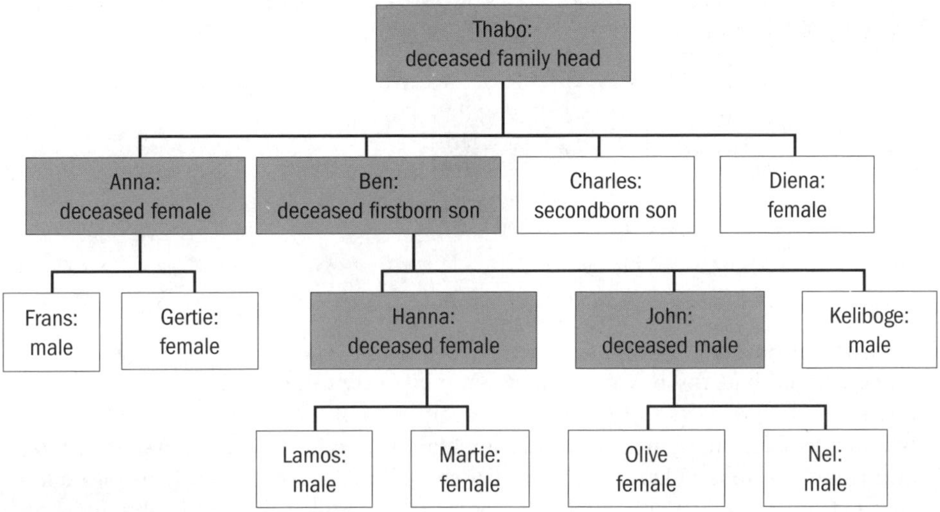

Monogamous family without descendants

Keeping the general rules in mind, the following situations may prevail in Figure 2.16:

- In this example, the deceased Thabo has no descendants and the next successor in line is his father.
- If Thabo's father were also predeceased, successsion moves to the side of the great wife (or left-hand wife) of the father.
- The brother, Anton, is predeceased and his daughter, Dina, cannot inherit.
- The brother, Ben, is predeceased and his eldest daughter cannot inherit, but he also has a predeceased son, Fanus, who has a son, Gert, who is still alive, and according to the rules, Gert will be the successor.
- If Gert were also dead, Thabo's sister Celia is excluded from inheritance (she is female), and succession moves to the right-hand wife to seek a successor.
- In the case of the right-hand wife, the eldest son, Hans, is still alive and he will thus inherit. If he were deceased, the successor will be the second brother, Ignus, and then finally the youngest brother, John.

Figure 2.16 How an estate devolves in a monogamous family without descendants

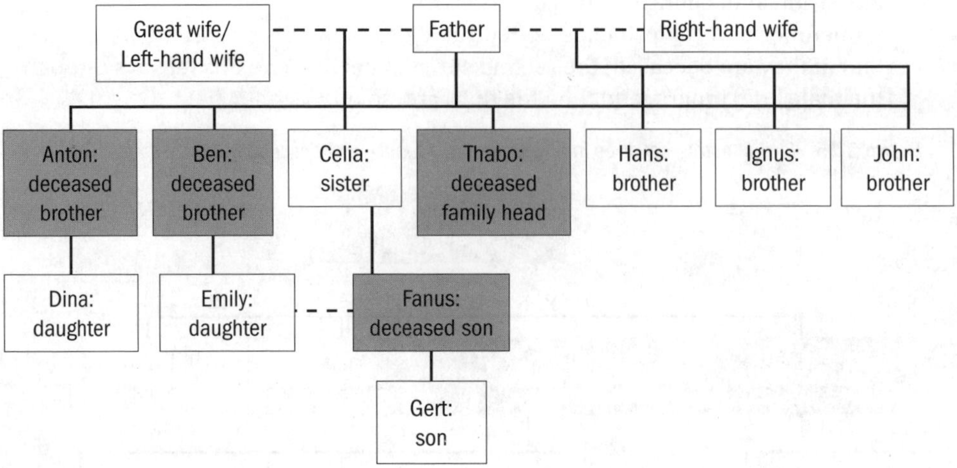

Polygynous family[55]

The deceased had three wives – his great wife, a right-hand wife and a house affiliated to the great wife's house. The descendants of the deceased from his great wife are Anna, his daughter, Ben and Dan, his sons, Celia, the daughter of Ben, Elias and Fanie, the sons of Dan, and Gert, the son of Fanie. The descendants of the deceased from his right-hand wife are his sons, Karel and Leon, and Ria, the daughter of Karel. The descendants of the deceased from his wife affiliated to his great wife are his son, Hans, his daughter, Ilze, and John, the son of Ilze. Piet is the father of the deceased. Olaf and Riaan are the brothers of the deceased from the great house of his father. Olaf has two children, namely a son, Zanor, and a daughter, Quile. Riaan has a daughter, Sonile. Tys and Willem are the half-brothers of the deceased from the right-hand house of his father. Tys has a daughter, Ulinge. Ulinge has a son, Vos. Willem has two children, namely a daughter, Xandi, and son, Yuli.

Keeping the general rules in mind, the following situations may prevail in Figure 2.17:

- If Ben and Dan are predeceased, the house property of the great wife will devolve upon Elias; the house property of the right-hand house will devolve upon Karel; and the property of the affiliated house will devolve upon Hans.
- If all the descendants of the deceased's great wife are also predeceased, the property will devolve upon Hans, the eldest son of the affiliated house.
- If Hans and Karel were also dead, the property will devolve upon Leon, the eldest son of the right-hand wife.
- If the deceased dies without descendants, the property will devolve upon Piet, the deceased's father.
- If Piet, Olaf, Riaan, Tys and Willem are also predeceased, the property will devolve upon Zanor, the son of the eldest son of the deceased's father's great wife.
- If Zanor is also predeceased, the property will devolve upon Yuli, the only son of a son of the right-hand house of the deceased's father.

55 This example is based on Rautenbach et al *LAWSA* para 144(a).

- If the deceased dies without male beneficiaries and no sons were conceived through other customs, the property will devolve upon the traditional leader.

Figure 2.17 *How an estate devolves in a polygynous family*

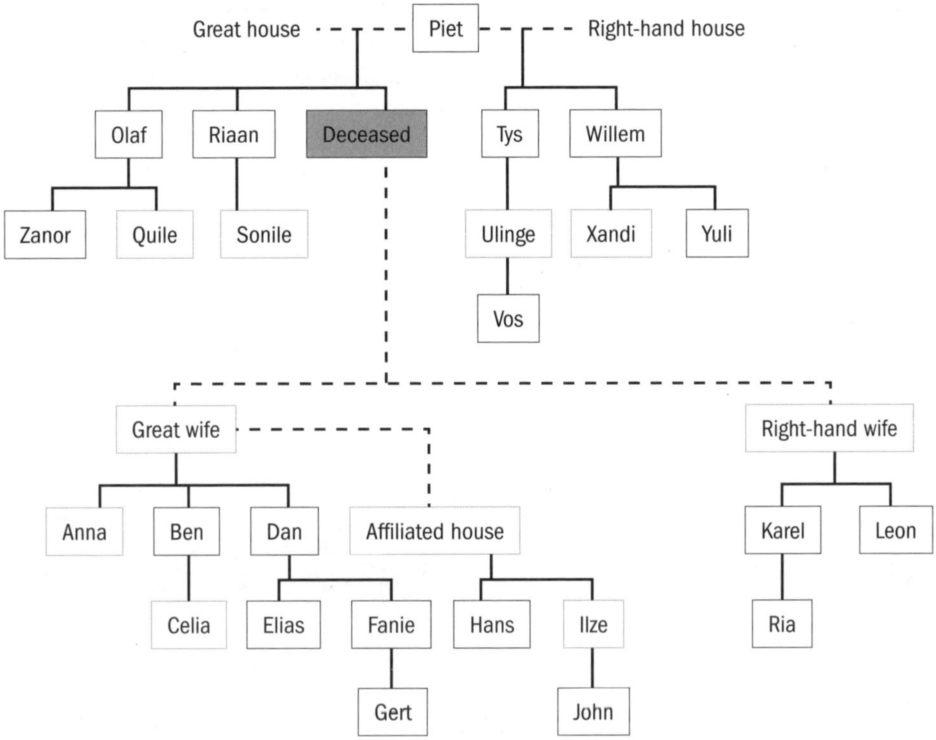

THIS CHAPTER IN ESSENCE

1. The law of intestate succession only applies where the testator has not left a valid will, testamentary provisions contained in a valid *pactum successorium* such as an antenuptial contract, or where he or she leaves a will but the will fails for some or other reason.
2. In the past certain intestate estates of African people were distributed according to the 'official customary law' as entrenched in the Black Administration Act and the regulations thereto whilst the Intestate Succession Act applied to the rest of the population.
3. Initially the word 'spouse' in the Intestate Succession Act was restrictively interpreted to mean those spouses who had contracted a marriage in terms of the Marriage Act 25 of 1961. This restrictive interpretation has now been extended by case law.
4. The Intestate Succession Act together with the Children's Act[56] has extended the categories of persons who may be intestate succession heirs. For example, all natural persons irrespective of whether they are adopted, extramarital, conceived as result of an artificial insemination procedure or born as a result of a surrogacy arrangement nowadays have capacity to inherit.

56 38 of 2005.

5. While the Intestate Succession Act is important, one cannot discount case law when determining the rules of intestate succession. Furthermore, if and when the RCLSA is promulgated into law, then it, too, will be relevant for determining our intestate succession laws.
6. A testator living under a system of customary law may still use his or her freedom of testation to stipulate that the customary law of succession must be applicable to his or her estate and, in such a case, it would be necessary to apply the customary law of succession to the deceased estate.
7. If the customary law of succession is applicable, it is important to distinguish between the order of succession in a monogamous and polygynous household.

Chapter 3

Testate succession – general rules

What are the general rules for the law of testate succession?

3.1	Introduction	47
3.2	Wills, codicils and testamentary writings	48
3.3	Joint and mutual wills	53
3.4	Adiation and repudiation	54
3.5	Doctrine of election	56
3.6	Customary law of succession	57
This chapter in essence		57

3.1 Introduction

The law of testate succession comprises those legal rules or norms that regulate the devolution of a deceased person's estate upon one or more persons according to the testator's wishes as expressed in a will. The law of testate succession therefore deals with wills.

A will is drafted and executed by a testator to regulate how his or her estate and other affairs should be dealt with after his or her death. As soon as a person dies, his or her will is submitted to the Master of the High Court and is scrutinised for validity. If it is accepted as validly executed, an executor is appointed to handle the liquidation of the estate.[1] A will must therefore comply with a number of general requirements as well as certain formalities stipulated in the Wills Act before it will be accepted as a valid will.

The complex system for executing wills that existed in South Africa prior to 1954 was rationalised by the enactment of the Wills Act (effective from 1 January 1954). This Act abolished all Roman-Dutch common law wills and repealed the separate legislation that applied in each of the four provinces. The Wills Act was amended in 1992 and, since then, our law has permitted only one kind of will, often referred to as the statutory will. The will-making formalities are set out in s 2(1)(a) of the Act and apply to all wills executed after 1 January 1954[2] where the testators died after 1 October 1992.[3] These formalities apply only to documents that are wills.

Any will that was properly executed at the time it was made in terms of the common law or pre-1953 legislation remains valid until revoked by the testator.

1 See Chapter 15 for a discussion of the administration of estates.
2 Being the date on which the Wills Act came into operation.
3 This is in terms of s 15 of the Law of Succession Amendment Act 43 of 1992.

3.2 Wills, codicils and testamentary writings

3.2.1 Definition of a will

The Wills Act defines a will as follows: ' "will" includes a codicil and any other testamentary writing.'[4] The purpose of this definition is solely to indicate which types of documents are relevant to the Act and especially which types have to conform to the formalities as stipulated by s 2(1)[5] of the Act. The Act's definition therefore does not indicate the essence of a will. Several writers have, however, provided their own definitions as illustrated in Table 3.1.

Table 3.1 Definitions of a will

Definition 1
'Testament is 'n eensydige en *vrywillige* wilsuiting wat op 'n regtens voorgeskrewe wyse plaasgevind het en waardeur 'n persoon bepaal wat met sy nalatenskap na sy dood moet gebeur.'[6] [Loosely translated: A will is a unilateral and voluntary expression of one's will which is made in a legally prescribed manner and by which one person provides what is to happen to one's estate after one's death.]
Definition 2
'A will can be defined as a written document in which a testator *voluntarily* sets out his instructions as to how his assets are to devolve following his death.'[7]
Definition 3
'A will or testament may be defined as a declaration in a document executed in the manner required by law by the person making it, the testator, in regard to the devolution of the testator's property[8] after the testator's death. ... Not every such document will necessarily be the result of a valid testamentary act. In order to be valid the act of testation must be free and voluntary.'[9]
Definition 4
'A last will and testament, commonly called a will, is a document executed in the manner prescribed by law by a person, called the testator, concerning the disposition of property and other matters within his control,[10] to take effect after his death.'[11]

The last definition best describes all the elements of a valid will but all of them make it clear that the act of drawing up a will must be voluntary. In other words, a will must be freely made with the intention of providing for the devolution of the testator's estate. The basic prerequisites for the validity of any testamentary document that may be gathered from these definitions are:

1. the testator must have the free and serious intention to execute a will (he or she must have *animus testandi*)
2. the testator must have made the declaration voluntarily.

4 Section 1.
5 The requirements of this section are discussed in Chapter 5.
6 Van der Merwe & Rowland at 15.
7 Pace & Van der Westhuizen 1, own italics.
8 Corbett et al, 34 n6 points out that the definition is incomplete as a will may not only concern the testator's property.
9 Corbett et al, 34.
10 Other matters within the control of the testator include, for example, the appointment of an executor or guardians.
11 Erasmus & De Waal *LAWSA* 31 para 221.

Certain requirements for a valid will are prescribed in the Wills Act, namely:

1. the testator must have testamentary capacity[12]
2. the will must comply with the formalities prescribed by s 2 of the Wills Act.[13]

3.2.2 Basic requirements for a valid will

3.2.2.1 *Animus testandi*

Animus testandi or the intention to make a will is a core requirement for the validity of a will. Beinart[14] sums up the principle as follows:

> *It is clear law that a will, before it can be given effect to as such, must be a conscious, serious and deliberate statement of intention, and therefore a mere indication of a testator's last wishes, or a statement for future use, or a mere note, or instructions for execution of the will is not an act of testation. There must be a serious and complete and final act of testation made* animo testandi, *of such a nature as to show testator [sic] intended his declaration to take effect as his will.*

The testator must not only intend to provide for the devolution of his or her estate, but must also have the intention of doing so in a will.[15]

> In *Sim v The Master,*[16] the Court decided that an unsigned document left by a testator which provided for several charitable bequests was not a valid charitable will as it appeared that the testator had intended to sign the document at a later stage. At that stage, charitable wills were seen as privileged wills which did not have to comply with the formalities required for other valid wills. The Court was of the opinion that the testator could have changed his mind before signing the document and consequently he did not have *animus testandi* towards that particular document. In this case, the Court saw the completion of the formalities as the expression of the deceased's *animus testandi*. In *In re Leedham,*[17] the Court reasoned differently and held that the deceased's intention to provide for the devolution of his estate was sufficient, regardless of whether he intended that the particular document should be his will.

Without the requisite *animus testandi,* a will created by a deceased is invalid *ab initio.*[18] This means that the will is invalid from the onset or beginning.

It is possible that a lack of *animus testandi* is caused by force or mistake. For example, if a testator mistakenly signs a document not knowing that it is a will, the necessary *animus testandi* to make a will is absent and the will is invalid *ab initio*. In such a case, the testator's mistake leads to a total lack of *animus testandi*. On the other hand, where a testator makes a will because of a mistake in the testator's motivation, he or she still has *animus testandi* and the will is not invalid. Evidence may be led in court to establish whether the deceased

---

12 This requirement will be discussed in Chapter 4.
13 Formalities will be discussed in Chapter 5.
14 1959 *Acta Juridica* 200.
15 *Sim v The Master* 1913 CPD 187; *Burton-Moore v The Master* 1983 (4) SA 419 (N).
16 1913 CPD 187.
17 (1901) 18 SC 450.
18 *Van Wyk v Van Wyk's Executor* (1887–1888) 5 SC 1; *In re Winter* (1894) 15 NLR 287; *Sim v The Master* 1913 CPD 187; *Ex parte Saunders* 1927 SWA 122.

had the requisite *animus testandi* if this issue is disputed.[19] A similar situation exists where a testator executes a will whilst in a state of fear due to duress – he or she does not have the requisite *animus testandi* and the will is also invalid *ab initio*.

PAUSE FOR REFLECTION

Duress, force and mistake

The principles regarding duress, force and mistake are well known in the law of contract and are discussed in *BOE Bank Bpk v Van Zyl*[20] where the nature of duress in the law of contract is considered. These principles may be extended to the law of succession.

Circumstances where the will was made because of fraud or duress need to be distinguished from those where the testator was under undue influence when the will was made. In the case of fraud or duress, the will is always invalid because of a lack of *animus testandi*. In the case of undue influence, however, the question is always whether the influence was such that the testator did not have *animus testandi*, or whether the influence was such that the testator no longer expressed his or her own free will even if he or she did have *animus testandi*.[21]

3.2.2.2 Volition (or choice)

From the definitions of a will given above, it is clear that the expression of a testator's own free will is an important element for establishing a valid will.[22] If a document does not express a testator's own free will, the document does not comply with the definition of a will and cannot be seen as valid. A testator must decide completely of his or her own volition how his or her estate is to be divided. There are various factors that can influence a testator's free will such as coercion, fraud or undue influence. If it can be proven that a testator made a will as a result of one of these factors, such a will is invalid because it expresses someone else's will or volition.[23]

PAUSE FOR REFLECTION

Freedom and capacity

Factors that may play a role in the exercising of a testator's free will should not be confused with factors that may influence a testator's testamentary capacity. A lack of free will and a lack of testamentary capacity are separate grounds for invalidity of a will.[24]

In *Spies v Smith*,[25] the Court explains the role of undue influence and asserts that not each and every interference with a testator's volition amounts to a ground for invalidity.[26] The Court indicates that it is not forbidden to convince a testator by way of flattery, declarations of love or even humiliation to make a will in a certain way. However, when these actions take the form of fraud or

19 The principles are set out in *Van Wyk v Van Wyk's Executor* (1887–1888) 5 SC 1; *In re Winter* (1894) 15 NLR 287; *Sim v The Master* 1913 CPD 187; *Ex parte Saunders* 1927 SWA 122; *Burton-Moore v The Master* 1983 (4) SA 419 (NPD).

20 1999 (3) SA 813 (C).

21 See the discussion below and *Millward v Glaser* 1949 (4) SA 931 (A); *Preller v Jordaan* 1956 (1) SA 483 (A); *Spies v Smith* 1957 (1) SA 539 (A); *Kirsten v Bailey* 1976 (4) SA 108 (C).

22 *Craig v Lamoureux* 1920 AC 349 (PC); *Finucane v MacDonald* 1942 CPD 19; *Spies v Smith* 1957 (1) SA 539 (A).

23 *Spies v Smith* 1957 (1) SA 539 (A); *Kirsten v Bailey* 1976 (4) SA 108 (C).

24 See the discussion of testamentary capacity in Chapter 4.

25 1957 (1) SA 539 (A); see also *Preller v Jordaan* 1956 (1) SA 483 (A); *Kirsten v Bailey* 1976 (4) SA 108 (C); *Thirion v Die Meester* 2001 (4) SA 1078 (T).

26 *Spies v Smith* 1957 (1) SA 539 (A) at 546.

when the testator's will is substituted by the will of the person guilty of these improper actions, there is undue influence which leads to invalidity of the will.[27] The mere fact that parties are in a particular relationship towards one another is also not enough to indicate undue influence. It is, nevertheless, a factor to be taken into account along with other factors such as the testator's emotional state, his or her capacity to withstand pressure and the amount of time between the influence and the execution of the will.[28]

From *Kirsten v Bailey*[29] it is also clear that testamentary capacity and lack of volition are two separate grounds for invalidity, but that undue influence may play a role when the testator is already no longer compos mentis:[30]

I am satisfied on all the evidence that the testatrix's supervening physical infirmity had by then so diminished and enfeebled her congenitally limited intellectual faculties, and had so disturbed and confused what remained of her mind and memory, that she was no longer possessed of the disposing mind and memory required for testamentary capacity. In my view the role which the first defendant played aggravated the confusion in the mind of the testatrix.

[I] am furthermore of the opinion that they [the wills] were in any event obtained as a result of undue influence exerted upon the testatrix by the first defendant and that they could, for this reason also, be set aside.[31]

Considering the discussion above, the differences between *animus testandi* and volition are represented in Table 3.2.

Table 3.2 The differences between animus testandi *and volition*

Animus testandi	**Volition (or choice)**
• the intention to make a will	• the testator's own free will
• force or coercion, mistake, fraud or duress can invalidate a will because of a lack of *animus testandi*	• force or coercion, fraud or undue influence can influence volition
• undue influence only considered after ascertained that testator did have *animus testandi*, where the question then becomes one of volition	• undue influence could affect volition so that the testator no longer expresses his or her own free will

3.2.3 Codicil and testamentary writing

The definition of the term 'will' contained in the Wills Act does not attempt to be comprehensive, but merely clarifies that a codicil also qualifies as a will.[32] In Roman and Roman-Dutch law a difference existed between a will and a codicil, especially with regard to the formalities. This differentiation has been eradicated in modern law. Although the term

27 *Spies v Smith* 1957 (1) SA 539 (A) at 547.
28 *Spies v Smith* 1957 (1) SA 539 (A) at 547; see also *Executors of Cerfonteyn v O'Haire* (1873) 3 Buch 47; *Thirion v Die Meester* 2001 (4) SA 1078 (T).
29 1976 (4) SA 108 (C).
30 The mental status of a testator plays a role when one deals with the question of testamentary capacity – see Chapter 4.
31 *Kirsten v Bailey* 1976 (4) SA 108 (C) at 111.
32 Section 1 of the Wills Act reads 'will' but includes a codicil and any other testamentary writing.

'codicil' is often used to refer to an addendum to an existing will, a codicil is a separate will that has to comply with the same formalities as a will.

A testator made a will on 1 August 2000 and, in clause 5, he gave his daughter a gift of R50 000. If he later wanted to increase the amount of this gift, he could write a simple codicil along the following lines: 'I refer to my will of 1 August 2000 and direct that the amount of the bequest in clause 5 shall be increased from R50 000 to R100 000, and I hereby confirm my said will of 1 August 2000 in all other respects.'

This simple codicil would constitute a will for the purposes of the Wills Act and would have to be executed with the same formalities as any other will.

Another term that is used by the Wills Act is 'testamentary writing.' The Act refers to this term in order to indicate which documents have to conform to the formalities required by s 2 of the Act.

In *Ex parte Davies*,[33] the testator had bequeathed a sum of money 'to a certain person who will not be named in this will but whose name will be disclosed by me in a separate note of hand addressed to my executors'. When he executed his will, he handed his attorney a sealed envelope which was opened after his death and which contained a letter identifying the secret beneficiary. One of the questions which the Court had to determine was whether this letter was a valid identification of the beneficiary named therein. It was argued by counsel that the gift of the property itself was contained in the will and that, therefore, the letter, which merely identified the recipient of the gift, was not a testamentary writing. This argument was rejected because the identification of the beneficiary is one of the essential components of a testamentary disposition. Accordingly, the letter constituted a testamentary disposition which was invalid because of a failure to comply with the formalities for a valid will.

Although the act does not define the meaning of testamentary writing, it was decided by the Court that it means a document which describes any one of the three necessary elements of a bequest, namely:

1. the identity of the property bequeathed
2. the extent of the interest bequeathed, for example ownership, usufruct or fideicommissum
3. the identity of the beneficiary.

A document which identifies any one of these three elements is consequently a testamentary writing which has to comply with the requirements of the Wills Act.

Thandi makes provision in her will to leave her jewellery, of which she attaches photographs, to her niece, Ayanda. The will itself is signed by the testator and two witnesses. The question is whether the attached photographs qualify as testamentary writings and whether they should also be signed by the testator and the witnesses. In this scenario, the photographs identify the jewellery to be inherited by the niece. Because they describe the 'property bequeathed,' the photographs qualify as testamentary writings which have to comply with the formalities required by the Act.

33 1957 (3) SA 471 (N) at 472H.

In *Oosthuizen v Die Weesheer*[34] the testator had attached a sketch plan of the bequeathed property to the will. The Court decided that the sketch plan qualified as a testamentary writing and therefore had to comply with the same formalities as the will. Consequently, a list of assets for distribution which are attached to a will, will have no effect if the list does not comply with the same formalities required for a valid will. The reason is that such a list qualifies as a 'testamentary writing' because it expresses the testator's intention to bequeath the property described in such a list. Such a list therefore contains one of the elements of a testamentary writing and consequently has to comply with the formalities required for a will to be valid.

Another issue concerns the question whether a trust deed must comply with the formalities of a will if the identity of a beneficiary is to be found in the trust deed of an inter vivos trust which comes into being during the testator's lifetime if the testator bequeaths further assets to the trust in his or her will, which takes effect on the death of the testator.[35] Simply stated, an inter vivos trust is created in the following way – the trust founder enters into an agreement with another person (the trustee) in which the founder undertakes to donate certain assets to the trustee on condition that the trustee uses the assets for the benefit of a third person (the trust beneficiary), and the trustee undertakes to receive and hold the assets on this basis. The setting up of an inter vivos trust is not done with compliance with the will-making formalities because the inter vivos trust deed is a contract, not a will.

In *Kohlberg v Burnett*[36] the testator bequeathed assets in his will to a trust that he had formed on the same day as he executed his will but before he signed his will. A person who stood to benefit if the bequest was invalid challenged the formal validity of this bequest. It was argued that the identity of the beneficiaries of the bequest was to be found in the trust deed. The deed could not be regarded as part of the will as this would constitute an unlawful incorporation by reference of the terms of the trust deed into the testator's will because the trust deed was not executed as a will. The Court ruled, however, that the bequest of assets to a trust constitutes a bequest to the trustee of the trust in his capacity as such, and that the trust beneficiaries benefit in terms of the trust deed, not in terms of the will. Accordingly, the arrangement was acceptable.

3.3 Joint and mutual wills

If two or more testators decide to make their wills in one single document,[37] this is known as a **joint will**.[38] If testators mutually benefit each other in such a will, it is called a **mutual will**. A mutual will is always a joint will but a joint will is not necessarily a mutual will. Joint wills are especially popular amongst couples married in community of property but may be made by anyone.

Two sisters, Catherine and Debbie, decide to make their wills but to save on attorney's fees they decide to do so in one document. Catherine leaves her entire estate to her niece, Xandile, and Debbie leaves her entire estate to her cousin, Yolanda.

---

34 1974 (2) SA 434 (EC).

35 For a discussion of testamentary trusts, see Chapter 11.

36 1986 (3) SA 12 (A).

37 *In re Murray's Estate: Ex parte Mulhearn* (1901) 18 SC 213 (where the parties were married out of community of property); *Estate Koopmans v Estate De Wet* 1912 CPD 1961 (where the parties were sisters).

38 *Secretary SA Association v Mostert* (1873) 3 Buch 31.

The will is therefore a joint will, but if Catherine had left her entire estate to Debbie and Debbie had left her estate to Catherine, the will would then have been a mutual will.

A joint or mutual will need only be executed once. In other words, only the multiple testators and two witnesses need sign the document.[39] Such a document is, however, seen as the separate will of each of the testators, and each testator may unilaterally revoke or amend the will with regard to his or her dispositions and may even do so without the knowledge of the other testator or testators.[40] The will may also be invalid with regard to one testator, but valid with regard to the other.[41]

3.4 Adiation and repudiation

Adiation means to accept a benefit from the estate of the testator or deceased either under intestate succession or under testate succession. Repudiation, on the other hand, means to decline such a benefit. In South African law a beneficiary is free either to adiate or repudiate any benefit. No one is obliged to accept or reject any benefit under the law of succession.[42]

With regard to adiation it is generally assumed that the beneficiary will adiate a benefit in terms of either a will or the rules of intestate succession depending on the circumstances.[43] As a result, there are normally no formalities required for adiation. However, there is at least one situation which requires adiation to be in writing, and that is when an obligation is attached to the benefit.

'I bequeath my farm to my son Peter, but he has to pay the amount of R100 000 to his sister Jane.'

In this example, there is an obligation attached to the benefit: Peter cannot accept (adiate) the farm and reject (repudiate) the responsibility to pay an amount to Jane. As it is not simply presumed that a beneficiary has adiated a benefit together with an obligation, Peter's act of adiation would need to be reduced to writing.

In most cases, adiation is inferred from the beneficiary's conduct and, upon adiation, the beneficiary acquires a vested personal right to claim delivery or transfer of the bequeathed benefit from the testator's executor when the estate has been wound up.[44]

Repudiation, on the other hand, is not readily inferred from conduct and written proof is usually required. If a beneficiary does not expressly repudiate a benefit but resigns himself or herself to the fact that he or she is not going to receive something that he or she was entitled to in terms of a will, such conduct may be construed as repudiation. The courts, however, will not readily accept that a beneficiary loses the right to enforce the provisions in a will by simply

39 *Thienhaus v The Master* 1938 CPD 69.

40 *Estate Gonsalves v Pataca* 1957 (4) SA 585 (T) at 589; *Estate McIntyre v Burne* 1957 (4) SA 488 (N); *Van Rensburg v Van Rensburg* 1963 (1) SA 505 (A).

41 *Ex parte Maurice* 1995 (2) SA 713 (C); *Theron v The Master of the High Court* [2001] 3 All SA 507 (NC).

42 *Colonial Treasurer v Rand Water Board* 1907 TS 479 at 484; *Weiner v The Master* (1) 1976 (2) SA 830 (T) at 837–838; *Kellerman v Van Vuren* 1994 (4) SA 336 (T).

43 *Crookes v Watson* 1956 (1) SA 277 (A) at 298; *Weiner v The Master (1)* 1976 2 SA 830 (T) at 838–839; *Secretary for Inland Revenue v Estate Roadknight* 1974 (1) SA 253 (A) at 260 .

44 *Estate Smith v Estate Follett* 1942 AD 364 at 383; *Greenberg v Estate Greenberg* 1955 (3) SA 361 (A).

doing nothing.[45] If a beneficiary expressly repudiates a benefit, such repudiation is final and will only be reversed by the court if it was made 'in excusable ignorance of his or her rights'.[46]

The effect of repudiation by a beneficiary may vary according to the provisions of the will and the particular circumstances. If the will makes provision for substitutes to inherit in the place of the repudiating beneficiary, direct substitution will take place and the substitutes will inherit in the place of the repudiating beneficiary. Under certain circumstances, accrual may take place and the repudiated benefit may be added to the shares of the other testate heirs in accordance with the right of accrual.[47] It is also possible that the repudiated benefit may fall into the residue of the testator's estate, to be inherited by the residual heirs. Finally, the repudiated benefit may devolve in accordance with the rules of intestate succession if no residual heir was appointed.

Table 3.3 *The differences between adiation and repudiation*

Will or intestate succession: beneficiary may	
adiate • no action needed • executor transfers benefit • must accept in writing when benefit is linked to an obligation	**repudiate** • must reject in writing • beneficiary receives no benefit • benefit devolves to the residual heir or according to rules of substitution, accrual or intestate succession

PAUSE FOR REFLECTION

How the benefit devolves if repudiated

Theuns included the following provisions in his will:

1. 'I leave my farm to my son, Sean. If he does not want the farm, it must go to my granddaughter, Dina.'
2. 'I leave my 1967 motorcycle to my friend, Candice.'
3. 'I leave the residue of my estate to my nephew, John.'

Considering the implications of the different bequests, the following scenarios could exist:

- At the time of Theuns' death, Sean repudiates the legacy of the farm. Dina has been named as direct substitute and will therefore inherit the farm. If Dina then repudiates the benefit, it will fall into the residue of the estate to be inherited by John.
- If Candice repudiates the bequest of the motorcycle, it falls into the residue of the estate as a substitute has not been named to receive the benefit should the instituted beneficiary repudiate. John, as the residual heir, will then receive the motorcycle.

45 *Ferreira v Otto* (1883–1884) 3 SC 193; *Galant v Mahonga* 1922 EDL 69; *Watson v Burchell* (1891–1892) 9 SC 2 at 5; *Wepener v Estate Henning* 1921 CPD 814 at 823; *Moyce v Estate Taylor* 1948 (3) SA 822 (A) at 829.

46 *Oxenham v Oxenham's Executor* 1945 WLD 57; *Ex parte Estate Van Rensburg* 1965 (3) SA 251 (C); *Swift v Pichanick* 1982 (1) SA 904 (ZS) at 906; *Bielovich v The Master* 1992 (4) SA 736 (N).

47 Substitution and accrual are discussed in Chapter 10.

- If John refuses to inherit the residue of the estate, it will be divided amongst the intestate heirs of Theuns. If all three of the named beneficiaries therefore repudiate, the entire estate will be divided amongst Theuns' intestate heirs.

3.5 Doctrine of election

The doctrine of election is applicable in all cases where acceptance of a benefit from a will at the same time holds some kind of burden or obligation (such as a modus or a condition) for the beneficiary. In other words, a beneficiary has to elect or choose to accept a benefit which imposes a burden. The beneficiary may accept the benefit (adiation) but is then obliged to accept the associated responsibility. There is no possibility for the beneficiary to adiate partially: the benefit has to be accepted as a whole.

It is important to know when or in what cases the doctrine of election comes into play because in cases where the choice (that is, whether to adiate or to repudiate) has to be exercised in writing, a written adiation or repudiation certificate must be submitted to the Master of the High Court together with the estate account.

If a beneficiary elects to repudiate a benefit, he or she will receive nothing. According to *Ex Parte Estate Van Rensburg*[48] a beneficiary must accept the whole will in as far as it is applicable to him or her. He or she may repudiate any bequest he or she does not like, but then may not receive any benefit under the will.[49]

The doctrine of election does not simply mean that a beneficiary has to choose whether he or she wants to inherit a benefit or not. The doctrine only applies if a burden (such as a modus or a condition) has been placed on the beneficiary by the testator.

PAUSE FOR REFLECTION

The doctrine of election in practice

Example 1

Thembela's will contains the following provision:

'I leave my farm, Mooiplaats, to my brother, Ben, on condition that the entire farm, Mooibosch, of which Ben and I each own half a share, be transferred to my son, Siyabonga.'

Ben has to decide whether he is going to accept the farm, Mooiplaats, under the condition that he transfers his half of the farm, Mooibosch, to Siyabonga. Since the bequest to him (the farm, Mooiplaats) is now burdened with the responsibility to transfer some of his own property (half of Mooibosch) to someone else (Siyabonga), he has to apply the doctrine of election: Should he decide to adiate the bequest of the farm, Mooiplaats, he has to give up his share of the ownership of Mooibosch. If he decides to repudiate the bequest of the farm, Mooiplaats, he will lose his right to inherit Mooiplaats, but will keep his half-share of Mooibosch. Mooiplaats will then be inherited by the residual heirs of Thembela's estate.

48 1965 (3) SA 251 (C).
49 See Van der Merwe & Rowland 412; Cronjé & Roos 490.

Example 2

Tom bequeaths his farm unconditionally to his only son, John. He also bequeaths his beach house to John subject to the burden to pay his three sisters each the sum of R100 000. John is put to election: He may not adiate the farm, or the beach house whilst refusing to pay each of his sisters the R100 000. If he repudiates the beach house because he does not want to pay the R100 000 to his sisters, he would also not receive the farm.

The doctrine of election plays a specific role in estate massing and will be discussed in more detail later.[50]

3.6 Customary law of succession

As already explained, testamentary succession according to a will is fairly unknown in customary law.[51] A family head may, however, dispose of property during his lifetime and he also has limited powers to give instructions on his deathbed about the distribution of some assets. Nevertheless, this is not the same as freedom of testation as discussed above.

In light of new developments in the customary law of intestate succession,[52] the possibility that testators might increasingly make use of wills to regulate the division of customary law property is not excluded. Testators could easily use the notion of freedom of testation to ensure that property is devolved according to the customary law of succession by stipulating so in a will. However, in such a case, the requirements of the Wills Act and other common law rules have to be complied with to prevent the will being invalid.

THIS CHAPTER IN ESSENCE

1. In this chapter the following general principles underpinning the law of testate succession have been explained:
   - the definition of a will
   - the basic requirements for the validity of a will (*animus testandi* and volition)
   - the difference and commonalities between joint and mutual wills
   - the meaning of adiation
   - the meaning of repudiation
   - the meaning and effect of the doctrine of election.
2. When dealing with a will which may have been executed under suspicious circumstances, it is important to investigate whether the testator wanted to execute a will and whether he or she did so freely.
3. Once these requirements have been fulfilled and it has been established that the formalities have been complied with, the executor is appointed and he or she has to deal with the general winding-up of the estate.

50 Estate massing is discussed in Chapter 9.
51 See the discussion in Chapter 1.
52 See the discussion in Chapters 2 and 15.

4. Adiation and repudiation form the basis of succession as it is important to know whether a beneficiary adiates or repudiates a benefit before the executor can begin with the final liquidation and distribution of an estate.
5. Nowadays, a testator living under customary law also has freedom of testation regarding customary law property.

Chapter 4

Testamentary capacity

Who is competent to make a valid will?

4.1	Introduction	59
4.2	Testamentary capacity	59
4.3	Customary law of succession	63
This chapter in essence		64

4.1 Introduction

A will is a unilateral legal act and, in principle, all persons who are capable of performing legal acts should be capable of making wills. In South Africa, the age at which a person is able to perform legal acts (legal capacity) such as entering into contracts is normally 18 years of age. (The required age was 21 years before its amendment by the Children's Act.) However, the age at which a person has the ability to make a legally valid will (testamentary capacity) is only 16 years of age. Testamentary capacity is governed by the Wills Act[1]. Any document drawn up and executed by a person without testamentary capacity cannot be valid even if it complies with the other formalities required by the Wills Act.[2] Consequently, testamentary capacity is a prerequisite for making a will.

4.2 Testamentary capacity

4.2.1 What is testamentary capacity?

Section 4 of the Wills Act defines testamentary capacity as follows:

> *Every person of the age of sixteen years or more may make a will unless at the time of making the will he is mentally incapable of appreciating the nature and effect of his act, and the burden of proof that he was mentally incapable at that time shall rest on the person alleging the same.*

4.2.2 Prescribed age

It is clear from the Wills Act that a testator must be 16 years of age to execute a valid will. As the making of a will is a unilateral legal act which is dependent upon the forming of one's own

1 Section 4.
2 These formalities are discussed in Chapter 5.

volition, a person under the age of 16 is incapable of making a will, even with the assistance of a parent or guardian.

PAUSE FOR REFLECTION

Why the difference in ages for contractual and testamentary capacity?

The fact that legal and testamentary capacity are not the same leads to some interesting questions. For example, why is the age for executing a valid will 16 years, whilst the age for concluding a contract is 18 years? Why can a minor ratify a contract that he or she concluded on becoming an adult but a will remains invalid and cannot be ratified, only re-executed?

The question is what is the reasoning behind this difference in law and are there any policy considerations that caused this difference? The difference between the ages required for contractual capacity and testamentary capacity arose historically. In Roman times, minors were often placed in the position of the *paterfamilias* as they inherited a whole family at an early age. The tradition was that the eldest son inherited the whole estate - including people (slaves and others who were seen as assets) and other assets and liabilities. He therefore also needed the capacity to make a will at an early age.

As the law and society developed, it became clear that minors often do not have the capacity to make responsible decisions and therefore several rules regarding contractual capacity were developed. Until recently (2005) the required age for full contractual capacity was 21.

In modern times, the reasoning behind the age difference is still the fact that third parties' rights and duties are affected in a contractual relationship with a minor, much more so than if a minor makes a will.

4.2.3 Mental capabilities

Section 4 of the Wills Act makes it clear that, apart from the age requirement, the only requirement for testamentary capacity is whether the testator, at the time of executing the will, was 'mentally incapable of appreciating the nature and effect of his act'. The only test required to prove testamentary capacity is whether or not the testator had all his or her wits about him or her (in other words, was sane or compos mentis)[3] when he or she executed the will.[4]

The courts have identified the following factors that need to be considered when determining whether a testator had testamentary capacity at the time of executing a will:

- general mental and physical condition
- general intelligence, memory and capacity to understand the legal implications of their acts
- general conduct.[5]

These factors should be distinguished from factors indicating that the testator did not exercise his or her own free will in making the will.[6]

3 *Tregea v Godart* 1939 AD 16 at 38.
4 *Essop v Mustapha and Essop* 1988 (4) SA 213 (D) 222; *Katz v Katz* [2004] All SA (4) 545 (C).
5 *Tregea v Godart* 1939 AD 16; *Kirsten v Bailey* 1976 (4) SA 108 (C); *Essop v Mustapha and Essop* 1988 (4) SA 213 (D).
6 See the discussion in Chapter 3 and *Spies v Smith* 1957 (1) SA 539 (A); *Kirsten v Bailey* 1976 (4) SA 108 (C).

The testator's testamentary capacity should be established at the time of execution of the will – Section 4 of the Wills Act specifically requires the testator to have had the necessary testamentary capacity at the time the will was executed. This means that the testator must be of sound mind when he or she and the witnesses sign the will. The testator's mental condition at the time of giving the instructions for the drafting of the will is therefore irrelevant.[7]

De Waal and Schoeman-Malan[8] draw a helpful distinction to explain the requirements for capacity to make a will and the factors that may influence a testator's free will. 'Formal' capacity (as provided for in the Act) is distinguished from the factors that influence free expression of the testator's will (as recognised by the common law), namely coercion, undue influence and fraud.

In *Spies v Smith*,[9] the Court separated the grounds for invalidity argued before it in favour of a finding that Spies had no testamentary capacity. The Court indicated that it was argued as the first ground for invalidity of the will that Spies, because of his mental disabilities, did not understand the nature and effect of his actions. This, however, was not proved and the will was not held to be invalid due to a lack of testamentary capacity.[10] As the second ground,[11] it was argued that the will was invalid because of undue influence that was exercised upon the testator. On this ground, the Court held that the influence was not of such a nature that the will no longer contained the free will of the testator[12] and consequently, the will was also not invalid on this ground.

These grounds or factors influencing the validity of a will were also distinguished clearly in *Kirsten v Bailey*.[13] The testatrix had made three wills shortly before her death. In terms of the first and third wills, the defendant was the only beneficiary. These wills were contested by her intestate heirs, who were the beneficiaries under the second will. The testatrix had been sickly almost all her life and the Court found that she lacked testamentary capacity when she made all three wills.[14]

The Court further found that the defendant had unduly influenced the testatrix as she had become convinced that everyone else had abandoned her and that he was going to marry her. The Court therefore found the first and the third wills to be invalid on the ground of undue influence as well.

A clear example of the application of the factors used to establish whether the testator had the necessary capacity or whether he or she exercised his or her own free will in executing the will can be found in *Katz v Katz*.[15] The plaintiffs argued that:

1. at the time of the execution of the will in question, the testator was mentally incapable of making a will as a result of a stroke; or
2. the will was executed as a result of undue influence brought to bear on the testator by his second wife; and
3. the will did not comply with the required formalities.

---

7 *Essop v Mustapha and Essop* 1988 (4) SA 213 (D) at 222.
8 At 40 and 44.
9 1957 (1) SA 539 (A).
10 *Spies v Smith* 1957 (1) SA 539 (A) at 543.
11 *Spies v Smith* 1957 (1) SA 539 (A) at 545.
12 *Spies v Smith* 1957 (1) SA 539 (A) at 547.
13 1976 (4) SA 108 (C).
14 See the quotation on p 51.
15 [2004] All SA (4) 545 (C).

The Court decided that there was sufficient evidence that the testator's mind was clear enough for him to dispose of his estate in a coherent way. The Court went on to apply the two grounds for invalidity set out in *Spies v Smith*[16] and found that there was no justification for the inference that the testator's second wife had influenced him in any way. Lastly, it was also found that the formalities had been complied with and that the will was therefore valid.

Certain categories of persons such as prodigals under curatorship,[17] the deaf and dumb, and the insane were identified under common law as persons who lacked testamentary capacity and therefore could not execute valid wills. Of these categories, certain persons, such as the insane or those under the influence of drugs and/or alcohol are still identified as persons without the necessary testamentary capacity. Their capacity must, however, be judged according to the relevant circumstances in each particular case.

Section 4 of the Wills Act creates a rebuttable presumption that every person is mentally sane, and the onus to prove the contrary is on the person alleging such lack of mental capacity.[18]

What must be done to prove that a testator was mentally insane, and thus incapable of executing a will was set out in *Smith v Strydom*:[19]

- the testator did not understand the nature and consequences of the testamentary act he or she performed
- the testator did not know or could not remember that he or she owned bequeathable property
- the testator did not have the mind (thinking capacity) to distinguish between the entitlements of persons to whom he or she should bequeath property and to judge between their entitlements.

A person suffering from a mental disorder is incapable of making a will even if he or she has not been declared insane by a court.[20] The onus or burden of proof is on the person who wants to prove that the testator was mentally insane. On the other hand, it will be easier for someone to prove that a person is mentally insane when such a person has been declared insane by a court.

It is possible for a person who suffers from a mental disorder, or who has been declared insane, to make a valid will during a lucid interval,[21] but it has to be proved that he or she did indeed experience a lucid interval. Because a person who has a mental disorder or is mentally insane is not capable of making a valid will, such a person must die intestate. It is not possible for someone else to make a will on behalf of such a person.

A person who is so intoxicated or under the influence of drugs that he or she is not in possession of all his or her faculties is, like an insane person, incapable of making a will,[22] but again the onus of proof will be on the person alleging such an intoxication or influence.

---

16 1957 (1) SA 539 (A).
17 Today the will of a prodigal is valid in terms of s 4 of the Wills Act. See *Ex parte F* 1914 WLD 27.
18 *Rapson v Putterill* 1913 AD 417; *Lewin v Lewin* 1949 (4) SA 241 (T); *Smith v Strydom* 1953 (2) SA 799 (T); *Essop v Mustapha and Essop* 1988 (4) SA 213 (D); *Geldenhuys v Borman* 1990 (1) SA 161 (E).
19 1953 (2) SA 799 (T) at 802.
20 *Smith v Strydom* 1953 (2) SA 799 (T).
21 *In re Kemp* (1844) 2 Menzies 435.
22 *Thirion v Die Meester* 2001 (4) SA 1078 (T).

Theo and his friends are having a wild party on a Saturday night. In a drunken stupor, he jokingly writes the following on the back of a cigarette packet: 'I leave everything I own to my girlfriend, Debbie'. He signs at the bottom of the carton and two of his friends sign next to his signature as witnesses. On his way home, he dies in a car accident. Although Debbie is devastated by his untimely death, she is nevertheless delighted at the prospect of inheriting from Theo. In light of the circumstances, the question is whether Debbie will be entitled to inherit Theo's estate.

In this scenario the will may be disputed as invalid on the following two grounds:

Firstly, Theo never had a serious intention to execute a will – he jokingly wrote the provision on a cigarette packet. He, therefore, did not have the necessary *animus testandi*[23] to execute a valid will.

Secondly, he did not have the necessary testamentary capacity as he was so intoxicated that he did not understand the nature and effect of his actions. This fact will, of course, have to be proven but the balance of probabilities would indicate that he was indeed so intoxicated that he did not have testamentary capacity.

4.2.4 *Animus testandi*, volition, testamentary capacity and freedom of testation

As we have seen in Chapter 3, a testator has to have the intention to make a will and he or she must exercise this intention freely. These are the two general requirements for the validity of a will. The testator must, furthermore, have the necessary capacity to make a will as prescribed by s 4 of the Wills Act. This requirement relates to his or her age as well as to his or her mental capabilities and is a formal requirement for the validity of a will. These concepts must be distinguished from the concept of freedom of testation which relates to the testator's freedom to make any provision, whatever he or she wishes, in his or her will.[24]

4.3 Customary law of succession

The mere fact that someone lives under a system of customary law does not mean that he or she has no freedom of testation or the capacity to make a will. However, s 23(1), (2) and (3) of the Black Administration Act restricted a black person's freedom of testation regarding customary property by stipulating the following:

> (1) *All movable property belonging to a Black and allotted by him or accruing under Black law or custom to any woman with whom he lived in a customary union, or to any house, shall upon his death devolve and be administered under Black law and custom.*
>
> (2) *All land in a tribal settlement held in individual tenure upon quitrent conditions by a Black shall devolve upon his death upon one male person, to be determined in accordance with tables of succession to be prescribed under subsection (10).*
>
> (3) *All other property of whatsoever kind belonging to a Black shall be capable of being devised by will.*

23 Remember the discussion in Chapter 3.

24 Freedom of testation will be discussed in Chapter 8.

Accordingly, customary property either had to devolve according to the rules of customary succession if it was movable property obtained in terms of customary law, or in accordance with certain tables of succession prescribed by legislation if it was communal or quitrent land. These stipulations created the interesting situation that a black person had testamentary capacity (he or she could make a will), but no freedom of testation (no freedom to make provisions in a will regarding certain property).

Section 23 was declared unconstitutional by the Constitutional Court in *Bhe v Magistrate, Khayelitsha*[25] and was repealed by the Repeal of the Black Administration Act and Amendment of Certain Laws Act.[26] Nowadays, a black person has the freedom to bequeath customary property if he or she has the capacity to do so (in other words, if he or she is at least 16 years of age and is not mentally impaired).

THIS CHAPTER IN ESSENCE

1. This chapter looked at testamentary capacity – the minimum age and the mental capacity required to make a valid will (see s 4 of the Wills Act). Evidence concerning a testator's mental capabilities is taken into account when determining the validity of a will.
2. The Master of the High Court will accept that the will that he or she receives from the executor was executed with the necessary testamentary capacity. The issue of a testator's testamentary capacity will only arise if someone approaches a court with an application regarding the capacity of the testator to make a will.
3. The Master only determines whether the formal requirements of the will have been met and does not concern himself or herself with the other formalities regarding capacity.
4. It is important to distinguish testamentary capacity from the testator's free expression of his or her will (volition) as well as from freedom of testation which will be discussed in Chapter 8.
5. Under a system of customary law, people have freedom of testation just like anyone else and also need to comply with the requirements of testamentary capacity.

25 See the discussion in Chapters 2 and 15.
26 28 of 2005. See the discussions in Chapters 2 and 15.

Chapter 5

Formalities for a will

What are the formalities for a valid will and what are the consequences if a will does not comply with the prescribed formalities?

5.1	Introduction	65
5.2	Formalities in terms of s 2(1)(a) of the Wills Act	66
5.3	Formalities for the amendment of wills	77
5.4	Section 2(3) of the Wills Act	78
5.5	Customary law of succession	84
This chapter in essence		84

5.1 Introduction

When a testator signs or executes his or her will, it has to be done in accordance with certain rules set out in the Wills Act. Lawyers refer to these rules as the formalities for the execution of a will. The execution of a will is the process whereby the testator and other parties comply with all the formalities required to bring a valid will into existence.

A will that is not executed in accordance with the formalities required by the Act is invalid. In other words, it is of no force or effect, and its contents are ignored unless there is a court order that, in terms of s 2(3) of the Act, the will be given effect to as if it had been validly executed. In this way, the law attempts to ensure that there is reliable and permanent evidence of the testator's testamentary intentions. Section 2(3) will be discussed later in this chapter, but it is important to note at this stage that it is not always possible to obtain a court order giving effect to a defectively executed will. Furthermore, even when it is possible, the process is time consuming and expensive. For this reason, it is vitally important that testators comply with the formalities in the Act when they execute their wills.

Even if a will is formally valid, it is possible that the contents of the will do not comply with the law in some way. For example, if a testator bequeathed his or her entire estate to an international terrorist organisation for the purposes of advancing its unlawful aims, the will would be formally valid if it was properly executed, but its contents would be unlawful and invalid, and would not be implemented. Such a will is said to be substantively invalid. Formal validity and substantive validity are entirely different concepts – formal validity refers to whether or not the will complies with the formalities while substantive validity refers to whether or not the contents of the will are lawful. This chapter only looks at the formal validity of wills.

5.2 Formalities in terms of s 2(1)(a) of the Wills Act

The execution formalities required by s 2(1)(a) of the Wills Act may be summarised as follows:

- The will must be signed at the end thereof by the testator himself or herself, or an amanuensis – someone who signs the will on behalf of the testator.[1]
- If the will comprises more than one page, every page other than the last must be signed anywhere on the page by the testator or the amanuensis.[2]
- The signature of the testator or the amanuensis must be made (or acknowledged) in the presence of two or more competent witnesses.[3]
- Such witnesses must attest and sign the will in the presence of the testator and each other, and (where applicable) of the amanuensis.[4]
- Where the testator signs with a mark, or an amanuensis signs for the testator, a commissioner of oaths must be present and certification formalities apply.[5]

Table 5.1 shows who needs to be present at the execution of a will.

Table 5.1 Persons required at the execution of a will

Method of execution	Persons present
Testator signs with own signature	Testator and two witnesses
Testator signs with a mark	Testator, two witnesses, and commissioner of oaths
Amanuensis signs for testator	Testator, amanuensis, two witnesses, and commissioner of oaths

5.2.1 Requirement of a written document

In the past, it may have been regarded as unnecessary repetition to speak of a written document. How else would writing exist but in a document? However, with the advent of word processing and the general recognition given to documents stored as computer files, this is no longer so.

The Wills Act does not expressly require that the will be in the form of a written document nor does it specify how it should be written. However, the requirement of a written document is implied from the requirement that the will must be signed by the testator in certain specified places,[6] and from the reference to pages of the will.[7] Accordingly, handwriting, typing, and printing (or a combination of these) are all acceptable. Even writing in pencil is acceptable although not advisable for obvious reasons.

An oral will is not possible. Nor would a will in the form of a video or DVD recording, or saved in electronic format as a computer file on a hard drive be permitted. None of these can comply with the signature requirements. Even if an electronic signature constituted a

1 Section 2(1)(a)(i).
2 Section 2(1)(a)(iv).
3 Section 2(1)(a)(ii).
4 Section 2(1)(a)(iii).
5 Section 2(1)(a)(v).
6 Sections 2(1)(a)(i) and (iv).
7 Section 2(1)(a)(iv) and (v).

signature for the purposes of the Wills Act, which is unlikely, it is not possible to comply with the requirements regarding where the signatures of the testator and witnesses must be placed. For the same reason, a will composed as an SMS on a cellphone could not comply with the execution formalities.

PAUSE FOR REFLECTION

Electronic communication

The general thrust of the Electronic Communications and Transactions Act[8] is to place documents that exist as computer files on the same legal footing as their more traditional paper counterparts, but wills are not covered by this Act. The question is therefore whether wills should be treated in the same manner?

1. Are the current methods for executing a will outmoded? Should they be replaced with provisions that allow for the execution of wills in electronic format as data files? A number of potential difficulties arise in connection with the execution of wills in electronic format, for example:
   - the danger of interference by computer hackers and viruses
   - the danger that an unauthorised person might delete the computer file so that it appears that the testator revoked the will
   - the danger that an unauthorised person might 'undelete' a computer file that the testator had intentionally deleted so that it appears that the testator had not revoked the will
   - the danger that testators' wills could disappear without trace when they replace their computers from time to time.
2. Would the use of witnesses be accommodated in an electronic will and, if so, how would that be done?
3. If parliament wished to provide for an electronic will, could this be achieved by modifying the existing framework of rules for executing a valid will, or would an entirely new set of formalities appropriate to an electronic document have to be developed?

5.2.2 Meaning of 'sign' and 'signature', and the concept of a 'mark'

The Wills Act requires that the will be signed by various persons in various places. The definition of 'sign' in the Act does not attempt to be comprehensive. Prior to 1 October 1992, this definition stated merely that, in the case of a testator, sign includes the making of a mark but it does not include the making of a mark in the case of a witness. The word 'signature' has a corresponding meaning. The Act accordingly drew a distinction between a signature in the ordinary sense of the word[9] and other devices or characters on the page, referred to as marks, that might be used by a person to function as a signature (for example, a thumbprint on the page). The use of a mark is reserved for the testator alone and when the testator uses a mark, the Act requires certification of the will by a commissioner of oaths.[10]

A difficult issue that arose was whether or not initials qualify as a form of mark. If initials were recognised as a form of mark, they could not qualify as signatures when used by a

8 25 of 2002.
9 This kind of signature is often referred to as a signature *strictu sensu.*
10 Section 2(1)(a)(v).

witness, and when used by the testator, the will would have to be certified by a commissioner of oaths. This issue gave rise to much litigation, with conflicting judicial views. It culminated in the decision of the Appellate Division in *Harpur v Govindamall,*[11] where the Court ruled that initials constitute a form of mark. Consequently, the Court held that a witness's signature using initials invalidated the will.

However, before the delivery of the judgment in *Harpur v Govindamall,*[12] parliament stepped in and revised the definition of 'sign' to state that sign includes 'the making of initials and, only in the case of the testator, the making of a mark'. The term 'signature' has a similar meaning.[13] This now means that the testator, witnesses, amanuensis, and a commissioner of oaths may sign by means of initials whenever they are required to sign a will, but that only the testator may sign by means of a mark, and when the testator does so a commissioner of oaths must certify the will.

The Act does not require that a person must sign with his or her ordinary or customary signature, nor does it require a person to sign in the same way on every page.

> In *Jhajbhai v The Master*[14] it was said that 'sign' includes the accustomed mode of signature of a witness, as well as any other mode adopted by him (not being a mark) to write or sign his name. It may or may not be his full name. The intention of the witness in writing or signing his name is the criterion. If he intends his mode of writing or signing his name to represent his signature, it is effective as such.

This seems to be so even if the signature is illegible. Note, however, that the use of any writing other than the person's name does not qualify as a signature in the ordinary sense and constitutes a mark.

Where the testator wishes to execute the will using a mark, it is common and acceptable for the testator to write a simple cross on the will. The use of a thumbprint has also received judicial approval.

> In *O'Connor v The Master of the High Court,*[15] the testator signed <u>using a thumbprint</u> but the requisite certificate was defective. The Court found that 'the only shortcoming in the execution of deceased's will was ... that the certification of the will was defective.' In other words, the use of the thumbprint was acceptable.

It seems that a mark may take other, more exotic forms such as the descriptor 'Your loving mother' at the end of the will[16] but this is not recommended.

5.2.3 Where must the testator sign?

The Wills Act requires the testator to sign at the end of the will which raises the issue of where the will ends. Suppose that the last paragraph of the testator's two-page will ends half way down an A4 sheet of paper – where is the ending of the will? At the end of the writing, half way down the page? Or at the bottom of the sheet of paper? It has been held that the will consists of the words, not the paper, and therefore the will ends at the end of the last paragraph of

11 1993 (4) SA 751 (A).
12 1993 (4) SA 751 (A).
13 Section 1.
14 1971 (2) SA 370 (D) at 372A–C.
15 [1999] 3 All SA 652 (NC) at 660 para 3: own emphasis.
16 *In the estate of Cook (deceased) Murison v Cook* [1960] 1 All ER 689 (PDA).

the writing.[17] This means that the testator must sign the will as close as reasonably possible to the concluding words of the will and a failure to do so invalidates the will. The purpose of this strict approach is to prevent the fraudulent insertion of words at the end of the will after the testator's signature.

In *Kidwell v The Master*[18] the Court had to consider the effect of (amongst others) a nine centimetre gap between the end of the writing and the testator's signature and held that such a gap meant that the signature was not as close as reasonably possible to the concluding words of the will and that the will was invalid.

The formulation 'reasonably close' is of course imprecise and it is not clear how great a gap is acceptable. It is submitted that in assessing whether or not the gap is too great, account should be taken of the objective of the provision, the layout of the will on the page, the size of the typeface, and the paragraph- and line-spacing used in the will.

PAUSE FOR REFLECTION

How close is close?

In *Kidwell v The Master*,[19] the Court said the testator's signature must appear as close as reasonably possible to the 'concluding words of the will'. Murray[20] has pointed out that this reference to the concluding words is ambiguous because the concluding words could be any of the following:

- the last substantive provision of the will (such as the appointment of a guardian for minor children)
- the end of the words that record when and where the will was signed, in other words, the attestation clause (which Murray calls the *testamonium*)
- the end of the portion of the will that states that the testator and witnesses were present together when the will was signed (the attestation clause).

Murray suggests that the Court in *Kidwell v The Master* thought that the will ends at the end of the *testamonium*. If this is so, it could mean that many wills are invalid because the signature line on which the testator signs is usually placed near the end of the attestation. However, the legislature was aware of how wills are usually typed when it enacted the requirement that a will be signed at the end. In the circumstances, therefore, it is submitted that when the testator's signature is adjacent to the attestation or close to the end of the attestation, this constitutes signature 'at the end thereof' as required by the Act. To hold otherwise means that the will drafter must dispense with *testamonium* or attestation, or the testator must sign above the *testamonium*. Both these outcomes would be absurd and it is unlikely that they correspond with the legislature's intentions.

If the will comprises more than one page then, in addition to signing the end of the will, the testator or amanuensis is also required to sign each of the other pages of the will. They can do so anywhere on these pages.[21] Where a will is written on two sides of a single sheet

17 *Tshabalala v Tshabalala* 1980 (1) SA 134 (O) at 137D–F.
18 1983 (1) SA 509 (E) at 513G.
19 1983 (1) SA 509 (E) at 513G.
20 1983 *Annual Survey of South African Law* 255–256.
21 Section 2(1)(a)(iv).

of paper, both sides must be signed.[22] The side on which the will ends must be signed at the end of the will and the other side can be signed anywhere on the page.

5.2.4 Signature by an amanuensis

Section 2(1)(a)(i) of the Act requires that the will be signed at the end by 'the testator *or by some other person in his presence and by his direction*.'[23] The other person referred to is known as an amanuensis.[24] In this way the Act makes provision for a testator who does not, for example, have the use of his or her hands, or who may be illiterate, to execute a will through the medium of the amanuensis.

Since the amanuensis is simply the physical vehicle by which the testator executes the will, he or she should sign the testator's name, and not his or her own. This would avoid confusion as to the identity of the testator that might arise if the signature on the will is not the same as the testator's name recorded in the will. In *Oosthuizen v Sharp*[25] and *Ex parte Fourie's Estate*,[26] wills that were signed with the testators' names by an amanuensis were held to have been correctly executed in terms of the formalities then applicable.

PAUSE FOR REFLECTION

Whose name?

Some authorities state that it would also be acceptable for the amanuensis to sign his or her own name on behalf of the testator. If the amanuensis signs with his or her own name, it would be wise to write the abbreviation p.p. (*per procurationem*) after the signature. This is the customary means of indicating that one signs not for one's self but in a representative capacity for someone else. However, since there is case authority to support the use of the testator's own name, this would seem to be the wiser course of action.

Where an amanuensis is used the will must be signed in the presence of a commissioner of oaths as well as in the presence of the usual witnesses, and the commissioner is required to certify the will. The certification formalities are discussed on pages 72–75.

5.2.5 Who is required to witness a will?

The Act requires that a will be witnessed by two competent witnesses. A competent witness is any person above the age of 14 years who is not incompetent to give evidence in a court of law.[27]

> In the English case of *Re Gibson (deceased)*,[28] the Court held that '[the term] "witness" means ... in regard to things visible, one who has the faculty of seeing. The signing of a will is a visible matter.' Accordingly, it was held that a blind person did not qualify as a competent witness because he or she could not testify to the signature of the will and the will could not truly be said to have been signed in his or her presence.

22 *Van Huyssteen v Die Meester* 1975 (4) SA 449 (W).
23 Emphasis added.
24 Section 2(1)(a)(iv), which requires the testator to sign all the other pages of the will, also makes provision for the use of an amanuensis.
25 1935 WLD 22.
26 1927 EDL 185.
27 Section 1 under the heading 'competent witness.'
28 [1949] 2 All ER 90 at 436–437.

Section 4A of the Wills Act stipulates that the witness to a will, and his or her spouse at the time of witnessing, lacks capacity to inherit under that will. However, this provision does not mean that a beneficiary does not have the capacity to witness – a will witnessed by a beneficiary remains formally valid although the witness/beneficiary is deprived of the inheritance.[29]

5.2.6 The meaning of witnessing

There are two aspects to witnessing a will – the physical presence whilst the testator, or amanuensis, signs (or the testator acknowledges his or her signature), and the actual signing of the will by the witnesses themselves. Two competent witnesses, both present at the same time, must be present when the testator, or amanuensis, signs each page of the will.[30] Alternatively, if one or both witnesses is not present when the testator signs, then the testator must acknowledge his or her signature in the presence of both witnesses after such signing. In addition to being present, the witnesses themselves must sign the will.[31]

Where the testator has executed a will comprising two or more pages as a single juristic act, the same two witnesses who attest and sign the last page of the will must be present as witnesses to the testator's signature of the earlier pages.[32] However, since 1 October 1992 the witnesses need not sign all the pages and it will be sufficient if they sign only the last page. It is, however, recommended that witnesses sign all pages of the will, because the changes introduced in 1992 have not yet been fully judicially interpreted and because doing so enhances the security of the will. In *Liebenberg v The Master*,[33] a case involving a one-page will which the witnesses had signed near the top of the page, the Court held that witnesses need not sign near or below the testator's signature but may sign anywhere on the page. However, the witnesses' signatures must not appear where the testator's signature ought to be at the end of the will because this would result in a failure by the testator to sign in the correct place.

Chronologically speaking, witnesses must sign after the testator has signed because they cannot attest to a signature that has not yet taken place. If a witness signs before the testator, the will is invalid.[34] The position of the witness' signature on the page, higher or lower on the page than the testator's signature, does not prove when the witnesses signed.

In view of the requirement that the testator and two witnesses be present when the will is signed (or when the testator acknowledges his or her signature to them), it is relevant to consider the meaning of the word 'presence'. Under one of the pre-1953 statutes which contained a similar requirement of simultaneous presence, this requirement was held to have been satisfied when the witness was in the same room as the testator and either actually saw him or her sign or could or might have done so.[35] In other words, it is not necessary to prove that the witness actually saw the act of signing if he or she was in a position to have seen it.

It has been held that it is not necessary for witnesses to know the contents of the will[36] or even that the document being executed is a will.[37]

---

29 Unless one of the three exceptions provided for in s 4A of the Wills Act can be established; see discussion in Chapter 7.
30 Section 2(1)(a)(ii).
31 Section 2(1)(a)(iii).
32 *The Leprosy Mission v The Master of the Supreme Court* 1972 (4) SA 173 (C) at 180F–181F.
33 1992 (3) SA 57 (D).
34 *Sterban v Dixon* 1968 (1) SA 322 (C) at 324H–325A.
35 *King v Nel* 1922 CPD 520 at 524–525.
36 See *Liebenberg v The Master* 1992 (3) SA 57 (D) at 58I–J; *Sterban v Dixon* 1968 (1) SA 322 (C) at 325A–C.
37 *Ex parte Suknanan* 1959 (2) SA 189 (N) at 190H; *In re Estate of W.R.Shaw* (1905) 26 NLR 3; *King v Nel* 1922 CPD 520 at 525–526.

5.2.7 Acknowledging a signature

Although the Act requires the testator to sign in the presence of the witnesses, it makes provision for the situation where the testator may have signed the will in advance by permitting the testator to acknowledge his or her signature to witnesses. The testator must do this in the presence of two witnesses.

The Act makes no provision for the testator to make a mark, or for an amanuensis to sign, in the absence of the commissioner of oaths. In other words, there is no provision for the mark or amanuensis' signature to be acknowledged *to* the commissioner of oaths.[38]

PAUSE FOR REFLECTION

Acknowledging a mark

In terms of the Wills Act, acknowledging a mark or the signature of an amanuensis is problematic. This is because of a mismatch between two sections, namely between the section that provides for acknowledgement to witnesses (s 2(1)(a)(ii)) and the section that provides for certification by the commissioner of oaths (the proviso to s 2(1)(a)(v)). The latter section does not expressly contemplate a will executed in terms of the former section because it only refers to wills executed in terms of subparas (i), (iii), and (iv) of s 2(1)(a), and not to wills executed in terms of subpara (ii). This would seem to be the result of an oversight in the drafting of the Act.

5.2.8 Must a will be dated or have an attestation clause?

The attestation clause is the final paragraph of the will which records and provides evidence of the date and place of signature and that the testator and witnesses signed in each others' presence. For example:

> Signed at Johannesburg on this twenty-fourth day of January 1994 in the presence of the undersigned competent witnesses present at the same time and who have attested and signed this will in the presence of myself and of each other.[39]

The absence of an attestation clause does not invalidate the will[40] but the clause has evidential value. Where appropriate, evidence may be adduced to contradict the information in the clause.[41] Note that the absence of a date does not invalidate a will.

5.2.9 Additional formalities associated with a mark or an amanuensis

When the testator signs with a mark, or when an amanuensis signs for the testator, the Act requires that the will be signed in the presence of a commissioner of oaths who must be present together with the two witnesses and the amanuensis if one is used.[42] Magistrates, advocates, attorneys, and police officers are amongst those who have been designated as commissioners of oaths by the Minister of Justice.[43]

---

38 Section 2(1)(a)(v).

39 Kahn, Ellison *1994 Supplement to the Law of Succession in South Africa*, 1994 at 35.

40 *Sterban v Dixon* 1968 (1) SA 322 (C) at 324H.

41 *Burton-Moore v The Master* 1983 (4) SA 419 (N).

42 Section 2(1)(a)(v)(aa) read with ss 2(1)(a)(i), (iii) and (iv).

43 Justices of the Peace and Commissioners of Oaths Act 16 of 1963 read with GN 903 in *GG* 19033 of 10 July 1998 read with s 1 of the Criminal Procedure Act 51 of 1977 under the heading 'peace officer'.

The commissioner of oaths must:

- satisfy himself or herself as to the identity of the testator
- satisfy himself or herself that the will so signed is the will of the testator[44]
- make a certificate on the will itself in which he or she certifies that he or she has so satisfied himself or herself[45]
- record in the certificate that he or she has done so in his or her capacity as a commissioner of oaths.[46]

The certificate can be written on the will by hand, typed or printed on the will, or impressed on the will with a rubber stamp.

Following a number of cases in which it was held that the commissioner's certificate was not compliant with the Act (resulting in an invalid will), specimen certificates were inserted into the Act to use when certifying an execution or amendment.[47] It is not necessary for the commissioner's certificate to follow the precise wording of the Act,[48] or for the specimen certificate to be used,[49] but the use of the specimen is advisable.

Figure 5.1 *A specimen certificate*

CERTIFICATE IN TERMS OF SECTION 2(1)(a)(v)

I, (full name) ....

of (full address)..

....

in my capacity as commissioner of oaths certify that I have satisfied myself as to the identity of the testator (full names) ....

and that the accompanying will is the will of the testator.

....

....

Signature

Commissioner of Oaths

....

Capacity

Place.. Date..

The requirements of the Wills Act regarding certification have been applied strictly by the courts. Furthermore, although the statute does not require in so many words that the commissioner of oaths must record his or her capacity as such in the certificate, it has been held that this is a requirement, and that failure to do so invalidates the will.

44 Section 2(1)(a)(v).
45 Section 2(1)(a)(v) of the Wills Act.
46 *Radley v Stopforth* 1977 (2) SA 516 (A) at 528H.
47 See Schedules 1 (for use when a will is executed) and 2 (for use when a will is amended).
48 *Radley v Stopforth* 1977 (2) SA 516 (A) at 527F.
49 *O'Connor v The Master of the High Court* [1999] 3 All SA 652 (NC) at 656.

In *Radley v Stopforth*,[50] an administrative officer of the Transvaal Provincial Administration at Vereeniging Hospital who was, in fact, a commissioner of oaths, signed a certificate in which an imprint made on the page with a rubber stamp intimated that he was an administrative official of the hospital. The will was held to be invalid because the commissioner of oaths had not stated his capacity as such.

Similarly, in *Jeffrey v The Master*,[51] where a stamp below the certifying officer's signature described him as a practising attorney, the will was invalid in spite of the fact that all practising attorneys are commissioners of oaths. It was held that the certificate itself must indicate that the certifying officer was functioning in his capacity as a commissioner of oaths at the time he carried out his duties.

Although strict compliance with the certification requirements is still necessary, it may now be possible to handle problems of this nature by application of s 2(3) of the Act which allows a court to order that a defectively executed will be accepted as if it were validly executed, provided that the requirements of s 2(3), can be satisfied.[52]

COUNTER POINT

Capacity as commissioner

The view adopted by the Appellate Division in *Radley v Stopforth*[53] that the certifying officer's capacity as a commissioner of oaths must be included in the certificate has been challenged by Jamneck[54] who has expressed doubt as to whether the courts are correct in insisting on this requirement. She has pointed out that the actual words of the section do not mention such a requirement.

However, the judgment in *Radley v Stopforth*[55] is a unanimous judgment of the Appellate Division and the following statement by Rumpff CJ carries considerable weight: 'Ek het geen twyfel nie dat die Wetgewer bedoel het dat die sertifiseerder se besondere amp, waarvolgens hy optree, op die testament vermeld moet word.'[56] Whether it creates a binding precedent of the Appellate Division on this point is another matter, because Rumpff CJ mentions immediately before this that counsel for the appellant conceded this point in the course of oral argument. In principle, a concession of counsel cannot create a binding precedent. Since Rumpff CJ gave no reasons for his opinion, it is arguable that his decision did not create a binding precedent on this point and that the issue is open to challenge along the lines of Jamneck's argument.

The commissioner of oaths must sign the certificate itself and each of the other pages of the will anywhere on the page.[57]

Before the 1992 amendments it was required that the certificate appear at the end of the will. However, this requirement has been removed and the certificate may now appear on

50 1977 (2) SA 516 (A).
51 1990 (4) SA 759 (N).
52 Section 2(3) is discussed on page 78ff.
53 1977 (2) SA 516 (A).
54 Jamneck 1991 *THRHR* 671.
55 1977 (2) SA 516 (A).
56 *Radley v Stopforth* 1977 (2) SA 516 (A) at 528H; this loosely translates as 'I have no doubt that the Legislature intended that the certifying officer's particular authority, in terms of which he acts, must be mentioned in the certificate.'
57 Section 2(1)(a)(v).

any page of the will. Since it is required to be on a page of the will,[58] it is doubtful whether writing it on the blank reverse of one of the pages would be compliant.

A number of decisions previously permitted the commissioner of oaths to function in a dual capacity as both a witness and a commissioner of oaths. It seems that this is no longer possible because the witnesses must sign in the presence of the commissioner of oaths.

In terms of the Act, the certificate must be made 'as soon as possible' after the will has been marked by the testator or signed by the amanuensis.[59] Prior to the 1992 amendments, it was held in *Radley v Stopforth*[60] that certification must be completed before the death of the testator because certification forms part of the execution requirements themselves, and execution must be completed by the testator during his or her lifetime.[61] The Act now provides, however, for the certificate to be made or completed after the death of the testator, provided that the commissioner acts as soon as possible.[62] The formulation 'as soon as possible' does not allow a great deal of leeway for delay and the commissioner of oaths should complete the execution of the will immediately it has been marked or signed.

PAUSE FOR REFLECTION

Defective execution

Section 2(3) of the Act, which permits a court to condone the defective execution of a will, is discussed later in this chapter but note that although s 2(3) can generally be used to resolve difficulties relating to certification where the testator has signed using a mark, it seems that it may not be possible to do so when the testator has used an amanuensis unless the will was personally drafted by the testator. Accordingly, it is preferable for a testator who is unable to execute the will with a signature to use a mark if this is possible, rather than relying on an amanuensis.

PAUSE FOR REFLECTION

The need to guard against fraud

The formalities for a valid will and their strict enforcement represent an attempt to guard against fraud which is a particular danger in the case of wills because the person most intimately connected with the will is not able to testify. As both society and technology change with time, the question should constantly be asked whether or not the present formalities are adequate, and whether or not other measures should be introduced to protect against fraud.

58 Sections 2(1)(a)(v) and 2(1)(a)(v)(bb) both contain the words 'page on which his certificate appears'.
59 Section 2(1)(a)(v)(aa).
60 1977 (2) SA 516 (A).
61 *Radley v Stopforth* 1977 (2) SA 516 (A) at 529A–530H.
62 Section 2(1)(a)(v)(bb).

LEGAL THINKING

Has a will been properly executed or not?

How should one go about analysing whether a will has been properly executed or not?

Because every will must be considered on its own merits and facts, it is not possible to produce an exhaustive list of questions that examine all the issues relevant to a particular will.

The questions that follow are designed for a will executed after 1 January 1954 when the testator died after 1 October 1992.

1. Is the will in documentary form?
2. Is the page on which the will ends signed by the testator and two or more witnesses?
3. Is the signature of the testator on that page as close as reasonably possible to the end of the will?
4. Did the testator sign all other pages of the will?
5. In each case, did the testator sign with a mark or was the testator's signature made by an amanuensis? If so:

- Has a commissioner of oaths made a certificate on the will?
- Is the certificate on the will itself? (It is a debatable point whether placing the certificate on the blank reverse of a page or on a separate page is compliant with the Act.)
- Does the content of the certificate satisfy the three requirements of the Act?
- Has the certificate been signed or initialled by the commissioner?
- Have all other pages of the will on which the certificate does not appear, also been signed or initialled by the commissioner?

6. Is there evidence that the testator and witnesses were not present together when each signed the will? If so, were the formalities for the testator to acknowledge his or her signature followed?
7. If the testator signed with a mark or an amanuensis signed for the testator, is there evidence that the commissioner of oaths was not present together with the testator, amanuensis, and witnesses when they signed the will?
8. Is there evidence that one or more witnesses signed the will before the testator had done so?
9. Is there evidence that the commissioner of oaths failed to append his or her certificate as soon as possible after the testator made a mark or the amanuensis signed?
10. Has the commissioner of oaths functioned in a dual capacity, as both certifying officer and witness?
11. Is there evidence that the testator was not legally competent to make a will at the date of execution?
12. Is there evidence that one, or more, of the witnesses was not a legally competent witness at the date of execution?
13. If the will is defective in any of the above respects, can the defect be remedied by an application to court in terms of s 2(3) and what are the prospects of the application succeeding?

5.3 Formalities for the amendment of wills

A will once executed is not written in stone. The testator is free to alter his or her will at any stage. Changes to a will can be made by executing a codicil which gives effect to the changes the testator wants to make. It is also possible for the testator to amend an existing will by interfering with the writing of it. It is this method of amendment that is the subject of this section.

The rules governing the amendment of a will are determined by the date on which the will that is being amended was executed.[63] This section deals with the amendment of wills executed on or after 1 January 1954 (the commencement date of the Wills Act) where the testator died after 1 October 1992 (the commencement date of the Law of Succession Amendment Act 43 of 1992 which introduced substantial changes).

It may be that a testator who is about to execute a will chooses to amend it in some way before signing it, for example by altering some of the words with a pen so as to increase the amount of a legacy or to change the name of a beneficiary. Such an amendment is referred to as a pre-execution amendment and requires no formalities in order to be lawful because the altered wording is already in place when the testator executes the will. Nevertheless, a pre-execution amendment should be signed by the testator and the two witnesses because the Act provides that any amendment to the will shall be rebuttably presumed to have been made after the will was executed,[64] and after the death of the testator it may not be possible to establish that the amendment was in fact made before execution. A rebuttable presumption is one that will stand as a fact unless proven otherwise.

Amendments made to a will that has already been executed (post-execution amendments) are governed by s 2(1)(b) of the Wills Act, and failure to comply with the requirements of this section will mean that the amendment is ineffective. This section requires an amendment of a will to be identified by the signature of the testator and two witnesses. Because the amendment is a new act of testation, the witnesses need not be the same witnesses as were present at the execution of the will that is being amended. The Act does not stipulate how the identification by signature is to take place, but it seems that this can be achieved by placing the signatures of the testator and witnesses close to the amendment.

The Wills Act makes provision for the testator to use a mark or an amanuensis to execute the amendment. In such event, a commissioner of oaths must be present when the amendment is executed. In addition, the commissioner of oaths is required to certify that:

- he or she is satisfied as to the identity of the testator
- the amendment has been made by or at the request of the testator
- the commissioner has functioned in his or her capacity as a commissioner of oaths in so certifying.

The commissioner must sign the certificate, but there is no provision for the commissioner of oaths to sign all the other pages of the will. The Act does not stipulate that the amendment be identified by the signature or certificate of the commissioner of oaths, nor where in the will the certificate should be made. It makes sense, however, for the certificate to be made near the amendment since it needs to be clear to which amendment the certificate refers. It also makes sense to include a reference identifying the amendment to which the certificate refers, although this is not a requirement of the Act. Even if there is only one amendment,

63 Section 2(1)(b) of the Wills Act.
64 Section 2(2) of the Wills Act.

the possibility cannot be ignored that further amendments might be made which could introduce confusion.

There are many ways in which a testator can amend his or her will, including:

- inserting additional paragraphs into the will
- writing additional words between the existing lines of the will
- altering words or numbers in the will
- drawing lines through words, numbers, or whole paragraphs of the will so as to delete them, whether or not new material is inserted in their place.

In terms of the Wills Act, each of the following actions brings about an amendment and requires compliance with the formalities for amendment that are described above:[65]

- additions
- alterations
- interlineations (inserting new words between the lines of the will)
- deletions, cancellations, and obliterations in whatever manner effected except where they contemplate the revocation of the entire will.

The reference to 'deletions, cancellations, and obliterations in whatever manner effected' includes acts such as erasing, cutting out, pasting over, or removing with something such as correction fluid. The exception relating to a deletion, cancellation, or obliteration which contemplates the revocation of the entire will was necessary to preserve the testator's right to revoke his or her will by destroying it in some way, without the need to comply with formalities of any kind.[66]

5.4 Section 2(3) of the Wills Act

The Act gives the High Court the power to order the Master to accept a will which does not comply with the execution or amendment formalities if it is satisfied that the testator intended the defectively executed document to be his or her will or an amendment to it. This power of the Court is often referred to as the power of condonation and is contained in s 2(3) of the Act. If the provisions of s 2(3) are satisfied, the Court makes an order directing the Master to accept the will or amendment as if it were validly executed.

The provisions of s 2(3) are peremptory. In other words, if the requirements of the section are satisfied by proof on a balance of probabilities, then the Court must make an order directing the Master to accept the will.[67] It does not have any discretion not to do so. Similarly, if there is insufficient proof that the requirements of the section are satisfied, the Court cannot make an order in terms of s 2(3), even if it believes that the document is consistent with the testator's wishes.

A number of issues resulted in extensive litigation and divergent judicial opinion regarding the scope of s 2(3), which reads as follows:

> *If a court is satisfied that a document or the amendment of a document drafted or executed by a person who has died since the drafting or execution thereof, was intended*

65 Section 1 under the headings 'amendment' and 'deletion'.

66 Revocation by destruction will be discussed in Chapter 6.

67 *Harlow v Becker* 1998 (4) SA 639 (D) at 642I–643E.

to be his will or an amendment of his will, the court shall order the Master to accept that document, or that document as amended, for the purposes of the Administration of Estates Act, 1965 (Act No. 66 of 1965), as a will, although it does not comply with all the formalities for the execution or amendment of wills referred to in subsection (1).

The first issue of interpretation that arose is whether or not the rescue provision can be used to give effect to a will that was completely unsigned, or whether some degree of compliance with the formalities is a prerequisite for the rescue of a will. If some degree of compliance is required, does this mean that there must be substantial compliance?

The view that some degree of compliance is required originated in the judgment in *Webster v The Master*,[68] in which Magid J held that the section was not intended to validate a document that does not comply with any of the formalities of the Act.[69] He reasoned that the history of the section showed that its purpose was to remedy technical non-compliance with the execution formalities, not to give effect to a completely unsigned document'.[70]

The second issue of interpretation was that if the rescue provision can be applied to an unsigned document, does the reference in the section to a document 'drafted or executed by a person who has died' mean that this can only be done if the testator had drafted the will personally, rather than using an attorney or other advisor to draft it?

At first, the courts followed two contradictory approaches – the strict approach and the flexible approach. The strict approach was followed by Magid J, in *Webster v The Master*,[71] who held that the words of the section refer to a document drafted or executed by 'a person who has died' (in other words, the testator himself or herself), and mean that the '[l]egislature did not intend to endow an unsigned document, drafted by someone other than the testator, even an attorney, with the status of a will'.[72] Magid J pointed to the contrast between the wording of s 2A, which permits the court to complete an act of revocation that the testator had 'caused to be done' (that is, using an agent), and the wording of s 2(3) that requires a 'document drafted or executed by a person who has died'. He concluded that the change in wording indicated that s 2(3) calls for conduct of the testator personally, and does not encompass conduct through an agent.

The flexible approach to s 2(3) was followed in *Back v Master of the Supreme Court*[73] in which Van Zyl J granted an order in terms of s 2(3) with respect to a will that had been drafted by the testator's attorney, and had been read to and approved by the testator who delayed signing it pending counsel's opinion on the tax consequences of the will. The testator died before he could execute the will. Van Zyl J was of the opinion that the difference in wording between s 2(3) and s 2A[74] that Magid J relied on in *Webster v The Master*[75] was not relevant because the two sections deal with different things. He held that the requirement of a document 'drafted' by the deceased must be flexibly interpreted in view of the purpose of s 2(3), which was to prevent the testator's

---

68 1996 (1) SA 34 (D) at 42F–G.

69 The same approach was followed in *Olivier v Die Meester: In re Boedel Wyle Olivier* 1997 (1) SA 836 (T) at 843 H–I.

70 *Webster v The Master* 1996 (1) SA 34 (D) at 41F–42G.

71 1996 (1) SA 34 (D).

72 *Webster v The Master* 1996 (1) SA 34 (D) at 41D–E.

73 [1996] 2 All SA 161 (C).

74 Section 2A reads as follows: 'If a court is satisfied that a testator has – (a) made a written indication on his will or before his death caused such indication to be made; (b) performed any other act with regard to his will or before his death caused such act to be performed which is apparent from the face of the will; or (c) drafted another document or before his death caused such document to be drafted, by which he intended to revoke his will or a part of his will, the court shall declare the will or the part concerned, as the case may be, to be revoked.' See Chapter 6 for a discussion of s 2A.

75 1996 (1) SA 34 (D).

> wishes from being nullified by non-compliance with technical formalities. It followed, he held, that the acceptance of the draft by the testator, who had approved it 'to its finest detail',[76] was tantamount to the testator drafting it himself and therefore a s 2(3) order should be made.

A number of other decisions followed in which courts made s 2(3) orders with respect to completely unsigned documents not personally drafted by the testator.[77]

In essence, those courts that subscribed to the flexible approach treated proof that the testator intended the document to be his or her will as the sole requirement for the application of the section. This flexible approach was, however, brought to an abrupt end in 2003 by the decision of the Supreme Court of Appeal in *Bekker v Naudé*[78] in which that Court refused an order in terms of s 2(3) with respect to a will that had been drafted by a bank official at the request of the deceased, and posted to him, but which he had not executed by the time of his death. The central issue was whether the document was drafted by the deceased.

Delivering the judgment of the Court, Olivier JA referred briefly to the decisions that have supported the strict and flexible interpretations respectively, and indicated that it was unnecessary for him to go through all the arguments used because, in his view, the strict interpretation was clearly the correct one. He based this conclusion on the basic principle that the ordinary, grammatical meaning of a word must be used unless that would lead to absurdity, inconsistency, or hardship, or result in an anomaly. None of these consequences was applicable here and, accordingly, approval of a document drafted by another person was not the equivalent of drafting the document oneself. His view was strengthened by the comparison between the wording used in ss 2(3) and 2A referred to above. The Court was further of the view that the requirement of a document drafted by the testator had been included, in unambiguous language, for good reason, namely to guarantee a degree of reliability by requiring evidence of personal conduct by the testator out of which his or her intention can be clearly deduced.

The result of *Bekker v Naudé* is that it is no longer possible to give effect to a completely unsigned will using the rescue provision unless the will was drafted by the testator in the strict sense of personal drafting. It should be noted that the requirement of personal drafting in this context amounts to a requirement that the testator be the author of the document because *Bekker v Naudé* seems to accept that a will composed by the testator and dictated to another person who writes or types it qualifies as a document personally drafted by the testator. The requirement of personal drafting narrows the scope for the use of the section with respect to unsigned wills because it seems likely that comparatively few testators draft their own wills. Nevertheless, this development keeps the rescue provision within proper limits as a tool for avoiding the harsh consequences of making a slip in complying with the execution formalities.

PAUSE FOR REFLECTION

What qualifies?

The question may be asked whether a document that has been dictated onto a dictaphone and typed by a typist during the testator's lifetime, which the testator never had an opportunity to revise or proofread, qualifies as a document drafted by the testator? If so, will it make a difference if the typist only types the document from the

76 *Back v Master of the Supreme Court* [1996] 2 All SA 161 (C) at 175f-g.
77 For example, *Ex parte Laxton* 1998 (3) SA 238 (N) and *Ex parte Williams: In re Williams' Estate* 2000 (4) SA 168 (T).
78 2003 (5) SA 173 (SCA).

dictaphone recording after the testator's death? There seems to be no sure answer to this question.

The requirement of s 2(3) is that there be a document that was 'drafted or executed' by the person who has died.[79] Accordingly, if the document was, in fact, *executed* by the testator, it will not matter that it was not personally drafted by the testator,[80] and it will be possible to use s 2(3) to give effect to the will if the formalities have not been strictly followed, provided that it can be shown that the testator intended the document to be his or her will.

COUNTER POINT

Unfair discrimination

It has been suggested that the decision in *Bekker v Naudé*[81] is unconstitutional as it discriminates unfairly against blind and illiterate people.[82] The argument is that they are less likely to be able to enjoy the benefits of s 2(3) than their sighted and literate counterparts because they need to use advisors to draft their wills. On the other hand, it seems likely that few people draft their wills personally, so the actual extent of the differential treatment – between those who are sighted and literate, and those who are unsighted or illiterate – is likely to be small. Unsighted testators are, in any event, still able to draft their wills personally if they wish to do so, by using suitable computer equipment or dictating their wills to someone else to write out or type for them. An illiterate person can execute a will by making a cross or thumbprint, which is all that is required to permit the making of an order in terms of s 2(3), provided that the document is intended to be a will. Section 2(3) does not undermine the dignity of unsighted people. Illiteracy is not a protected category in terms of the equality clause of the Bill of Rights. The requirement of personal conduct has a valid purpose – to diminish the possibility of fraud – and the negative effects of the requirement are very limited, as indicated above. The legislature cannot be expected to cater for all possibilities.

If the interpretation adopted in *Bekker v Naudé* is unfairly discriminatory, what is the solution? Should the operation of s 2(3) be extended to wills not drafted or executed by the testator personally, or should it be cut down so as to completely rule out the application of s 2(3) to unexecuted wills?

5.4.1 Executing a will

Since the decision in *Bekker v Naudé*,[83] it is likely that most applications for relief in terms of s 2(3) will relate to defectively executed documents that have not been drafted by the testator personally. This will shift the focus to the alternative requirement that there be a document '*executed* by a person who has died'.[84] The term 'execute' in relation to a document usually means to go through the formalities necessary to give it validity, but this can hardly be the intended meaning in the context of s 2(3), which is aimed at providing relief where there has been a failure to go through those requirements.

79 That was intended to be his or her will.
80 *Mdlulu v Delarey* [1998] 1 All SA 434 (W) at 442, last paragraph.
81 2003 (5) SA 173 (SCA).
82 See Paleker 2004 *SALJ* 27 at 32–33.
83 2003 (5) SA 173 (SCA).
84 Emphasis added.

PAUSE FOR REFLECTION

Execution of a will

In *Ex parte De Swardt*,[85] the testatrix's draft will comprising several pages was read and approved by her before she signed the will. Unfortunately, one page of the will was accidentally omitted when the document was printed for signing, and was, therefore, not executed with the rest of the will. An order was granted in terms of s 2(3) on the basis that the testatrix had read and approved the draft will and could, therefore, be regarded as having drafted the will herself, including the missing, unsigned, page. Now that *Bekker v Naudé*[86] no longer permits the use of such an argument to justify the use of s 2(3), the interesting question arises whether it would be possible to satisfy the requirements of s 2(3) in those circumstances on some other basis, such as that the testatrix 'executed' the will personally. But can one correctly say that she executed the will when one whole page of her testamentary wishes was absent from the document that she executed? The situation is problematic and one cannot predict the outcome with certainty.

A further situation to consider is whether it is possible to use s 2(3) to give effect to a document that existed only in the form of a computer file at the time of the deceased's death.

In *Macdonald v The Master*,[87] the deceased had typed his will on his office computer and saved it as a computer file, without printing it. He then committed suicide and left a note alerting his family to the existence of the computer file containing his will. In the presence of the police, his wife accessed this computer file which was then printed and deleted from the computer. The security arrangements around the deceased's computer were such that there was no doubt that the computer file had been drafted by the deceased. An order in terms of s 2(3) was granted by Hattingh J, who favoured the liberal approach and who stated that '[the] deceased's will was indeed a document that was stored in his computer in accordance with his instructions. On a flexible interpretation of s 2(3), it may be regarded as having been drafted by him personally.'[88] In this way, the Court avoided possible debate over the issue whether at the time the deceased died, there was a document in existence in the everyday sense of the word 'document'.

5.4.2 Intention requirement of section 2(3)

In addition to the litigation surrounding the contentious issues discussed above, there have been a number of cases relating to s 2(3) concerning the requirement that there be a document that the testator 'intended to be his will.'

To establish intention it must be shown that the document was, at the time it was made,[89] the final expression of the deceased's wishes, not subject to change except by a new will or codicil.[90] This required degree of finality is not present in the case of written instructions, or letters of instruction, given by the deceased to an attorney, bank, or other advisor, because the testator does not intend that the instructions themselves should serve as his or her will. Rather, the testator intends that a further document will be produced for his or her approval, based on the written instructions.

85 1998 (2) SA 204 (C).
86 2003 (5) SA 173 (SCA).
87 2002 (5) SA 64 (O).
88 *Macdonald v The Master* 2002 (5) SA 64 (O) at 71I–J.
89 *Van Wetten v Bosch* 2004 (1) SA 348 (SCA) at para 21.
90 *Anderson and Wagner v The Master* 1996 (3) SA 779 (C) at 784G–785A.

In *Ex parte Maurice*,[91] the testator had written out a draft will after exhaustive discussions with his wife as to what the contents of their joint will should be, and had sent the will to a friend who had experience in the drafting of wills, with the request that the friend 'knock it into shape'. When the testator died before the will could be finalised, it was held that a s 2(3) order could not be made with respect to the draft prepared by the testator because the testator had envisaged that the document might well be changed on the basis of his friend's advice and, therefore, he had not intended it to be the final expression of his wishes.

Similarly, in *Letsekga v The Master*,[92] notes were found amongst the testator's possessions that appeared to be notes of future changes to his will. For example, '1 (d) This amount to be increased to R50 000'. The prospective tone of the notes ('to be increased' rather than 'is hereby increased') coupled with certain other factors indicated that these were notes of changes that the testator was contemplating making to his will. The notes themselves were not intended to be a codicil to his will. Accordingly, a s 2(3) order could not be made with respect to the notes.

It is, however, vital to pay attention to the intention of the testator with respect to the writing, not merely to the form that the writing takes. Thus, in *Van Wetten v Bosch*,[93] a s 2(3) order was granted with respect to a letter addressed to the testator's attorney containing instructions for the drafting of a will. What distinguished this case from *Ex parte Maurice* was that the testator had left the letter in the possession of a friend with instructions that the letter was only to be given to the testator's attorney if something should happen to the testator, which the Court interpreted as a reference to the testator's death. Since it would be futile to give instructions for the drafting of a will after one's death, the Court concluded that the letter itself was intended to function as the final expression of the testator's wishes, notwithstanding that it was in the form of a letter of instructions.

It has been held that it is the testator's intention at the time he or she made the document that is relevant.[94] A subsequent change of intention is irrelevant unless it is manifested in a testamentary document, or in one of the recognised methods of revoking a will, or part of a will.[95] In *Van Wetten v Bosch*,[96] when the deceased's wife sought to bring evidence to court to show that by the time of the deceased's death, he no longer intended the letter to his attorney to be his will, this evidence was held to be irrelevant to the testator's intention at the time he made the document and was regarded as inadmissible.

It has been held that it is not necessary to show that the testator believed that he or she had succeeded in making a valid will.[97] In other words, even if the testator was familiar with the will-making formalities and was well aware that the document did not comply with them, a court can find that the testator intended the document to be his or her will for the purposes of s 2(3).

The applicant for a s 2(3) order does not have to establish testamentary capacity, merely testamentary intention.[98] This is because testamentary capacity and testamentary intention are different things[99] and s 2(3) only calls for proof of intention. For example, a testator may

---

91 1995 (2) SA 713 (C).

92 1995 (4) SA 731 (W).

93 2004 (1) SA 348 (SCA).

94 *Van Wetten v Bosch* 2004 (1) SA 348 (SCA) at paras 20 & 21; *De Reszke v Maras* 2006 (2) SA 277 (SCA) at para 11.

95 Regarding revocation of wills, see Chapter 6.

96 2004 (1) SA 348 (SCA) at paras 20 & 21.

97 *Ex parte Williams: In re Williams' Estate* 2000 (4) SA 168 (T) at 179D–G.

98 *Harlow v Becker* 1998 (4) SA 639 (D), especially at 643G–647C; *Thirion v Die Meester* 2001 (4) SA 1078 (T) at 1091D–E.

99 *Harlow v Becker* 1998 (4) SA 639 (D) at 644C–645J.

have a clear understanding of a draft will submitted to him or her and may approve of it, but if his or her memory is so defective through disease that he or she was unaware of the existence of his or her blood relations and, as a result, chose strangers to be beneficiaries, then that will is invalid for lack of testamentary capacity.[100] The person who contests the validity of a document on the basis that the testator lacked testamentary capacity bears the onus of proving the absence of capacity once the testamentary intention has been established.[101]

If the document is incomplete, in the sense that it does not contain all the testator's testamentary wishes at the time he or she approves it, then it cannot be said that the testator intends it to be his or her will. In *Webster v The Master,*[102] the testator asked his attorney to add a legacy to his draft will appointing his children as his heirs but died before the new will was prepared. One of the several reasons for refusing a s 2(3) order that would have given effect to the draft benefiting the children, was that the draft was not the testator's complete will.

5.5 Customary law of succession

Since the decision of the Constitutional Court in *Bhe v Magistrate, Khayelitsha,*[103] and the subsequent repeal of s 23 of the Black Administration Act, persons living under a system of customary law are free to execute wills regarding customary property. As a result, the requirements discussed in this chapter will apply to all wills made by such persons.

THIS CHAPTER IN ESSENCE

1. The only way in which a testator can make a valid will is by strictly complying with the detailed requirements of s 2(1) of the Wills Act.
2. Similar execution requirements apply when the testator amends an existing will by making changes on the will itself. A codicil that amends an existing will must also be made in accordance with the requirements of s 2(1) of the Wills Act.
3. In terms of s 2(3) of the Wills Act, a court may order that a document that has not been executed in strict compliance with the will-making formalities shall nevertheless be treated as if it were a valid will. To obtain such an order, it is essential to prove that the testator intended the document to be his or her will, and that the document was personally drafted by the testator, or personally executed by the testator.
4. Despite the existence of s 2(3), it remains vital for wills to be properly executed in accordance with the requirements of s 2(1) because the lengthy delays and financial expense involved in obtaining a court order that a defective document be treated as a will can be disastrous for the testator's family. In addition, it may not always be possible to satisfy the requirements for such an order, even when the testator's intentions can be clearly established.

100 *Battan Singh v Amirchand* [1948] 1 All ER 152 at 155H.
101 *Harlow v Becker* 1998 (4) SA 639 (D) at 647B–D; the concept of testamentary capacity is discussed in Chapter 4.
102 1996 (1) SA 34 (D) at 40F–G.
103 2005 (1) SA 580 (CC).

Chapter 6

Revocation and revival of wills

What are the legal principles applicable to the revocation and revival of wills?

6.1	Introduction	85
6.2	Methods of revoking a will	86
6.3	Presumptions concerning the revocation of wills	89
6.4	Doctrine of dependent relative revocation	91
6.5	Revival of wills	92
6.6	Revocation by the court: section 2A	93
6.7	Customary law of succession	98
This chapter in essence		98

6.1 Introduction

Revocation is the act by which a testator cancels a will, or part of a will so that it is no longer valid. Revocation is the only way in which a will can be undone by a testator. It is also possible for a testator to revoke only part of his or her will, leaving the remainder of the will valid. This is referred to as partial revocation. Oral revocation of a will is not recognised and will be ineffective.[1]

A testator is free to revoke his or her will at any time during his or her lifetime,[2] and any agreement that attempts to restrict this freedom is unenforceable.[3] There are only two exceptions:

1. Where a mutual will establishes estate massing,[4] the surviving testator who accepts the benefit of the massing cannot subsequently alter the testamentary disposition of the massed assets stipulated in the mutual will.[5]
2. Testamentary provisions contained in a duly registered antenuptial contract cannot be unilaterally departed from or altered.

1 *Louw v Engelbrecht* 1979 (4) SA 841 (O) at 849H–850E; *Marais v The Master* 1984 (4) SA 288 (D) at 291H–292B; *Ferreira v Die Bybelgenootskap van Suid-Afrika* 1994 (2) Juta's Supreme Court Digest 9 (CPD 15 October 1993 Case 1652/93 (unreported); *Mdlulu v Delarey* [1998] 1 All SA 434 (W) at 449–452.

2 *Mdlulu v Delarey* [1998] 1 All SA 434 (W) at 445.

3 *James v James's Estate* 1941 EDL 67; *Van Jaarsveld v Van Jaarsveld's Estate* 1938 TPD 343.

4 For a discussion of estate massing, see Chapter 9.

5 *Joubert v Ruddock* 1968 (1) SA 95 (E) at B–D.

There are two essential elements for the revocation of a will:

1. an intention to revoke (*animus revocandi*)
2. a legally recognised act by which this intention is manifested.

Only when both essentials are satisfied does revocation take place. If the intention to revoke is present but is not manifested in a legally recognised act of revocation, then it may be possible for the court to order that the will be revoked in terms of s 2A of the Wills Act.

The revocation of wills is governed by the common law and the provisions of the Wills Act.[6] Revocation of a will that expressly or impliedly revokes an earlier will does not revive the earlier will. In other words, it does not bring the earlier will back into operation.[7]

6.2 Methods of revoking a will

South African common law recognises the following four methods of revocation.

6.2.1 Revocation by destruction of the whole will

Destruction of the whole will *animo revocandi* (with intention to revoke) revokes the will, and no formalities are required.[8] Accidental destruction of the will does not revoke it because the intention to revoke is absent and, in spite of its physical destruction, the provisions of the destroyed will will be given effect. Evidence would have to be led as to the contents of the will. Such evidence may be available from persons who have read the will, or from the attorney who prepared it. Destruction of only part of the will involves different rules, which are discussed below.

Destruction of a will can be physical (for example, the will may be burnt or torn up), or symbolic, for example:

- defacing the writing of the will by drawing lines across it[9]
- writing the words 'cancelled' or 'revoked' across the face of the will[10]
- destroying the testator's signature on the will[11]
- destroying the signature of a witness on the will.

A will can be destroyed by any means such as tearing, burning, or scribbling over it and defacing it with a pen. Because a testator is required to sign the end of a will as well as all the other pages, destruction of his or her signature at the end of the will would revoke the will. However, destruction of the testator's signature on an earlier page of a multiple paged will is problematic because the testator may have merely intended to revoke that particular page and, if so, the partial revocation will not be recognised unless the rules for the partial amendment of wills were satisfied.

As far as destruction of a witness' signature is concerned, witnesses are now only required to sign the last page of the will, so only the destruction of a witness' signature on the last page would revoke the will. Furthermore, the destruction would have to reduce the number of witnesses to less than two, which is the required minimum number of witnesses.

6 *Marais v The Master* 1984 (4) SA 288 (D) at 291F; *Mdlulu v Delarey* [1998] 1 All SA 434 (W) at 446.
7 *Fram v Fram's Executrix* 1947 (1) 787 (W) at 789; *Le Roux v Le Roux* 1963 (4) SA 273 (C), especially at 284C; *Raabe v The Master* 1971 (1) SA 780 (T) at 781G–H.
8 *Senekal v Meyer* 1975 (3) SA 372 (T); *Marais v The Master* 1984 (4) SA 288 (D) at 291G–H.
9 *In re Nortje* 1956 (4) SA 180 (C); *Senekal v Meyer* 1975 (3) SA 372 (T).
10 *In re Nortje* 1956 (4) SA 180; *Senekal v Meyer* 1975 (3) SA 372 (T).
11 *Fram v Fram's Executrix* 1947 (1) SA 787 (W) at 789.

According to Corbett et al,[12] merely writing the words 'cancelled' or 'revoked' in any of the four margins of the will would not constitute destruction of the will and would not revoke it because there would be no interference with the words of the will.

The limits of what symbolic acts are recognised as destruction of a will are governed by common law[13] and are not clearly defined. This allows the courts a measure of flexibility in deciding whether a will has been revoked by destruction.

In *Senekal v Meyer*,[14] acts of symbolic destruction were carried out on a duplicate original of the will. The other original was inaccessible to the testator because it was locked in his attorney's strongroom over a weekend. Even though the other original in the attorney's possession was still physically intact, the acts of destruction carried out on the duplicate original were held to revoke the will. (A duplicate original will is a second printing of the will that is executed with all the requisite formalities simultaneously with the execution of the first printing.)

In *Marais v The Master*,[15] the will was held to be revoked by acts of destruction carried out on a copy of the will in the testator's possession. As in *Senekal v Meyer*,[16] the original was in his attorney's possession out of the testator's reach. Although the original was physically unaffected by the destruction of the copy, it was held that the testator's conduct with respect to the copy showed what he would have done to the original had it been in his possession, and this was sufficient to revoke the will.[17]

It seems that if the act of destruction is on a duplicate original or copy there must be an explanation as to why the testator left a properly executed original of the will physically intact. The fact that the testator has left the original of his or her will intact suggests an intention that the will remain in force.[18]

6.2.2 Destruction of part of a will

A will can also be partially revoked by destruction of the relevant part *animo revocandi* (for example, drawing lines across a paragraph of the will, cutting a paragraph out of the will with scissors, or drawing lines through the name of one of the heirs appointed in the will). Partial destruction constitutes an amendment of the will and, as a result, the formalities for the amendment of wills apply.[19] However, the application of s 2A should be kept in mind - see section 6.6.

6.2.3 Express revocation (including informal revocation)

The testator can revoke a previous will or wills by including an appropriate revocation clause in a duly executed will, or in a document that is executed as a will but contains only a revocation clause. Executing a new will without including a revocation clause does not revoke previous wills.[20]

---

12 *Law of succession* (2001) at 97.
13 *Marais v The Master* 1984 (4) SA 288 (D) at 291.
14 1975 (3) SA 372 (T).
15 1984 (4) SA 288 (D).
16 1975 (3) SA 372 (T).
17 *Marais v The Master* 1984 (4) SA 288 (D) at 294D-F.
18 For a discussion of a number of important rebuttable presumptions relating to the revocation of wills, including presumptions concerning the destruction of wills, see pages 89-90.
19 See the discussion in Chapter 5.
20 In some circumstances the execution of a new will may impliedly revoke a previous will; see the discussion of implied revocation in paragraph 6.2.4.

A typical revocation clause that would revoke all previously executed wills might read as follows: 'I hereby revoke all wills and other testamentary writings previously made by me.'

PAUSE FOR REFLECTION

Is an express revocation in an informal document valid?

Oral revocation of a will is not possible. Nor is it possible to give effect to an oral revocation using the provisions of s 2A. An important question is whether an express revocation contained in a document that is not executed with the formalities for a will is effective to revoke previous wills. Sonnekus[21] has argued that an express revocation in an informal document is valid and effective if two requirements are met:

1. The intention to revoke is clearly apparent from the writing.
2. It is sufficiently clear from the document that it is the testator who has done the act of revocation (for example, the testator identifies the cancellation with his or her signature).

However, the limited judicial authority on this point does not carry much weight and it is unlikely that revocation in this manner would be allowed.[22]

Where a revocation clause has been inserted in a signed will without the knowledge of the testator, evidence is admissible to establish the true intentions of the testator and the court will order that the revocation clause be treated as *pro non scripto.*[23] *Pro non scripto* means as if it had not been written.

6.2.4 Implied revocation

6.2.4.1 Execution of a later conflicting will

The execution of a new will does not automatically revoke the testator's previous wills. As far as possible, the wills in force at the testator's death must be read together. It may be, however, that the provisions of a more recent will conflict irreconcilably with the provisions of an earlier will. In this case, the provisions of the earlier will are impliedly revoked in so far as they are inconsistent with the later will or cannot stand together with any provision in the later will.[24] This is referred to as implied or tacit revocation.

In *Vimpany v Attridge,*[25] the testator left two wills, the earlier will appointing his children as his heirs, and a later will appointing the respondent, Attridge, as his sole heir. The later will was held to have revoked the earlier will although it did not contain any express words of revocation because it was not possible to reconcile the appointment of the children as heirs if the respondent was to be the sole heir.

In *Price v The Master,*[26] the testatrix had also made two wills, the later will containing no express words of revocation. Although, at a simple level, it was possible to read some of the provisions together (for example, a legacy in the earlier will gave the testatrix's brother a bequest of R10 000, and a legacy in the later will gave him a parcel of shares), the Court held that the later will was

21 1982 *TSAR* 230 at 242–243.
22 *Louw v Engelbrecht* 1979 (4) SA 841 (O); *Narshi v Ranchod* 1984 (3) SA 926 (C); *Marais v The Master* 1984 (4) SA 288 (D).
23 *Ex parte Lutchman* 1951 (1) SA 125 (T), especially at 129C–E; *Ex parte Olfsen* 1976 (1) SA 205 (W).
24 *Bredenkamp v The Master and Bredenkamp* 1947 (1) SA 388 (T) at 389; see also *Vimpany v Attridge* 1927 CPD 113.
25 1927 CPD 113.
26 1982 (3) SA 301 (N).

intended to revoke the earlier will in its entirety because in both wills the testatrix set about disposing of her entire estate, and the overall scheme of the later will was completely new and different from that of the earlier will.[27]

6.2.4.2 Ademption

Revocation by ademption occurs where a testator voluntarily alienates a particular asset which he or she has given to a beneficiary in a legacy in the testator's will. Alienate is a broad term that covers all modes of disposing of an asset, for example selling or donating. The testator is rebuttably presumed to have revoked the bequest of the asset.[28] A bequest which is revoked in this way is said to have lapsed by ademption. Ademption is discussed in Chapter 9.

6.3 Presumptions concerning the revocation of wills

If a will is found in the testator's possession in a damaged state, such as would be sufficient to revoke the will if done with *animus revocandi*, then it is rebuttably presumed that the damage was done by the testator with such intention and the will is accordingly revoked. The operation of this presumption may be illustrated by the decision in *Fram v Fram's Executrix.*[29] In this case a will was presumed to have been revoked by the testator by destruction because the will was found amongst the testator's possessions, after his death, with his signature cut out of the paper.

If it is shown that the testator's will was in his or her possession but, after diligent search following his or her death, the will cannot be found, it is rebuttably presumed to have been revoked by the testator. The presumption is actually two-fold:[30]

1. There was an act of destruction.
2. This was done with an intention to revoke (*animus revocandi*).[31]

This presumption as to missing wills is illustrated by the decision in *Le Roux v Le Roux*[32] in which the evidence was that a will made by the testator in January 1960 had been seen on his desk at home later that year but could not be found after his death in 1961. There was no other evidence as to what had become of the will and it was presumed to have been revoked.[33]

In *Ex parte Warren,*[34] it was stated that the rationale behind the presumption is the probability that a testator would usually take steps to preserve his or her will, and that, if it is lost or accidentally destroyed, then he or she would be aware of it and take steps to make a new one.[35]

With respect to a will damaged or lost whilst in the possession of a third party, such as the testator's attorney or the trustee department of a bank, it has been held that the presumption that the will was revoked does not apply, and it is presumed that the destruction was not done

27 *Price v The Master* 1982 (3) SA 301 (N) at 304B–H.
28 *Barrow v The Master* 1960 (3) SA 253 (E), especially at 256H–257A; and 257D–E regarding possible rebuttal of the presumption.
29 1947 (1) 787 (W) at 788.
30 It can be argued that there is a third element, namely that the destruction was carried out by the testator.
31 *Fram v Fram's Executrix* 1947 (1) 787 (W) at 788.
32 1963 (4) SA 273 (C).
33 *Le Roux v Le Roux* 1963 (4) SA 273 (C) at 277A–F.
34 1955 (4) SA 326 (W).
35 *Ex parte Warren* 1955 (4) SA 326 (W) at 327C.

with revocatory intention.[36] It seems likely that the position will be the same if the will went missing whilst in the possession of a third party, since the rationale for the presumption as to missing wills will not be present.

COUNTER POINT

Duplicate original wills

In both *Senekal v Meyer*[37] and *Ex parte Warren*,[38] the testator's will had been executed in duplicate original and one of the duplicates was being held by the testator's attorney when the testator died. In *Senekal v Meyer*, the duplicate that had been in the testator's possession was found symbolically destroyed, but the Court held that the presumption as to damaged wills could not be relied on to establish revocation. The Court cited Voet as authority[39] but, as it turned out, there was sufficient evidence to establish that the testator had revoked the will without relying on the presumption.

In *Ex Parte Warren*, the duplicate original that had been in the testator's possession could not be found after his death and the Court relied on the presumption as to missing wills to come to its conclusion that the will had been revoked. The Court held that the rationale behind the presumption, namely that a testator would take care to reinstate a lost will if it was intended to be operative, applies also to a missing duplicate original that was in the testator's custody.[40] It seems unsatisfactory that different rules should apply to the two presumptions when duplicate originals are still in existence after the testator's death because the presumptions are closely analogous. The reason given in *Ex Parte Warren* for applying the presumption as to missing wills when there is a duplicate original safe in the hands of a third party is not convincing. A testator who realises that one of a pair of duplicates is missing may well simply take comfort from the fact that the other duplicate is safely in the hands of his or her attorney.

The approach adopted by Voet with respect to a damaged duplicate original is preferable, and should apply equally to both presumptions. When only one of a pair of duplicate original wills is either damaged by the testator, or cannot be found after the testator's death having previously been in the possession of the testator, the onus would be on the person alleging that revocation of the will has taken place to prove it. However, as has been indicated above, the Court in *Ex Parte Warren* takes a different approach to the lost duplicate original.

According to De Waal and Schoeman-Malan,[41] the presumption as to missing wills does not operate where the testator had possession of both duplicate original wills, and after his or her death only one can be found, but the authors cite no case authority for this view. This conclusion is, however, consistent with the approach taken in *Senekal v Meyer*.

Both presumptions, where applicable, are rebuttable by direct evidence of the testator's conduct or intentions, or by inference from the circumstances.[42]

36 *Prinsloo v The Master of the Supreme Court (OFS)* 1960 (3) SA 882 (O) at 884E–H, applying Voet 28.4.4.
37 1975 (3) SA 372 (T).
38 1955 (4) SA 326 (W).
39 Voet 28.4.1.
40 *Ex Parte Warren* 1955 (4) SA 326 (W) at 327D.
41 At 94.
42 See *Davis v Steel and Eriksen* 1949 (3) SA 177 (W) at 183; this case concerned the presumption as to missing wills but the same principle should apply to the presumption as to damaged wills.

6.4 Doctrine of dependent relative revocation

An essential requirement for a valid revocation is that the testator must have had *animus revocandi*. Suppose a testator, believing that he or she has just successfully executed a new will, destroys his or her previous will (either physically or symbolically) without realising that the new will does not comply with the formalities for a will and lacks legal efficacy. In this example, the testator's revocatory intention is based on a supposition that proves to be wrong - the new will is not valid. In other words, the intention is defective and the destroyed will is not revoked. This is in terms of the doctrine of dependent relative revocation or, more simply, the principle of conditional revocation.[43]

> A testator makes a new will in 2009 and then destroys an earlier will made in 1999. Although her intention was to revoke the 1999 will, the revocation will not be effective if it turns out that the 2009 will is defectively executed and invalid (unless an order is made in terms of s 2(3) giving effect to the defectively executed 2009 will). The 1999 will stands and, if necessary, evidence as to its contents can be led in court. This is because true *animus revocandi* will be lacking with respect to the revocation of the 1999 will since it was based on the mistaken belief that the testator had succeeded in making a new will.

The principle of conditional revocation has been applied in a number of different circumstances. In *Le Roux v Le Roux*,[44] where the testator had destroyed his second will in the mistaken belief that this would revive an earlier will, the second will was held not to have been revoked.[45] In *Prinsloo v The Master of the Supreme Court (OFS)*,[46] the testatrix destroyed her first will with the intention of executing a new will to replace it. For some reason, she never actually executed a new will and the destroyed will remained in force in spite of the fact that it had been destroyed. If the testator wants the destroyed will to be revoked even though he or she is acting on the basis of some supposition that is false, the testator's revocatory intention is absolute even though it is informed by a false supposition and the will is, therefore, revoked.

> In *Raabe v The Master*,[47] the testator made a will in 1966 just before he and his wife travelled overseas. In his will, he bequeathed his estate to a close friend. It appeared from oral statements made at a later stage that he had done so because he had no children and wanted to provide for the devolution of his estate should he and his wife die in an air crash. After his return from overseas, the testator destroyed his 1966 will in the mistaken belief that this would revive his previous will, executed in 1964 which included provision for his wife.
>
> The destruction of the 1966 will was informed by a mistaken supposition that the 1964 will would automatically be revived. Although the supposition was incorrect, the Court had no difficulty in coming to the conclusion that the testator's intention to revoke his 1966 will was absolute.[48] In other words, the testator would have destroyed the 1966 will even if he knew that this would not

43 For an extensive discussion of the doctrine and the cases on which it is based, see *Davis v Steel and Eriksen* 1949 (3) SA 177 (W).

44 1963 (4) SA 273 (C) especially at 284B–D.

45 *Le Roux v Le Roux* 1963 (4) SA 273 (C) at 284B–D.

46 1960 (3) SA 82 (O), especially at 886B–D.

47 1971 (1) SA 780 (T).

48 *Raabe v The Master* 1971 (1) SA 780 (T) at 786A–F.

revive the 1964 will because the 1966 will was only intended to operate in the event that he and his wife died during their journey overseas.

6.5 Revival of wills

Revival of a will occurs when a previously revoked or lapsed will is given legal force again. Before we look at how revival can be brought about, it should be re-emphasised that the destruction of a will that expressly or impliedly revoked an earlier will does not bring about the revival of the earlier revoked will.[49]

For some years, since the decision of the Appellate Division in *Moses v Abinader*,[50] there was uncertainty over the permitted methods for reviving a revoked will. Clearly, the re-execution of a revoked will, that is signing the will afresh in the presence of two witnesses in full compliance with the will-making formalities, serves to revive the will.

In *Moses v Abinader*, although the bench agreed that there had been no revival in that particular case, there was a difference of opinion amongst the judges over why revival had not taken place and, in particular, over whether it was possible to revive a will by referring to it in a subsequent document that is executed as a will. Van den Heever JA held that this method of revival would be unlawful in South Africa because the pages of the old will are not signed together with the pages of the new will but are only referred to in the new will (this is called incorporation by reference).[51] Schreiner JA, on the other hand, distinguished between revival and incorporation by reference. He held that if the required intention to revive was present, it is permissible to revive a will by referring to it in a later valid will.[52] This uncertainty was resolved in *Wessels v Die Meester*,[53] in which the Supreme Court of Appeal ruled, in a unanimous judgment, that it is permissible to revive a lapsed or revoked will by referring to it in a subsequent, validly executed will because effect must be given to a testator's wishes expressed in a duly executed document. It was further held that revival in this way is not equivalent to incorporation by reference[54] – just because a will has been revoked or has lapsed does not mean it was improperly executed, and the original valid execution is a historic fact that does not fall away. Accordingly, *Wessels v Die Meester*[55] held that revival of a lapsed or revoked will takes place if the following three requirements are satisfied:

1. The lapsed or revoked will must have been validly executed when it was originally made.
2. It must be incorporated by reference into a new validly executed will (for example, 'I refer to my will dated 1 October 2003, since revoked, and now direct that it shall again have full force as my last will and testament').
3. The testator intended to revive the will.

49 *Le Roux v Le Roux* 1963 (4) SA 273 (C) at 284C.
50 1951 (4) SA 537 (A).
51 1951 (4) SA 537 (A) at 551F–552D.
52 1951 (4) SA 537 (A) at 543A–544C.
53 [2007] SCA 17 (RSA).
54 This is implicit in the Supreme Court of Appeal's preference for the approach of Schreiner JA over that of Van den Heever JA in *Moses v Abinader* 1951 (4) SA 537 (A): see at paras 21 & 22.
55 [2007] SCA 17 (RSA) at para 22.

COUNTER POINT

Revoked by physical destruction

According to a number of writers, a will that has been revoked by physical destruction cannot be revived.[56] A possible reason for this is the objection to giving effect to a will that no longer exists either in law as a will or merely physically as a paper.

Regarding the intention requirement, it must be shown that when the testator executed the new will, he or she knew that the will that it was meant to revive was no longer valid. If the testator believed that the original will was still in force, it is impossible to establish that he or she intended to revive the will.[57]

> In *Wessels v Die Meester*,[58] the testator's will of 18 January 2002 lapsed on the death of his wife because there was no provision in the will for the devolution of his estate if he survived her. The provisions of the will were all predicated on the testator predeceasing his wife. However, in May 2003, the testator executed a short will which described itself as a codicil to his 2002 will. The codicil modified one of the bequests in the 2002 will and concluded '[t]he rest of my will remains unaltered'.[59] It was held that this showed that the testator had executed the 2003 codicil in the mistaken belief that the will of 2002 was still in force and that this necessarily excluded an intention to revive it (one cannot intend to revive what one does not know is dead), and therefore the testator died intestate.[60]

6.6 Revocation by the court: section 2A

In s 2(3), the Wills Act makes provision for a court to order that a defectively executed will be treated as if it were a valid will provided, amongst other things, that the court is satisfied that the defective will was intended by the testator to be his or her will.[61] Section 2A is a parallel provision which empowers a court to complete a defective attempt by a testator to revoke his or her will. Section 2A reads as follows:

> *If a court is satisfied that a testator has –*
>
> *(a) made a written indication on his will or before his death* caused *such indication to be made;*
> *(b) performed any other act with regard to his will or before his death* caused *such act to be performed which is apparent from the face of the will; or*
> *(c) drafted another document or before his death* caused *such document to be drafted,*
>
> *by which he intended to revoke his will or a part of his will, the court shall declare the will or the part concerned, as the case may be, to be revoked.*[62]

56 See Corbett et al at 110; De Waal & Schoeman-Malan at 109; Cronjé & Roos at 104; and Van der Merwe & Rowland at 204.
57 *Wessels v Die Meester* [2007] SCA 17 (RSA) at para 26.
58 63 [2007] SCA 17 (RSA).
59 *Wessels v Die Meester* [2007] SCA 17 (RSA) at para 4; this is a translation from the original Afrikaans.
60 *Wessels v Die Meester* [2007] SCA 17 (RSA) at para 26.
61 See the discussion in Chapter 5.
62 Emphasis added.

Once a court is satisfied that the requirements of this section have been satisfied, it is obliged to make an order revoking the will, or part of the will, as the case may be. Because the section is peremptory and involves a court in undoing the testator's (original) wishes, it has been held that courts must adopt a cautious approach in determining that the testator intended to revoke his or her will.[63]

It follows from the section that a court can only grant an order in terms of s 2A if there is proof on a balance of probabilities that the testator intended to revoke the will (or a part of the will), and that one of the acts described in s 2A(a)–(c) was performed by the testator, or by another person on the testator's behalf with the testator's authority, for the purpose of revoking the will. These acts are:

1. making a written indication on the will (such as drawing lines across the face of the will)
2. performing another act, not being writing, with regard to the will that is apparent from the face of the will (such as cutting out a witness's signature on page one of a two-page will, which would not revoke the will at common law because earlier pages are not required to be signed by witnesses)
3. drafting another document by which it is intended to revoke the will (such as writing an informal document that purports to revoke the will, but that does not comply with the requirements for a will).

When a document referred to in Section 2A(c) is relied upon, the testator's intention must have been that the document itself would revoke, or partially revoke, the will. This follows from the decision in *Letsekga v The Master*[64] in which it was held that notes of changes that the testator proposes to make to his or her will in future do not justify an order revoking part of the will - the notes themselves are not intended to revoke or amend the will.[65] The intention of the testator in such a case is that a further document will be made in due course that will bring about the revocation. In *Henwick v The Master*,[66] a s 2A order was refused because there was insufficient proof that a bank that had drafted a codicil revoking part of the testator's will had done so on the instructions of the testator, rather than on those of his wife.

PAUSE FOR REFLECTION

Written or not?

In *Mdlulu v Delarey*,[67] it was held that the document relied upon to establish the testator's revocatory intention must be produced to the Court so that the Court is able to inspect it and come to its own conclusion as to the testator's revocatory intentions.

Unfortunately, after stating unequivocally that a 'written document' is required by s 2A, the Court muddied the waters later in the judgment by stating that '[a]bsent the document before the Court (and for the purposes of this consideration I envisage that a document may include a video or film of the testator)' the Court cannot be satisfied as to the revocatory intention of the testator.[68] (The comment concerning videos and films is obiter.) In view of the Court's earlier emphatic statement that a written document is required, and the words 'for the purposes of this consideration' in the passage just

63 *Mdlulu v Delarey* [1998] 1 All SA 434 (W) at 448.
64 1995 (4) SA 731 (W).
65 *Letsekga v The Master* 1995 (4) SA 731 (W) at 737E–F.
66 1997 (2) SA 326 (C).
67 1995 (4) SA 731 (W) at 454.
68 *Mdlulu v Delarey* [1998] 1 All SA 434 (W) at 454; see the rhetorical question at 455.

quoted, it seems possible that the Court may simply have envisaged that the written document, and the testator's intentions arising from it, may be proved by video or film evidence.

It is also important to note that s 2A cannot be used to give legal effect to an oral revocation.[69]

An important question relating to paras (a) and (b) is whether the word 'will' includes a copy of the testator's will. In other words, can a written indication or other act carried out with respect to a mere copy of the will provide the basis for a revocation order in terms of s 2A?

In *Webster v The Master*,[70] the testator had marked up changes to his will on a copy of it to show his attorney the deletions that he wanted to implement. It was held that the will could not be revoked by the Court in terms of s 2A(a) because the writing was on a copy of the will and not the original. However, the Court held that the will could be revoked in terms of s 2A(b). The decision is difficult to understand because para (b) requires the 'other act' referred to there to be apparent from the face of the 'will'. The Act would seem to require that for the purposes of both ss 2A(a) and (b) conduct on the original will is required.

In *Marais v The Master*,[71] a Court interpreting the common law requirements for the revocation of wills treated acts of symbolic destruction carried out on a copy of the will as sufficient to revoke the will because they showed what the testator would have done to his or her original will had it been in his or her possession.

However, the courts enjoy a greater leeway in their application of the common law rules than they do in the case of statutory provisions. With statutes, courts are limited by the intention of the legislature as expressed in the words of the statute, and their starting point is the ordinary meaning of the language used. The ordinary sense of the word 'will' does not include a mere copy thereof. On the other hand, it would include a duplicate original will.

PAUSE FOR REFLECTION

Cancelling a will

Suppose that a testator neatly writes the word 'cancelled' at the top of each page of a photocopy of his or her will, the original being in the possession of the testator's attorney. It seems that at common law this would not be an effective revocation by symbolic destruction because the testator has not interfered with the writing of the will in any way. Would it be possible to obtain an order revoking the will in terms of s 2A, relying on the testator's actions? The writing is not written on the original will itself which seems to exclude the use of s 2A(a). It also does not fall under s 2A(b) both because it does not qualify as 'any other act' in the context of para (b), and because it is not done on the will itself. Could the word 'cancelled' be regarded as 'another document' in the context of s 2A(c)? It is certainly drafted by the testator and would appear to have been done in order to bring about the revocation of the will.

69 *Mdlulu v Delarey* [1998] 1 All SA 434 (W).
70 1966 (1) SA 34 (D).
71 1984 (4) SA 288 (D).

In *Olivier v Die Meester: In re Boedel Wyle Olivier*,[72] the Court was faced with a validly executed will and a codicil which was unsigned, but which purported to revoke certain provisions of the testator's will, and to substitute new provisions for the revoked material. The codicil could not be rescued in terms of s 2(3) because the testator had neither drafted it nor signed it. The Court also refused to implement separately the revocatory aspects of the codicil in terms of s 2A even though s 2A does not require personal drafting or execution.

On the particular facts of the case, this decision seems, with respect, to have been correct because it is unlikely that the testator would have intended the separate implementation of the revocatory aspects of the codicil. However, the reason for the Court's decision is ambiguous. The Court commented that there is a potential conflict between s 2(3) and s 2A in that, although a partial revocation of the will would bring about an amendment of the will, the requirements for an order under s 2A implementing a partial revocation of a will are quite different from the requirements for an order under s 2(3) that an invalid codicil be treated as valid.[73] The Court appeared to be of the view that in order to resolve this potential conflict between the two interrelated provisions of the Act, applications for revocation in terms of s 2A must be limited to pure revocations in which no additional matter is simultaneously introduced into the will, and all other applications for revocation must be handled in terms of s 2(3).[74] However, the Court also stated that on a proper interpretation of the will and the unsigned codicil, portions of the will could not be revoked unless the Court also gave effect to the codicil.[75]

Nortjé[76] has suggested that the judgment is ambiguous and that it is possible that the Court was not laying down a general rule regarding when s 2A can be used, but was simply holding that where the provisions were intended by the testator to comprise one transaction (this intention being objectively determined from the will and admissible evidence of surrounding circumstances), then s 2A cannot be used.

If the Court in *Olivier v Die Meester: In re Boedel Wyle Olivier* was laying down a general rule limiting the use of s 2A, then it would follow, for example, that an application for the removal of a paragraph from the will and its substitution by another would have to be adjudicated solely in terms of s 2(3), even if the testator had an absolute intention to remove the paragraph not dependent on successfully introducing the new materials. However, this rigid approach is not necessary if one recognises the possibility that a substitution (the removal of words and their replacement with other words) may be partially valid in appropriate circumstances.

A testator wishes to disinherit his former spouse and provide a legacy for his new spouse. He asks his friend, who is more literate than he is, to attend to this. The friend writes a new clause into the will providing a legacy for the new spouse and draws lines on the will deleting the bequest to the former spouse. There is no compliance with the formalities for the amendment of a will. The testator does not want his former spouse to inherit from him in any circumstances whatsoever. His intention to disinherit her is absolute and is in no way dependent on the successful creation of a legacy in favour of his new spouse.

---

72 1997 (1) SA 836 (T).

73 *Olivier v Die Meester: In re Boedel Wyle Olivier* 1997 (1) SA 836 (T) at 844H–845D.

74 *Olivier v Die Meester: In re Boedel Wyle Olivier* 1997 (1) SA 836 (T) at 845A–D, and in particular the statement that 'myns insiens kan die bepalings van arts 2(3) en 2A net met mekaar versoen word as die herroeping beoog ingevolge art 2A nie 'n wysiging as sodanig is nie.' [This roughly translates as: 'In my view the provisions of ss 2(3) and 2A can only be reconciled if the revocation contemplated in s 2A is not an amendment as such.']

75 *Olivier v Die Meester: In re Boedel Wyle Olivier* 1997 (1) SA 836 (T) at 841I–J & 844H–845A.

76 1998 *SALJ* 6 & 9–10.

In terms of the approach provided for in *Olivier v Die Meester: In re Boedel Wyle Olivier*, the entire transaction must be adjudicated in terms of s 2(3), which means that neither the revocation nor the new legacy will be given effect to because the amendments do not comply with the required formalities and s 2(3) requires that they be drafted by the testator personally if he has not signed them.

On the other hand, if use of s 2A is not restricted in the way suggested in *Olivier v Die Meester: In re Boedel Wyle Olivier*, the bequest to the former wife can be revoked by the Court (because s 2A provides for the situation where the testator has caused a written indication on the will to be made by which his revocatory intention is shown) even though the legacy in favour of the new spouse cannot be given effect to in terms of s 2(3). In this scenario the testator's revocatory intention was absolute. It was not dependent on the validity of the substitute legacy so there can be no objection to this outcome in principle. If, however, the testator's revocation of part of his will was conditional on the successful insertion of new materials, then an order under s 2A would not be made unless a s 2(3) order could be made too.

Since the words of ss 2(3) and 2A do not require the restrictions implied by the approach in *Olivier v Die Meester: In re Boedel Wyle Olivier*, it may be argued that s 2A should not be limited in the manner suggested in that case. Nortjé[77] pointed out that although no decisions have expressly decided that the revocatory element of a substitution can be separately adjudicated in terms of s 2A, a number of decisions have applied s 2A to acts that contemplated substitutions.

LEGAL THINKING

When can a will be revoked?

The issue whether s 2A can be used to revoke a will can be approached in the following way:

1. Was the will in question validly executed, or if invalid, could a court make an order under s 2(3) that it be treated as if it were validly executed? (If not, there is no question of revoking it.)
2. When was the will executed? (There is some debate whether a will executed before 1 January 1954 can be revoked in terms of s 2A.)
3. When did the testator die? (Section 2A cannot be used if the testator died before 1 October 1992.)
4. Has one of the following three acts, required by s 2A, taken place?:
   - a written indication on the will itself purporting to revoke the will (An indication on a mere copy of the will is not enough.)
   - another act in relation to the will itself, that is apparent from the face of the will, which purports to revoke the will (The act must be apparent from the face of the original will, not from the face of a copy thereof.)
   - the drafting of a new document that purports to revoke the will, either expressly or impliedly.
5. Was any of these acts done by the testator himself or herself?
6. If not, is there sufficient proof that the act was done with the testator's authority?

77 Nortjé 1998 *SALJ* 8.

7. Did the testator intend that the doing of the act should bring about the revocation of the will? Or was the act merely a preliminary step which was to be followed by a revocatory act at a later stage?
8. If there was revocatory intention, was this intention conditional? If so, was the condition fulfilled?
9. Does the act involve the introduction of new testamentary material? If so:
   - Does *Olivier v Die Meester: In re Boedel Wyle Olivier*[78] prevent the use of s 2A in such circumstances?
   - Is the reasoning in *Olivier v Die Meester: In re Boedel Wyle Olivier* correct on that point?
   - Will the court hearing the s 2A application be bound by *Olivier v Die Meester: In re Boedel Wyle Olivier* in terms of the principles of judicial precedent?

6.7 Customary law of succession

The will of a person living under a system of customary law is governed by the common law and the Wills Act. Accordingly, such a testator has the freedom to make and revoke a will, and the provisions of s 2A and s 2(3) of the Wills Act as well as the principles regarding revival of wills that have been discussed in this chapter and in Chapter 5 will apply.

THIS CHAPTER IN ESSENCE

1. When a testator executes a document in accordance with the formalities for a will, the document remains in existence as the testator's will until such time as the testator:
   - decides to revoke it
   - manifests this revocatory intention in one of the recognised acts of revocation.
2. Even a document that does not comply with the execution formalities but was intended by the testator to be his or her will must be revoked by the testator in one of the recognised ways to avoid the possibility that a court may make an order in terms of s 2(3) directing that the document be accepted as the testator's will.
3. If the testator intends to revoke his or her will but does not carry out one of the recognised acts of revocation, a court can make an order in terms of s 2A revoking the will for the testator if there is proof of the testator's revocatory intention, provided that the requirements of s 2A are satisfied.
4. The requirements for a court to intervene in terms of s 2A are different from those that apply in terms of s 2(3). The issue of whether or not s 2A can be applied in circumstances where the testator revokes a portion of his or her will and simultaneously introduces new testamentary provisions in place of the revoked provisions is problematic.

78 1997 (1) SA 836 (T); see discussion on pages 96–97.

Chapter 7

Capacity to inherit

When is a beneficiary capable of inheriting from a deceased person?

7.1	Introduction	99
7.2	Persons capable of inheriting: Natural persons	99
7.3	Persons capable of inheriting: Juristic persons	104
7.4	Persons disqualified from inheriting	105
7.5	Customary law of succession	113
This chapter in essence		113

7.1 Introduction

One of the ground rules of inheritance is that the beneficiary must be competent to inherit. Capacity to inherit (an heir's ability to inherit) must be distinguished from testamentary capacity (the ability of a testator to engage in the act of testation; see Chapter 4). The general rule is that all juristic or natural persons, born or unborn, are competent to inherit either testate or intestate regardless of their legal capacity.[1] The South African law of succession clearly defines categories of beneficiaries who have capacity to inherit as well as the circumstances under which beneficiaries are disqualified from inheriting. The capacity to inherit is relevant in both the common and the customary law.

7.2 Persons capable of inheriting: Natural persons

A natural person, irrespective of his or her age, mental or legal standing,[2] has capacity to inherit. In other words, every natural person is capable of acquiring a *vested* right to an inheritance. It is important to note that a vested right to an inheritance should not be confused with the right to enjoy an inheritance.[3] The capacity to inherit is the ability to acquire a vested right whether or not the beneficiary is able to enjoy the inheritance. This distinction between a *vested* right and the ability to *enjoy* an inheritance becomes relevant when considering the position of, for example, a minor beneficiary, a beneficiary who suffers from a mental disability, or a beneficiary whose legal standing is impaired on account of, for example, insolvency.

1 Corbett et al at 79.
2 Legal standing may be affected by insolvency or prodigality, although prodigality is treated in the same vein as mental incapacity for the purposes of this Chapter.
3 Vesting is discussed in Chapters 1 and 9, and see also the discussion of usufruct in Chapter 10.

7.2.1 Major beneficiary of sound mind with legal standing

A person who is a major (that is, a person of 18 years and older[4]), who is of sound mind, is not insolvent, and who does not repudiate an inheritance, will not only acquire a vested right to an unconditional inheritance, but will also be able to exercise unrestricted enjoyment of the inheritance.

7.2.2 Minor beneficiary

A minor (that is, a person under 18 years of age) has capacity to inherit, but his or her ability to enjoy the inheritance is restricted. Inherited property will be administered for the benefit of the minor by the minor's guardian, with the office of the Master of the High Court exercising a supervisory function. Where no guardian is available, enjoyment of the property will be regulated by a court-appointed guardian or curator.[5]

There is a difference in the way that the movable and immovable property of a minor is administered. Where a minor is bequeathed movable property, such as a sports car, he or she will acquire a vested right to the property when the deceased dies. Should the minor die after the deceased, the property will form part of the minor's estate and will be transferrable to his or her heirs, unless there is a contrary indication in the deceased's will. Because the minor's capacity to exercise all the rights of ownership in respect of the property is limited, the movable property concerned will, however, not be delivered to the minor but to the minor's guardian who will have to ensure that the property is used for the minor's benefit or kept safely for the minor's future use.[6]

If money (also a form of movable property) is left to a minor, the minor acquires a vested right to the money but it will not be physically given to him or her in case he or she spends the money carelessly. For the same reason, however, money will also not be deposited with the minor's guardian. The Administration of Estates Act requires that money be placed into what is known as the Guardian's Fund.[7] The Guardian's Fund is administered by the office of the Master of the High Court. The minor's guardian is permitted, from time to time, to withdraw money from the Guardian's Fund to take care of the minor's maintenance.[8] The Master may not disburse funds towards the maintenance of a minor, 'without the sanction'[9] of a court, if the amount required exceeds 'the amount determined by the Minister from time to time by notice in the *Gazette* of the capital amount received for account of the minor ...'[10] At present the stipulated amount is R100 000.[11]

PAUSE FOR REFLECTION

A disadvantage of the Guardian's Fund

Although the purpose of depositing money into the Guardian's Fund is to protect the minor, it has to be noted that, from an estate planning point of view, this is not the best vehicle to protect the financial interests of a minor. Experience has shown that money placed into the Guardian's Fund usually attracts nominal interest and the investment options available to the Master's office are extremely limited. This is why most estate

4 Section 17 of the Children's Act.
5 Section 43(1) of the Administration of Estates Act.
6 Section 43(1) of the Administration of Estates Act.
7 Section 43(2)(a) read with s 90(1).
8 See, for example, *Hughes v The Master* 1960 (4) SA 936 (C) at 939 regarding the needs of the minor.
9 Interested parties would have to make application to the High Court.
10 Section 90.
11 GN R1318 in *GG* 25456 of 19 September 2003.

planners encourage testators to create a testamentary trust in the event of any beneficiary being a minor at the time of the testator's death.

Immovable property inherited by a minor is treated altogether differently to movable property or money. Immovable property is not transferred to a minor's guardian but is immediately registered in the minor's name in the deeds registry.[12] This does not mean that the minor can alienate, pledge, cede or mortgage the property concerned.

In terms of the Administration of Estates Act, the minor's guardian, tutor or curator will administer the property of the minor until he or she becomes a major.[13] (A tutor is normally a third person appointed in a will by a natural parent or parents where such a parent or parents (who would ordinarily act as the minor's guardian) is or are unavailable, for whatever reason, to act as guardian.) If the guardian, tutor or curator wants to alienate or mortgage the property, he or she must either obtain authorisation from the Master of the High Court or the High Court itself. If the value of the property or the mortgage does not exceed the amount determined by the Minister from time to time by notice in the *Gazette* (currently R100 000), the Master's consent would be sufficient. However, if the value of the property or the mortgage exceeds the stipulated amount, an order of the High Court authorising the mortgage or alienation would be necessary. The Master may authorise a mortgage not exceeding R100 000 if the 'mortgage is necessary for the preservation or improvement of the property or for the maintenance, education, or other benefit of [the] minor ...'[14] In the case of alienation, the Master has to be satisfied that the alienation is in 'the interest of the minor'.[15] Similar considerations would apply when bringing an application to the High Court.[16]

7.2.3 *Nasciturus* (or unborn)

South African law, under the influence of its Roman and Roman-Dutch law heritage, recognises that an unborn child (referred to as a *nasciturus* in Latin) is capable of inheriting.[17] The fiction used to apply this principle is called the *nasciturus* fiction and has been interpreted as follows:

- The child must have been conceived at the time of the devolution of the benefit.
- The inheritance has to be to the advantage of the unborn child.
- The child has to be subsequently born alive.

The last requirement is important. The mere conception of a *nasciturus* is no automatic guarantee that he or she will inherit. For the fiction to become reality, it is necessary for the *nasciturus* to be born alive - even if only for one second. Thus, if a child is stillborn, he or she will inherit nothing.

An intestate inheritance (subject to the exception in *Harris v Assumed Administrator, Estate MacGregor*[18]) usually devolves on the death of the deceased. Therefore, as long as the

12 Section 25 of the Deeds Registries Act 47 of 1937; read with ss 39 and 43 of the Administration of Estates Act.
13 Section 76.
14 Section 80(2)(b) of the Administration of Estates Act.
15 Section 80(2)(a) of the Administration of Estates Act.
16 *Ex parte Visagie* 1940 CPD 42; *Ex parte Blomerus* 1936 CPD 368; *Ex parte Jeffrey* 1922 CPD 260.
17 *Ex parte Administrators Estate Asmall* 1954 (1) PH G4 (N); *Ex parte Boedel Steenkamp* 1962 (3) SA 954 (O).
18 1987 (3) SA 563 (A). For a detailed discussion of this case, see Chapter 2, pages 20–21.

nasciturus is conceived at the time of the deceased's death and is subsequently born alive, he or she will inherit his or her intestate share. If the *nasciturus* survives momentarily after birth and then dies, he or she is still considered to have been born alive and is therefore capable of inheriting intestate. The inheritance that he or she would have received will be transmissible to his or her intestate heirs.

When it comes to testate succession, things are a little more complicated. For testate succession s 2D(1)(c) of the Wills Act applies. According to this section:

> *(1) In the interpretation of a will, unless the context otherwise indicates – ...*
>
> *(c) any benefit allocated to the children of a person, or to the members of a class of persons, mentioned in the will shall vest in the children of that person or those members of the class of persons who are alive at the time of the devolution of the benefit, or who have already been conceived at that time and who are later born alive ...*

PAUSE FOR REFLECTION

Application of the fiction

The assumption is always that the testator would have wanted the *nasciturus* fiction to apply unless there is a contrary intention in the will. If the will, either expressly or impliedly, suggests that the testator did not want the fiction to apply, this assumption must be disregarded.

In testamentary succession the time when a benefit devolves can be either conditional or unconditional. Because of this, s 2D(1)(c) of the Wills Act does not only refer to a beneficiary concerned being alive or conceived at the time of the deceased's death, but also to the beneficiary being *alive at the time of the devolution of the benefit,* or having *already been conceived at that time and ... later born alive.*

A *nasciturus* who is conceived at the time of the devolution of a benefit, is subsequently born alive, and who inherits either under testate or intestate succession is, to all intents and purposes, in the exact same position as a minor beneficiary and is subject to the same limitations.

Consider the following clause in a will:

'On my death the sum of R500 000 shall be invested in a fixed deposit, and on the fifth anniversary of my death, this money must go to my grandchildren.'

This testamentary provision presents an interpretational conundrum. When does the benefit devolve on the grandchildren? Does the benefit devolve on the deceased's death or does it devolve on the fifth anniversary of the deceased's death?

If the benefit devolves on the deceased's death, then it goes without saying that all living and conceived (and subsequently born alive) grandchildren at the time of the deceased's death will acquire a vested right to the inheritance. All that will be postponed is the enjoyment of the inheritance.

However, if the benefit devolves on the grandchildren on the fifth anniversary of the testator's death, it would mean that vesting of the inheritance will be postponed in its entirety until the fifth anniversary of the deceased's death. Delaying devolution in this way will enable any grandchild alive at the time of the testator's death, born in the interim period, or conceived on or before the date of the fifth anniversary of the deceased's death (and later born alive) also to inherit.

7.2.4 Illegitimate children

Under the common law children born of incestuous, adulterous or extramarital relationships could only inherit under certain circumstances. Section 1(2) of the Intestate Succession Act[19] and s 2D(1)(b) of the Wills Act[20] now afford these children (all referred to as illegitimate children) the same status as legitimate children when it comes to testate and intestate succession.

7.2.5 Persons of unsound mind

Persons of unsound mind include more than the insane or the delusional - the causes of mental infirmity are much broader. Those who act perpetually irrationally on account of drugs, alcohol or disease may also be regarded as being of unsound mind.

In terms of the law of succession, a person of unsound mind has capacity to inherit. However, this does not necessarily mean that he or she will be able to enjoy the inheritance free of any restrictions. If a beneficiary is declared of unsound mind, a court-appointed *curator bonis* will administer the inheritance on the beneficiary's behalf.[21] Any property will be managed as if he or she were a minor. If there is no pre-existing court order or if a court order is not granted after an application has been made to court, the beneficiary, irrespective of his or her behaviour, will be treated as a person of sound mind. When making application to court, the onus is on the applicant to prove on a balance of probabilities that the beneficiary is unable to administer the property in a sensible manner.[22]

A prodigal (a spendthrift; someone who is characterised by excessive or imprudent spending) who is likely to land both himself or herself and his or her family in a state of poverty is not regarded as being of unsound mind. However, the ability of such a person to deal with his or her estate is limited and would require the appointment and assistance of a court-appointed curator.[23]

7.2.6 Insolvents

When someone is declared insolvent, he or she retains the capacity to inherit but any property which he or she owns falls into the insolvent estate and must be administered by a trustee for the benefit of the creditors.[24] In all likelihood, property received will have to be sold and the proceeds paid to creditors according to the order of preference mentioned in the Insolvency Act.[25]

---

19 See Chapter 2 for a detailed discussion of the relevant provision.
20 See Chapter 13 for a detailed discussion of the relevant provision.
21 Section 43 of the Administration of Estates Act; see Chapter 1 for a description of *curator bonis.*
22 Uniform Rule of Court 57(10), (12).
23 Du Bois (ed), Wille's Principles at 385.
24 Section 20 of the Insolvency Act 24 of 1936.
25 Sections 96–103 of the Insolvency Act 24 of 1936.

PAUSE FOR REFLECTION

Can an insolvent repudiate an inheritance?

For quite some time there was uncertainty in our law as to whether an insolvent could repudiate an inheritance. This question was eventually settled in *Wessels v De Jager*.[26] The Supreme Court of Appeal held that when an inheritance becomes due and owing to an insolvent, the latter acquires a competence to inherit but not a right per se. A beneficiary may repudiate an inheritance and by so doing, does not cause any prejudice to creditors. The Court held that if a beneficiary has not expressly or impliedly accepted an inheritance, it cannot be said that the inheritance forms part of his or her estate. Since an insolvent has limited legal capacity, the insolvent retains the right either to accept or to reject an inheritance. This right does not pass to his or her trustee.

As a matter of estate planning, it is better for a testator to stipulate in a will that if any of his or her heirs are insolvent or provisionally insolvent at the time of the devolution of the inheritance, the heir concerned will forfeit the inheritance in favour of a named substitute beneficiary, or even a trust. Such a clause is not considered against public policy.[27]

7.3 Persons capable of inheriting: Juristic persons

In terms of the Intestate Succession Act, only natural persons can inherit intestate. However, there is nothing in statute or the common law precluding a testator from nominating a company or a close corporation as a beneficiary in a will. The right to claim the inheritance will vest in the company or close corporation unless an authorised[28] company director or a member of a close corporation repudiates the inheritance. The repudiation would have to be exercised within a reasonable time after the company acquires the capacity to inherit. If a company or close corporation is insolvent or under judicial management, it is an open question in our law – as it was not expressly decided in the case of *Wessels v De Jager*[29] – whether the directors of the company or the members of the close corporation would be able to repudiate the inheritance. It may be argued that to repudiate the inheritance to the detriment of creditors would constitute a breach of the fiduciary duties of directors and members.

PAUSE FOR REFLECTION

Are other entities capable of inheriting?

Trusts, voluntary associations, syndicates, firms, and partnerships, though not juristic persons, may also be nominated as beneficiaries in a will. What happens to inherited property if one of these entities goes insolvent, is quite a complex question to which there is no definite answer and which is best left to the law of insolvency. Whether these entities, acting through their human agents, may repudiate an inheritance on insolvency was also not considered in *Wessels v De Jager*. It may be argued that as long as these entities do not have juristic corporate personality and are nothing more than fronts for natural persons, the persons behind these entities should be able to repudiate an inheritance by majority vote or special resolution.

26 2000 (4) SA 924 (SCA).
27 *Ruskin v Sapire* 1966 (2) SA 306 (W).
28 Authority would be gained by general resolution.
29 2000 (4) SA 924 (SCA).

7.4 Persons disqualified from inheriting

In terms of the common law, a person may not benefit by his or her own wrongdoing.[30] Accordingly, there are a number of categories of persons who, on account of their actions, are precluded from inheriting.

7.4.1 Beneficiary who caused the death of the deceased or the *coniunctissimi* of the deceased

A beneficiary who is responsible for the death of the deceased or the *coniunctissimi* (people closely related to the deceased) of the deceased is precluded from inheriting either testate or intestate from the deceased. According to the common law, even a beneficiary who gives assistance or counsel to a killer is disqualified from inheriting. The rule precluding a killer from inheriting finds application in the Roman-Dutch law maxim, *de bloedige hand neemt geen erf* (literally meaning the bloody hand takes no inheritance).[31]

The operation of the *bloedige hand* maxim is absolute. It does not matter whether the deceased was killed intentionally or negligently. Thus a beneficiary who commits culpable homicide (the unlawful and negligent killing of a human being) is as equally disqualified from inheriting as a person who commits murder (the unlawful and intentional killing of a human being). It would seem that the courts are reluctant to relax the operation of the *bloedige hand* maxim without legislative intervention.[32]

Someone responsible for the death of the deceased or the *coniunctissimi* of the deceased will not automatically be disqualified from inheriting and the Master does not have the authority to disqualify him or her.[33] An order of court is required in this regard.

PAUSE FOR REFLECTION

The *bloedige hand* maxim

In *Casey v The Master*,[34] a beneficiary was charged with and convicted of culpable homicide. He accidently shot and killed his wife whilst handling his gun. It was common cause that even though he was intoxicated at the time, his level of intoxication was such that he was still able to appreciate what he was doing. The Court, in finding him guilty, took into account the circumstances leading to his wife's death as well as other mitigating factors and imposed, rather than mandatory jail time, a sentence of three years imprisonment, wholly suspended. When he was subsequently disqualified from inheriting, the beneficiary approached the High Court to relax the *bloedige hand* maxim. His counsel argued that the maxim was obsolete in the case of a negligent killing. The Court did not agree and the disqualification remained.

The Court referred to several cases[35] where courts made indirect reference to death caused by negligence as a ground for disqualification. Although the Court saw no reason on the facts to deviate from previous cases upholding the application of the maxim for a negligent killing, the Court did refer to the views expressed by Lee and Honoré,[36]

30 *Casey v The Master* 1992 (4) SA 505 (N) at 507G; *L. Taylor v A.E. Pim* (1903) 24 NLR 484 at 491; Van Leeuwen *RDL* 3.3.9.
31 *Casey v The Master* 1992 (4) SA 505 (N) at 507E.
32 See discussion of *Casey v The Master* 1992 (4) SA 505 (N) below.
33 See in this regard *Ferreira v Die Meester* 2001 (3) SA 365 (O) at 370F–H.
34 1992 (4) SA 505 (N) at 507G.
35 For example, *L. Taylor v A.E. Pim* (1903) 24 NLR 484 at 492, 496–497; *Ex parte Steenkamp and Steenkamp* 1952 (1) SA 744 (T) at 748C; *Caldwell v Erasmus* 1952 (4) SA 43 (T) at 49D–G.
36 At para 560 note 2.

and Van der Walt and Sonnekus[37] to the effect that the *bloedige hand* rule should be relaxed in certain cases. These academic writers have argued for the relaxation of the rule in so-called 'technical negligence' cases. The common example identified by the writers where the rule should be relaxed was in motor vehicle accidents. Although the Court was sympathetic to the relaxation of the rule in circumstances identified by the academic writers or in other cases where public policy favoured the amendment of the rule, it nevertheless held that if the rule was harsh and out of touch with the spirit of our times, it was the responsibility of the legislature to reform the law and not the courts. Van der Walt and Sonnekus[38] have suggested that legislation alleviating the position of the beneficiary who negligently causes the death of the testator is unnecessary in cases of technical negligence. The moral blameworthiness of the killer is a matter for judicial discretion because they argue that such determination takes the form of an objective assessment of the community's feelings of what is morally objectionable.

7.4.1.1 Onus and evidence

In *Casey v The Master*,[39] there was a dispute regarding who bore the onus of proof - was it the party alleging the disqualification or was it the party who sought not to be disqualified on account of the killing? Because of the general rule that any person can benefit under a will, the Court held that the onus of proof is always on the party that maintains that another party is disqualified from taking a benefit under a will. A further issue considered in this case was whether a criminal conviction is a prerequisite for disqualification. The Court firmly held that 'a conviction on a criminal charge arising from the death of another is not a prerequisite for the applicability of the maxim'.[40] Even if a person is acquitted on a criminal charge, he or she can still be disqualified from inheriting if it can be established on a balance of probabilities that he or she unlawfully caused the death of the deceased.

PAUSE FOR REFLECTION

Evidence in the civil matter

The question has been raised whether one can rely on a guilty finding in a criminal case to disqualify a beneficiary from inheriting on the ground that he or she unlawfully caused the death of the deceased or of the *coniunctissimi* of the deceased. In *Leeb v Leeb*[41] the only evidence placed before the Court by the applicant was that the respondent had been convicted of murdering the deceased. The Court held that the conviction of the beneficiary was in itself not sufficient evidence that she murdered the deceased. The Court held that evidence had to be led anew in the civil matter to prove on a balance of probabilities that she committed the murder.

37 1981 *TSAR* 30.
38 1992 *TSAR* 147.
39 1992 (4) SA 505 (N).
40 *Casey v The Master* 1992 (4) SA 505 (N) at 511D. See also *Caldwell v Erasmus* 1952 (4) SA 43 (T) at 49; *Ex parte Vonzell* 1953 (1) SA 122 (C) at 125.
41 [1999] 2 All SA 588 (N).

7.4.1.2 Tricky questions relating to causation

Whilst a beneficiary who unlawfully causes the death of another can be disqualified from inheriting, the element of causation is not as well developed in the law of succession as it is, for example, in the law of delict or criminal law.

PAUSE FOR REFLECTION

Who's to blame?

If a beneficiary wounds a testatrix who subsequently dies in an ambulance accident on the way to hospital, should a distinction be drawn, as it would in the law of delict or in criminal law, between legal and factual causation? Would the ambulance accident constitute a new action that breaks the chain of events and makes the beneficiary not responsible for the testatrix's death? Remember, if the deceased had survived the wound and died of natural causes many years later, the beneficiary might still have inherited provided, of course, that the deceased was benevolent enough not to disinherit him or her. How the law of succession will treat such vexing questions seems uncertain. The only reported case that deals with causation for the purposes of the law of succession is the case of *Ex parte Steenkamp and Steenkamp*.[42]

In this case, the testators bequeathed a farm and certain movables to their grandchildren. The grandchildren's father (Steenkamp) murdered both testators. He was convicted and sentenced to life imprisonment. At the time of the testators' deaths, the accused's wife (the testators' daughter) was pregnant. The child was born alive but did not live for long. Steenkamp and his wife, as parents of the deceased grandchild, applied to Court for an order declaring them the child's intestate heirs. The Master objected and raised the question whether it was appropriate for Steenkamp to inherit property from his child's estate considering that he had murdered the grandparents. The Court noted that the facts presented quite a novel scenario and that the common law was not clear about what to do in such a situation. The Court considered whether Steenkamp benefited directly from the murders and thought it improbable that Steenkamp, at the time when he committed the murders, would reasonably have foreseen the possibility of his child dying before him as this was not an ordinary and natural occurrence. The Court found that there was no causal relationship between the murder and the enrichment because the factual cause of the enrichment was the birth and death of the child and not the murder of the testators. The birth and death of the child constituted a new action, breaking the chain of events between the murder and the enrichment. The result was that Steenkamp was not incompetent to inherit from his daughter.

The judgment was criticised by Hahlo[43] who did, however, concede that the birth and the death of the child were the immediate cause of the murderer's enrichment. He argued that if Steenkamp had not murdered the testators, they most certainly would have survived the child and Steenkamp would not have succeeded, directly or indirectly, to the inheritance. He questioned the position that the murder was not a direct cause of the enrichment and submitted that the murder and the enrichment were sufficiently connected to bring the case within the *bloedige hand* maxim and the principle that no one may benefit by his or her own wrongdoing.

42 1952 (1) SA 744 (T).
43 Hahlo 1952 *SALJ* 138–139.

Another tricky question is whether or not the *coniunctissimi* of the deceased (people closely related to the deceased) also include grandparents, grandchildren or other persons related to the deceased.

In *Ex parte Steenkamp and Steenkamp*,[44] the question was whether the categories of *coniunctissimi* could be extended when applying the *bloedige hand* maxim. In terms of the common law, a beneficiary would be disqualified for killing the deceased's spouse, parents or children. However, could the beneficiary be disqualified if he or she killed the deceased's grandparents or grandchildren? In *Ex parte Steenkamp and Steenkamp*, the *curator ad litem*, appearing on behalf of the deceased child, argued that since Steenkamp had murdered the grandparents of the beneficiary (the child), he was disqualified from inheriting. The *curator* argued that even though the common law referred to specific categories of persons when making reference to the *coniunctissimi* of the deceased, the list was not a closed one and could be extended to accommodate the legal convictions of society. However, the Court was unwilling to agree to the *curator's* request. The Court noted, with a measure of reluctance, that perhaps it was possible to include grandparents and grandchildren as *coniunctissimi* of the deceased where the grandchildren were raised by grandparents. However, it was unwilling to rule firmly on this issue as the facts in *Ex parte Steenkamp and Steenkamp*[45] did not support such a conclusion.

7.4.1.3 Extension of the *bloedige hand* maxim

A notable feature of the *bloedige hand* maxim is the manner in which it has been extended in recent years.

In *Makhanya v Minister of Finance*,[46] the deceased was employed by the South African Police Services. The deceased's spouse was convicted of his murder. On the deceased's death, certain benefits became payable to his dependants in terms of the Government Service Pension Act.[47] The deceased's wife, who was his sole heir, petitioned the Department of Finance for payment of the deceased's pension benefits. When the Department refused to pay any of the pension benefits to the applicant or the deceased's estate, the deceased's daughter (the applicant) instituted proceedings in the High Court to disqualify the deceased's spouse from receiving any of the pension benefits. Her counsel relied on the *bloedige hand* maxim to justify the disqualification.

The Court acknowledged that the issue in question was a novel one as there was no case in which the *bloedige hand* maxim was utilised to disqualify a person from benefiting in terms of a statutory enactment. Despite the lack of precedent, the Court held as follows:

> *The rule is one of public policy that precludes a person who has unlawfully killed another from acquiring a benefit in consequence of the killing, and I can think of no cogent reason why this should be limited to benefits accruing directly from the estate of the victim.*[48]

The Court found that since the spouse was convicted of murder and did not dispute the conviction, public policy required the rule to be extended to cover all benefits accruing to the spouse as a consequence of the deceased's death. This, held the Court, included his pension benefits.

---

44 1952 (1) SA 744 (T).
45 1952 (1) SA 744 (T) at 750–752.
46 2001 (2) SA 1251 (D).
47 57 of 1973.
48 *Makhanya v Minister of Finance* 2001 (2) SA 1251 (D) at 1254D.

PAUSE FOR REFLECTION

The *bloedige hand* maxim, matrimonial property and maintenance

The question has arisen whether a spouse who is responsible for the death of the other spouse can be precluded from benefiting in accordance with the applicable matrimonial property regime.

Ordinarily, a surviving spouse who was married in community of property is entitled to a half-share of the joint estate. Similarly, a surviving spouse who was married out of community of property with the application of the accrual system may be entitled to claim half the difference between the amounts by which their respective estates increased while they were married.

Previously, the courts have refused to extend the *bloedige hand* maxim to preclude spouses from taking their matrimonial benefits, as decided in *Nell v Nell*[49] and *Ex parte Vonzell*.[50] However, in the more recent case of *Leeb v Leeb*,[51] the Court came to a different conclusion. In this case, the wife had already been convicted of the murder of her husband, to whom she had been married in community of property, and the Court held as follows:

> *It would seem to me that there is good reason for applying the principles of unworthiness also to the benefits of the marriage in community of property so as to deprive the unworthy spouse of those benefits. At common law the spouse through whose fault the marriage ends in divorce forfeits the benefits of the marriage in community of property. There seems to be every reason why the spouse who chooses to obtain his freedom through murder rather than divorce, should be in no better position.*[52]

While the case of *Leeb v Leeb*[53] dealt with a marriage in community of property, the rationale for the decision could also be applied to a marriage out of community of property subject to the accrual system.

The above outcome could also be extended to the application of the Maintenance of Surviving Spouses Act. In this regard, it will be interesting to note whether the courts may find that a spouse with blood on his or her hands is precluded from claiming maintenance from the estate of the other spouse.

7.4.2 *Indignus* (unworthy person)

A person who unlawfully causes the death of the deceased or the *coniunctissimi* of the deceased is automatically considered an *indignus*, a person who is unworthy or lacking in merit. The term *indignus* is, however, not limited solely to killing. It also applies to all types of conduct perpetrated against the deceased which would be viewed as despicable according to prevailing notions of public policy.

The *indignus* principle is perhaps best illustrated by the case of *Taylor v Pim*:[54]

49 1976 (3) SA 700 (T).
50 1953 (1) SA 122 (C).
51 [1999] 2 All SA 588 (N).
52 [1999] 2 All SA 588 (N) at 595.
53 [1999] 2 All SA 588 (N).
54 (1903) 24 NLR 484.

The deceased, Rebecca Bingham, was married to Edward Bingham. Together they established a successful business. Edward died in 1900 leaving his estate, including the business, to his wife. Shortly after her husband's death, the deceased took up residence with a married man, the defendant, a certain Mr Pim. Shortly after moving in together, the deceased started consuming unusually high quantities of liquor, much to the consternation of her medical advisers. In 1901, the deceased executed a will in which she appointed Pim as the executor and sole heir of her estate. Whilst on a vacation, she suffered a cerebral haemorrhage and died. It appeared that at the time of her death, she was heavily intoxicated and that Pim only allowed a doctor and a nurse to be called in when the hotel manager insisted. On her death, the deceased's sister, Taylor, brought an action in which she sought an order declaring the deceased's will null and void on the following grounds:

- that the deceased was not of sound mind and memory at the date when she executed the will
- that she was coerced into signing the will under the influence of Pim
- that she 'acquired the habits of intemperance which were encouraged by Pim' which ultimately led to her death
- that she was fraudulently induced by Pim to execute the will in contemplation of a promised marriage.[55]

The Court found that the evidence was unable to establish that the deceased lacked testamentary capacity at the time that she executed the will or that she was unduly influenced by Pim to benefit him in terms of the will. What was left to be decided was whether or not Pim was to be regarded as an *indignus*. The Court concluded that Pim was indeed an *indignus* because he was the cause of Rebecca's 'fall from a virtuous and honourable life to a degraded and immoral one'.[56]

PAUSE FOR REFLECTION

Forgery of a will

The list of causes which render a person unworthy to inherit could be limitless. This was recently illustrated in *Pillay v Nagan*.[57] In this case, the son of the deceased forged his mother's signature on a document purporting to be her will and tried to pass it off as her last will to the rest of his siblings. He later admitted the error of his ways to some of his family members, the plaintiffs. In Court, the evidence conclusively established that he had forged his mother's will. The plaintiffs contended that he should be disqualified from inheriting on account of the forgery. The Court noted that South African law was silent regarding the question as to whether a person responsible for forging a will could be disqualified from inheriting. After referring to *Taylor v Pim*,[58] and Voet[59] who states that if a legatee has hidden the last will of a testator, the legatee should be disqualified from inheriting and the inheritance should pass to the heir he sought to defraud, the Court held it appropriate to disqualify the beneficiary and his share accrued to his brothers and sisters.[60] Although *Pillay v Nagan* deals with forgery of a will, disqualification would also be applicable to someone who destroys or conceals a will.

55 (1903) 24 NLR 484 at 486.
56 (1903) 24 NLR 484 at 495.
57 2001 (1) SA 410 (D).
58 (1903) 24 NLR 484.
59 34.9.2.
60 *Pillay v Nagan* 2001 (1) SA 410 (D) at 424I.

From *Taylor v Pim* and *Pillay v Nagan* a number of salient principles regarding the *indignus* can be extracted:

1. The *indignus* principle is firmly rooted in South African law by virtue of its express recognition in the common law.
2. The instances when a beneficiary would be considered an *indignus* are referred to in the common law. However, these instances of disqualification must be looked at in the light of prevailing values of public policy and must agree with prevailing laws. If the common law is silent on a particular act committed by a beneficiary, the courts nevertheless have discretion to regard someone as an *indignus* if prevailing values of public policy so require.
3. If a person is rendered an *indignus*, he or she will be disqualified from inheriting in terms of both testate and intestate succession.

7.4.3 Persons involved in the execution process

A beneficiary may not benefit from a will if he or she was involved in the execution of that will in terms of s 4A of the Wills Act. Section 4A(1) provides that any person who signs a will as a witness or as an amanuensis,[61] or anyone who writes out the will or any part thereof in his own handwriting, and the person who is the spouse of such person at the time of the execution of the will, shall be disqualified from receiving any benefit from that will.

PAUSE FOR REFLECTION

The written or spoken word

It is interesting to note that s 4A(1) only provides for the disqualification of the person who has written the will 'in his own handwriting'. In other words, if the testator dictated the provisions of his or her will to a beneficiary, and if the beneficiary typed the will, the disqualification does not apply.

Section 4A(3) further provides that the nomination in a will of a person as executor, trustee or guardian shall be regarded as a benefit to be received by such person from that will and therefore s 4A(1) and (2) also apply to these persons.

If a beneficiary is disqualified in terms of s 4A(1), he or she may yet be capable of inheriting provided the requirements in s 4A(2) are present. The central provision in s 4A(2) is contained in para (b). Where a beneficiary is disqualified for any of the reasons mentioned in s 4A(1), it is important to decide whether or not the disqualified beneficiary would have been an intestate heir of the testator had the testator died intestate. If the disqualified beneficiary would have been an intestate heir and the share which he or she would have received in terms of the will is equal to or less than what he or she would have received had the testator died intestate, the disqualification will be lifted, the beneficiary will inherit in terms of the will, and there will be no need to apply either paras (a) or (c) of s 4A(2). Furthermore, where a beneficiary is entitled to more than what he or she would have received according to the rules of intestate succession, but elects to receive an amount equal to or less than his or her intestate share, he or she will also not be disqualified from inheriting. The Master can make a determination in terms of s 4A(2)(b) and the involvement of the High Court is unnecessary to lift a disqualification where the requirements of s 4A(2)(b) are met. However,

61 See Chapter 5.

if what the beneficiary would have received in terms of the will is more than what he or she would have received had the deceased died intestate and he or she does not reduce his or her inheritance accordingly, the disqualification will stand. It will then become necessary to apply the remaining provisions in s 4A(2).

If a beneficiary is disqualified because he or she witnessed a will, s 4A(2)(c) permits the disqualification to be disregarded if there are at least two competent witnesses who do not stand to inherit. Ordinarily, only two competent witnesses attest and sign a will.[62] Therefore, for s 4A(2)(c) to apply, there would have to be one or more superfluous witnesses who participated in the execution of the will and who do not stand to inherit, and the Master can make a determination in terms of the section.

Where neither ss 4A(2)(c) nor (b) applies, the only remedy available will be to bring an application to court and to satisfy the court that the requirements of s 4A(2)(a) have been met (in other words, to prove that the disqualified beneficiary did not unduly influence or defraud the testator). Once the court finds in favour of the beneficiary, the disqualification will be lifted and the beneficiary will be permitted to inherit.

***Figure 7.1** Diagrammatic summary of section 4A*

<table>
<tr><td colspan="4">Disqualified from inheriting because of s 4A(1)?
Section 4A(2)(b)
Two questions:
FIRST QUESTION: Is the disqualified beneficiary a potential intestate heir?</td></tr>
<tr><td colspan="2">If the answer is YES
SECOND QUESTION: Is the amount which the disqualified beneficiary stands to inherit equal to or less than what he or she would have received on intestacy?</td><td colspan="2">If the answer is NO</td></tr>
<tr><td>If the answer is YES, the disqualification is lifted; there is no need to go to court for relief; the Master of the High Court can make the determination</td><td>If the answer is NO and the beneficiary refuses to reduce the benefit to what he or she would have received had the deceased died intestate</td><td colspan="2">One would have to apply s 4A(2)(c) and if that does not work, one would have to apply s 4A(2)(a)</td></tr>
<tr><td colspan="2"></td><td>Section 4A(2)(c):
Master can make the determination</td><td>Section 4A(2)(a):
Application will have to be made to the High Court</td></tr>
</table>

7.4.4 Consequences of disqualification

Under the common law, when a beneficiary was disqualified for whatever reason, his or her progeny ad infinitum were disqualified from inheriting. However, this common law position was ameliorated by the legislature as it was deemed unfair to visit 'the sins of the father on the children.' Section 2C of the Wills Act and s 1(7) of the Intestate Succession Act contain similar provisions in this regard. These sections provide for substitution *ex lege* and are discussed in Chapter 2 (in the case of s 1(7)) and in Chapter 10 (in the case of s 2C).

62 Section 2(1)(a)(ii) of the Wills Act.

7.5 Customary law of succession

In situations where the Wills Act and the Intestate Succession Act apply to the estate of persons living under a system of customary law, the principles regarding the capacity of beneficiaries to inherit in terms of the testate and intestate law of succession discussed in this chapter also applies to these estates.

There are a few customary rules that influence the capacity of a beneficiary to inherit in terms of the customary law, some of which are listed below:

- The principle of primogeniture disqualifies almost all other beneficiaries (male and female) apart from the eldest son (or his eldest male descendant) from inheritance. In a polygynous household, this principle is qualified by the fact that the senior or general heir is the eldest son of the great wife, even if he is not the first son of the family head.
- The position of illegitimate children is quite interesting. In general, an illegitimate son may never inherit from his mother, but an illegitimate son may ultimately inherit from his father if there are no legitimate beneficiaries to inherit. This is an over-simplification of the rules but since neither the Intestate Succession Act[63] nor the Wills Act[64] distinguish between legitimate and illegitimate children anymore, any discrimination between children on these grounds would be regarded as unfair discrimination and would therefore be disallowed if detected.
- A family head may during his lifetime, under certain circumstances, and according to the prescribed formalities, disinherit his son and exclude him from succession. If, for example, the son is guilty of serious misconduct (such as a serious crime) making him unworthy to succeed his father as family head, he may be disinherited.[65]

THIS CHAPTER IN ESSENCE

1. Every person has capacity to inherit. There are, however, various factors that may influence a beneficiary's capacity to inherit. Persons who have limited legal capacity are still capable of inheriting. However, their ability to enjoy their inheritance as they see fit is affected.
2. There are common law and statutory grounds for disqualification that prevent beneficiaries from inheriting and the courts have, over time, developed the law relating to these.
3. Although the customary law of intestate succession has been abolished to a great extent by means of court judgments, there are customary law impediments influencing a beneficiary's capacity to inherit in terms of the customary law of succession. Cognisance must be taken of certain rules if a testator uses the principle of freedom of testation to stipulate in his or her will that the customary law of succession must apply.

63 Section 1(2).
64 Section 2D(1)(b).
65 *Mhlonhlo v Mhlonhlo* 3 NAC 114 (1913).

Chapter 8

Freedom of testation

What are the scope and application of freedom of testation in the law of succession?

8.1	Introduction	115
8.2	Limitations on freedom of testation	116
8.3	Power of appointment	126
8.4	Customary law of succession	129
This chapter in essence		130

8.1 Introduction

The expression 'freedom of testation' refers to the freedom of a person to make any provision he or she wants to make in a valid will, and to the right to have his or her estate divided in whatever manner he or she wishes. A testator is free to appoint as beneficiary whoever he or she wants to appoint. In other words, freedom of testation is a person's freedom to execute a valid will to govern the transmission and use of property, and regulate the activities and lives of others after his or her death.

In South African law, testators may decide freely on the succession of their estates and may make almost any provision they please in a will. A testator may leave his or her estate to his or her family or may disinherit them entirely, and the court must enforce the provisions of the will according to the maxim *voluntas testatoris servanda est,* meaning the will of the testator has to be complied with.

The High Court has no general authority to consent to alterations to a testator's will against his or her express intention.[1] The Court may only rectify a will in certain specified cases.[2] Even if all the beneficiaries agree to it, the Court may not change the binding clauses of a will.[3]

Schnetler v Die Meester[4] gives a sad but appropriate example of a testator's freedom of testation. After making several bequests to his brother and other parties, the testator provided:

'Aan my Kinders, Wilna, Ronel en Simon vir wie ek so lief was wat my heeltemal vergeet het, het ek van vergeet.' (translation 'To my children Wilna, Ronel and Simon whom I loved dearly and who have forgotten me totally, I have forgotten too.')

---

1 *Ex parte Trustees Estate Loewenthal* 1939 TPD 250; *Jewish Colonial Trust Ltd v Estate Nathan* 1940 AD 163; *Ex Parte Jewish Colonial Trust Ltd: In re Estate Nathan* 1967 (4) SA 397 (N); *Ex parte Kruger* 1976 (1) SA 609 (O).

2 See rectification in Chapter 13.

3 *Bydawell v Chapman* 1953 (3) SA 514 (A); *Ex parte Watling* 1982 (1) SA 936 (C).

4 1999 (4) SA 1250 (C) at 1264.

The principle of freedom of testation is, however, subject to a few restrictions.[5] The court will not give effect to bequests that are illegal or against public policy, or that are too vague or uncertain to be enforced. The Immovable Property (Removal or Modification of Restrictions) Act limits the testator's freedom by limiting his or her powers to prohibit the alienation of immovable property. The Constitution also limits a testator's freedom by prohibiting discriminatory clauses. Furthermore, claims for maintenance indirectly limit a testator's freedom of testation. The fact that a child has been disinherited does not deprive him or her of a claim for maintenance. The testator's surviving spouse may also claim maintenance from the estate in terms of the Maintenance of Surviving Spouses Act.

A testator must, as a general rule, also exercise his or her freedom of testation personally and may not leave it up to someone else to appoint his or her beneficiaries. This power of appointment may only be delegated in certain exceptional circumstances. The first exception is in respect of bequests for charitable purposes, and the second is that a testator may authorise the bearer of an interim right to nominate the eventual beneficiaries.

8.2 Limitations on freedom of testation

8.2.1 Statutory limitations

A testator's freedom of testation is limited by certain statutory provisions,[6] the Immovable Property (Removal or Modification of Restrictions) Act being perhaps the most important. In terms of this Act, a testator cannot prevent the alienation of land by means of long-term fideicommissa or other long-term provisions in his or her will. Sections 6, 7 and 8 of this Act provide that such long-term provisions are restricted to two fideicommissaries.[7] Sections 2 and 3 of the Act also indirectly restrict the testator's freedom by providing that the court may, on application from the beneficiaries, remove any restrictions on immovable property if such a removal will be to the advantage of the person entitled to the property.[8]

In 1968, Thembeka left her 5 000 m^2 property on the outskirts of Paardeberg to her son, Xavier, and provided that no more than two dwellings may be built on the property. This restriction was registered against the title deed of the property when it was transferred to Xavier. In 2008, a developer approached Xavier and offered him a partnership in developing the land, which was now situated in the centre of town. He suggested that they could build at least 30 townhouses on the property with a value of R30 million. The restriction registered against the title deed, however, prohibits this development.

In terms of the Act, Xavier can approach the High Court to remove the restriction placed on the property by the testator. Adjacent properties are now developed in a similar fashion and it is clear that the removal of the restriction will be to the financial benefit of Xavier.

5 All these restrictions will be discussed hereafter.

6 These include the Immovable Property (Removal or Modification of Restrictions) Act 94 of 1965 (discussed here), the Subdivision of Agricultural Land Act 70 of 1970, the Mineral and Petroleum Resources Development Act 28 of 2002, the Pension Funds Act 24 of 1956, and the Close Corporations Act 69 of 1984.

7 See Chapter 10 for a discussion of the fideicommissum.

8 *Ex parte Schnehage* 1972 (1) SA 300 (O); *Ex parte Stranack* 1974 (2) SA 692 (D).

Section 33(1) of the General Law Amendment Act[9] also gives the court the power to authorise the alienation or mortgage of immovable property which is subject to any restriction imposed by a will when an unborn person will become entitled to the property. The High Court may consent to the alienation or mortgage of any such property on behalf of the unborn person as if he or she was alive and a living minor.

8.2.2 Common law limitations

The courts will not enforce conditions in a will that are seen as *contra bonos mores* or against public policy.[10] Public policy or that which the community sees as immoral does, however, change with the times. It is therefore possible that what was seen as *contra bonos mores* fifty years ago is now seen as acceptable.

In *Minister of Education v Syfrets Trust Ltd*,[11] the testator, a Mr Scarbrow, made a will in 1920 and a later codicil in which he (in brief) provided that a trust fund created after his death should be applied to provide bursaries for deserving white, non-Jewish male students who wished to study overseas. In 2002 the Minister of Education brought a court application requesting the deletion of the discriminatory provisions in the will. This application was based on three grounds:

1. section 13 of the Trust Property Control Act 57 of 1988, which confers upon the court the power to vary a trust provision if the provision brings about consequences that were unforeseen by the trust founder (the testator) and that are in conflict with the public interest
2. common law, which prohibits bequests that are illegal, immoral or contrary to public policy (in other words, *contra bonos mores*)
3. the Constitution, specifically the equality and anti-discriminatory provisions.

The counter-argument was that the contested provisions of the will were valid because of the high value attached to a testator's freedom of testation in our law. The Court pointed out that the principle of freedom of testation has never been absolute and unfettered. Over the years various restrictions have been placed on this by common law and statute:

- **Public policy:** One of the restrictions on freedom of testation is the principle that the courts will refuse to give effect to a testator's directions that are contrary to public policy. This concept changes over time as social conditions change. In South Africa today, public policy is rooted in the Constitution and the fundamental values it protects. In *Minister of Education v Syfrets Trust Ltd*,[12] therefore, the Court had to look at the constitutional values of human dignity, achievement of equality and the advancement of non-racialism and non-sexism.
- **Equality:** According to s 9 of the Constitution, no one may unfairly discriminate directly or indirectly against anyone on the basis of race, gender, sex, religion or several other factors. The Court, however, did not apply the Constitution directly to the facts. The Constitution was applied indirectly - the Court's decision was based on its common law powers to remove provisions that are contrary to public policy. As such, the Court was of the opinion that if it were to hold that the provisions amounted to unfair discrimination, it could also hold them to be against public policy.

9 62 of 1955.
10 See *Ex parte President of the Conference of the Methodist Church of Southern Africa: In re William Marsh Will Trust* 1993 (2) SA 697 (C) and the cases discussed hereafter.
11 2006 (4) SA 205 (C). Note that this case is also relevant with regard to race and gender clauses as discussed hereafter.
12 2006 (4) SA 2005 (C).

- **Unfair discrimination:** The condition in Mr Scarbrow's will that limited eligibility to white males of 'European descent' amounted to indirect discrimination based on race and colour. The provision that excluded Jews and women amounted to direct discrimination on the grounds of religion and gender. In terms of s 9(5), these provisions are presumed to be unfair discrimination unless the contrary is proved.

The Court consequently held that the provision constituted unfair discrimination and based on its common law power to delete provisions in a will that are against public policy, ordered that the offending provisions of the will be deleted.

PAUSE FOR REFLECTION

Freedom of testation

In *Minister of Education v Syfrets Trust Ltd* the Court pointed out that the principle of freedom of testation cannot be ignored. The Court, however, reinforced an existing limitation on freedom of testation, namely the common law principle that provisions that are *contra bonos mores* may be deleted. Although provisions that constitute unfair discrimination are contrary to public policy, not all clauses in wills or trust deeds that differentiate between different groups of people are invalid. It is only where the differentiation can be considered to be unfair discrimination (for example, on the grounds of race, gender and faith) that it can be held invalid and be deleted.

There are two types of condition which have frequently been challenged in our courts as possibly being *contra bonos mores*:

1. conditions that interfere with a beneficiary's marital relationship
2. conditions limiting a beneficiary's freedom of movement.

8.2.2.1 Conditions that interfere with a beneficiary's marital relationship

In terms of the common law a testator cannot leave a benefit to a beneficiary who has never been married on the condition that the beneficiary never gets married. Such a condition is void as being *contra bonos mores* since it encourages the beneficiary to continue in the unmarried state.[13]

In *De Wayer v SPCA Johannesburg*,[14] the testator provided that the residue of her estate shall go to her son 'on condition that he remains unmarried after [her] death'. If he did get married, he would only be entitled to the movable assets and the rest of the estate would go to the SPCA. The son applied for the removal of the condition, and the Court decided that it is settled law that a general restraint on marriage is *contra bonos mores*. The will clearly placed a general restraint on the son to marry any woman at any time and it was the intention of the testator to discourage her son from marriage.[15] The condition was therefore held to be *contra bonos mores* and *pro non scripto*.

The effect of a condition being held *contra bonos mores* and *pro non scripto* is that the beneficiary inherits the benefit without any condition attached. In *De Wayer v SPCA*

13 *Aronson v Estate Hart* 1950 (1) SA 539 (A) at 564–566; *De Wayer v SPCA Johannesburg* 1963 (1) SA 71 (T).
14 1963 (1) SA 71 (T).
15 1963 (1) SA 71 (T) at 79.

Johannesburg, this meant that the son inherited the estate unconditionally and that the SPCA had no claim of any kind to it.

Under the common law, there was an exception to the general rule that a condition which prohibits a person from marrying is void for being *contra bonos mores* – it is not considered *contra bonos mores* to prohibit someone who has been married before to marry again. If a testator therefore bequeaths something to his surviving spouse subject to the condition that the surviving spouse does not remarry, such a condition will be valid.[16] The reasoning behind this exception is that the testator's motive might have been that if his widow remarried, his children may suffer.[17]

In *Ex parte Gitelson*,[18] the applicant was the sole heir of her husband's estate 'subject to the condition that ... should she remarry, she shall, ... pay to each of my four children a sum equal to one-fifth of the value of my estate as at the date of my death'. The applicant wanted to sell a farm which was part of the estate but the registrar refused to register the transfer without authority from the Court or security furnished by the applicant to cover the inheritance in the event of her remarriage. The applicant was unable to provide security and asked for an order authorising her to sell the property without providing the security. The Court held that the condition was valid and that the applicant had to provide the relevant security.

A condition is also considered to be *contra bonos mores* if the intention of the testator is to destroy an existing marriage.[19] Such a condition will only be considered *pro non scripto* if it is the intention of the testator to destroy the marriage and not if the destruction of the marriage is simply incidental to the application of the condition.[20] In other words, if a bequest results in the breakdown of a marriage without this having been the testator's purpose, such a bequest will not be invalid.

In *Levy v Schwartz*,[21] the testator provided that one of his daughters would only receive her benefits if her marriage was dissolved by death or 'any other cause'. The Court held that this provision was calculated to bring about the break up of the applicant's existing marriage and was therefore *contra bonos mores* and against public policy. The condition was removed and the applicant inherited her benefits unconditionally.

In *Ex parte Swanevelder*,[22] certain farms were left to the applicant with a fideicommissum in favour of her children. The will provided that the proceeds of the farms be divided amongst the applicant's siblings or their descendants should she die without children. If, however, the applicant's husband were to predecease her, these conditions would lapse. The applicant applied for an order declaring the conditions null and void as they caused discord between herself and her husband. The Court held that the intention was not to cause the dissolution of the marriage

16 *Ex parte Marks' Executors* 1921 TPD 284; *Ex parte Administrators Estate Lesser* 1940 TPD 11; *Fram v Fram* 1943 TPD 362; *Scott v Estate Scott* 1943 (NPD) 7; *Barnett v Estate Schereschewske* 1957 (3) SA 679 (C); *Stevenson v Greenberg* 1960 (2) SA 276 (W).

17 *Ex parte Gitelson* 1949 (2) SA 881 (O) at 887; *Rubin v Altschul* 1961 (4) SA 251 (W).

18 1949 (2) SA 881 (O).

19 *Ex parte Isaacs* 1964 (4) SA 606 (GW); *Levy v Schwartz* 1948 (4) SA 930 (W); *Ex parte St Clair Lynn* 1980 (3) SA 163 (W); *Oosthuizen v Bank Windhoek* 1991 (1) SA 849 (Nm).

20 *Ex parte Higgs: In re Estate Rangasami* 1969 (1) SA 56 (D); *Ex parte Swanevelder* 1949 (1) SA 733 (O); *Barclays Bank DC v Anderson* 1959 (2) SA 478 (T).

21 1948 (4) SA 930 (W).

22 1949 (1) SA 733 (O).

and as the will only referred to the death of the husband, it was difficult to see how the conditions caused discord between the parties. The conditions were held to be valid.

In *Barclays Bank DC v Anderson*,[23] the testator left certain portions of a farm to his children provided that they personally and permanently occupy such land. Two of his daughters were experiencing health problems and their husbands had business interests which made it difficult for them to live on the farms. The executor applied for an order declaring that they had lost their rights to the properties. The daughters, however, maintained that the provisions of the will were void as they tended to create a separation between husband and wife. The Court held that there was no evidence that it was the testator's intention to create a separation between the husbands and their wives, and that it was not even evident that the separation would be an inevitable consequence of the provisions. The respondents therefore forfeited their rights.

Under common law it was in principle possible for a testator to place a restriction on a beneficiary with regard to the person he or she was allowed to marry. Initially it was accepted that a testator may make it a condition of a bequest that a beneficiary may not marry a certain person or that the beneficiary may not marry a person who subscribed to a certain faith.[24] Such clauses were attacked on the ground that they were against public policy but this ground was not upheld by the courts. In some cases, the court did not doubt the validity of such conditions and thus did not regard it necessary to decide upon this ground.[25] In *Wasserzug v Administrators of Estate Nathanson*,[26] it was held that the condition that the beneficiary should not marry 'out of the Jewish faith' was too uncertain and therefore void for vagueness. This view was, however, overturned by the Appellate Division in *Aronson v Estate Hart*,[27] when it held that a condition that the beneficiary 'should not marry a person not born in the Jewish faith or should not forsake the Jewish faith' was not void for vagueness[28] nor was it against public policy.

PAUSE FOR REFLECTION

Faith clauses

Consider what the core question in cases such as the so-called faith clauses should be when deciding on the validity of such clauses. This question lies at the heart of the moral dilemma faced in *Aronson v Estate Hart*.[29] The question was answered more than fifty years ago by Hahlo as follows:[30]

But, with respect, the question is not whether intermarriage between Jew and Christian is a good or a bad thing nor whether the testator believes it to be a good or a bad thing. The question is whether it is contrary to our notions of propriety that a testator should be allowed to use the power of the purse to force his descendants for one, two or more generations to profess a faith which they may no longer hold ...

23 1959 (2) SA 478 (T).
24 *Ex parte Administrators Estate Lesser* 1940 TPD 11; *Fram v Fram* 1943 TPD 362; *Scott v Estate Scott* 1943 (NPD) 7.
25 See *Ex parte Marks' Executors* 1921 TPD 284; *Ex parte Administrators Estate Lesser* 1940 TPD 11; *Fram v Fram* 1943 TPD 362.
26 1944 TPD 369. This case was followed in *Ex parte Estate Hack* 1945 TPD 414; *Ex parte Perel* 1948 (3) SA 195 (GW).
27 1950 (1) SA 539 (A).
28 *Aronson v Estate Hart* 1950 (1) SA 539 (A) 543 at 545; see also *Standard Bank of SA Ltd v Betts Brown* 1958 (3) SA 713 (N) and *Ex parte Administrator Estate Sandler* 1976 (4) SA 930 (C).
29 1950 (1) SA 539 (A).
30 1950 *SALJ* 231 at 240.

This answer points to the undeniable fact that public policy changes with the times. The question is not simply whether such marriages are to be allowed or not. One cannot use the old authorities to hold that such clauses are against public policy as they may have considered such marriages to be undesirable whilst it is no longer the case in modern times. However, if one looks at the question of whether a testator should be allowed to control his descendants by financial means, it has long since been considered improper and still is.

8.2.2.2 Conditions limiting a beneficiary's freedom of movement

The testator may provide that a beneficiary must live in a certain place or on a certain property and the court is obliged to give effect to such provisions if they are clear and unambiguous. Under common law such provisions are regarded as valid and enforceable.[31] If the clause is vague, effect will not be given to it. These are, however, good examples of how unfair such provisions can be towards the beneficiaries. In *Ex parte Mostert: In re Estate late Mostert,*[32] a prohibition was created without a discernible indication of the consequences that would follow on a breach of the clause. The clause was held to be void to that extent.[33]

PAUSE FOR REFLECTION

How fair are conditions limiting a beneficiary's freedom of movement?

In *Ex parte Higgs: In re Estate Rangasami,*[34] the will provided that the testator's four sons would forfeit their inheritance if they chose to move out of the family home. The sons and the testator's widow applied for an order declaring the condition invalid or, in the alternative, impossible, not reasonably capable of being obeyed, or not binding upon the sons. They argued that the family home had become too small for the sons and their families to all live together and the situation had become a health risk. They wanted to divide the property so as to afford each son the opportunity to build his own house on the property. The Court held that the condition was not void as it was not calculated to break up existing marriages nor was it calculated to discourage any possible future marriages. The testator's intention seemed to have been to keep his home and family intact and the Court found nothing *contra bonos mores* in that. Furthermore, the Court found that it was not impossible to carry out the terms of the condition - the sons could simply add additional space to the existing house.

If similar facts to *Ex parte Higgs: In re Estate Rangasami* were to appear before the court today, do you think that a similar decision would be reached? Might the guarantees provided in the Constitution with regard to freedom of movement and freedom of association affect the outcome? Only time will tell.

Under common law clauses requiring a beneficiary to change his or her name, or to give his or her children certain names are valid.[35] In this regard, it is interesting to note the

31 *Ex parte Dodds* 1949 (2) SA 311 (T); *Ex parte Kock* 1952 (2) SA 502 (C); *Ex parte Higgs: In re Estate Rangasami* 1969 (1) SA 56 (D).

32 1975 (3) SA 312 (T).

33 See also *Ex parte Sieberhagen* 1946 CPD 83.

34 1969 (1) SA 56 (D).

35 *Ex parte Estate Edwards* 1964 (2) SA 144 (C); *Loock v Steyn* 1968 (1) SA 602 (A).

comments of Wiechers[36] a mere five years after the decision in *Loock v Steyn*.[37] He reiterates that public policy and opinion of what is *contra bonos mores* change constantly, that there is no clear test to determine what is regarded as *contra bonos mores*, and that testators should not be allowed to saddle their beneficiaries with certain names. In *Minister of Education v Syfrets Trust Ltd*,[38] the Court held that public policy is now rooted in the Constitution and the fundamental values it protects. The Court therefore has to look at constitutional values when determining public policy.

8.2.3 Constitutional limitations

In modern society, changes in public policy and what is seen as being *contra bonos mores* are embodied in the Constitution. There is, therefore, also a possibility that certain conditions may be declared invalid in terms of the Constitution. Section 9(3) of the Constitution lists factors that may not be used to discriminate unfairly against a person. Furthermore, according to s 9(4), read with s 9(3), no one may discriminate unfairly directly or indirectly against anyone on the basis of race, gender, sex, pregnancy, marital status, ethnic or social origin, colour, sexual orientation, age, disability, religion, conscience, belief, culture, language, or birth. Section 9(4) operates horizontally between all natural and juristic persons. Furthermore, ss 18 and 21 of the Constitution guarantee a person's freedom of association, freedom of movement, and freedom of residence. It is therefore quite possible that provisions such as those prohibiting a person from marrying a person of a certain race or faith, or requiring a beneficiary to live in a certain place will be regarded as against public policy and the *boni mores*, and may be found to be invalid.

The case of *Minister of Education v Syfrets Trust Ltd*[39] discussed above, provides a useful set of facts that illustrate how the Constitution could have a direct impact on a testator's freedom of testation.

8.2.4 Indirect limitations

8.2.4.1 Maintenance of children

Although a testator has complete freedom to disinherit his or her children, the maintenance and education of minor children remains an obligation on the estate and does not die with the testator.[40] This is a common law obligation which is dependent upon need and ends when the child is able to support himself or herself.[41] The amount of the maintenance is determined by the standard of living of the child and, if necessary, continues until majority. A major child who is unable to support himself or herself adequately is entitled to claim support from his or her deceased parent's estate.[42] The obligation to pay maintenance falls primarily upon the living relatives of the child before the parent's estate will be liable.[43]

36 1973 *De Jure* 54 at 56.
37 1968 (1) SA 602 (A).
38 2006 (4) SA 205 (C).
39 2006 (4) SA 205 (C).
40 *Carelse v Estate De Vries* (1906) 23 SC 532; *Ex parte Burstein* 1941 CPD 87; *Ex parte Insel* 1952 (1) SA 71 (T); *Glazer v Glazer* 1963 (4) SA 694 (A); *Bank v Sussman* 1968 (2) SA 15 (O); *Hoffmann v Herdan* 1982 (2) SA 274 (T); *Ex parte Jacobs* 1982 (2) SA 276 (E).
41 *Carelse v Estate De Vries* (1906) 23 SC 532.
42 *Davis' Tutor v Estate Davis* 1925 WLD 168; *Hoffmann v Herdan* 1982 (2) SA 274 (T); *Ex parte Jacobs* 1982 (2) SA 276 (O).
43 *Bank v Sussman* 1968 (2) SA 15 (O).

In *Ex parte Jacobs*,[44] a major daughter claimed maintenance from her deceased father's estate. It was held that the duty to support her rested in the first place on her husband and only if he was incapable of fulfilling this obligation, could a claim for maintenance against her father arise.

A child's claim for maintenance follows that of creditors in order of preference[45] but is preferred to those of legatees and heirs.[46]

8.2.4.2 Maintenance of the surviving spouse

In terms of the Maintenance of Surviving Spouses Act,[47] if a marriage is dissolved by death, the survivor shall have a claim against the estate of the deceased spouse for the provision of his or her reasonable maintenance needs until his or her death or remarriage, but only insofar as he or she is unable to provide this from his or her own means and earnings.[48] In determining the reasonable maintenance needs of the surviving spouse the following factors, in addition to any other relevant factor, are taken into consideration:

- the amount in the estate of the deceased spouse that is available for distribution to heirs and legatees[49]
- the existing and expected means, earning capacity, financial needs and obligations of the surviving spouse and the subsistence of the marriage[50]
- the standard of living of the survivor during the subsistence of the marriage and his or her age at the death of the deceased spouse.[51]

A claim for maintenance by a surviving spouse against the estate of the deceased spouse occupies the same position of preference as a claim for maintenance by a dependent child of the deceased spouse. If a claim of the survivor and that of a dependent child compete with each other, those claims shall be reduced proportionately.[52] Where there is a conflict of interests because the survivor, in addition to his or her own claim for maintenance, also has to institute a claim for maintenance on behalf of a minor dependent child of the deceased spouse, the Master may defer the claim for maintenance until the court has decided on the dependent's claim.[53] The executor of the deceased spouse's estate is empowered to enter into agreements with the survivor, heirs and legatees who have an interest in such an agreement. These may include the creation of a trust, transferring of assets of the deceased estate, or a right in the assets, to the survivor or the trust, or imposing an obligation on an heir or legatee in settlement of the claim of the survivor.[54]

8.2.4.2.1 The meaning of 'spouse'

Although the provisions of the Maintenance of Surviving Spouses Act[55] seem relatively simple, a shift in public policy with regard to marriages and life partnerships has resulted in a number

44 1982 (2) SA 276 (O).
45 *Ritchken's Executors v Ritchken* 1924 WLD 17; *In re Estate Visser* 1948 (3) SA 1129 (C).
46 *Davis' Tutor v Estate Davis* 1925 WLD 168; *Goldman v Executor Estate Goldman* 1937 WLD 64; *Ex parte Estate Pitt-Kennedy* 1946 (NPD) 776.
47 27 of 1990.
48 Section 2(1).
49 Section 3(a).
50 Section 3(b).
51 Section 3(c).
52 Section 2(3)(b).
53 Section 2(3)(c).
54 Section 2(3)(d).
55 27 of 1990.

of problems. The main problem has been that the Act confers rights on spouses who have been predeceased by their husbands or wives but does not define the word 'spouse'. In terms of s 1, only the word 'survivor' is defined – 'the surviving spouse in a marriage dissolved by death'. As a result, the Constitutional Court had to decide on the meaning of the words 'spouse' and 'survivor' as used in the Act, specifically in relation to Muslim marriages[56] and persons living in a permanent heterosexual life partnership.[57]

The meaning of these words (spouse and survivor) as used in the Intestate Succession Act also came up for decision in respect of Muslim marriages[58] and persons living in a same-sex life partnership.[59]

In *Daniels v Campbell*,[60] a couple was married by Muslim rites in 1977. The marriage was never solemnised by a marriage officer appointed in terms of the Marriage Act,[61] but had been monogamous for thirty years until the husband died. No children had been born of the union but both parties had children from previous marriages. The deceased died intestate and the main asset was a house that Mrs Daniels had lived in for 30 years. She and her first husband had acquired this house on a rental basis from the city council. Shortly after she divorced her first husband, tenancy of the house was assigned to her in her own name. However, when she married the deceased, the tenancy of the house was registered in the deceased's name. After Mr Daniels' death, Mrs Daniels continued to reside in the house with her children and she frequently paid the rental and levies that were owed.[62] After her husband died, her family claimed the house as the Master of the High Court was of the opinion that she was not the deceased's spouse in terms of the Intestate Succession Act because she had been married under Muslim rites. A claim for maintenance against the estate was rejected on the same basis. Mrs Daniels therefore approached the Court and the Court held that a party to a monogamous Muslim marriage is a 'spouse' and a 'survivor' in terms of the Intestate Succession Act and in terms of the Maintenance of Surviving Spouses Act.

In 2008 the Cape High Court expanded this decision to include polygamous Muslim marriages. In *Hassam v Jacobs*[63] the Court held that the word 'survivor' as used in the Maintenance of Surviving Spouses Act includes a surviving partner to a polygamous Muslim marriage. The Court also held that the word 'spouse' as used in the Intestate Succession Act includes a surviving partner of a polygamous Muslim marriage. The effect of these decisions is that surviving spouses in all Muslim marriages, irrespective of whether they were de facto monogamous or not, can inherit in terms of intestate succession law from their deceased spouse's estate and also have a claim for maintenance in terms of the Maintenance of Surviving Spouses Act.[64] The judgment of the Cape High Court was confirmed by the Constitutional Court in *Hassam v Jacobs*.[65]

56 *Daniels v Campbell* 2004 (5) SA 331 (CC).
57 *Volks v Robinson* 2005 (5) BCLR 446 (CC).
58 *Daniels v Campbell* 2004 (5) SA 331 (CC); *Hassam v Jacobs* [2008] 4 All SA 350 (C); see also Chapter 2.
59 *Gory v Kolver* 2007 (4) SA 97 (CC); see also Chapter 2.
60 2004 (5) SA 331 (CC).
61 25 of 1961.
62 *Daniels v Campbell* 2004 (5) SA 331 (CC) at paras 3–5.
63 [2008] 4 All SA 350 (C) at para 19.
64 The order of the Court has been referred to the Constitutional Court for confirmation; see also Chapter 2.
65 Unreported case CCT 83/08 [2009] ZACC 19 on 15 July 2009.

PAUSE FOR REFLECTION

Surviving spouses

In *Volks v Robinson*,[66] a woman who had lived with a man in a life partnership for almost 12 years prior to his death, claimed maintenance from his deceased estate in terms of the Maintenance of Surviving Spouses Act. The executor rejected the claim, whereupon she approached the Cape Provincial Division of the High Court for relief. The High Court declared s 1 of the Maintenance of Surviving Spouses Act to be unconstitutional because it fails to include permanent life partners within the ambit of the Act. The Court found that this violates the equality clause of the Constitution and infringes the right to dignity of surviving life partners.[67]

The case was referred to the Constitutional Court for confirmation. The majority of the judges of the Constitutional Court, however, did not agree with the High Court. They found that differentiating between a spouse and a heterosexual life partner by excluding the heterosexual life partner from a maintenance claim against the estate of his or her deceased life partner in circumstances where a spouse would have had such a claim does not constitute unfair discrimination, nor does it violate the surviving life partner's right to dignity. They pointed out that although the Bill of Rights does not include the right to marry and to found a family, s 15(3)(a)(i) recognises marriage as an institution. Furthermore, the Constitutional Court has already recognised that marriage and family are important social institutions in our society[68] and marriage is also recognised internationally. They therefore concluded that the law may distinguish between married and unmarried persons, and may afford benefits to those who are married that it does not afford to those who are unmarried. The Court held that the distinction between married and unmarried people could not be said to be unfair when considered in the broader context of the rights and obligations that are uniquely attached to marriage. In the case of heterosexual life partnerships, the law does not impose an automatic duty of support upon the life partners during the subsistence of the life partnership as it does in the case of marriage. As the law does not impose such a duty of support during a life partner's lifetime, the Constitution does not impose such an obligation on the estate of a deceased partner in circumstances where there was no intention on the part of the deceased to undertake such an obligation. The majority of the Constitutional Court therefore held that it is not unfair to distinguish between surviving spouses and surviving heterosexual life partners.

The effect of *Volks v Robinson* is that a heterosexual life partner is not automatically regarded as a spouse or a survivor in terms of the Maintenance of Surviving Spouses Act, and cannot claim maintenance from the deceased life partner's estate. It is interesting to note the underlying current of the majority judgment in this case. Clearly, the majority was of the opinion that public policy has, as yet, not developed to the point that it sees a life partnership as placing the same rights and duties on the partners as those afforded to partners of a marriage. According to this approach, public opinion wants to protect and preserve the

66 2005 (5) BCLR 446 (CC).
67 See *Robinson v Volks* 2004 (6) BCLR 671 (C).
68 *Dawood v Minister of Home Affairs; Shalabi v Minister of Home Affairs; Thomas v Minister of Home Affairs* [2000] (8) BCLR 837 (CC); 2000 (3) SA 936 (CC); *Du Toit v Minister for Welfare and Population Development* [2002] (10) BCLR 1006 (CC).

marriage relationship. In the view of the minority judgment, on the other hand, public policy regards the constitutional purpose of the prohibition on discrimination on the ground of marital status as more important than the preservation of the marriage relationship as such, and therefore held that it is unfair to discriminate between relationships to which the law attaches the obligations of support and cohabitation and those relationships to which the law does not attach such consequences. To decide whether one agrees with the majority or with the minority, one has to weigh one's own beliefs and decide whether one regards the preservation of marriage as an institution or non-discrimination on the ground of marital status as the most important principle to be upheld.

8.2.4.2.2 The Civil Union Act and the meaning of 'spouse'

In terms of s 1 of the Civil Union Act the elements of a civil union are:

- the voluntary union
- of two persons
- who are both 18 years of age or older
- which is solemnised and registered by way of either a marriage or a civil partnership
- in accordance with the procedures prescribed in that Act
- to the exclusion, whilst it lasts, of all others.

According to s 13(1), the legal consequences of a civil union are the same as those of a marriage in terms of the Marriage Act, but with such changes as may be required by the context. Marriage is therefore no longer restricted to persons of the opposite sex.

The Act further provides that any reference to marriage in any other law (common law and customary law) includes, with such changes as may be required by the context, a civil union. Also, the words 'husband,' 'wife' or 'spouse' in any other law include, with such changes as may be required by the context, a civil union partner. This means that a partner in a civil union will be entitled to claim maintenance in terms of the Maintenance of Surviving Spouses Act, and such a partner will also be able to inherit in terms of the Intestate Succession Act.

8.3 Power of appointment

Testators enjoy a wide freedom of testation in South African law. They have the power to appoint whoever they wish as beneficiaries but this power, known as testamentary power, must be exercised by the testator himself or herself. It is a fundamental rule of the law of succession that 'a testator must himself make his will and cannot commit the discretion as to who shall be beneficiaries under his will to others.'[69] Except for a few exceptions, a testator may not leave it to someone else to decide who will inherit under his or her will.[70] A testator may also not leave it to the discretion of a beneficiary to decide whether he or she will retain the property himself or herself or pass it on to other beneficiaries.[71]

69 *Estate Watkins-Pitchford v Commissioner for Inland Revenue* 1955 (2) SA 437 (A) at 458. See also *Estate Orpen v Estate Atkinson* 1966 (4) SA 589 (A) at 596; *Braun v Blann and Botha* 1984 (2) SA 850 (A).

70 *Marks v Estate Gluckman* 1946 AD 289; *Estate Watkins-Pitchford v Commissioner for Inland Revenue* 1955 (2) SA 437 (A); *Ex parte Henderson* 1971 (4) SA 549 (D); *Administrators, Estate Richards v Nichol* 1996 (4) SA 253 (C).

71 *Pritchard's Trustee v Estate Pritchard* 1912 CPD 87 at 96; *Harter v Epstein* 1953 (1) SA 287 (A) at 293.

Consider the following:

1. Ben provides in his will that he leaves his estate to his daughter, Bernadine, 'and the division thereof is entirely in her hands'.
2. Ayanda provides in her will that her estate will be inherited by the descendants of her daughter, Dineo.
3. Schalk provides in his will that his daughter, Delores, must appoint beneficiaries to Schalk's estate in her will.

In the first example, power of appointment has not been validly conferred as Ben did not exercise his own testamentary power. In the second example, Ayanda exercised her power of appointment herself by providing who the beneficiaries to her estate will be even though she did not mention them by name and they might not yet have been born when she made the provision. This form of power of appointment is recognised as special power of appointment – the beneficiaries must be chosen from certain persons or from a certain class of persons. In the third example, Schalk left it up to his daughter, Delores, to decide who the beneficiaries of his estate will be. In this case, he did not exercise his testamentary power himself but delegated it to Delores. This delegation of his power of appointment in this manner is known as a general power of appointment and confers upon the beneficiary the freedom to choose the beneficiaries. The position regarding the validity of such general power is not entirely clear. The effect of any invalid power of appointment will depend on the intention of the testator.[72]

There are, however, exceptions to the rule that the testator may not delegate his or her power of appointment. The exceptions to the rule are:

1. **Bequests for charitable purposes (*ad pias causas*).** In the case of such bequests, the testator may authorise a beneficiary, or the executor or administrator of his or her estate to appoint specific beneficiaries.[73]

   Stefano creates a trust in his will 'for the benefit of animals in distress' and provides that the trustee of the trust should choose two beneficiaries from organisations that look after the welfare of animals.

   In this case the testator does not mention specific beneficiaries from which the trustee should choose, but the trustee may choose the beneficiaries within the broad charitable purpose provided for in the will. A provision such as this is not regarded as an invalid conferment of a power of appointment.[74]

2. **Delegation to the bearer of an interim right.** Bearers of interim rights are beneficiaries who only have limited rights to the assets of a testator's estate and who are obliged to hand the assets or certain rights over to other beneficiaries. Examples of such bearers of interim rights are the fiduciary in a fideicommissum or the usufructuary in a usufruct. In modern times, the trustee may also have the power of appointment although he or she will be limited to choosing the beneficiaries from a designated group of people.[75] The testator may give the bearer of an interim right the power to nominate the eventual

72 See *Arkell v Carter* 1971 (3) SA 243 (R).
73 *Ex parte Henderson* 1971 (4) SA 549 (D).
74 *Ex parte Henderson* 1971 (4) SA 549 (D).
75 See *Braun v Blann and Botha* 1984 (2) SA 850 (A).

beneficiaries, or to determine what each beneficiary is to receive, or the manner in which they are to inherit.

In the past the conferment of a power of appointment was possible only in the context of a fideicommissum.[76] Today, however, the power of appointment may also be conferred upon a usufructuary[77] as well as upon a trustee.[78]

Mrs Oliver is appointed as the fiduciary of a farm belonging to her father, Mr Terrouge. Mr Terrouge's will further provides that upon Mrs Oliver's death, the farm will go to the person/s she appoints as beneficiaries in her will. In this case a valid power of appointment has been conferred upon Mrs Oliver as she is the holder of an interim right (the fiduciary) and therefore the farm will go to any beneficiary which she appoints in her will.

In *Estate Orpen v Estate Atkinson*,[79] similar facts occurred. In this case, however, the beneficiary who had been appointed as fiduciary in the testator's will, died before the testator. The Court held that she could not validly exercise the power of appointment conferred upon her in the testator's will as the general rules applicable to a fideicommissum applied when she exercised her power and, as she predeceased the testator, she had not yet been the fiduciary.

The reason for the acceptance of a valid conferment of the power of appointment upon a bearer of an interim right was the view that such a person had a beneficial interest in the property.[80] For this reason also, the view was formerly held that a power of appointment could not be delegated to a trustee as he or she did not have such a beneficial interest. In *Braun v Blann and Botha*[81] however, the Appellate Division held that such a power may be conferred upon a trustee but with the proviso that the testator has to indicate a specified class of persons from which the trustee should appoint the beneficiaries.

The person who receives the power of appointment exercises it in accordance with the provisions of the will in which it is created.[82] If the will, for example, provided that the beneficiary may only divide the assets amongst his or her lawful issue, extramarital children would not be beneficiaries.[83] They could, of course, argue that such a clause would discriminate against them and that it is a *contra bonos mores* stipulation which should be declared invalid. However, it is doubtful whether the courts would go so far to limit a testator's freedom of testation. In essence, many stipulations in a will have the potential to infringe upon the human rights of a beneficiary, but to disallow infringements of any kind would be a denial of a testator's freedom of testation.

76 *Union Government (Minister of Finance) v Olivier* 1916 AD 74; *Westminster Bank v Zinn* 1938 AD 57.
77 *Commissioner for Inland Revenue v Lukin's Estate* 1956 (1) SA 617 (A) 623; *Estate Orpen v Estate Atkinson* 1966 (4) SA 589 (A) at 594.
78 *Braun v Blann and Botha* 1984 (2) SA 850 (A).
79 1966 (2) SA 639 (C).
80 *Estate Orpen v Estate Atkinson* 1966 (2) SA 639 (C); *Braun v Blann and Botha* 1984 (2) SA 850 (A).
81 1984 (2) SA 850 (A).
82 *Smit v Du Toit* 1981 (3) SA 1249 (A); *Ferreira v Smit* 1981 (3) SA 1264 (A).
83 *Ferreira v Smit* 1981 (3) SA 1264 (A); *Ex parte Reay: In re McGregor's Estate* 1982 (4) SA 27 (C).

8.4 Customary law of succession

Section 23(1) of the Black Administration Act provided for a limitation on the freedom of testation of a person living under customary law. It read as follows:

> *All movable property belonging to a Black and allotted by him or accruing under Black law and custom to any woman with whom he lived in a customary union, or to any house, shall upon his death devolve and be administered under Black law and custom.*

In effect, this provision prohibited a person living under customary law from making a will pertaining to customary property[84] but nothing prohibited a testator from disposing of personal property by means of a will.

Section 23 was declared invalid by the Constitutional Court in *Bhe v Magistrate, Khayelitsha*,[85] and was consequently repealed by the Repeal of the Black Administration Act and Amendment of Certain Laws Act[86] on 12 April 2006. This means that a testator has freedom of testation regarding customary property subject to the normal limitations that exist in terms of the common and statutory law as discussed above.

In essence, there is nothing that prohibits a testator living under a system of customary law from stipulating in his or her will that the customary law of succession should apply to the devolution of his or her estate. One should, however, be cautious of such a stipulation as it would, in all probability, entail that someone other than the testator (who is already dead) has to decide who the customary law beneficiaries are. This could be regarded as delegation of power of appointment which is not allowed in terms of the common law.

PAUSE FOR REFLECTION

Customary law and freedom of testation

The will of a testator stipulates the following: 'The whole of my estate must devolve amongst the beneficiaries according to the rules of the customary law of succession of the Tswana people.' In essence, there is nothing wrong with this stipulation because the testator has freedom of testation. However, the succession rules of the Tswana people are not readily accessible, and usually someone from the community (mostly an elder or expert on Tswana law) has to explain how the devolution of the estate should take place. In other words, someone other than the deceased (the executor of the will) has to indicate who the beneficiaries will be in terms of customary law. This could amount to the delegation of the testamentary power of the testator (power of appointment), which is prohibited in terms of the common law.[87]

A stipulation in the will that the customary law of succession must apply to the deceased estate will bring the rule of male primogeniture into operation. This means that there will be an uneven distribution of the deceased estate between beneficiaries based on gender and age which was found to be unconstitutional because of its unequal results in *Bhe v Magistrate, Khayelitsha*.[88] Nevertheless, the common law concept of freedom of

84 See Chapter 1 for a definition of customary property.
85 See Chapter 2.
86 28 of 2005.
87 See para 8.3 where the power of appointment is discussed.
88 2005 (1) SA 580 (CC).

testation might be strong enough to allow a testator to discriminate between his or her family members (especially between his or her children), because in principle there is nothing in terms of the common law that prevents a parent from discriminating against one or more of his children by excluding some or all of them from inheriting.

THIS CHAPTER IN ESSENCE

1. While testators in South Africa enjoy a wide freedom of testation, this freedom is subject to certain limitations.
2. These limitations can be divided into statutory and common law limitations and include conditions that interfere with a beneficiary's marital relationship and conditions limiting a beneficiary's freedom of movement.
3. The common law limitations are also entrenched in the Constitution and certain indirect limitations, such as those imposed by the maintenance of children and the Maintenance of Surviving Spouses Act, may also be found.
4. The testator may also delegate his or her freedom of testation to a certain extent by conferring the power of appointment upon other persons.
5. A person living under a system of customary law is free to make a will regarding customary property. The principles regarding power of appointment should, however, be kept in mind in such instances.

Chapter 9

Content of wills – absolute bequests, conditions, the modus and estate massing

What is the typical content one can expect to find in a will?

9.1	Introduction	131
9.2	Vesting of rights	132
9.3	Bequests	134
9.4	*Nudum praeceptum*	140
9.5	Modus or obligation	141
9.6	Estate massing	143
9.7	Customary law of succession	147
This chapter in essence		149

9.1 Introduction

In South African law, testators enjoy an almost unlimited freedom of testation. Because of this, the content of wills may vary greatly. A testator may stipulate whatever he or she wishes in a will, and may use any wording that he or she pleases. Through the years, certain concepts which recur in wills have been identified and given names. These legal concepts have been defined by our courts and legal writers, and their consequences have been discussed and explained repeatedly. All the concepts have certain consequences on the vesting of testamentary beneficiaries' rights and may affect the way in which a beneficiary is allowed to deal with his or her inheritance after the testator's death.

When drafting a will, it is therefore important to take the consequences of certain stipulations into consideration. It goes without saying that it is important to consider the legal ramifications of each concept, but it is also important to consider the practical consequences for the beneficiaries after the testator's death.

Given that testators have freedom of testation as to what stipulations they can include in their wills, it is almost impossible to examine all possible stipulations. It is also difficult to predict the outcome of the interpretation of a concept in every single will as the use of these concepts and their meaning depend greatly on the testator's intention. For this reason, the precedent system is of limited assistance when interpreting these concepts.

The **precedent system** is also known as ***stare decisis***—'to stand by that which is decided'. South Africa follows the principle of *stare decisis* which means that when a court makes a decision, it establishes a precedent that has to be followed by other courts in their future judgments. The precedent system is especially utilised in common law systems where judges are greatly involved in making law; when judges interpret the law, it leads to a common understanding of how law should be interpreted.

9.2 Vesting of rights

When a benefit is left to a beneficiary, the beneficiary obtains certain rights or interests to the benefit after the testator's death. For example, if a house is left to a beneficiary, the right to ownership vests in the beneficiary. The word 'vesting' means that a person becomes the holder of a right.[1]

Although the focus here is on testate succession, the principles concerning vesting are also applicable to intestate succession.

> Testator Tom's will provides:
> 'I leave my house to my daughter, Delia.'
>
> When the rights to the house have unconditionally vested in Delia, she becomes the holder of all the competencies and rights of ownership to the house. In other words, she may use, enjoy and alienate the house after vesting of ownership has taken place.

The date when vesting will take place depends on the intention of the testator as indicated in the will.[2] The fact that a right has vested in a beneficiary does not necessarily mean that the right to enjoy or exercise the right already exists.[3] Vesting consists of two sub-moments, namely *dies cedit*, the time when a beneficiary gets a vested right to claim delivery of the bequeathed benefit unconditionally, and *dies venit*, the time at which the beneficiary's right to claim delivery of the benefit becomes enforceable. The testator may postpone either *dies cedit* or *dies venit*, or both, to any moment after the date of his or her death.[4]

Unless there is an explicit stipulation to the contrary in a testator's will, it is presumed that he or she intended the bequeathed benefit to vest in the beneficiary immediately on his or her death.[5] Both *dies cedit* and *dies venit* are therefore presumed to arrive immediately upon the testator's death.

PAUSE FOR REFLECTION

Vesting

Nowadays the process of the administration of estates takes some time to complete and one has to keep in mind that vesting will be affected by this process.[6] In *Greenberg v*

1 *Jewish Colonial Trust Ltd v Estate Nathan* 1940 AD 163 at 175–176; *Konyn v Viedge Bros (Pty) Ltd* 1961 (2) SA 816 (E) at 823. Although delivery is required for ownership, the explanation here is kept in simple terms in order to clarify *dies cedit* and *dies venit*.

2 *Wasserman v Sackstein* 1980 (2) SA 536 (O) at 540D–E; *Webb v Davis* 1998 (2) SA 975 (SCA) at 981H–I.

3 *Jewish Colonial Trust Ltd v Estate Nathan* 1940 AD 163 at 175–176; *Konyn v Viedge Bros (Pty) Ltd* 1961 (2) SA 816 (E) at 823.

4 *Estate Cato v Estate Cato* 1915 AD 290; *Greenberg v Estate Greenberg* 1955 (3) SA 361 (A) at 364; *Ramsumer v The Master (NPD)* 1978 (4) SA 877 (N) at 881; *Durandt v Pienaar* 2000 (4) All SA 77 (C).

5 *Estate Cato v Estate Cato* 1915 AD 290 at 306; *McEwan's Estate v McEwan's Estate* 1933 CPD 489 at 496–497.

6 Administration of estates is discussed in Chapter 15.

Estate Greenberg,[7] the Court explains that a beneficiary does not obtain the ownership of the property immediately on the death of the testator, but instead obtains a vested right to claim delivery of the inherited property from the testator's executor at some future date, namely after confirmation of the liquidation and distribution account. However, for convenience sake, it is generally stated that vesting takes place at the time of the death of the testator.

It is important to take note of the time when vesting takes place as it has several effects:

1. The time of vesting (*dies cedit*) affects whether a beneficiary may transfer rights he or she has received from the testator's estate.

Toby provides in his will:
'I leave my house to my son, Xeno. My wife may, however, live in the house for ten years after my death.'

In this example, *dies cedit* takes place for Xeno on Toby's death – he gets a vested right to the ownership of the house. (In fact, he only gets this ownership after the administration process has been completed.) He may, however, not enjoy his vested right for a period of ten years as the right to live in the house has been given to someone else.[8] In this example, Xeno's right to claim physical delivery or enjoyment of the house (*dies venit*) has been postponed. If Xeno should die before the expiry of the ten-year period, the fact that *dies cedit* has occurred means that his vested right to the house will form an asset in his estate and will be transferred to his heirs. He may also bequeath the house to his own choice of heir in his own will.

Contrast the following example:
'I leave my house to my son, Xeno, if he obtains an LLB degree.'

Until Xeno obtains the LLB degree, *dies cedit* does not take place for him. If Xeno dies before obtaining the degree, the house cannot be transferred to his heirs as the rights have not vested in him (*dies cedit* has not taken place).

2. Accrual does not operate once a beneficiary's rights have vested.[9]

Ted provides in his will:
'I leave my house to my friends, Xavier and Yolanda.'

If Xavier dies before Ted, the question would arise whether his share in the house may accrue to Yolanda, in other words whether accrual may take place. In this example, the wording indicates that the testator would have wanted Yolanda to inherit the house in its entirety in the event of Xavier being unable to inherit his share. If, however, Xavier died two months after Ted, *dies cedit* and *dies venit* would have already taken place and consequently Xavier's heirs and not Yolanda, would be entitled to inherit Xavier's share in the house.

---

7 1955 (3) SA 361 (A) at 364; see also *Galliers v Rycroft* (1900) 17 SC 569; *Durandt v Pienaar* 2000 (4) SA 869 (C).

8 See the discussion of usufruct in Chapter 10.

9 *Steenkamp v De Villiers* (1892–1893) 10 SC 56; *Mijiet's Executors v Ava* (1897) 14 SC 511; *Bradfield v Bradfield's Executors* 1914 CPD 147; *Ex parte Wessels* 1946 OPD 123 at 131. See the discussion of accrual in Chapter 10.

3. Vesting can be a determining factor in the solution of problems relating to the distribution of surplus capital or income amongst trust beneficiaries.

   If Thabiso creates a testamentary trust and provides that the income from the trust must be distributed amongst his three sons annually on 1 March, it means that vesting (*dies cedit* and *dies venit*) to the income takes place every year on 1 March. If he further provides that the capital be distributed when his youngest son turns 25, *dies cedit* and *dies venit* take place when the youngest turns 25 and the capital will then be shared amongst the three sons.

4. Vesting can also determine whether the acceleration of interests in cases of repudiation or renunciation by a beneficiary should take place.

   Theresa left her farm to her husband, William, on condition that it should pass to her son, Jonty, if William ever remarries. Upon Theresa's death, William repudiates the farm. The question is now whether acceleration of the interest in the farm to Jonty may take place. In other words, may Jonty become the owner of the farm immediately? In such an example, it is likely that the testator's intention was to provide for her husband until he remarried and as William has repudiated, she would have wanted vesting in Jonty to take place immediately.

9.3 Bequests

Figure 9.1 shows the ways in which a testator may make bequests in his or her will. An absolute or unconditional bequest is the simplest and most straightforward way for a testator to make a bequest. A conditional bequest, on the other hand, is one which postpones the vesting of rights. In other words, vesting will only take place if and when an uncertain future event occurs. A conditional bequest may also be one which terminates a beneficiary's rights upon the happening of an uncertain future event.

Figure 9.1 *Different ways of making bequests*

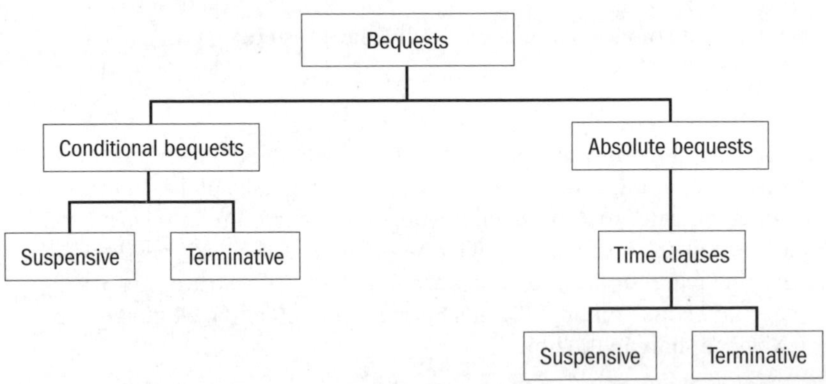

9.3.1 Absolute bequests

An absolute bequest is a bequest which does not contain any conditions. It is the simplest way of making a bequest and the effect of such a bequest is that vesting normally takes place upon the testator's death.

Bongani provides in his will:
'I leave my house to my daughter, Donna.'

In this example, there are no conditions attached to the bequest and the beneficiary's rights vest immediately upon the death of the testator. Both *dies cedit* and *dies venit* take place at the same time and the beneficiary becomes owner of the benefit. There is also no possibility that the benefit left to the beneficiary will perhaps cease to be his or hers in future if a specific uncertain event takes place. It is an absolute bequest and, as such, the subject matter of the bequest forms part of the estate of the beneficiary and will pass on to his or her heirs.

Where the testator leaves a specific asset to a beneficiary, such as a house, a farm, or a specific amount of money, the bequest is known as a **legacy**. The beneficiary of a legacy is called a **legatee**. A legatee always inherits a specific asset or a specific sum of money.

Where a testator leaves his entire estate, a specific share thereof or the residue thereof to a certain beneficiary, such a bequest is called an **inheritance** and the beneficiary is called an **heir**. If a testator leaves his or her entire estate to a single person, the beneficiary is called a **sole heir**.

John Mayor has the following bequests stipulated in his will:

'I leave my farm Boschkop to my son, Ben.'
'I leave my motor car and R10 000 cash to my daughter, Crystal.'
'My wife, Wendy, is to receive R100 000 in cash.'
'My shares in ABC (Pty) Ltd are to go to my friend, Molly.'
'The residue of my estate is to be shared equally between Crystal and Ben.'

There are four beneficiaries and they can be further classified as follows:

- Ben is a legatee because he inherits a specific benefit or a legacy, namely a farm.
- Crystal is a legatee because she inherits a specific benefit or a legacy (the motor car is one legacy and the specific amount of money (R10 000) is another legacy).
- Wendy is a legatee because she inherits a specific amount of money or a legacy (R100 000).
- Molly is a legatee because she inherits a specific benefit or a legacy (the shares).
- Crystal and Ben are both also heirs because they inherit the residue of the estate.

In this example, there is no sole heir. Had John left his entire estate to Ben, Ben would have been the sole heir.

The question whether a beneficiary is a legatee or an heir depends upon the language and the surrounding circumstances of each will.[10] The difference between heirs and legatees is important for the process of administration of the estate as it affects the order of payment of beneficiaries and collation.[11] Legacies always enjoy preference over inheritances. After the executor has paid the testator's debts, he or she must first transfer the legacies to the legatees before transferring inheritances to heirs. If the legacies are of equal value to the value of the estate after the creditors have been paid, nothing will be left for the heirs. It is also possible to create a pre-legacy in a will. Such a pre-legacy has precedence over all other legacies and inheritances.

> 'I leave R1 million to my wife Marcia which has to be paid to her before all other beneficiaries receive their bequests.'
>
> With this provision the testator can ensure that his wife receives her legacy before any of the other legatees receive theirs.

In the example given above, John Mayor stipulated that the residue of his estate was to be shared equally between Crystal and Ben. The **residue** of an estate (or **residuary estate**) is the property that remains in the deceased's estate after all legacies have been paid out and all debts, taxes, administrative fees and other administration costs have been paid. It is what is left in the estate after everything has been paid out or transferred and it includes all bequests that have failed or lapsed.

> The gross value of John Mayor's estate was R2 million. After deducting debts and costs from this amount, the executor has to deduct the value of the legacies, namely the farm (R1 million), the value of the motor car (R100 000), cash for Crystal (R10 000), cash for Wendy (R100 000), and shares in ABC (Pty) Ltd for Molly (R15 000). If the debts and other costs, for example funeral costs, administration costs, and taxes amount to R50 000, the amount left over after the legacies are deducted (R725 000) will be divided equally between Crystal and Ben as residuary heirs.

If the funds in the estate are not sufficient to pay the creditors and the legatees, the heirs receive nothing. If the debts exceed the funds available in the residue of the estate, the legacies will be proportionately reduced and the heirs will receive nothing.

> In the example above, had John Mayor's debts and administration costs amounted to R775 000, Crystal and Ben would not have received anything from the residue of the estate and only the legatees would have inherited their legacies after the creditors had been paid. Had the debts exceeded the R775 000 still available in the estate, the legacies would have had to be proportionately reduced as well.

A further important reason to distinguish between heirs and legatees involves collation. Heirs may be compelled to collate certain benefits (in other words, to account for the benefits they received during the testator's lifetime), while legatees are not obliged to collate.[12]

10 *Ex parte Macdonald* 1947 (2) SA 150 (C); *Cohen v Roetz* 1992 (1) SA 629 (A); *Els v Els* 1993 (2) SA 436 (E).
11 See Chapter 1 for the distinction between a legacy and an inheritance.
12 See collation in Chapter 12.

9.3.1.1 When does a legacy lapse?

If, for some reason or other, effect cannot be given to the legacy, it depends on the intention of the testator whether the legacy will fail or not.[13] In general, a legacy will lapse or fail in the following circumstances:

- Ademption
  Ademption is a form of tacit revocation of a legacy. If a testator voluntarily alienates the object of a legacy during his or her lifetime, the legacy fails. If a testator therefore sells the object of a legacy solely for reasons of convenience, ademption takes place.[14] If the alienation of the bequeathed asset was not voluntary, for example if the testator sold the asset because he or she had pressing debts to discharge or because of some similar necessity, the bequest will not be revoked.[15] In such a case, the executor of the testator's estate will be under an obligation to purchase the asset for the estate in order to implement the legacy, or to pay the legatee the value of the asset if it is not possible to acquire it.[16] The cost of implementing the legacy in this way will reduce the amount of the residue of the estate that goes to the heirs and will, of course, be dependent on sufficient funds being available in the estate. Clearly, ademption will not occur if an asset is attached by the Sheriff of the Court and sold to satisfy a judgment. However, necessity is something more than simply avoiding inconvenience.

In *Barrow v The Master*,[17] the testator had bequeathed a half-share of the farm *Longridge* to his son who managed the farm. Because of the considerable distances that his son had to travel each day to reach *Longridge*, the testator later sold that farm and purchased the farm *Patchwood* in its place. The testator did not alter his will to refer to *Patchwood* and, on his death, it was held that the legacy of a half-share of *Longridge* had lapsed by ademption. The son's argument that the sale had been made out of necessity because of the impracticality of travelling the considerable distance to *Longridge*, was rejected. The sale was seen as a matter of convenience, not necessity. This conclusion was fortified by the fact that the testator had been able to put off selling until he was able to obtain the price that he had set.

Tulani left her house in Parktown to her son, Dumi, in her will. About two years before her death, she experienced financial difficulties and the house was sold in execution. She never changed her will and the bequest remained in her will. Approximately one year before her death, Tulani managed to recover from her financial difficulties and, in fact, died a wealthy woman. As her house in Parktown had been sold in execution, the object of the legacy had been alienated. However, the testator did not have the intention of revoking the bequest. Dumi, the legatee, is therefore entitled to the value of the legacy or to the bequest itself if the executor is able to recover it.[18]

---

13 *Barrow v The Master* 1960 (3) SA 253 (E) at 256G–H.
14 *Sorge v Estate Preuss* 1933 CPD 61 at 65; *Barrow v The Master* 1960 (3) SA 253 (E) at 257.
15 *Barrow v The Master* 1960 (3) SA 253 (E) at 257A.
16 See *Attridge v Lambert* 1977 (2) SA 90 (D) regarding the executor's obligations when the testator knowingly bequeaths property that does not belong to him.
17 1960 (3) SA 253 (E).
18 *Attridge v Lambert* 1977 (2) SA 90 (D); *Dempers v The Master (1)* 1977 (4) SA 44 (SWA); *Jowell v Bramwell-Jones* 1998 (1) SA 836 (W).

- **Legatee dies before the legacy vests in him or her.** This is obvious in light of the ground rule that a beneficiary must be alive in order to inherit.[19] If s 2C of the Wills Act applies, the legatee will be substituted ***ex lege*** ('by virtue of law') and the legacy will not fail.[20]
- **Legatee repudiates the legacy.** If a legatee repudiates the legacy and a substitute has not been named in the will, and if s 2C of the Wills Act does not apply, the legacy will fall into the residue of the estate to be shared by the residuary heirs.
- **Legatee is incapable of inheriting.**[21] If a legatee is incapable of inheriting, for example because he had murdered the testator, and neither substitution nor accrual is possible, the legacy will fall into the residue of the estate.
- **Bequeathed object is destroyed.** If the object of the legacy is destroyed and there is nothing which can be inherited, it is assumed that the testator revoked the bequest.
- **Testator's estate is insolvent.** If the testator's estate is insolvent, there can be no transfer of legacies to the legatees because all the assets of the estate must be used to repay the creditors of the estate.

9.3.1.2 Time clauses

Although absolute bequests are made with no conditions attached, they may be made subject to a time clause or term. Such a time clause may be either suspensive or terminative, and exactly when the time will be may be certain or uncertain.

If a bequest is subject to a time clause, it is subject to an event that will certainly happen in the future, although it may be certain or uncertain when it will arrive. A **bequest subject to a suspensive time clause** is a bequest by which the beneficiary will receive the benefit only at a certain future time. A bequest subject to a suspensive time clause is thus a bequest where the beneficiary will have to wait (he or she is kept in suspense) until a certain time to receive the benefit.

A **bequest subject to a terminative (resolutive) time clause** is one in which the beneficiary's rights are terminated when a certain time arrives. According to a terminative time clause, a beneficiary's already established rights terminate when a certain time arrives.

> Tintswalo provides in her will:
>
> 'I leave my farm to my son, Siyabonga, but it shall only be transferred to him when he reaches the age of 21.'
>
> This is a suspensive time clause because it is certain. It is not a condition as vesting is not postponed until the happening of an uncertain future event nor do the rights terminate upon the happening of an unceratin future event. If the testator's son should die after the testator but before he turns 21, his heirs would be entitled to take the farm. The reason for this entitlement is that *dies cedit* takes place for the son on the death of the testator, but *dies venit* is postponed until he turns 21. He therefore receives a vested right to claim delivery of the bequeathed benefit unconditionally (*dies cedit*) at the time of the testator's death. The time at which this right becomes enforceable (*dies venit*) is, however, postponed until a certain time, namely when he turns 21.

19 See Chapter 1.
20 See the discussion of direct substitution in Chapter 10.
21 Circumstances of incapacity are discussed in Chapter 7.

'I leave my farm to my son, James. When he dies or reaches the age of 60 years, it is to go to the National Research Institute to be used as an agricultural research station.'

James will acquire ownership of the farm subject to a terminative time clause. Although it is uncertain when he will die, it is certain that he will reach 60 or that he will die. In this example, *dies cedit* as well as *dies venit* take place for James on the testator's death, but his rights terminate when he either dies or reaches the age of 60. Consequently, it is certain that James' ownership will terminate and his heirs will never inherit the farm.

9.3.2 Conditional bequests

A **conditional bequest** is one which depends on a future event which is uncertain in the sense that it may or may not occur. Conditional bequests often contain words such as 'if' or 'should.' In order to be valid, a condition must be clear and possible. In addition, it may not be illegal or *contra bonos mores*. If a condition fails in one of these respects, it is invalid and void, and held to be *pro non scripto*. This means that the condition falls away and the bequest becomes unconditional.[22]

There are two kinds of conditions found in wills, namely resolutive or suspensive conditions. It is important to consider the effect of both these kinds of condition on the vesting of rights before deciding on the wording to be used in a will.

9.3.2.1 Resolutive (or terminative) conditions

A **bequest subject to a terminative condition** is one in which the bequest is made to terminate in the event of a particular uncertain future state of affairs.[23]

Tebogo provides in his will:
'I leave my farm to my wife, Ayanda. Should she remarry, my farm is to go to SANParks.'

This is a resolutive condition as it is uncertain whether the widow will remarry or not. If she does remarry, her rights to the farm will terminate and she will no longer own the farm. Upon the happening of this uncertain future event, the condition will be fulfilled and the farm will become the property of SANParks. If the testator's wife does not remarry, the farm will remain her property until she dies, and it will then go to her heirs and not to SANParks.

In this example, both *dies cedit* and *dies venit* take place for Tebogo's wife upon his death but her rights terminate if the resolutive condition is fulfilled. In the same example, it will be a suspensive condition for SANParks – see discussion further on.

9.3.2.2 Suspensive conditions

When a **bequest is made subject to a suspensive condition**, the beneficiary does not acquire a vested right to the object of the bequest unless and until a particular uncertain future state of affairs comes to pass. The vesting of the beneficiary's rights is therefore suspended

22 See *Grusd v Grusd* 1946 AD 465; *Aronson v Estate Hart* 1950 (1) SA 539 (A); *De Klerk v De Witt* 1973 (3) SA 865 (NC); *Ex parte Dessels* 1976 (1) SA 851 (D) and the discussion in Chapter 4.

23 *Grusd v Grusd* 1946 AD 465; *Ex parte Fleishman* 1983 (4) SA 866 (E) at 871.

(postponed) until the uncertain future event occurs. Until the condition is fulfilled, the beneficiary has no transmissible right that would form an asset in his or her estate upon death or insolvency.[24]

> Chandana provides in her will:
> 'I leave my racehorse stud farm to my son Pavan should he win the Durban July Handicap.'
>
> If Pavan has not won the race by the time the testator dies, it is uncertain whether he will ever win it. If he does not win the race before his own death, the farm never becomes his property – *dies cedit* and *dies venit* never take place for him and his heirs cannot inherit the farm from him. If, however, he does win the race, the farm becomes his immediately after winning.

The effect of a suspensive condition is usually to postpone *dies cedit* while a resolutive condition does not do so. However, the possibility does exist for a beneficiary to lose his or her vested right to a bequest if a resolutive condition is fulfilled.

A suspensive condition usually has a corresponding resolutive condition. Consider the example used above again:

> Pavan's right to the farm is subject to his winning the Durban July Handicap. It is therefore subject to a suspensive condition. However, there is also a resolutive condition in this bequest. Before the suspensive condition is fulfilled, the stud farm falls into the residue of the estate and the residuary heirs inherit the farm in the interim. In turn, their rights to the stud farm are subject to a resolutive condition – if Pavan wins the Durban July Handicap, they lose their rights to the farm.
>
> A result of the use of a condition is that a fideicommissum is created. The fiduciary's right is always subject to a resolutive condition while the fideicommissary's right is subject to a suspensive condition. The use of these conditions implies that the person subject to the resolutive condition (the fiduciary) has to pass the benefit to the person subject to the suspensive condition (the fideicommissary). This statement also holds true where resolutive and suspensive time clauses are used.
>
> In the example above, the residuary heirs are the fiduciaries who are obliged to hand over the farm to Pavan (the fideicommissary) as soon as the resolutive condition applicable to them is fulfilled (in other words, as soon as Pavan wins the race).

9.4 *Nudum praeceptum*

If a testator bequeaths property to a beneficiary but prohibits him or her from dealing with the property in a certain way (for example alienating the property), such a prohibition will only be valid if someone else has been nominated by the testator to take the property should the beneficiary contravene the prohibition.[25]

---

24 *Jewish Colonial Trust Ltd v Estate Nathan* 1940 AD 163 at 176; *Commissioner for Inland Revenue v Sive's Estate* 1955 (1) SA 249 (A) at 269; *Wasserman v Sackstein* 1980 (2) SA 536 (O).

25 *Jewish Colonial Trust Ltd v Estate Nathan* 1940 AD 163 at 180; *Van Soelen v Van Soelen* 1964 (4) SA 24 (O); *Ruskin v Sapire* 1966 (2) SA 306 (W); *Ex parte Roads* 1978 (4) SA 649 (O).

If no provision is made for a substitute or 'gift over' in the event of contravention of the prohibition, the prohibition is called a ***nudum praeceptum*** or **nude prohibition** and is not legally binding.[26]

The following bequest is an example of a *nudum praeceptum* because a substitute is not indicated:

'I leave my trout farm to my son, Philani. He may not leave the farm permanently during his lifetime.'

The following bequest contains a valid prohibition beause it provides a substitute:

'I leave my trout farm to my son, Philani. If he leaves the farm permanently during his lifetime, my daughter, Sithelo, will inherit the farm.'

This principle is also important in the creation of a valid fideicommissum as a fideicommissum cannot exist without a proper 'gift over'.[27]

9.5 Modus or obligation

If a testator makes a bequest subject to a burden or obligation, this provision is called a **modus**. A modus is a qualification added to a gift or testamentary disposition whereby the person benefited is required to devote the property he or she receives, or the value thereof, in whole or in part to a specific purpose.[28]

Including a modus in a bequest does not make the bequest conditional nor does it postpone the vesting of a beneficiary's rights.[29] The difference between a modus and a suspensive condition is that when a modus is used, vesting of the beneficiary's rights is not postponed unlike the position when a suspensive condition is used, but takes place immediately upon the testator's death.[30] The modus also does not affect the beneficiary's rights if he or she does not comply with it although the beneficiary does, in certain circumstances, render himself or herself liable to a personal action if he or she does not comply with the modus.[31]

9.5.1 Types of modus

The testator may have different objectives for adding a modus to a bequest:

- **The modus may be in the interest of the beneficiary.**

  'I leave R500 000 to my son, Petrus, to be used to pay for his LLB studies.'

---

26 *Pritchard's Trustee v Estate Pritchard* 1912 CPD 87; *Vickers' Trustees v Cloete* 1914 CPD 575; *Estate Freedman v Freedman* 1962 (3) SA 79 (W); *Morley v Standard Bank Trustees Department* 1970 (4) SA 299 (W); *Ex parte Roads* 1978 (4) SA 649 (O); *Vorster v Steyn* 1981 (2) SA 831 (O); *Smit v Du Toit* 1981 (3) SA 1249 (A).

27 See the discussion of the fideicommissum in Chapter 10.

28 *Jewish Colonial Trust Ltd v Estate Nathan* 1940 AD 163 at 176; *Ex parte Mouton* 1955 (4) SA 460 (A); *Wessels v DA Wessels en Seuns (Edms) Bpk* 1987 (3) SA 530 (T); *Kerkraad van die Nederduitse Gereformeerde Kerk, Douglas v Loots* 1990 (3) SA 451 (NK).

29 *British South Africa Company v Bulawayo Municipality* 1919 AD 84; *Wessels v DA Wessels & Seuns (Edms) Bpk* 1987 (3) SA 530 (T) at 538.

30 *Holley v Commissioner for Inland Revenue* 1947 (3) SA 119 (A).

31 *Ex parte Strümpfer* 1945 OPD 268; *Ex parte Esterhuyse* 1971 (4) SA 261 (O); *Wessels v DA Wessels en Seuns (Edms) Bpk* 1987 (3) SA 530 (T) at 538.

In this example the modus (the obligation to use the money to study) is solely for the benefit of the beneficiary.

If a modus is solely for the benefit of the beneficiary who has been burdened with it, the beneficiary is not obliged to carry out the modus and no one will enforce it. He or she simply has a moral obligation to comply with the modus but non-compliance will not affect his or her rights to the bequeathed benefit.[32]

- **The modus may be in the interest of a third person.**

This form of modus is often used where a testator has fixed assets but not much other capital and wishes to benefit all his or her children without dividing the assets.

'I leave my stud farm to my son, Vusi, but he must pay R200 000 to my daughter, Nonyameko, within three years of my death,' or

'I leave my beach house to my son, Charlie, but he must pay R500 000 into my estate which has to be equally divided amongst my other three children.'

The beneficiary in whose favour the testator has made the modus then has a personal right against the beneficiary on whom the modus rests.

'I leave my fynbos farm to my son, Norman, but he must pay R200 000 to my daughter, Ilka, within three years of my death.'

Ilka may claim the R200 000 from Norman in a personal action if Norman does not pay her the money within three years of the testator's death.

Performance (in other words, the execution of the modus) may be demanded from the burdened beneficiary by the testator's executor, the Master, or by the person in whose favour the modus was made.[33] The executor may reclaim the bequeathed benefit from the beneficiary concerned if the latter refuses to carry out the modus. This takes place in the same way that a property is attached in an execution process – the benefit is attached following the enforcement of the third party's personal right. It is even possible for those persons in whose favour the modus was made to ask for security to be furnished by the beneficiary for performance of the modus.[34]

- **The modus may be for the furtherance of an impersonal object.**

'I leave R200 000 to my cousin, PJ, to be used for the decoration of my grave,' or

'I leave R200 000 to my stepson, Jody, to be used for the publication of the book I have been writing for the past ten years.'

32 *Ex parte Gardner* 1940 EDL 175 at 178.
33 *Ex parte The Dutch Reformed Church of Dewetsdorp* 1938 OPD 136; *Ex parte Wessels* 1946 OPD 123 at 132.
34 *Ex parte Gitelson* 1949 (2) SA 881 (O) at 888; *Benoni Town Council v Minister of Agricultural Credit and Land Tenure* 1978 (1) SA 978 (T).

In practice, the problem with this type of modus is that there is nobody to supervise the beneficiaries and make sure that they perform as required.[35] It is impossible for either the Master or the executor to enforce the obligation as they have no rights, personal or otherwise, that may be used to force the beneficiary to carry out the modus.[36]

9.5.2 Difference between a modus and a condition

As outlined above, the difference between a modus and a condition is that the modus does not affect the beneficiary's rights. While a suspensive condition postpones the vesting of the beneficiary's rights, a modus has no effect on the vesting of rights to the benefit. This means that the important difference between a modus and a suspensive condition is that if the burdened beneficiary dies before the performance of the modus, the bequeathed benefit still devolves upon his or her beneficiaries. This is not the case when a suspensive condition is in force. The modus will therefore form part of the estate of the burdened beneficiary, which means that any personal right obtained against the deceased by virtue of a modus may be enforced against his or her estate by the holder of the personal right. In the case of the modus for an impersonal purpose or for the benefit of the beneficiary himself or herself, the modus will not be enforceable.

In the same vein, there is also a difference between a modus and a terminative condition. In the case of a modus, the personal right that the third party has against the burdened beneficiary vests in him or her at the testator's death. At the same time, the rights of the burdened beneficiary to the benefit also vest in him or her and these vested rights will not be lost if the modus is not carried out. The third party may, however, institute a personal action against the burdened beneficiary in terms of the personal right. In a terminative condition, on the other hand, the beneficiary loses the vested rights if the condition is fulfilled.

9.6 Estate massing

Estate massing is a popular concept used in joint or mutual wills in South Africa. The basic idea is that two or more testators (in practice, almost without exception two spouses) mass the whole or parts of their estates into one consolidated economic unit for the purpose of testamentary disposal. Normally, the disposal becomes effective upon the death of the first testator.

Couples married in community of property often use estate massing as a tool to ensure that the survivor will continue to be in control of the massed estates during his or her lifetime and thus continue to enjoy the same standard of living. It is, however, not a prerequisite for the operation of estate massing that the testators be married in community of property, nor that they be married at all.[37] In *Estate Koopmans v Estate De Wet*,[38] for example, the parties who consolidated their estates were sisters.

The requirements for estate massing to take place are:

- the intention of the parties to consolidate their estates

---

35 *Donaghy v Estate Hablutzel* (1905) 22 SC 162; *Bagnall v Colonial Government* (1907) 24 SC 470; *Dalrymple v Colonial Treasurer* 1910 TPD 372; *The Town Council of Bloemfontein v Bloemfontein Licensing Board and John Duff* 1917 OPD 34 at 41.

36 *Ex parte Strümpfer* 1945 OPD 268; *Estate Freedman v Freedman* 1962 (3) SA 79 (W).

37 *In re Murray's Estate: Ex parte Mulhearn* (1901) 18 SC 213 at 216; *Rhode v Stubbs* 2005 (5) SA 104 (SCA).

38 1912 CPD 1961.

- the first-dying testator must have disposed of the survivor's share of the joint estate as well as of his or her own.[39] (Where a testator has disposed of his or her own estate only in a will, there can never be any question of estate massing.[40])
- the surviving testator must adiate the massing.

For this reason, estate massing is traditionally seen as a manifestation of the doctrine of election or choice. The doctrine of election is applicable in all cases where acceptance of a benefit in a will holds some kind of burden or obligation for the beneficiary. The beneficiary has to make a choice - to adiate both the benefit and the burden or obligation, or not to repudiate the benefit and burden or obligation attached to the benefit.[41]

Estate massing imposes a burden on the survivor because the estate of the survivor will also devolve in terms of the mutual will whilst he or she is still alive.[42] This means that the survivor loses his or her freedom of testation regarding his or her own estate. In order to accept the benefits left to him or her, the survivor must give effect to the mutual will. If the survivor changes his or her mind and no longer wants estate massing to take place, he or she may repudiate the bequest and not accept any benefit under the will. He or she then retains his or her own property and may do with it as he or she pleases.[43]

PAUSE FOR REFLECTION

Estate massing

The motive for instituting estate massing is often to protect the children born of the marriage of the testators whilst at the same time providing for the survivor. Estate massing ensures the preservation of the joint or consolidated estate and makes it possible for the surviving spouse to educate and support any minor children in accordance with the standard of living to which the family was accustomed.

9.6.1 How can estate massing be effected?

Estate massing can be effected through the use of different legal institutions. The rights of the survivor and the rights of the beneficiaries of the first-dying testator, in all instances, depend on the legal institution used, namely a usufruct, a fideicommissum or a trust.

1. **Usufruct.** Anna and Bill mass their estates and stipulate that upon the death of the first-dying, the whole massed estate will go to their son, Charlie, subject to a lifelong usufruct in favour of the surviving spouse.
2. **Fideicommissum.** Corne and Delilah mass their estates and stipulate that upon the death of the first-dying, the massed estate will go to the survivor, and upon the death of the survivor, to their children in equal shares. In this example, a fideicommissum is created, with the survivor as fiduciary and the children as fideicommissaries.
3. **Trust.** Elise and Frank mass their estates and stipulate that, upon the death of the first-dying, the massed estate shall be transferred to a trust to be administered

39 *The Receiver of Revenue Pretoria v Hancke* 1915 AD 64 at 72.
40 *Ex parte Gouws* 1952 (3) SA 793 (E) at 798; *Ex parte Malan* 1951 (3) SA 715 (E) 721.
41 See discussion in Chapter 3.
42 See again Chapter 1 where the exceptions to the ground rules for succession were discussed.
43 *Harvey v Estate Harvey* 1914 CPD 892 at 896; *The Receiver of Revenue Pretoria v Hancke* 1915 AD 64 at 72; *Rhode v Stubbs* 2005 (5) SA 104 (SCA).

by an appointed trustee. During the lifetime of the survivor, he or she receives an income (in other words, he or she is an income beneficiary), and following the death of the survivor, the trust capital (corpus) goes to their children in equal shares.

4. **Unlimited rights.** Gita and Husani mass their estates and stipulate that the family home will go to the survivor and the rest of the estate property to the children in equal shares.

The rights which are vested upon the death of the first-dying (in other words, the rights of the survivor and other beneficiaries) depend on the relevant legal institution used in the massing. In the first example, the surviving spouse is the usufructuary (holder of the usufruct) and the son, Charlie, becomes the remainderman. In the second example, the survivor is the fiduciary and the children are the fideicommissaries as in any fideicommissum.[44] In the third example, the survivor is simply the income beneficiary, the children are capital beneficiaries and, upon the death of the first-dying, their rights are established accordingly. In these three examples, the survivor only obtained a limited right (a usufruct, fiduciary right or trust income) but in the fourth example, the survivor obtains an unlimited right in the house and can leave it to whoever he or she pleases in his or her will. This last example is not covered by s 37 of the Administration of Estates Act[45] and may be referred to as common law estate massing.

9.6.2 Section 37 of the Administration of Estates Act

Section 37 of the Administration of Estates Act regulates estate massing and its effects. The requirements are the following:

- There must be a mutual will. Section 37 will not apply to estate massing in an antenuptial contract or in a will of a sole testator, although there is no logical reason why the ultimate beneficiaries should be in a better position merely because their benefits are contained in a mutual will.
- There must be two or more persons who are parties to the mutual will; they need not be married to each other.
- Some or all of the property of each testator must be consolidated into a single mass and this mass, or part of it, must be disposed of by the mutual will.

  The mutual will must give the survivor 'a limited interest in respect of any property in the massed estate'. Such limited interest may be in the form of various legal institutions, such as usufruct, fideicommissum or trust[46] (see the examples above). An outright bequest of the property of the first-dying which does not form part of the massed estate will not be sufficient to bring s 37 into operation (see example 4 above).
- The survivor must adiate the bequest. In *Rhode v Stubbs*[47] it was made clear that estate massing only takes effect once the survivor has accepted the benefit.

44 See the discussion in Chapter 10.
45 See the discussion below.
46 See Chapter 10.
47 *Rhode v Stubbs* 2005 (5) SA 104 (SCA).

- The disposition must take place at some time on or after the death of the first-dying. Although s 37 specifically refers to 'after' the death of the first-dying, it probably includes a disposition taking place on the death of the first-dying.[48]

9.6.3 Consequences of estate massing

It should be clear by now that estate massing will only occur once all the requirements have been met. A survivor may adiate or repudiate estate massing.

9.6.3.1 Consequences of adiation

Firstly, one of the most important consequences of adiation is that the surviving testator loses the power to alter or revoke the joint (mutual) will after adiation. Once the survivor accepts a benefit under the mutual will, he or she loses the ability to revoke the will or to make a will which is in conflict with the provisions of the mutual will. Thus, by accepting a benefit under such a will, the surviving testator renounces the power to dispose of his or her own estate in a manner different from that in which the first-dying testator has already disposed of it in the will. This is because the survivor's estate becomes part of the massed estate which has already been disposed of.[49] This is a serious infringement on the survivor's freedom of testation, and there exists a presumption against estate massing resulting from the common law rule that no one can deprive himself or herself of the power to make a last will freely.

If there is any reasonable doubt that the testators had intended to achieve estate massing, the will is interpreted in a manner that allows the greatest possible measure of freedom of testation. In addition, it will be seen as if the first-dying testator has disposed of his or her estate only.[50] In *Rhode v Stubbs,*[51] the Court also makes it clear that the fact that testators who were married in community of property made a mutual will does not mean that they intended to effect estate massing. According to the common law rules of interpretation, when interpreting a joint or mutual will of parties married in community of property one has to start off with the premise that one is dealing with two separate wills of the parties until the contrary becomes clear.

Secondly, at common law the beneficiaries other than the survivor (called the 'ultimate beneficiaries' - in the examples above, the children) were not entitled to claim any real rights in that part of the massed property which the survivor contributed. They had personal rights only against the survivor. This meant that the children had no *dominium* or ownership (real right) in the survivor's bequest and acquired such *dominium* only on the death of the survivor. If, therefore, the survivor was sequestrated after having accepted benefits under the will creating the estate massing, these beneficiaries would have only a concurrent claim in the property which the survivor contributed to the consolidated mass of property.[52]

This position was changed by s 37 of the Administration of Estates Act. The ultimate beneficiaries of the massed property now obtain the same rights in respect of the survivor's part of the massed property as they do to the property of the first-dying. If, therefore, a

48 In *Rosenberg v Dry's Executors* 1911 AD 679 the disposition to the children took place on the death of the first-dying; see also *Greenberg v Estate Greenberg* 1955 (3) SA 361 (A); *Standard Bank of SA Ltd v Estate C.J. van Rooyen* 1927 (NPD) 300.

49 *Secretary SA Association v Mostert* (1869) 2 Buch 231 at 264; *The Receiver of Revenue Pretoria v Hancke* 1915 AD 64 at 72; *Rhode v Stubbs* 2005 (5) SA 104 (SCA).

50 *D'Oyly-John v Lousada* 1957 (1) SA 368 (N) at 373; *Kruger v Terblanche* 1978 (2) SA 198 (T) at 205; *Brummund v Brummund's Estate* 1993 (2) SA 494 (Nm) at 500; *Rhode v Stubbs* 2005 (5) SA 104 (SCA).

51 2005 (5) SA 104 (SCA) at para 22.

52 *Rosenberg v Dry's Executors* 1911 AD 679.

mutual will of spouses married in community of property provides that the whole joint estate is to be consolidated into one mass and bequeathed to the children subject to a usufruct in favour of the surviving spouse, the children will not only be entitled to claim ownership of the first-dying's share of the joint estate from the executor, but they will also be entitled to claim ownership of the half that belongs to the survivor. Section 37, therefore, gives the children the same rights in respect of both the survivor's and the first-dying's share of the joint estate. The children would be entitled to claim transfer of both halves of any immovable property concerned.[53]

9.6.3.2 Consequences of repudiation

If, on the death of the first-dying testator, the survivor elects not to take any benefit under the will, the effects are as follows:

- The surviving testator may not receive any benefit whatsoever under the will from the estate of the first-dying testator.[54]
- The surviving testator retains his or her own estate and may dispose of it in any way he or she wishes.[55]
- The mutual will, as the will of the first-dying testator, relates to the estate of the first-dying testator only, subject to the provision that the surviving testator may not receive any benefit from the estate of the first-dying testator.[56]

From *Rhode v Stubbs*,[57] it is clear that the principles of estate massing are difficult to apply and that, if there is any reasonable doubt as to the testators' intention, the Court would rather steer clear of estate massing.

9.7 Customary law of succession

Nothing prevents a testator living under a system of customary law to make a will and to stipulate in his or her will whatever he or she wishes. A family head living under a system of customary law may make use of estate massing in a will to ensure that the family property remains within the family.[58] The Recognition of Customary Marriages Act[59] provides that the matrimonial consequences of a customary marriage concluded before the commencement of the Act (15 November 2000) are still governed by customary law. In other words, the marriage is neither in community of property, nor out of community of property, and the family head has the responsibility to see to it that all the houses (if a polygynous marriage exists) are kept separate with their separate house property. In the case of marriages concluded after the commencement of the Act, the marriage will generally be in community of property except if the spouses concluded an antenuptial contract or if a court made a new division in the case of a polygynous marriage. The family head together with his spouse (in the case of a monogamous marriage) or spouses (in the case of a polygynous marriage) could stipulate

53 Section 39 of the Administration of Estates Act. See *Rampathy v Krumm* 1978 (4) SA 935 (D) for the application of the principles regarding the rights of the respective beneficiaries.

54 *Watson v Burchell* (1891–1892) 9 SC 2 at 6–7; *Van der Merwe v Van der Merwe's Executrix* 1921 TPD 9 at 14, 17.

55 *The Receiver of Revenue Pretoria v Hancke* 1915 AD 64 at 72.

56 *The Receiver of Revenue Pretoria v Hancke* 1915 AD 64 at 72.

57 2005 (5) SA 104 (SCA).

58 See Chapter 1 for a definition of house and family property.

59 120 of 1998, which came into operation on 15 November 2000.

in a mutual will that the estates of the first-dying and surviving spouse or spouses must consolidate upon the death of the first-dying to be distributed as follows: a lifelong usufruct to the wife or wives whilst the rest of the family and house property devolves according to the rules of customary law. There is, however, no guarantee that the wishes of the family head (to mass the estate and devolve it according to the customary law of succession) will be honoured by the surviving spouse or spouses, because she or they can always decide to repudiate the massing and to forfeit the usufruct in favour of her or their portion of the estate in terms of the matrimonial rules.

In *Gumede v President of the Republic of South Africa*,[60] the following facts were before the Constitutional Court:

Elizabeth Gumede (the applicant) married Amos Gumede (the fifth respondent) on 29 May 1968 in terms of customary law. Their marriage was concluded before the Recognition of Customary Marriages Act[61] came into operation and, as a result, the matrimonial property of their marriage was still regulated in terms of customary law. The parties lived in KwaZulu-Natal under Zulu law and as a result the KwaZulu Act on the Code of Zulu Law[62] and the Natal Code of Zulu Law,[63] which set out the customary law position, applied to them. In terms of this legislation, the family head is the owner of all the property acquired during the course of the marriage. In other words, the couple is married neither in community of property nor out of community of property.

Mr and Mrs Gumede had a monogamous relationship which lasted many years before breaking down. Mr Gumede instituted divorce proceedings against Mrs Gumede in 1993. Mrs Gumede realised that she was going to lose everything as a result of Zulu law and she approached the High Court for an order that the Recognition of Customary Marriages Act[64] was unconstitutional because it differentiates between those marriages concluded before the operation of the Act and those concluded afterwards. The result of such differentiation is that the discriminatory consequences of the Zulu law in the case of matrimonial property are endorsed by the Act and only marriages after the commencement of the Act are protected. The Court agreed with this contention, and held that ss 7(1) and (2) of the Recognition of Customary Marriages Act[65] are unconstitutional and invalid insofar as they exclude a marriage concluded prior to commencement of the Act from being in community of property. The Court also declared those customary rules contained in the KwaZulu Act on the Code of Zulu Law and the Natal Code of Zulu Law insofar as it affords full ownership of property during the marriage of the parties to the family head only, unconstitutional. The order of the High Court was referred to the Constitutional Court that confirmed the High Court order with retrospective effect. It is notable that this order is only applicable to monogamous customary marriages concluded in terms of Zulu law.

60 2008 ZACC 23. To date the case is unreported and this is the reference of the Constitutional Court who delivered its judgment on 8 December 2008.

61 120 of 1998.

62 16 of 1985.

63 Proc R151 of 1987 in *GG* 10966 of 9 October 1987.

64 120 of 1998.

65 Section 7(1) makes provision for in community of property for all monogamous customary marriages concluded after the Act came into operation, and s 7(2) excludes marriages concluded before the Act came into operation.

THIS CHAPTER IN ESSENCE

1. A South African testator has almost unlimited freedom of testation and may stipulate in his or her will whatever he or she wishes. As a result, the contents of wills may vary greatly.
2. Various concepts have been identified, named, defined and documented, for example conditions, time clauses, modus, fideicommissum, usufruct, estate massing, and substitution. Each and every concept has specific requirements and consequences.
3. The terms *dies cedit* and *dies venit* are very important when dealing with vesting of rights.
4. A testator may postpone *dies cedit* or *dies venit*, or both, by means of conditions or time clauses (terms) and can make a specific benefit dependent on a condition or link it to a term or period of time.
5. There is a distinction between legacies and inheritances and this distinction plays an important role in the final distribution of an estate.
6. When a legacy fails because the legatee does not want to or cannot inherit his or her benefit (for example, he or she repudiated the legacy or he or she dies before the testator), there are three possibilities:
   - a substitute may be provided for in the will or *ex lege*,
   - accrual may take place, or
   - the bequest may fall into the residue of the estate and will be inherited by the residuary heirs.
7. Should a legacy fail and the testator has not appointed a substitute or accrual is not possible, the legacy will form part of the residue of the estate or it will form part of the intestate estate to be inherited by the intestate beneficiaries.
8. There is a distinction between suspensive and resolutive conditions with regard to their influence on *dies cedit* and *dies venit*.
9. There is also a distinction between suspensive and resolutive time clauses with regard to their influence on *dies cedit* and *dies venit*.
10. The modus has to be distinguished from a condition. The modus can manifest itself in different forms, namely:
    - in the interest of the beneficiary himself or herself
    - in the interest of a specific person
    - in the interest of an impersonal purpose.
11. If a testator places a prohibition on a bequest but fails to say what should happen with the bequest if the prohibition is contravened, it is said that the prohibition is nude (*nudum praeceptum*). In other words, the prohibition is of no effect and the beneficiary will receive the bequest free from any prohibitions.
12. Estate massing takes place when two or more testators combine or mass the whole or parts of their estates into one consolidated unit and then dispose of it in terms of their mutual will:
    - In the case of common law estate massing, a real right is transferred to the survivor.
    - In the case of statutory estate massing (s 37 of the Administration of Estates Act), a limited right is transferred to the survivor.
13. Since estate massing places a burden on the survivor, the doctrine of election comes into play - the survivor has to adiate or repudiate the massing before there can be any legal consequences.
14. The same principles are applicable to testators living under a system of customary law.

Chapter 10

Content of wills – substitution, usufruct and accrual

What are substitution, usufruct and accrual and how do they operate?

10.1	Introduction	151
10.2	Substitution	151
10.3	Direct substitution	152
10.4	Fideicommissary substitution (fideicommissum)	156
10.5	Statutory restriction on the fideicommissum	159
10.6	Legal position of the parties to a fideicommissum	159
10.7	Presumption against a fideicommissum	162
10.8	Usufruct	162
10.9	Accrual	163
10.10	Customary law of succession	167
This chapter in essence		167

10.1 Introduction

In the previous chapter we started discussing the content of wills and identified some arrangements that a testator may use in a will. In this chapter we will continue this discussion with particular reference to various forms of substitution and usufruct. We will also discuss the right of accrual.

10.2 Substitution

Substitution is an arrangement in which a testator appoints a beneficiary to inherit a benefit but simultaneously nominates another beneficiary to take the place of the appointed beneficiary (legatee or heir) upon the occurrence of an event, usually the death of the appointed beneficiary. Substitution may take place either in the alternative (direct substitution), or successively, where one beneficiary receives the benefit after another beneficiary (fideicommissary substitution or fideicommissum).

Figure 10.1 A schematic description of substitution

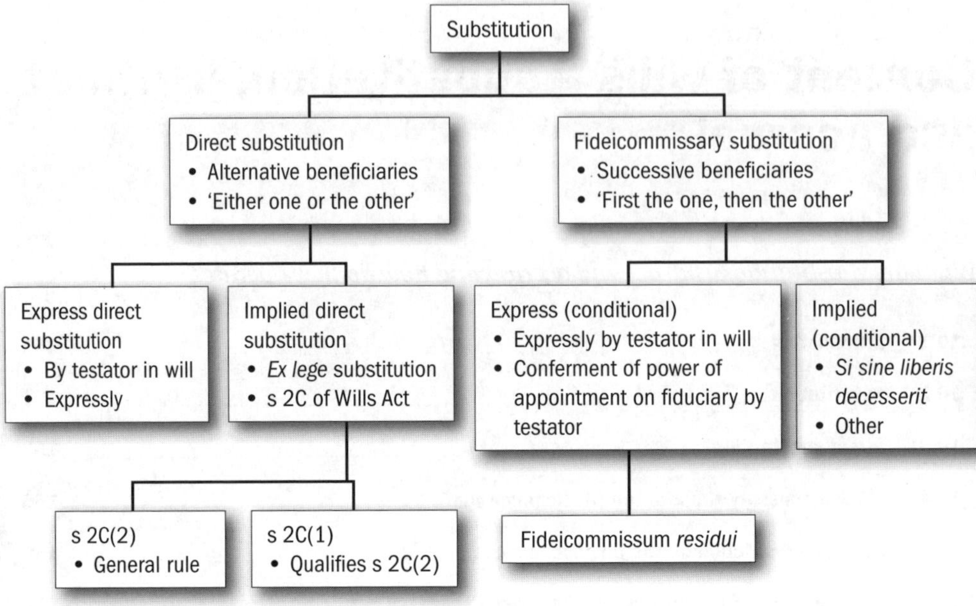

10.3 Direct substitution

If a testator nominates a beneficiary to inherit a benefit and also nominates an alternative beneficiary to take the benefit in the event that the first beneficiary does not take the benefit, it is called direct substitution. Direct substitution occurs where one or more beneficiaries are instituted in the alternative to make provision for instances where the appointed beneficiary:

- has predeceased the testator
- is disqualified from benefiting
- has repudiated the benefit
- cannot take the benefit because of the non-fulfilment of a condition.

Direct substitution can take two forms, namely express direct substitution stipulated by the testator in the will, or direct substitution implied by law (*ex lege*) in terms of s 2C of the Wills Act, where the testator has not provided for substitution. Testators use direct substitution to:

- avoid the benefit devolving in terms of the rules of intestate succession under the circumstances mentioned above (in the case of heirs)
- prevent certain assets from falling into the residue of the estate (in the case of legatees)
- exclude the right of accrual (see discussion of accrual below).

10.3.1 Express direct substitution by the testator

A clause that makes provision for direct substitution might read:

'I bequeath my house to my son, Xanor. If Xanor predeceases me, repudiates the benefit, or otherwise cannot receive the benefit, the house must pass to my daughter, Yolandi.'

The testator makes provision for beneficiaries in the alternative. Xanor is the instituted beneficiary and Yolandi is the substitute beneficiary. If Xanor is alive upon the testator's death, adiates the benefit and has capacity to inherit, Yolandi will not receive it and her interest in the house is extinguished. If, on the other hand, Xanor predeceases the testator, repudiates the benefit or is disqualified, Yolandi (if alive) will be Xanor's direct substitute and will receive the house. The respective interests of the instituted beneficiary (Xanor) and the substituted beneficiary (Yolandi) are therefore alternative and mutually exclusive. The bequest would pass directly from the testator to either Xanor or Yolandi.

PAUSE FOR REFLECTION

Ambiguous clauses

It is important that the wording of direct substitution clauses reflects the intention of the testator in a clear and unambiguous way. For example, 'I bequeath my house to my son, Constantine. Upon his death, it must pass to his sister, Erica'. This clause does not make the testator's intentions clear as it may be interpreted in two ways,[1] namely:

- as a direct substitution by Erica in the event of Constantine predeceasing the testator
- as a fideicommissary substitution whereby the house must first vest in Constantine, and then after Constantine's death, in Erica.

In order to make provision for direct substitution, the testator (drafter of the will) must indicate that the benefit will pass to Erica only if Constantine predeceases the testator. In case of doubt whether the testator intended direct or fideicommissary substitution, substitution is presumed to be direct rather than fideicommissary.[2]

10.3.2 Direct substitution implied by law (*ex lege*): Section 2C

Direct substitution may be implied by law in circumstances where the testator has not expressly made provision for substitution. This is regulated by s 2C of the Wills Act as follows:

- **So-called 'Statutory accrual':** Section 2C(1) provides that if a descendant of a deceased person (excluding a minor or mentally ill descendant) who is entitled to a benefit in terms of a will, renounces his right to receive such a benefit, it will vest in the surviving spouse.
- **So-called 'Statutory representation':** Section 2C(2) provides that if a descendant, whether as a member of a class or otherwise, would have been entitled to a benefit if he or she had not predeceased the testator, or had not been disqualified from inheriting, or had not after the testator's death renounced his or her right to receive such benefit, the descendants of that descendant shall, subject to the provision of section 2C(1), *per stirpes* be entitled to the benefit, unless otherwise indicated by the context of the will.

1 Corbett et al 201.

2 See, however, the warning posed by the Court in *Van Zyl v Van Zyl* 1951 (3) SA 288 (A); see the discussion of this case on page 162.

Section 2C(2) can possibly be seen as the general rule or point of departure in deciding what must happen with a benefit should a descendant of the testator be the beneficiary but:

- predeceases the testator
- renounces his or her benefit
- be disqualified to benefit.

Section 2C(2) is, however, qualified by s 2C(1). The differences and similarities between the two sections has been set out in Table 10.1.

Table 10.1 The differences and commonalities between section 2C(1) and section 2C(2)

Section 2C(2)	Section 2C(1)
1. Section 2C(2) applies to descendants of the testator who cannot or do not wish to inherit.[3]	1. Section 2C(1) only applies to a major descendant who is not mentally ill and only where such a descendant is 'together with the surviving spouse of the testator entitled to a benefit' in terms of the provisions of the will, and he or she repudiates his or her benefit.[4]
2. Section 2C(2) provides that the descendants of a descendant of the testator who has been appointed as a beneficiary in a will can represent or be substituted for that descendant where the descendant predeceases the testator or is disqualified from inheriting. Such representation can also occur where the descendant repudiates in circumstances where s 2C(1) is not applicable (for example, where the descendant is not entitled to a benefit together with the surviving spouse).[5]	2. Section 2C(1) states that the benefit of the major descendant who repudiates his or her benefit, will accrue to the surviving spouse of the testator.
3. Section 2C(2) relates to all descendants of the testator and not only children. In other words, grandchildren can, for example, be represented by great-grandchildren. Section 2C(2) makes provision for class bequests and bequests to a descendant directly.	3. Section 2C(1) applies to all descendants who repudiate, provided they were 'together with the surviving spouse entitled to a benefit'.
4. Section 2C(2) applies only to a descendant and not to other beneficiaries such as ascendants or collaterals of the testator.[6]	4. Section 2C(1) also applies only to a descendant and not to other relatives of the testator.

3 See example (c) hereafter.
4 See examples (c) and (d) hereafter.
5 See example (a) hereafter.
6 See example (b) hereafter.

Section 2C(2)	Section 2C(1)
5. A descendant may be represented only if he or she would have become entitled to a benefit under the will. For example, if Tina appointed her 'children' as her heirs in her will, and Tina's daughter died before Tina executed her will, the child of Tina's daughter would not be entitled to inherit *per stirpes* in the place of her parent.[7] Tina's daughter would not have become entitled to a benefit under the will because she died before the will was executed.[8]	5. Uncertainty exists as to when the spouse and descendant(s) will 'together be entitled to a benefit.' It could refer to them being mentioned in one will (with regard to different benefits) or to them being mentioned together in respect of a specific bequest (narrow interpretation). The narrow interpretation is favoured by most commentators.

The principles are applied as follows:

(a) 'I bequeath my house to my son, George.'

George predeceases the testator but is survived by a son, Douglas. Douglas will inherit the house in terms of s 2C(2).

(b) 'I bequeath my house to my brother, Bill.'

Bill predeceases the testator but is survived by a son, Harry. Harry will not inherit in terms of s 2C(2) because Bill is not a descendant of the testator.

(c) 'I bequeath my house to my son, Robson, and wife, Tilly.'

Robson (an adult) repudiates his benefit upon the testator's death. Robson has a son, Andre. Section 2C(1) will be applicable. Robson is an adult descendant who, together with the surviving spouse, is entitled to a benefit in terms of the will. Robson repudiates his benefit and therefore it will accrue to Tilly, the surviving spouse of the testator.

(d) 'I bequeath my house to my son, Sibu, and wife, Meg.' Sibu is disqualified to receive the benefit upon the testator's death. Sibu has a son, Tiny.

Section 2C(2) is applicable because s 2C(1) only applies to a situation where a major descendant repudiates his or her benefit. Tiny will therefore receive Sibu's benefit in terms of s 2C(2).

(e) 'I bequeath my house to my son, Fuad. If he cannot inherit, the house must go to his sister, Yasmina.'

Fuad predeceases the testator but leaves a son, Faizel. Section 2C(2) will not be applicable since a contrary intention as to who must receive the benefit under these circumstances appears from the will. (One can also argue that the testator expressly made provision for substitution.)

7 *Nel v The Master* 1975 (3) SA 271 (T).
8 *Verseput v De Gruchy* 1977 (4) SA 440 (W).

(f) 'I bequeath R10 000 to my wife, Anne, and R10 000 to my son, Calvin.'

Calvin repudiates his benefit. Calvin has a son, Damian. There is uncertainty whether Anne will inherit under these circumstances. Although Calvin and Anne are 'together entitled to a benefit', it is not the same asset.

Notwithstanding the possible solutions, the testator's intention must always be determined.

10.4 Fideicommissary substitution (fideicommissum)

In its simplest form, a testamentary fideicommissum is an arrangement in which a testator leaves property to one person (fiduciary) but provides that the property shall go to another beneficiary (fideicommissary). The bequest to the fiduciary is usually subject to a provision that transfers ownership to the fideicommissary on the death of the fiduciary, at a definite time, or upon the fulfilment of a condition. The different successors therefore inherit the same property from the testator, one after the other.

'I leave my house to my son, Heston. Upon his death (after mine), it must go to my grandson, Gordon.' This is a typical clause creating a fideicommissum or fideicommissary substitution.

This characteristic of a fideicommissum, namely that there is always a succession of owners, distinguishes fideicommissary substitution from direct substitution, in which either one beneficiary or the other becomes owner, once and for all.

There are always at least three people involved in a fideicommissum, namely the testator, the fiduciary and the fideicommissary. The fiduciary is the first person to receive the property, and he or she has to hand it over to the second person called the fideicommissary. There may be more people involved in a fideicommissum if a series of successive fideicommissaries have been nominated.

In the following clause, there would be a fiduciary and two fideicommissaries:
'I leave my house to my son, Simeon. Upon his death (after mine) it must pass to his son, Dan ①, and upon Dan's death, it must pass to Dan's eldest son ②.'[9]

Figure 10.2 Schematic exposition of the persons involved in a fideicommissum

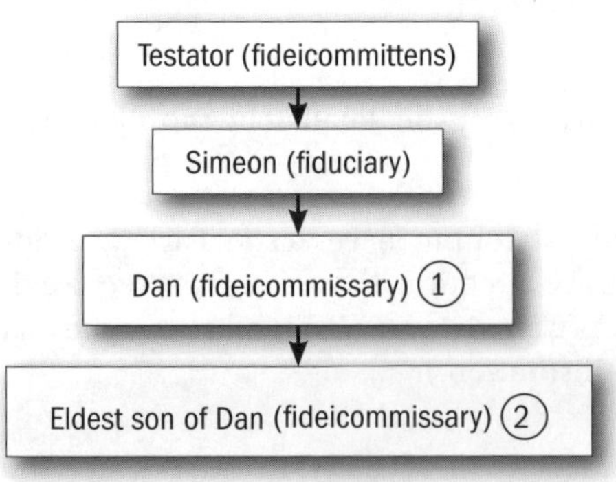

9 Keep in mind, however, the restrictions placed on fideicommissa by the Immovable Property Act 94 of 1965 as discussed hereafter.

In the above example, there is not only a fideicommissum, but also a time clause. It is therefore possible to have more than one legal concept in a single clause.

Where several fideicommissaries have been nominated to inherit one after the other, each fideicommissary becomes owner of the fideicommissary property subject to the burden of handing it over to the next, whilst the last beneficiary becomes full owner.

The advantage of the fideicommissum is that it enables a testator to retain assets (such as the family house) within the family circle for successive generations. From an estate planning point of view, the purpose of a fideicommissum can be achieved through other means such as a trust without the disadvantages attached to the fideicommissum.[10]

10.4.1 Various forms of the fideicommissum

10.4.1.1 Fideicommissum expressly created

A fideicommissum is usually expressly created in the testator's will and has many manifestations.

10.4.1.1.1 Conditional fideicommissum

The first manifestation of a fideicommissum is referred to as a conditional fideicommissum or fideicommissum *conditionale* because the passing on of the property to a subsequent beneficiary is dependent on the fulfilment of a condition (an uncertain future event).

> 'I bequeath my house to my wife, Veronica. Upon her remarriage, the house is to go to my son, Wian.'

The second manifestation of a fideicommissum is where the passing on of the property to a subsequent beneficiary could depend on a future date, definite (after 10 years) or indefinite (at the death of the fiduciary). This form of fideicommissum is called a fideicommissum *in diem* and is also a manifestation of a conditional bequest. If the fideicommissary is not alive when the time (definite or indefinite) has lapsed, the fiduciary will remain owner and on his or her death the property will form part of his or her estate.

> 'I bequeath my house to my wife, Venus. Ten years after my death, the house is to go to my son, Jude.'

10.4.1.1.2 Special power of appointment

The testator can confer a special power of appointment on the fiduciary to appoint the fideicommissary.[11]

> 'I bequeath my house to my wife, Betty. She has to determine which of our children must receive the house upon her death (after mine).'

10.4.1.1.3 Fideicommissum *residui*

Another form of an express fideicommissum that may appear in wills is the fideicommissum *residui*. This is a special type of fideicommissum which is created when a testator bequeaths property to a fiduciary, subject to the condition that the residue (as much of the property as may be left upon the termination of the fiduciary interest – usually upon the death

10 See the discussion of trusts in Chapter 11.

11 See the discussion on the delegation of testamentary power in Chapter 8.

of the fiduciary) shall devolve upon the fideicommissary. Words and phrases such as 'whatever should remain' or 'what is then to be found' can be indicative of this form of fideicommissum.[12]

> Such a clause might read: 'I leave my entire estate to my wife and what is left of it upon her death must go to our children in equal shares.'

After the death of the testator, the fiduciary has the power to alienate the fideicommissary property but may, however, alienate only three-quarters of it – the other quarter must be left for the fideicommissary – unless the testator granted the fiduciary the power to alienate the whole of the inheritance.[13] The fiduciary may only dispose of the property inter vivos and may not dispose of any part of the fideicommissary property by will.[14]

10.4.1.2 Fideicommissum created impliedly

An implied (or tacit) fideicommissum arises when, after considering the will as a whole (and in spite of the general presumption against fideicommissa[15]), it is clear from the language used that the testator wishes to burden the disposition with a fideicommissum, although the testator has not expressly done so.

10.4.1.2.1 *Si sine liberis decesserit* clause

In a *si sine liberis decesserit* clause, a testator bequeaths his or her property to a beneficiary stipulating that if he or she dies after the testator leaving no children (*si sine liberis decesserit*), the property must pass to another.

> 'I leave my house to my daughter, Blom. If she dies without children, the house must go to my son, Boeta.'
>
> This fideicommissum in favour of Boeta is subject to a condition. The condition is that Blom must die without children. If Blom dies with children, the condition is not fulfilled and Boeta will not inherit the house. The question is whether the children are now tacit fideicommissaries, since the testator did not expressly provide that the house must go to them upon Blom's death after that of the testator.

In *Du Plessis v Strauss*[16] the Appellate Division held the following:

- A *si sine liberis* provision coupled to a conditional fideicommissum gives rise to a presumption that the testator impliedly appointed the children mentioned in the clause as fideicommissary beneficiaries, provided that they are the descendants of the testator.
- This inference, however, can be rebutted if a contrary intention appears from the rest of the will.
- Where the children mentioned in the *si sine liberis* clause are not descendants of the testator, such as in the following clause: 'I leave my house to my brother, Thabo. If he dies without children (after my death), the house must go to my uncle, Monchusi', then the mere fact

---

12 See *Coll v Murray* (1917) 38 NLR 222; *Ex parte Muller* 1949 (4) SA 429 (O).
13 Voet 36 1 54; *Ex parte Berrange* 1938 WLD 39.
14 *Brown v Rickard* (1883–1884) 2 SC 314; *Ex parte Berrange* 1938 WLD 39.
15 See discussion on page 162.
16 1988 (2) SA 105 (A) at 145D.

that the children are mentioned in the condition does not create a presumption that a tacit fideicommissum was created in their favour.

- It may be that such children of the brother are instituted as tacit fideicommissaries, but then there will have to be other indications in the rest of the will that such was the intention of the testator.

In *Du Plessis v Strauss*, the children were descendants of the testator and therefore the presumption operated in their favour. There were no indications that the testator did not intend a tacit fideicommissum in their favour. On the contrary, there were sufficient indications that he did intend such tacit fideicommissum.

10.4.1.2.2 Other forms

It is also possible for a *si sine liberis decesserit* clause itself to be implied when the clause does not appear expressly. Such an implied clause is usually presumed if the fiduciary is a descendant of the testator but the designated fideicommissary is not. In *Du Plessis v Strauss,*[17] it was stated that the presumption regarding the tacit fideicommissum also applies in cases where a *si sine liberi decesserit* clause is implied. Where a testator disposes of property to a beneficiary, subject to a prohibition against alienation of the property by the beneficiary to third parties other than family members, he or she also impliedly creates a fideicommissum.

10.5 Statutory restriction on the fideicommissum

In the case of a fideicommissum on immovable property, the duration of the fideicommissum is statutorily limited to two successive fideicommissaries by s 6 of the Immovable Property (Removal or Modification of Restrictions) Act.[18] In terms of s 7, the Act has retroactive effect - a fideicommissum on immovable property created before the Act came into operation is also limited to two successive fideicommissaries. In such a case the second fideicommissary would eventually (if alive) hold the property as full unconditional owner and would be under no obligation to hand it to a third fideicommissary. In other words, the second fideicommissary may ignore the terms of the will to the extent that they relate to the third fideicommissary.[19]

Because the Act only affects a fideicommissum over immovable property, a fideicommissum over movable property is effective for as long as the testator wishes.

10.6 Legal position of the parties to a fideicommissum

The legal position of the parties to a fideicommissum (after the death of the testator) is summarised in Table 10.2.

17 1988 (2) SA 105 (A).
18 94 of 1965.
19 See *Ex parte Schnehage* 1972 (1) SA 300 (O).

Table 10.2 *The legal position of the parties to a fideicommissum*

General	
Legal position of the fiduciary	**Legal position of the fideicommissary**
1. The fiduciary becomes owner of the property upon delivery or registration. Both *dies cedit* and *dies venit* occur. As the owner of the fideicommissary property, the fiduciary can use and enjoy it, and keep the fruit.	1. The right of the fideicommissary is to receive the fideicommissary property, undiminished in value and extent, upon the fulfilment of the fideicommissary condition.
2. The fiduciary becomes owner subject to a resolutive condition.[20] His rights will terminate if the condition is met or the term arrives. If the fideicommissary predeceases the fiduciary, the fiduciary will become full owner.	2. The fideicommissary does not have to be alive at the time of the testator's death; in fact, it is possible that the fideicommissary may be born generations after the testator. It is, however, essential that he or she should be alive or already conceived at the time indicated by the testator as the moment for the transfer of the fideicommissary property to him or her by the fiduciary.
3. The fiduciary's ownership is limited in duration and extent: • As soon as the fiduciary condition or term is fulfilled, he or she is obliged to transfer the property to the fideicommissary. • Because the fiduciary's ownership is limited by the right of the fideicommissary, he or she may, as a general rule, not alienate the property or burden it with a mortgage bond, a pledge, or the grant of a servitude.	3. If the fideicommissary dies before the prescribed condition is fulfilled, the fideicommissum falls away, and unless the testator ordered otherwise in his or her will, the fiduciary acquires full ownership of the fideicommissary property and the fideicommissary's heirs acquire no rights.
	Specific nature of fideicommissary's rights while the fiduciary is still alive
4. The fiduciary may only alienate or mortgage the fideicommissary property with the cooperation of all the fideicommissaries if they are majors. Alienation or mortgage is also possible with the consent of the High Court.[22] The fiduciary can, however, alienate his or her fiduciary interest. Although the fiduciary would pass ownership of the property to the buyer, ownership would still be subject to the original resolutive condition.	4. It is usually inferred from the decision in *Barnhoorn v Duvenage*[21] that after the death of the testator, the fideicommissary has a personal right. What is important is that the Appellate Division stipulated that before fulfilment of the condition or expiry of the fideicommissary term, the fideicommissary is quite definitely the holder of an actual, existing right, although it is not a vested right in the sense that it would constitute part of his or her deceased estate.[23]

20 *Grusd v Grusd* 1946 AD 465.
21 1964 (2) SA 486 (A); see also discussion on page 161.
22 Section 2(1) of the Immovable Property (Removal or Modification of Restrictions) Act 94 of 1965.
23 See *Van der Merwe v Registrateur van Aktes* 1975 (4) SA 636 (T).

5. The fiduciary must use the fiduciary property in such way that it maintains its essential qualities until it is transferred to the fideicommissary. He or she is liable to the fideicommissary for damage caused by him or her. He or she can, however, claim compensation for expenses incurred on useful or necessary improvements to the fideicommissary property.	5. A fideicommissary can take steps to protect his or her interest as an interested party.[24]

PAUSE FOR REFLECTION

The legal position of the fideicommissary

The legal position of the fideicommissary has long been debated. The traditional view is that the fideicommissary has no right before fulfilment of the fideicommissary condition or expiry of the fideicommissary term, but only a hope or *spes*.[25] However, as an interested party, a fideicommissary can take steps to protect his or her rights. In the case of immovable property, his or her 'right' may be registered against the title deed of the property; he or she may have an interdict granted to him or her to prevent an impending alienation of the fideicommissary property; he or she may claim security from the fiduciary; he or she may cede his or her right,[26] and may, where the fiduciary has alienated the fideicommissary property without having a right to do so, in certain circumstances, on fulfilment of the fideicommissary condition, recover the property by means of the *rei vindicatio* from the person to whom it was alienated. It is clear that these are extraordinary remedies to confer upon a person who only has a *spes*. On the other hand, nothing will devolve upon the fideicommissary's heirs should he or she die before the fiduciary or before fulfilment of the condition.

The issue has, to a certain extent been resolved in *Barnhoorn v Duvenage*.[27] In later cases, however, the issue was again confused. In *Wasserman v Sackstein*,[28] the Court reverted to the view that the fideicommissary has only a *spes* fideicommissi. In *Kinloch v Kinloch*,[29] the *spes* of the fideicommissary is also mentioned, while in *Heymans v Van Tonder*,[30] a fideicommissary was given only a personal right or a *spes* fideicommissi.[31]

There is also a difference of opinion amongst writers about the nature of the right of the fideicommissary. Corbett et al[32] suggest that the fideicommissary has a personal right enforceable against the fiduciary or his or her estate upon the fulfilment of a (suspensive) condition (namely, if the fideicommissary survives the fiduciary). According to Van der Merwe & Rowland[33] the fideicommissary has a personal right subject to a resolutive condition – if he or she predeceases the fiduciary, his personal right terminates.

24 *Barnhoorn v Duvenage* 1964 (2) SA 486 (A).
25 *Reek v Registrateur van Aktes Transvaal* 1969 (1) SA 589 (T) at 592; *Wasserman v Sackstein* 1980 (2) SA 536 (O).
26 *Barnhoorn v Duvenage* 1964 (2) SA 486 (A).
27 1964 (2) SA 486 (A) – see above.
28 1980 (2) SA 536 (O).
29 1980 (2) SA 449 (N).
30 1983 (2) SA 242 (O) at 247.
31 See also *Kruger v Terblanche* 1978 (2) SA 198 (T) at 205H–206A.
32 At 319.
33 At 334–335.

10.7 Presumption against a fideicommissum

When interpreting wills, the question of whether a provision amounts to direct or fideicommissary substitution is important. The consequences of a fideicommissum limit the ownership of the fiduciary as well as all the fideicommissaries except the final one. Because they place unnecessary burdens on the beneficiaries, the common law is not in favour of fideicommissa. However, this presumption against fideicommissa only exists where there is doubt as to whether a testator intended direct or fideicommissary substitution.

There have been cases where the courts have carried the presumption against the creation of fideicommissa too far. Fortunately, in *Van Zyl v Van Zyl*,[34] the Appellate Division made it quite clear that effect must be given to a fideicommissary substitution where the wording of a will clearly incorporates it. It is only where there is reasonable doubt about whether the testator envisaged direct substitution that there is a presumption in favour of direct substitution and against fideicommissary substitution. The presumption against fideicommissary substitution does not apply where there is doubt whether the testator intended fideicommissary substitution or usufruct.[35]

10.8 Usufruct

Strictly speaking, usufruct is part of property law. However, it often occurs in wills when a testator bequeaths ownership to one person, but the right to use, enjoy, and take the fruits of the property to another. The owner is called the *dominus* or remainderman and the person with the user's rights is called the usufructuary. Because the owner is stripped of the normal competencies which accompany full ownership, he or she is also called the nude owner. Usufruct usually lasts for as long as the usufructuary lives. Usufruct is also known as a life interest.

10.8.1 Influence on *dies cedit* and *dies venit*

Normally, the *dominus* obtains a vested right of ownership (*dies cedit*) in the property bequeathed to him or her upon the death of the testator. However, the *dominus* is not entitled to enjoy and use the fruits of the property before a future date – *dies venit* is postponed until a certain future event (for example, the death of the usufructuary), or an uncertain future event (for example, remarriage of the usufructuary) occurs. The *dominus* owns the property unconditionally although the ownership does not include the right of enjoyment (it is *nudum dominium*). For the usufructuary, on the other hand, *dies cedit* and *dies venit* occur on the death of the testator. The usufructuary obtains a vested right in the property (although it belongs to the *dominus*) to enjoy and use its fruits.

> The testator bequeaths the ownership of his farm to Ralph but the lifelong right to use and enjoy the farm to his wife, Lillian. Ralph obtains ownership of the farm (*dies cedit*), but his right to use and enjoy the farm is postponed until a future event, namely the death of Lillian. Lillian has the right to enjoy and use the fruits (*dies cedit* and *dies venit)* of the farm until the future event happens, in which case her rights will cease to exist and be transferred to the *dominus* who will then have unlimited ownership of the property.

34 1951 (3) SA 288 (A).

35 See below and *Schaumberg v Stark* 1956 (4) SA 462 (A).

If the *dominus* dies before the usufructuary, the ownership of the property, subject to the usufruct, will pass to the beneficiaries of the *dominus*.

In the above example, if Ralph dies before Lillian, the farm will pass to the testate beneficiaries named in his will, or his intestate beneficiaries if he died without a valid will. It will, however, still be subject to the usufruct in favour of Lillian.

Although *dies cedit* and *dies venit* occur for the usufructuary on the death of the testator, the vested rights are different from the rights of the *dominus*. In this case, the vested rights are the right to use and enjoy the property subject to a term (resolutive term or time clause), or condition (resolutive condition). In other words, the rights of the usufructuary in the property resolve when the time has come or the condition has been fulfilled.

Dies cedit and *dies venit* occur for Lillian when the testator dies. She obtains the right to use and enjoy the fruits of the farm. However, when the term has lapsed (in this case, her death), her right of enjoyment goes to Ralph and he will not only have nude ownership of the farm, but also the right to use and enjoy it.

10.8.2 Difference between usufruct and fideicommissum

On the surface, usufruct and fideicommissum are similar - in both cases one person holds the right to use and enjoy the property (usufructuary and fiduciary respectively) while another person obtains full ownership at some or other time (*dominus* and ultimate fideicommissary respectively). However, the two concepts differ in important respects. In the case of a fideicommissum, the fiduciary obtains a real right in the fiduciary property, which passes to a fideicommissary when the time comes (resolutive term) or upon the occurrence of an uncertain future event (resolutive condition). In the case of a usufruct, the usufructuary never obtains a real right, but only a personal right (*ius in re aliena*) which must ultimately be transferred to the *dominus*.

Whilst it is not always easy to determine whether a bequest is a usufruct or a fideicommissum, effect must always be given to the intention of the testator as expressed in his or her will. If the intention of the testator was to vest ownership in the first beneficiary subject to a condition or term before it is transferred to the second beneficiary, it is usually a fideicommissum.[36] Conversely, if the intention of the testator was to vest only a personal right in the beneficiary subject to the condition that this right must pass on to the *dominus*, it is usually a usufruct. In the case of doubt, there is a presumption against a usufruct in favour of a fideicommissum.[37]

10.9 Accrual

Accrual is the right of a testator's beneficiaries, under specific circumstances, to inherit (an) asset(s) which another beneficiary might not want to inherit or is not capable of inheriting. The right of accrual is the right which co-heirs or co-legatees have of inheriting the share that their co-heir or co-legatee cannot or does not wish to receive. The right applies where a co-heir or co-legatee:

---

36 *Van Staden v Van Staden* 1984 (4) SA 507 (T).

37 *Schaumberg v Stark* 1956 (4) SA 462 (A).

- is predeceased (died before the testator)
- is disqualified to inherit
- repudiates the benefit
- was a beneficiary subject to a suspensive condition which was not fulfilled.

This is also known as common law accrual. Accrual can only operate if there is no provision made for substitution either by the testator himself or herself, or *ex lege* through the operation of s 2C(2) of the Wills Act.[38]

> Depending on the intention of the testator, accrual may or may not operate under the following circumstances:
>
> 'I hereby bequeath my boat and camping equipment to my brothers, Harvey and Zakes.'
>
> Assume Harvey predeceases the testator and is survived by a son, Nkosi, and that the testator did not amend his will. Upon the death of the testator, the question arises as to what should happen to Harvey's share in the benefit. Will it devolve upon Nkosi or will it accrue to Zakes? The answer depends on the intention of the testator as expressed in his or her will. Assume the clause, however, reads:
>
> 'I hereby bequeath my boat and camping equipment to my sons, Anton and Bernard.'
>
> Accrual will not operate under these circumstances. This example differs from the one above in that the beneficiaries are the descendants of the testator and therefore s 2C becomes relevant. If Anton predeceases the testator and he is survived by a child, Caspar, s 2C(2) of the Wills Act will apply. In terms of s 2C(2), Anton's descendants will inherit in his stead *per stirpes*. This is known as *ex lege* representation. Section 2C(2) applies to descendants of the testator who cannot or do not wish to inherit.
>
> Under the circumstances in the first example, accrual will not operate if the testator himself or herself made provision for a substitute. If the testator stipulated that another beneficiary, Zozo, should receive the benefit if either of his brothers, Harvey and Zakes, are not able or willing to receive it, Zozo (the substitute), would inherit and accrual would not take effect.

It is important that a will stipulates what should happen if beneficiaries (whether descendants, heirs or legatees) cannot or do not want to receive a benefit. Where the right of accrual does not operate, the share of a co-heir devolves upon the deceased's intestate heirs. The share of a co-legatee falls into the residue and devolves upon the deceased's heirs.

10.9.1 What is the intention of the testator?

Whether or not accrual operates in certain circumstances depends on the intention of the testator.[39] If the testator plainly states in his or her will that accrual must not take place, his or her intention is clear and the consequences discussed above will be applicable. Otherwise:

- in the event of co-heirs, if the testator intended that his or her entire estate be disposed of by will, accrual must operate

38 For a discussion of section 2C(2), see the discussion of substitution on page 153.
39 *Lello v Dales* 1971 (2) SA 330 (A).

- in the event of co-legatees, if the testator intended to dispose of the specific benefit as a whole, even if one of the legatees falls away, accrual must operate
- if the testator intended the benefit, or a share in the benefit, to revert back to his or her estate and therefore to devolve on the heirs, accrual must not operate.

The intention of the testator is, therefore, the point of departure in determining whether accrual should operate or not.[40]

10.9.2 Where the testator's intention is not clear

If it is not clear whether the testator intended accrual to take place, his or her (probable) intention must be deduced from clues or indications (*coniecturae*) in the will itself, or in the surrounding circumstances. These indications are only used to assist in working out what the testator's probable intentions were. They are not rules of law creating irrebuttable presumptions. In addition to the normal rules of interpretation of wills,[41] the mode in which the beneficiaries in question are joined in the will is an important indication in ascertaining the probable intention of the testator. Traditionally, we use the following Latin phrases to describe the different modes:

1. Joinder *re tantum* (joined by the thing)
   This mode occurs when a person is appointed as beneficiary of property in one clause and, in another clause, someone else is appointed as beneficiary of the same property without the allocation of shares to each.

   The testator stipulates in clause 3: 'I leave my house to Albert', and in clause 5: 'I leave my house to Ben.'
   Albert and Ben are joined by the house because the house is bequeathed to both of them. Such a joinder leads to an inference that accrual is intended (unless another intention appears from the will), should Albert or Ben predecease the testator.

2. Joinder *re et verbis* (joined by the words and the thing)
   This mode occurs when the same property has been left to different beneficiaries in the same clause of the will without specific shares of the property having been allocated to any of them.

   The testator stipulates: 'I leave the residue of my estate to my brothers and sisters.'
   The brothers and sisters are joined by the words and the thing in one sentence. Such a joinder also leads to an inference that accrual is intended should one beneficiary predecease the testator and no other intention appears from the will.

3. Joinder *verbis tantum* (joined through words alone)
   This mode occurs when the same thing has been bequeathed to different beneficiaries in the same clause in a will but specific shares have been allocated to specific beneficiaries.

40 See Chapter 13 on the interpretation of wills with regard to the question of how a testator's intention is determined.
41 Such as taking into account the scheme and terms of the will as a whole and the surrounding circumstances at the time of the making of the will, the presumption against partial intestacy, the presumption that a testator wishes to benefit his or her children equally, considerations of consistency and fairness and, several other factors – see Chapter 13.

> The testator has one of the following stipulations in his will: 'I bequeath the residue of my estate to my three brothers in equal shares,' or 'I bequeath the residue of my estate to my brothers, Chuck and Ivan, in the ratio 2:1,' or 'I bequeath my house to my sisters, Xandi and Bella, one half to Xandi and one half to Bella.'

In *Winstanley v Barrow* [42] this method of joinder was held to infer that accrual is not intended unless the will reveals a contrary intention. In *Lello v Dales,*[43] however, the Appellate Division emphasised that a joinder *verbis tantum* does not automatically lead to a presumption against accrual, but that in such a case the emphasis should be placed on the testator's probable intention.[44]

> In *Lello v Dales*[45] the testatrix had left her estate in trust to her son, Harry, who was to benefit as an income beneficiary. On Harry's death, the estate was to devolve upon his lawful issue. If Harry were to die without lawful issue, the will provided: '... the residue of my estate ... shall devolve as follows: half to my brother Edward ... and the other half in equal shares, share and share alike to my nephews and nieces, the children of my brothers'. Harry married but died childless and Edward had predeceased Harry. The question which arose was whether Edward's share lapsed and fell back into the residue, or, on the other hand, accrued to the nephews and nieces. The Appellate Division referred to *Winstanley v Barrow*[46] and emphasised that the question whether or not accrual takes place depends on the probable intention of the testator, as discovered from 'the scheme and terms of the will ... in the light of the relevant circumstances existing at the time of its making'.[47] The Court found that the beneficiaries had been joined *verbis tantum*, and recognised that the inference that accrual does not take place which flows from a joinder *verbis tantum* is not necessarily logical. The Court held that the probabilities strongly indicated that the testatrix intended accrual to take place and that what had been bequeathed to Edward accrued to the nephews and nieces in spite of the fact that the joinder of the bequests was *verbis tantum* in form.

PAUSE FOR REFLECTION

Intention

The intention of a testator can differ from case to case, and the same words or similar methods of joinder do not necessarily reflect the same intention. For these reasons, it is dangerous to approach a will with preconceived views regarding the importance of *coniecturae* and thereby substitute a real intention with an objective supposed intention. A joinder *verbis tantum* in equal or specific shares is not per se indicative of an intention for or against accrual.[48] *Lello v Dales*[49] puts *Winstanley v Barrow*[50] in the correct perspective and tempers the rule that accrual does not take place if beneficiaries are joined *verbis tantum* (unless another intention appears from the will).

42 1937 AD 75.
43 1971 (2) SA 330 (A).
44 See also *Stock v Keren Hayesod, Israel* 1978 (4) SA 92 (WLD); *Geft v Gelbart* 1984 (4) SA 515 (C); *Griessel v Bankorp Trust Bpk* 1990 (2) SA 328 (O).
45 1971 (2) SA 330 (A).
46 1937 AD 75.
47 *Lello v Dales* 1971 (2) SA 330 (A) at 335.
48 Van der Merwe & Rowland at 470.
49 1971 (2) SA 330 (A).
50 1937 AD 75.

10.10 Customary law of succession

The customary law of succession is in essence a system with intestate rules. However, there is nothing that prohibits a testator living under a system of customary law from executing a will containing some or all of the legal concepts dealt with in this chapter, particularly the fideicommissum. Although the principle of male primogeniture has been declared unconstitutional by the Constitutional Court in *Bhe v Magistrate, Khayelitsha*,[51] the fideicommissum can be applied to create a similar effect. Nothing prohibits a testator from stipulating in his or her will that the eldest male son in the male lineage must inherit the family property ad infinitum. By using the common law concept of fideicommissum, results similar to those created by the rule of male primogeniture can be obtained.

THIS CHAPTER IN ESSENCE

1. Substitution occurs when a testator appoints a beneficiary to inherit a benefit, but at the same time nominates another beneficiary to take the place of the appointed beneficiary (legatee or heir) upon the occurrence of an event, usually the death of the appointed beneficiary. Substitution may take place either in the alternative (direct substitution) or one beneficiary may receive the benefit after another beneficiary (fideicommissary substitution).
2. Direct substitution can be created by the testator himself or herself, or can operate by law (*ex lege*) in terms of s 2C of the Wills Act.
3. Fideicommissary substitution can be created expressly or impliedly. With regard to an implied fideicommissum, the so-called *si sine liberis* (meaning 'if you die without children') clause is examined.
4. The legal position of the parties to a fideicommissum is examined.
5. The fideicommissum *residui* is a form of fideicommissum which constitutes an exception to the general rule that the fiduciary may not alienate the fideicommissary property.
6. The nature of a fideicommissum is burdensome since it limits the ownership of the fiduciary and it is not favoured in South African common law. A presumption against *fideicommissa* exists but only where there is doubt as to whether a testator intended direct or fideicommissary substitution.
7. A usufruct, which is often confused with the fideicommissum, essentially forms part of the law of property although it is often used in wills. A testator bequeaths the property rights to one person (the *dominus* or remainderman) but the right to use, enjoy and take the fruits of the property to another (the usufructuary).
8. The right of accrual is the right co-heirs and co-legatees have of inheriting a share which a co-heir or co-legatee cannot, or does not wish to, receive. Accrual can, however, only operate if provision is not made for substitution either by the testator himself or herself, or *ex lege* through the operation of s 2C of the Wills Act.
9. Whether or not accrual operates in certain circumstances depends on the intention of the testator as it appears from the will. If the intention of the testator is not clear, his or her probable intention must be deduced from certain indications in the will itself, or from the surrounding circumstances. The mode in which beneficiaries are joined is only one of the indications, although an important one, in ascertaining the probable intention of the testator.

51 See Chapters 2 and 15 for a discussion of the case.

Chapter 11

Content of wills – trusts

What is a testamentary trust and what rules govern it?

11.1	Introduction	169
11.2	Brief historical perspective	171
11.3	Defining a trust	171
11.4	Legal nature of the testamentary trust	174
11.5	Requirements for the creation of a valid trust	176
11.6	Core elements of a trust	179
11.7	Trustees	180
11.8	Beneficiaries	185
11.9	Amendment of trust provisions	188
11.10	Termination of a trust	189
11.11	Customary law of succession	190
This chapter in essence		190

11.1 Introduction

A testamentary trust is a trust created within the context of the law of testate succession. It must be differentiated from a trust that is created by agreement during the lifetime of the founder. This is known as an inter vivos trust and forms part of the law of contract. As such, the inter vivos trust will not be dealt with in this chapter.

A testamentary trust is often used by a testator to provide for the needs of dependants upon his or her death without their having ownership and/or control[1] in or over the property.

> A typical clause creating a trust in this regard might read:
> 'I bequeath my estate to my trustee, Mr Xanadu, in trust. My wife, Yolandi, is the income beneficiary until her death. My children, Zozo and Zanor, are the capital beneficiaries.'

1 See definition of trust in Chapter 1 and on page 171 para 11.3.

In this example, the ownership and control of the assets lie with the trustee,[2] and he or she has to administer the trust property in terms of the provisions of the trust deed for the benefit of the trust beneficiaries.

A trust is also often used by spouses in a joint will to make provision for the disposition of assets should they die simultaneously or should the survivor die within a specified time after the first-dying.

A typical clause in this regard might read:

'The testator and the testatrix mutually appoint one another as sole heir of the first-dying. If, however, we should die simultaneously or within 90 days after one another, we mass our joint estate and bequeath it to our trustees to be held in trust and to be administered in terms of clause 10 for the benefit of our minor children.'[3]

A testamentary trust can also be created for beneficiaries with limited capacity or for an impersonal object.

A typical clause in this regard might read:

'I bequeath R100 000 to my trustee, Mr Xanadu, in trust to combat child abuse.'

The basic idea behind a trust is that ownership of property is bequeathed to another person for the benefit of a third or for the achievement of an impersonal object. This idea is referred to as the *treuhand* principle.

PAUSE FOR REFLECTION

The usufruct, the fideicommissum or the testamentary trust?

When a person wants to provide for the care of dependants and, at the same time, wants to protect the assets after his or her death, or keep them in the family for future generations, he or she can (traditionally) make use of the usufruct,[4] the fideicommissum,[5] or the testamentary trust. The benefits of a testamentary trust are apparent when compared to the consequences and disadvantages of the usufruct and fideicommissum. A special feature of the testamentary trust is its flexibility and adaptability. A testamentary trust is, as a general rule, better equipped to provide for changing circumstances, including changes in the financial position, health and educational needs of the beneficiaries. In terms of a testamentary trust, income may be awarded to the income beneficiary according to his or her needs and the rest retained for (other) contingencies. With a usufruct, the usufructuary is entitled to the entire income and provision is not made for unforeseen circumstances when large amounts may be required. A disadvantage of a fideicommissum, namely that a fideicommissum attached to immovable property is limited to two successive fideicommissaries,[6] can be avoided by a testamentary trust where the assets can be held in trust indefinitely. Usufructs and fideicommissa also impose limitations on the economic use of the property concerned. Property subject to a usufruct or fideicommissum will not readily be accepted as security for raising a loan

2 Take note, however, that the so-called *bewind* trust – see definition on page 173 in para 11.3 – is also possible.
3 This is also an example of estate massing as discussed in Chapter 9.
4 See Chapter 10.
5 See Chapter 10.
6 Section 6 of the Immovable Property (Removal or Modification of Restrictions) Act 94 of 1965.

to continue, for example, farming operations. For these reasons, in modern wills the tendency is to use a trust rather than a fideicommissum.

However, the testamentary trust is not an easy solution to the limitations of the usufruct and the fideicommissum, and should not be recommended without careful thought. Even a simple trust involves a good deal of work and a high degree of responsibility commensurate with the trustee's fiduciary duty towards the beneficiary. Compared to a usufruct or a fideicommissum, a testamentary trust costs more to administer. Trustees are entitled to remuneration which may be fixed in the will.[7] The trust's books have to be written up each year and tax returns submitted, which usually involves accounting fees. The cost of running a testamentary trust may mean that there is little left over for the beneficiary, and therefore the benefits of the testamentary trust must be carefully weighed up against these disadvantages.

11.2 Brief historical perspective

The common law trust, developed in English law, was introduced in South Africa after the commencement of British rule in the Cape in 1806. Although the terms 'trust' and 'trustee' are of English origin, the English law of trusts does not form the basis of South African trust law. South African courts have evolved, and are still in the process of evolving, South African trust law by adapting the trust idea to the principles of South African law.

An important development with regard to South African trust law was the introduction of the Trust Property Control Act.[8] The purpose of this Act is to regulate the control of trust property and to protect trust assets by ensuring that the administration of trusts is supervised by the Master of the High Court. The Act is not a complete codification of the law of trusts - aspects such as the requirements (*essentialia*) for a valid trust and the nature of the fiduciary office of the trustee are, for example, still dealt with in terms of common law.

11.3 Defining a trust

It is important to distinguish between a trust in the wide and narrow senses of the word. The Trust Property Control Act only applies to a trust in the narrow sense, which refers to only trusts inter vivos and testamentary (or *mortis causa*) trusts. The inter vivos trust will not be discussed in this chapter. Testamentary trusts can be divided into ownership and *bewind* trusts.[9] Ownership trusts can be discretionary or non-discretionary trusts.

7 Section 22 of the Trust Property Control Act 57 of 1988.

8 57 of 1988.

9 This terminology is, however, not found in the Act but relate to the two constructions in s 1 of the Act, paras (a) and (b) respectively.

Figure 11.1 The different types of trusts

TRUSTS

Wide sense	**Narrow sense**
Comprehensive concept to indicate any legal relationship where one person controls and administers property for another or an impersonal object	Ownership and/or control in/over property handed over to a trustee for the benefit of another or an impersonal object in terms of s 1 of the Trust Property Control Act
Separation between control over property and the benefit that derives from it	Separation between control over property and the benefit that derives from it is also a pertinent feature
Trustees can loosely be described as agents with fiduciary duties. Although trustees also hold a public office, it is not the office of trustee as intended in the Trust Property Control Act	Trustees are authorised by the Master to act in the capacity of trustee. Trustees hold a specific office and, as such, are subject to public control by the Master and the High Court
Trustees are not owners of property (representatives, tutors, curators, executors and directors)	Trustees do not act in their private capacities but in an official capacity other than one of the capacities applicable to the wide sense. Trustees can be the owners of trust property, but in their official capacities (ownership trust)
Unique rules and legislation applicable to these offices	Trust Property Control Act and common law applicable

Inter vivos	***Mortis causa***
Created during founder's lifetime	Created in founder's will

Ownership trust	***Bewind* trust**
Trustees own property	Beneficiaries own property (subject to trustee's control)

Discretionary	Non-discretionary

In terms of s 1 of the Trust Property Control Act 57 of 1988 a trust means:

> *... the arrangement through which the ownership in property of one person is by virtue of a trust instrument [the will] made over or bequeathed –*
>
> *(a) to another person, the trustee, in whole or in part, to be administered or disposed of according to the provisions of the trust instrument for the benefit of the person or class of persons designated in the trust instrument or for the achievement of the object stated in the trust instrument; or*
>
> *(b) to the beneficiaries designated in the trust instrument, which property is placed under the control of another person, the trustee, to be administered or disposed of according to the provisions of the trust instrument for the benefit of the person*

> *or class of persons designated in the trust instrument or for the achievement of the object stated in the trust instrument, ...*

In the case of the ownership trust,[10] the trustee becomes the owner of the trust assets, but for the benefit of the beneficiary or for an impersonal purpose. The trustee occupies a fiduciary office and, in this capacity, he or she must exercise his or her powers for the benefit of the trust beneficiaries or for the impersonal purpose.

> A typical clause creating an ownership trust might read:
> I bequeath the residue of my estate to my trustee, Mr Nkayi, in trust. My wife is the income beneficiary and the children born from our marriage are the capital beneficiaries in equal shares.

A question that arises is whether a beneficiary can have any rights with regard to the trust income and/or capital in view of the fact that the trustee is the owner of the trust property. The nature of the beneficiary's rights will depend on the intention of the testator. In the example above, while the trustee is the owner, the wife has a vested right (*dies cedit*) to the income and she can enforce it (*dies venit*) when the income becomes payable. Because no provision was made for substitution of the capital beneficiaries, they also have a vested right (*dies cedit*) in the capital upon commencement of the trust but will have to wait until dissolution of the trust before they can enforce their rights (*dies venit*).[11]

Under a *bewind* trust,[12] the beneficiaries are the owners of the trust assets, while the trustee acquires only the powers of control and disposal as determined by the trust instrument. These powers must necessarily be exercised to the advantage of the beneficiaries or for the impersonal purpose (to fulfil objectives other than the benefit of an individual).

> A clause creating a *bewind* trust might read:
> I bequeath my assets to my child, Zara. The assets must, however, be held in trust and be administered for Zara's benefit by my trustee, Mrs August, in terms of the provisions of clause 10.[13]

In a discretionary trust, the trustee (sometimes also a trust beneficiary) has the discretionary power to nominate the income and/or capital beneficiaries of the trust from a certain group.[14] The trustee is usually also given discretionary capacity to determine the ratio in which awards will be made to the beneficiaries.

The term 'non-discretionary trust' is used for a trust arrangement in terms of which the beneficiaries and their respective benefits are predetermined and fixed in the trust instrument and where the trustees have no discretion in this regard.

Trusts are often referred to as private trusts (or family trusts, if the trust is set up to take care of dependants), or trusts with an impersonal purpose or object (in other words, for public benefit). The names of these kinds of trusts usually refer to one of the trust's principal characteristics or to the object of the trust, for example 'the Kennedy Trust' or 'the Lung Cancer Trust'.

10 The description used in practice for the construction in terms of para (a) of the definition.
11 The rights of trust beneficiaries are dealt with on pages 185–186.
12 The description used in practice for the construction in terms of para (b) of the definition.
13 For a discussion of the nature of the beneficiary's rights, see pages 185–186.
14 *Braun v Blann and Botha* 1984 (2) SA 850 (A).

PAUSE FOR REFLECTION

Ownership of trust assets

The ownership trust (s 1(a) of the Trust Property Control Act), occurs more frequently in practice than the *bewind* trust (s 1(b)). Although the legal differences between the two constructions are material, the effect of both is that the property is administered by the trustee on behalf of the beneficiary in terms of the provisions of the trust instrument and the law. Even though the beneficiary in a *bewind* trust owns the assets, the trustee administers and controls the assets in the beneficiary's interest. The fact that the beneficiary has a real right to the assets strengthens his or her position in cases of non-compliance with the provisions of the trust document. However, a *bewind* trust has disadvantages if the beneficiary's estate is sequestrated.

The fact that it is possible for beneficiaries to have vested rights (in the income and/or capital) in an ownership trust, is reiterated by Corbett et al:[15]

Since the trustee does not enjoy a beneficial interest in the property, the bequest to the trustee, although conferring bare dominium, does not of itself debar an immediate vesting (that is, upon the taking of effect of the will) in the beneficiary ultimately entitled to the corpus.

11.4 Legal nature of the testamentary trust

A testamentary trust (trust *mortis causa*) is embodied in the will of the founder (testator) and is therefore the result of a unilateral legal act. The will is thus the trust instrument in which ownership is made over or bequeathed to the trustee or beneficiary depending on the chosen construction. At the earliest, a testamentary trust comes into existence upon the death of the testator although its commencement can be postponed until a later stage.

Traditionally, the testamentary trust was seen as a special version of the fideicommissum. In *Estate Kemp v MacDonald's Trustee*,[16] it was held that a testamentary trust is, in the phraseology of South African law, a fideicommissum and a testamentary trustee is a fiduciary. In *Braun v Blann and Botha*,[17] however, this was rejected and the trust was acknowledged as a separate legal concept with its own set of rules. Although it can be said that the office of trustee is fiduciary in nature, general distinctions can be drawn as illustrated in Table 11.1.

Table 11.1 *The differences between a trustee and a fiduciary*

Trustee	Fiduciary (in a fideicommissum)
Control or ownership separated from enjoyment – trustee only has administrative interest unless he or she also happens to be a beneficiary	Owner beneficially entitled to the fruits and use of property
Quasi-public office	No office
Court and Master supervise proper execution of trusts	Observance of fideicommissum left to fideicommissaries

15 At 389.
16 1915 AD 491 at 499.
17 1984 (2) SA 850 (A) at 858H–G.

Trustee	Fiduciary (in a fideicommissum)
If trust fails, trustee not beneficially entitled	If fideicommissum fails, fiduciary takes property free of burden
Trust may continue for indefinite period	Limited to two successive fideicommissarii (where the Immovable Property (Removal or Modification of Restrictions) Act[18] is applicable
Trust will not fail for want of trustee	Fideicommissum fails in absence of fiduciary

The trust, furthermore, does not have legal personality and it does not bear its own rights and responsibilities.[19]

COUNTER POINT

Legal persons

A problem that arises with trusts is that even though they are not (legal) persons, they are often treated as such in terms of legislation or by courts. De Waal[20] points to certain anomalies in South African trust law:

- the registration practice of immovable property in terms of s 40 of the Administration of Estates Act which creates an extraordinary method of transfer of ownership to the trustee
- taxation of a trust in terms of the Income Tax Act[21]
- sequestration of a trust where a trust is regarded as a debtor in the usual sense of the word within the meaning of the definition in s 2 of the Insolvency Act[22]
- an inter vivos trust as a beneficiary in terms of a will was held to be in order in *Kohlberg v Burnett*[23]
- section 102 of the Deeds Registries Act[24] (regarding the purchase of immovable property by trustees) has been amended to include a trust in the definition of a 'person' for purposes of the registration of immovable trust property.

If the trust is said to be a separate legal institution with its own set of legal rules, these anomalies need to be addressed. Either the trustees (in the event of the ownership trust) or the beneficiaries (in the event of the *bewind* trust) are the owners, and not the trust.

18 94 of 1965.
19 *Commissioner for Inland Revenue v MacNeillie's Estate* 1961 (3) SA 833 (A); *Kohlberg v Burnett* 1986 (3) SA 12 (A).
20 1993 *THRHR* 1.
21 58 of 1962.
22 24 of 1936.
23 1986 (3) SA 12 (A).
24 47 of 1937.

11.5 Requirements for the creation of a valid trust

11.5.1 Intention to create a trust

The intention to create a trust must be present. The testator must have the serious intention to bequeath ownership in property to a trustee or beneficiaries, in order that the property is administered according to the provisions of the will by the trustee for the benefit of the person or persons designated in the trust instrument or for the achievement of the object stated in the trust instrument.

11.5.2 Create a binding obligation

The intention must be expressed in such a way that it creates a binding obligation to set up a trust. There have been occasions when the use of precatory words (for example, 'I wish') by the founder or words merely empowering trustees to create (a further) trust under certain circumstances, were regarded by the courts as insufficient to create a binding obligation. This especially relates to the power sometimes given to trustees to create a so-called 'role-over' trust under certain circumstances.

PAUSE FOR REFLECTION

Braun v Blann and Botha

In *Braun v Blann and Botha*,[25] the testatrix 'empowered' her administrators (trustees) in certain circumstances to set up new trusts for her great-grandchildren for such periods and on such terms as the administrators determined, instead of distributing the capital on the death of her children. The Court held that it amounted to a delegation of will-making power which exceeded the power of appointment of income and/or capital beneficiaries from a specified group of persons. It was, in substance, a delegation of will-making power to her administrators which the testatrix should have exercised herself and it was therefore held to be invalid.

It is important that the testator does not empower trustees to set up new trusts or provide them with the discretion to do so, thereby making decisions the testator should make.[26]

11.5.3 Testamentary formalities

Since a testamentary trust is created by a will, the will has to comply with the formality requirements in s 2(1)(a) of the Wills Act.[27]

11.5.4 Determined or determinable trust property

The trust property must be determined or be capable of determination. The testator must therefore indicate what the trust assets are that have to be administered by the trustee. In terms of s 1 of the Trust Property Control Act, trust property is defined as movable or immovable property and includes contingent interests in property. The trust property may consist of assets, movable or immovable, corporeal or incorporeal such as a farm, furniture, shares, or copyright. If the description of the trust property is ambiguous, the ambiguity is

25 1984 (2) SA 850 (A).

26 See also *Administrators, Estate Richards v Nichol* 1996 (4) SA 253 (C) and in particular clause 12 of the will concerned at 256F–H; 258D–259A.

27 See the discussion in Chapter 5.

resolved like any other in a will.[28] In *Deedat v The Master,*[29] the Court decided that a charitable trust created inter vivos does not fail if the subject matter of the trust can be ascertained through admissible means of interpretation.

11.5.5 Clear trust object

The trust object or purpose must be clear. In the case of the typical family trust, this requirement means that the beneficiaries must be determined or capable of being determined. It is, subject to certain limitations, possible to grant the power to appoint beneficiaries to a trustee or trustees, or for an income beneficiary to appoint the capital beneficiary.[30] In *Braun v Blann and Botha,*[31] the Court acknowledged the delegation of testamentary power to a trustee to appoint income and/or capital beneficiaries from a designated class or group of persons provided to him by the testator. The conferment of a power of appointment to trustees is therefore restricted to so-called 'specific powers'. However, in the case of a bequest for charitable purposes (or a trust with an impersonal object), the trustee of a charitable trust may be given wide discretion in identifying beneficiaries or objectives within the broad charitable aims provided by the testator.[32] The rule that a trust with an impersonal object is interpreted in a benevolent fashion means that such a trust will not easily be declared invalid on the grounds that the trust object is not clear.

PAUSE FOR REFLECTION

What can be delegated?

It is one of the fundamental principles of the law of succession that the testator must exercise his or her testamentary power himself or herself and cannot delegate it to someone else. There are, however, a few exceptions to this principle. One exception arises in the context of a bequest for charitable purposes where a trustee of a charitable trust may be given wide discretion in identifying beneficiaries within the broad charitable aims outlined by the testator. Another exception is the conferment of a power of appointment to a trustee (in the case of an ordinary family trust) to appoint income and/or capital beneficiaries from a class of persons.[33] Any delegation of any power to a trustee will thus only be valid if it is covered by one of the mentioned exceptions.

If a testator thus makes it clear that his or her trust objective is to combat child abuse, bequeaths R100 000 and delegates to his or her trustees the **discretion** and **power** to decide which institutions to benefit (within the charitable aim), such a provision is valid. If the testator also stipulates that, after five years, the trustees will have the **power** and **discretion** to form a new trust (with the remaining capital available at that time) with a new trust objective and new beneficiaries, it will be an invalid delegation. It will be a delegation of testamentary power which exceeds the scope of a mere power of appointment of income/capital beneficiaries from a class of persons.

28 See Chapter 13 for a discussion of the interpretation rules.
29 1995 (2) SA 377 (A) at 354C–F.
30 See Chapter 8 where power of appointment is discussed.
31 1984 (2) SA 850 (A).
32 See *Ex parte Henderson* 1971 (4) SA 549 (D).
33 See *Braun v Blann and Botha* 1984 (2) SA 850 (A). For other exceptions see delegation of testamentary power in Chapter 8.

In *Administrators, Estate Richards v Nichol*,[34] the following clause in the will came under scrutiny:

On the death of the longest living beneficiary under the preceding portions of this will, I (the testator) empower and direct my trustees to create a trust upon such terms and governed by such constitution and for such period as they in their absolute discretion shall deem fit. The said trustees shall have the power to appoint the trustees for the mentioned trust. The residue of the estate shall thereupon vest in the trustees to be invested in such manner as shall be permitted and required by the constitution of the trust. The income derived from the trust shall be used to assist brothers and sisters of either myself or my wife.

It was common cause between the parties that the provision empowering the trustees to create a trust was invalid based on *Braun v Blann and Botha*. The essentials for a valid trust were, however, otherwise present, namely that the testator imposed an obligation on the trustees to create a trust. The fact that the testator left both the terms of creation and the constitution of the trust to the discretion of the trustees also constituted an invalid delegation of testamentary power. The invalid portions of the clause were, however, severable from the remaining provisions of the clause so that the trust as a whole did not need to fail.[35] The *essentialia* (validity requirements) were present:

- The intention of the testator to create a trust was expressed in a mode apt to create a binding obligation (direct).
- The trust property was defined with reasonable certainty (residue).
- The beneficiaries were determined (discretion to trustees to select beneficiaries from a specified class of persons).
- The trust object was lawful.

11.5.6 Lawful trust object

The trust object must be lawful. It is not possible to give an exhaustive list of trust objectives that will be regarded as lawful or unlawful but, in general, the object will be unlawful if it is illegal or *contra bonos mores*. Ultimately, each case will have to be judged in the light of its own facts and prevailing social norms or legal provisions. Section 9 of the Constitution stipulates grounds upon which nobody may be unfairly discriminated against.[36]

PAUSE FOR REFLECTION

Freedom of testation and the Constitution

The judgment in *Minister of Education v Syfrets Trust Ltd*[37] addresses the inherent conflict between freedom of testation and the principles enshrined in the Constitution. The question arises as to what is now left of freedom of testation which the Court accepted as being a component of the right to property in terms of s 25 of the Constitution? Specifically, will any bequest to any particular group survive the test set out by the Court?

34 1996 (4) SA 253 (C).
35 *Administrators, Estate Richards v Nichol* 1996 (4) SA 253 (C) at 258.
36 *Minister of Education v Syfrets Trust Ltd* 2006 (4) SA 205 (C). See the discussion of this case in Chapter 8.
37 2006 (4) SA 205 (C).

Previously it had been accepted that a trust may be created for a minority group, for example a religious or language group.[38] However, the danger is that any bequest to a particular group excludes other groups. What will the courts' attitude be towards a bequest in trust to a certain church or community? De Waal[39] is of the opinion that conditions or restrictions of this nature neither encroach upon the personal sphere of the recipients nor are they aimed at influencing the personal conduct of the recipients and, in this sense, freedom of testation, depending on the circumstances of each individual case, should perhaps prevail.

It is important to note the Court's remark that the conclusion reached does not mean that the principle of freedom of testation is now being negated. The Court held that there are many examples of differentiation in this field which will have to be considered by other courts on other occasions. The central issue is whether a bequest amounts, under the specific circumstances of a case, to fair or unfair discrimination.[40] The parameters of fair discrimination must be flexible in order to accommodate freedom of testation.[41]

In the (recent) judgment of *Ex parte BOE Trust Ltd*[42] a trust provided bursaries to 'White South African students who have completed an MSC degree ...'. The court was not satisfied that the provision was contrary to public policy.[43]

11.6 Core elements[44] of a trust

When a testator creates a testamentary trust, he or she wants to be certain that the trust assets and the beneficiary's interests are sufficiently protected. Protection is needed in the event of, for example, insolvency of the trustee, death, and divorce of a trustee, or a trustee acting in breach of trust, causing damage to the trust beneficiaries.

In essence, the core elements of a trust are the following:

1. **The fiduciary position of the trustee.** A breach of his or her fiduciary position will amount to a breach of trust which can result in a trustee being held personally liable.
2. **Separate estates.** The trustee (in the event of the ownership trust) holds separate personal and trust estates.[45] The trustee's private creditors and the trust beneficiaries therefore have claims against different estates.
3. **The principle of real subrogation.** This means that the proceeds of trust assets (if sold) or substitute assets (if something else is bought with the proceeds) will also be subject to the trust. Since South African law restricts this principle to lawful replacement of assets, the unlawful replacement of assets has to be dealt with in accordance with other private law remedies such as the doctrine of notice or principles of enrichment.

---

38 For example, *In re Denton's Estate* 1951 (4) SA 582 (N); *Ex parte Marriott* 1960 (1) SA 814 (D); *Ex parte Henderson* 1971 (4) SA 549 (D).

39 *Bill of Rights Compendium* (2005) 3G–27.

40 See in this regard the discussion of unfair discrimination by the Court in *Minister of Education v Syfrets Trust Ltd* 2006 (4) SA 205 (C) at paras 33–34.

41 With regard to the test for fair discrimination see *Harksen v Lane* 1998 (1) SA 300 (CC).

42 Case no 211/09 of 27 May 2009.

43 Para 14. The case was, however, decided on the Court's power to vary trust provisions in terms of section 13 of the Act. The court was not convinced that the will contained provisions which brought about consequences which the founder in her 2002 will did not contemplate or foresee as required by section 13, para [22].

44 Elements explaining the true nature and characteristics of the trust. For a full discussion see De Waal 2000 *SALJ* 548.

45 See also ss 11 and 12 of the Trust Property Control Act.

4. **Trusteeship as an office.**[46] The trust possesses a public element in the sense that the Master of the High Court supervises the administration of trusts.

These elements, together with the possibility of the *bewind* trust and the provision of security in terms of s 6 of the Trust Property Control Act, result in sufficient protection for the beneficiary.

11.7 Trustees

11.7.1 Appointment and authorisation

As holder of the office of trustee, the trustee is the person who controls trust property to the advantage of the trust beneficiaries or in pursuance of an impersonal purpose. Whilst the trustee is the owner of the trust property (in the case of the ownership trust) for purposes of administration of the trust, he or she has no beneficial interest. In a private trust, the beneficial interest relates to the trust beneficiaries, either as income beneficiaries or as capital beneficiaries.[47] Most natural persons and corporate bodies[48] qualify for appointment as trustees. No special requirement is imposed by law. Persons who lack contractual capacity and persons disqualified in terms of s 4 of the Wills Act are not qualified.

A trustee is appointed in accordance with the provisions of the will. A testator cannot delegate the power to appoint a trustee to another person.[49] If the office of trustee cannot be filled or becomes vacant, and in the absence of any relevant provision in the will, the Master shall, after consultation with as many interested parties as he or she may deem necessary, appoint any person as trustee.[50] A trustee's appointment will not become effective until he or she has accepted his or her appointment. Even if the trustee has been validly appointed in terms of the will and even if he or she has accepted the appointment, he or she may not act in that capacity until such time as written letters of authority have been issued to him or her by the Master.[51]

11.7.2 Duties of a trustee

The trustee's duties are determined by the trust instrument, the common law and the Trust Property Control Act. The duties which are laid down by the trust instrument differ from case to case. The common law and statutory duties of the trustee relate to the office which he or she holds. The trustee office places the trustee in a fiduciary relationship with the beneficiaries. This fiduciary relationship requires that a trustee must always act in the best interest of the beneficiaries and, consequently, brings about unique duties. The trustee's most important *ex lege*[52] duties include the following:

46 See ss 4, 6, 7, 13, 16 and 20 of the Trust Property Control Act.
47 *Braun v Blann and Botha* 1984 (2) SA 850 (A) at 859G/H.
48 Section 6(4) of the Trust Property Control Act.
49 *Administrators, Estate Richards v Nichol* 1996 (4) SA 253 (C) at 259B–C.
50 Section 7(1) of the Trust Property Control Act. The Master may also, if he considers it desirable, appoint co-trustees.
51 Section 6(1) of the Trust Property Control Act.
52 In terms of either common law or statutory provisions.

1. The trustee must see to the lodgement of the will,[53] payment of Master's fees[54] and notice of address.[55]
2. A trustee must as soon as possible acquaint himself or herself with the trust instructions and determine the nature and extent of his or her powers and duties.[56]
3. As soon as possible after the issue of the letters of authority, a trustee must obtain effective control over the trust property.
4. The trustee must administer the trust in accordance with the law and the provisions contained in the trust instrument.
5. In the performance of his or her duties and the exercise of his or her powers, a trustee must act with the care, diligence and skill which can reasonably be expected of a person who manages the affairs of another.[57] This implies a higher degree of care and skill than would be the case when the trustee manages his or her own personal affairs. Any provision in the will that exempts or indemnifies a trustee against liability for breach of trust where he or she fails to show the degree of care, skill and diligence required shall be void.[58]
6. Whenever a trustee receives money in his or her capacity as trustee, he or she must deposit such money in a separate trust account at a banking institution.[59]
7. Since trust assets do not form part of the trustee's personal estate,[60] it is important for the protection of third parties, such as the trustee's personal creditors and the beneficiaries, that trust property is identified as such and separated from the trustee's personal property.[61]
8. A trustee must, at the written request of the Master, give account to the Master for his or her administration of trust property.[62] The trustee is also obliged, on written request from the Master, to submit any book, record, account or document relating to his or her administration and disposal of trust property.[63] A trustee is also obliged to provide important information in connection with the trust to beneficiaries at their request and owes the utmost good faith towards all beneficiaries. A capital beneficiary is therefore entitled to a complete accounting by the trustee of the administration of the trust even for the period prior to the termination of the trust.
9. The trustee must act in good faith and must at all times avoid a conflict between his or her personal interests and his or her official and fiduciary duties. For example, a trustee is not allowed to make a profit, directly or indirectly, from the administration of the trust. Therefore, a trustee is not allowed in general (unless properly authorised) to buy trust property, to sell his or her private property to the trust, to borrow money from the trust, or to lend his or her money to the trust (especially on inadequate security).

---

53 Section 4(1).
54 Regulation 2 of R609 of 31 March 1989; presently set at R100.
55 Section 5 of the Trust Property Control Act.
56 *Tijmstra v Blunt-MacKenzie* 2002 (1) SA 459 (T).
57 Section 9(1).
58 Section 9(2).
59 Section 10.
60 Section 12.
61 Section 11.
62 Section 16.
63 Section 16.

PAUSE FOR REFLECTION

Voidable transactions

In general, legal transactions that contravene this no-profit principle are voidable, not void. Whether such voidable transactions will be set aside by the court depends on the circumstances and, in particular, on whether the transaction is entered into openly and in good faith. If a trustee entered into a transaction whereby trust property was transferred to him or her in his or her personal capacity for value with the full knowledge and consent of the co-trustees and the transaction was for the benefit of the trust, it has, on occasion, not been set aside by the court.[64]

10. The trustee may delegate the execution of his or her decisions to another, but he or she must take the necessary decisions and personally exercise his or her discretionary powers (for example, the appointment of beneficiaries from a group). If an agent acts on behalf of the trustee, the trustee is responsible to the beneficiaries for the agent's actions. A trustee who has been appointed on the basis of his or her special ability, however, may not delegate his or her capacity and duties to someone else.[65]
11. Trustees must ensure that debts due to a trust are collected with all reasonable diligence and a reasonable return must be obtained on property which is income producing.
12. A trustee must, for a period of five years, keep all documents which serve as proof of the investment, safe custody, control, administration, abandonment, or distribution of trust property.[66]

A trust instrument can also impose particular duties on a trustee such as the duty to invest trust funds, the duty to keep accounting books, and to have them subjected to an annual audit. The provisions may differ depending on the requirements set out in each will. It may be that the trustee must encumber assets, let assets, dispose of assets, make assets available to the beneficiaries, collect income, nominate beneficiaries, determine the extent of benefits awarded to beneficiaries, and transfer benefits to beneficiaries. In the absence of trust provisions to the contrary, trustees must act jointly in their dealings with outsiders because they are seen as co-owners in the case of the ownership trust.

11.7.3 Breach of fiduciary duty

A breach of the general fiduciary obligation which the trustee owes the beneficiary, or of any of the specific duties flowing from it, constitutes a breach of trust. If the elements of delictual liability are present, the trustee is personally liable to make good any loss. The position of a co-trustee in this regard is also of importance. In South African law, trustees are not vicariously liable for the actions of co-trustees – liability is based on own fault and therefore on the general principles of delictual liability. However, where two or more trustees commit a breach of trust, they will be held liable jointly and severally. Due to the nature of the trustee office it will, depending on the circumstances, be difficult for a co-trustee to escape liability by claiming he or she was not actively involved with the administration of the trust.[67]

64 See *Hoppen v Shub* 1987 (3) SA 201 (C).
65 *Hoosen v Deedat* 1999 (4) SA 425 (SCA).
66 Section 17.
67 *Boyce v Bloem* 1960 (3) SA 855 (T).

PAUSE FOR REFLECTION

A position of trust

A fiduciary position means a position of trust. The trustee must honour the trust placed in him or her and must always act in the best interest of the trust beneficiaries. He or she must attend to the administration of the trust in the utmost good faith.

In order to fulfil his or her fiduciary obligation, specific duties regarding the administration of the trust have been developed. Some of the common law duties have been incorporated into the Trust Property Control Act as well. A testator must be careful in his or her election of trustees, and trustees need to be made aware of the extent of their duties before they accept the appointment. Kernick[68] (in the context of the inter vivos trust) recommends that the Master must require of trustees to warrant that they have educated themselves on the seriousness of the duties they have taken on and on the consequences of falling down in their duties. According to the Court in *Land and Agricultural Bank v Parker*[69] (again in the context of inter vivos trusts), a trustee should be someone with proper realisation of the responsibilities of trusteeship and awareness that failure to observe these duties may risk action for breach of trust.

11.7.4 Powers of a trustee

A trustee's powers are determined mainly by the content of the trust instrument. However, a testamentary trust does not need to contain a comprehensive description of the trustee's powers in order to be valid, but the absence of such a description will make it difficult for trustees to administer the trust and they will probably have to apply for a declaratory order regarding their powers. Consequently, these powers will differ from case to case. The administration of a trust usually takes place over a long period of time during which unforeseen circumstances and new needs can arise. This means that a trustee needs wide powers to ensure proper administration and disposal of trust property at all times.

It is not easy for a trustee to exercise legally powers that are not expressly conferred by the trust instrument. If a specific power which a trustee wishes to exercise has not been expressly conferred on him or her, the proposed action may be invalid. It is especially important that formal acts, for example the sale, transfer and burdening of immovable property, should be expressly authorised in the trust instrument.

> In *Liebenberg v MGK Bedryfsmaatskappy (Edms) Bpk*,[70] the question was whether the trustees could bind the trust as surety and co-principal debtor for the debts of a third party. The Court[71] held that the terms of the trust deed have to be read against the common law background, namely that, unless otherwise provided in the trust deed, a trustee has no power to expose the trust assets to business or farming risks. A trustee who contends that such a power is necessary to preserve the value of the trust property must apply to court for the necessary power.

The extent of a trustee's powers to invest trust funds is dependent on the provisions of the trust instrument and the facts of each specific case, including changed circumstances. A trustee must always act like a *bonus et diligens paterfamilias* (with the care, diligence and skill which

68 2007 *De Rebus* 29.
69 2005 (2) SA 77 (SCA) at para 36.
70 [2002] 4 All SA 322 (SCA).
71 *Liebenberg v MGK Bedryfsmaatskappy (Edms) Bpk* [2002] 4 All SA 322 (SCA) 328 at para [8]b–c.

can reasonably be expected of a person who manages the affairs of another) in the choice of investment alternatives for trust funds. This implies a higher degree of care than would be the case when the trustee makes his or her own investments. Whether an investment in listed shares or unit trusts can be regarded as a prudent investment will depend on the facts of each case. There is no longer a fixed rule in our law that prohibits such investment (in shares or unit trusts) of trust funds in the absence of an explicit authorisation.

In *Administrators Estate Richards v Nichol*,[72] the Court provided the following practical criteria to serve as a guideline for a trustee's investment strategy:

[I]t must not be overlooked that every investment in shares (and unit trusts) carries with it the inherent risk of capital loss. A trustee exercising due diligence and care will bear this in mind ... He will accordingly avoid investments which are of a speculative nature ... Generally speaking, a trustee will as far as practicable seek to spread the investments of the trust over various forms of undertaking in order to obtain a balance of stability and growth in the capital value of the trust and the income it produces.

De Waal[73] emphasises, however, that this does not mean that the trustees have unrestricted power to engage in high-risk investments. The Court makes it clear that the question whether any investment will be acceptable or not will depend on the circumstances of each case.

In exercising his or her powers, a trustee is always subject to the inherent limitations associated with his or her trustee office. Firstly, the trustee office places the trustee under the control of the Master and the court in the performance of his or her functions. Secondly, the trustee holds a fiduciary position. Powers of trusteeship must always be exercised to the advantage of the beneficiaries or in pursuance of a specified impersonal object, and not to the advantage of the trustee in his or her personal capacity.

11.7.5 Termination of trusteeship

Trusteeship ends upon the death or resignation of a trustee or when the trust comes to an end. A trustee can also be removed by the Master[74] or the court.[75] Whenever trust assets are endangered and it is in the interest of the trust beneficiaries, a trustee should be removed. A trustee may be removed even though his or her actions were bona fide (good faith). *Mala fides* (bad faith) or even misconduct is not necessarily a requirement for the removal of trustees.

The case of *Tijmstra v Blunt-MacKenzie*,[76] illustrates the circumstances or grounds upon which a trustee can be removed from office by the court. In this case, all six trustees were removed from office although for different reasons. Specific grounds included:

- where the trustee, without furnishing any explanation for his or her conduct, removes trust funds from an apparently safe investment with a financial institution and transfers them to his or her personal account[77]

72 1999 (1) SA 551 (SCA) at 558H–I.
73 1999 *TSAR* 376.
74 Section 20(2).
75 Section 20(1).
76 2002 (1) SA 459 (T).
77 At 474C/D–D/E.

- where the trustee deliberately fails to comply with the trust deed which requires that if a decision is to be taken (especially the sale of immovable property), notice must be given to all the trustees so that they may decide together; such conduct may very well amount to *mala fide*[78]
- where the trustee does not ascertain from the trust deed what the rights and obligations of the office of trustee entail[79]
- where the trustee treats the trust and its assets as his or her own, for example by selling the trust assets without the proper approval of the other trustees as required by the trust deed[80]
- where the trustee expresses no independent views about matters affecting the trust, but relies entirely upon a dominant co-trustee and approves of his or her (wrongful) conduct[81]
- where the trustee, without objection, allows grave misconduct on the part of a co-trustee in the administration of trust property, and thus exercises no control at all over the trust property.[82]

11.8 Beneficiaries

11.8.1 Nomination and qualifications

Except where a trust with an impersonal object is created, there must be a specific trust beneficiary or a trust beneficiary who can be determined. The trust beneficiaries can be indicated in the trust instrument by name or by description in order that their identity may be established at a later stage (for example, my spouse, my eldest son, my grandchildren). The capacity to nominate beneficiaries can be delegated to the trustee or to an income beneficiary. If the capacity to nominate beneficiaries is delegated, however, it is essential that the class (for example, the children or the grandchildren of the testator) from which the beneficiaries are to be selected, be stated in the trust instrument.[83]

In a trust instrument a distinction is usually made between income beneficiaries and capital beneficiaries. The income beneficiaries are benefited by means of the income (for example rent, dividends, and interest) yielded by the trust capital. The capital beneficiaries are benefited by way of the trust property itself, usually when the trust is dissolved. An income beneficiary can also be a capital beneficiary and the other way round.

In the case of a trust with an impersonal object, the founder must indicate the trust object. The selection of the specific beneficiaries in accordance with the criteria of the trust instrument is usually left to the trustee.

The beneficiary can be a natural person or a juristic person. The beneficiary does not need to exist at the commencement of the trust. Also, it is not necessary for the beneficiaries to have contractual capacity. However, the trust document may lay down certain qualifications or disqualifications regarding beneficiaries.

11.8.2 Rights of beneficiaries

The origin, nature and extent of a beneficiary's rights are determined by:

- the existence of a fiduciary relationship

78 At 468H–J; 469A–B.
79 At 468H–J.
80 At 468B–C.
81 At 472A/B–C.
82 At 476D–477B.
83 *Braun v Blann and Botha* 1984 (2) SA 850 (A).

- the type of trust concerned
- provisions of the trust instrument.

The trustee holds an office which places him or her in a fiduciary relationship with the trust beneficiaries. Because of this fiduciary relationship, every trust beneficiary has a personal right to claim that the trustee should fulfil his or her trust duties and should not act contrary to his or her obligations. This personal right originates at the start of the trust. If a trustee fails to perform a duty, any person having an interest in the trust property (especially a trust beneficiary) may apply to the court for an order directing the trustee to perform.[84]

The intention of the testator regarding the vesting and enforcement of rights has to be determined from the wording of the will.

Figure 11.2 Types of beneficiaries and their rights

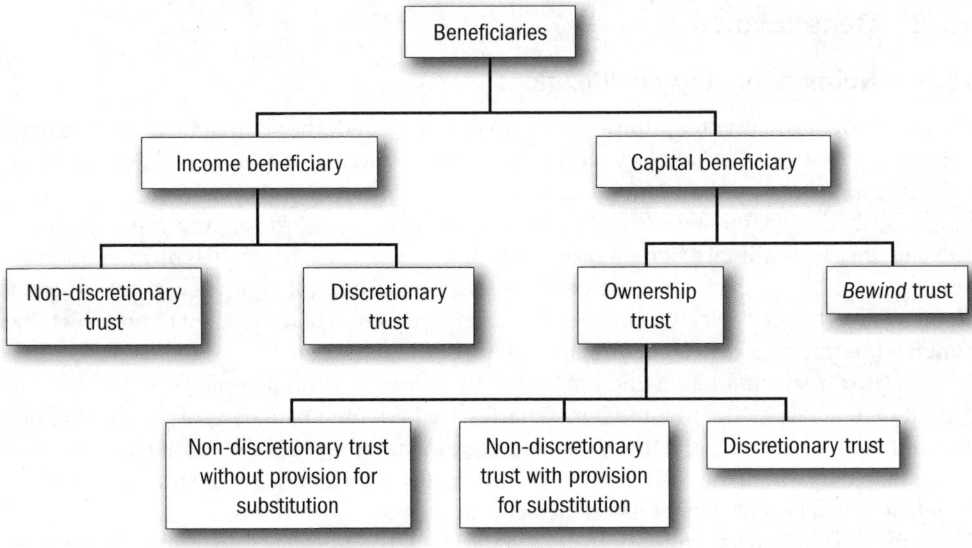

11.8.2.1 Income beneficiary

An income beneficiary's right in respect of the trust income is mainly determined by the nature of the trust, namely whether it is a discretionary or a non-discretionary trust.

11.8.2.1.1 Non-discretionary trusts

'I bequeath R100 000 and my shares in ABC company to the trustee, Mr Proudfoot, in trust. The income beneficiary is my wife, Zaza.'

- Zaza obtains a vested personal right against the trustee at the commencement of the trust.
- The content of her personal right is that she may claim payment of the income by the trustee as soon as it becomes distributable.
- In these circumstances, Zaza does not have to wait for anything to happen before she receives her income – the coming into being of her personal right is not dependent upon any exercise of discretion.

84 Section 19.

11.8.2.1.2 Discretionary trusts

> 'I bequeath R100 000 and my shares in ABC company to my trustee, Mr Maki, in trust. Mr Maki has the discretion to choose the income beneficiary(s) and the extent of his or her or their benefits from my grandchildren.'

- A specific grandchild only acquires a vested personal right against the trustee once the latter has exercised his or her discretion in favour of the beneficiary.
- The content of the personal right is that the beneficiary may claim from the trustee that the income which the trustee has awarded to the beneficiary will be paid out at the destined time.
- If the beneficiary should die after the discretion has been exercised in his or her favour but before the payment has been made, the personal right in respect of the particular income will constitute an asset in his or her deceased estate which can be exercised by his or her executor.
- Until the trustee actually exercises his or her discretion, the beneficiaries only have an expectation of being benefited.

11.8.2.2 Capital beneficiaries

With regard to the rights of beneficiaries in respect of the trust capital, it is necessary to distinguish between a *bewind* trust and an ownership trust.

11.8.2.2.1 *Bewind* trusts

> 'I bequeath my assets to my child, Zebulon. The assets must, however, be held in trust and be administered for Zebulon's benefit by my trustee, Mr Gordon, in terms of the provisions of clause 10.'

- At the creation of a *bewind* trust, the beneficiary acquires a vested personal right to the transfer or cession of the trust property to him or her.
- This personal right would normally be enforceable against the executor.
- On transfer or cession, the beneficiary becomes the owner of the trust property subject to the trustee's control.

11.8.2.2.2 Ownership trusts

In the case of an ownership trust, the provisions of the trust instrument will be decisive in determining the nature of the rights of the capital beneficiaries. It will be especially important to determine whether the ownership trust is a discretionary trust, and whether provision is made for direct substitution.

Non-discretionary trusts without provision for substitution

> 'I bequeath my assets to my trustee, Mr Kotze, in trust. The income beneficiary is my wife, Vinny. The capital beneficiary is my son, Bobo.'

- Bobo will acquire a vested (personal) right against the testator's estate when *delatio* takes place (which is usually at the moment of the testator's death) although he cannot enforce it (*dies venit*) before dissolution of the trust (the death of Vinny).
- Bobo does not automatically become owner of the trust property when the trust is dissolved. For this to take place, a transfer or cession by the trustee to Bobo is necessary.

- Should Bobo die before the dissolution of the trust, his vested right passes to his estate and can be enforced against the trustee by his executor at the dissolution of the trust.

Non-discretionary trust with provision for substitution

'The capital beneficiaries of the trust are my children. If a capital beneficiary should die before dissolution of the trust, such beneficiary's descendants will represent that beneficiary as capital beneficiaries. If the predeceased capital beneficiary leaves no descendants, he or she will be substituted by the other capital beneficiaries.'

- The effect of direct substitution is that the rights of the capital beneficiary will only vest upon the dissolution of the trust.
- Only if the capital beneficiary (who was originally nominated) is still alive at that stage, does he or she acquire a vested personal right against the trustee in respect of the trust property.
- Should the capital beneficiary die before the dissolution of the trust, there is no vested personal right that can pass to his or her estate. The substitute then benefits in his or her place.

Discretionary trust

'Trustee Du Preez can choose the capital beneficiary(s), and the extent of their benefits, from my grandchildren.'

- Until the trustee exercises his or her discretion, none of the grandchildren has a vested personal right in respect of the trust property; they only have the expectation of possible benefits.
- Once the trustee has exercised his or her discretion in favour of a particular grandchild, such beneficiary acquires a vested personal right against the trustee.
- The content of the personal right is that he or she can claim transfer or cession of the relevant trust property as soon as his or her vested personal right becomes enforceable. This usually occurs upon the dissolution of the trust. The beneficiary only becomes owner of the trust property when it is transferred or ceded to him or her.

11.9 Amendment of trust provisions

11.9.1 Common law

The court does not have a general capacity to amend trust provisions in terms of the common law - it is in the public interest that the intentions of testators are upheld. There are, however, certain specific exceptions to this general rule.

Firstly, the court may amend or delete provisions in a trust instrument if it is imperative to do so. Imperatives may arise from different circumstances, for example, legal requirements which bind the trustees, essential maintenance of trust assets, or the maintenance of minors. Secondly, if it is impossible or impractical to give effect to a trust in the manner prescribed by the founder, the court may authorise another method.[85]

85 See *Administrators, Estate Richards v Nichol* 1996 (4) SA 253 (C).

11.9.2 Section 13 of the Trust Property Control Act

The Trust Property Control Act confers a relatively wide power on the court to amend the provisions of a trust instrument. The trustee and any other interested party, such as a beneficiary, can apply to the court for a variation order. Section 13 reads as follows:

> *If a trust instrument contains any provision which brings about consequences which in the opinion of the court the founder of a trust did not contemplate or foresee and which –*
> *(a) hampers the achievement of objects of the founder; or*
> *(b) prejudices the interests of beneficiaries; or*
> *(c) is in conflict with the public interests,*
>
> *the court may, on application of the trustee or any person who in the opinion of the court has a sufficient interest in the trust property, delete or vary any such provision or make in respect thereof any order which such court deems just, including an order whereby particular trust property is substituted for particular other property or an order terminating the trust.*[86]

11.9.3 Validity of power to amend given to a trustee

A question has been posed as to whether a testator can give the trustee the power to amend a testamentary trust. The general consensus seems to be that the most that a testamentary trustee could be authorised to do is to change administrative provisions (for example, the frequency of trustee meetings). A trustee cannot change the beneficiaries, or the benefits that may accrue to them, or the powers a trustee can exercise. Power to change these kinds of provisions would be an invalid delegation of testamentary power as discussed earlier.

11.10 Termination of a trust

Factors which can lead to the termination of a trust include:

- the realisation of the trust objective
- the destruction of the trust assets without fault on the part of the trustee
- the failure of the trust for some or other reason
- the acceleration of rights to the capital beneficiary, for example, when the income beneficiary renounces his or her rights and no other intention is stated in the trust document
- a court order in terms of s 13 of the Trust Property Control Act
- the sequestration of the trust.

86 For an application of this section see *Ex parte President of the Conference of the Methodist Church of Southern Africa: In re William Marsh Will Trust* 1993 (2) SA 697 (C) and *Minister of Education v Syfrets Trust Ltd* 2006 (4) SA 205 (C); *Ex parte BOE Trust Ltd*, case no 211/09 of 27 May 2009.

11.11 Customary law of succession

Although the *mortis causa* trust is an unfamiliar concept in customary law, variations of the inter vivos trust have been both effectively and ineffectively applied to protect customary property rights over the years. One such example of an inter vivos trust is the KwaZulu-Natal Ingonyama Trust. This trust is a legal landowner of almost 2.8 million hectares of land in KwaZulu-Natal which has to be administered for the material benefit and social well-being of the individual members of the relevant communities.

Intestate customary law has been abolished to a large extent by recent developments in the customary law of succession.[87] However, the trust can be an effective instrument to ensure that family property remains in the family – the family head creates a trust in his or her will and then bequeaths the family property to the trust to be administered for the common good of the family. The administration of the trust could be entrusted to certain family members (for example, the elders) by appointing them as trustees. In such a case, the normal principles applicable to trusts have to be taken into consideration.

THIS CHAPTER IN ESSENCE

1. The chapter focuses on the trust as legal institution within the context of the law of testate succession, in other words, the testamentary trust or *mortis causa* trust.
2. A testamentary trust is most often used to provide for the needs of dependants or for an impersonal object. As an institution, it has certain advantages compared to the usufruct and fideicommissum.
3. The basic idea of a trust is that ownership is bequeathed to one person for the benefit of a third person (or people), or for the achievement of an impersonal object.
4. The Trust Property Control Act is only applicable to the trust in the narrow sense of the word, the main characteristic of which is that the trustee occupies an office as trustee.
5. Section 1 of the Act defines a trust and distinguishes between the so-called ownership trust and the *bewind* trust.
6. The requirements for the creation of a valid trust are:
   - the intention to create a trust
   - the intention must be expressed in such a way that it creates a binding obligation to set up a trust
   - the trust property and trust beneficiaries must be determined or be capable of determination
   - the trust object must be lawful.
7. There are certain core elements describing the true characteristics of a trust and which provide protection to the trust beneficiary.
8. The trustee's powers and duties are determined by the trust instrument, the common law and the Trust Property Control Act.
9. Trustees are not vicariously liable for a breach of trust by co-trustees. Liability is based on own fault and therefore on the general principles of delictual liability.
10. The origin, nature, and extent of a beneficiary's rights are determined by the existence of a fiduciary relationship, the type of trust concerned and the provisions of the trust instrument.
11. A trust instrument can be amended by a court under specific circumstances.
12. Various factors can lead to the termination of the trust.
13. The *mortis causa* trust is fairly unknown in customary law, but it can be a useful instrument for a testator who wants to preserve the family property within the family.

87 See the discussion in Chapter 2.

Chapter 12

Collation

When does collation come into play?

12.1	Introduction	191
12.2	Who participates in collation?	193
12.3	What benefits are collatable?	196
12.4	Valuation of collatable benefits	198
12.5	Customary law of succession	200
This chapter in essence		201

12.1 Introduction

Collation is a process by which the inheritances of certain of a deceased's heirs are adjusted to take into account the fact that they received substantial benefits from the deceased during his or her lifetime. Since collation does not in itself increase the actual value of the deceased's estate, the process of adjustment means that the inheritances of those heirs involved in collation are increased beyond what the will or the rules of intestacy would otherwise have given them, and the inheritances of other heirs are correspondingly reduced.[1]

Collation has been more formally defined by Corbett et al,[2] who state that:

> *[i]t is the duty incumbent on descendants (of either sex) who wish to share as heirs in the estate of an ascendant (of either sex), whether by will or* ab intestato, *of accounting to the estate for certain gifts or advances received from, or debts incurred to, their ascendant during the ascendant's lifetime.*

Collation is also known by the following terms: *collatio bonorum* in Roman law, '*inbreng*' in Roman-Dutch law, '*inbring*' in Afrikaans, and 'hotchpotch' in some foreign jurisdictions.

The rationale behind collation is to ensure that the deceased's children are all treated equally.[3] A secondary purpose, which applies when the testator has chosen not to benefit his or her children equally, is to ensure that the children benefit in the particular proportions chosen by the testator, and that those proportions are not upset by substantial benefits given

1 See *Abraham v Els* 1964 (2) SA 215 (C) at 219E–G.

2 At 21.

3 *Estate Van Noorden v Estate Van Noorden* 1916 AD 175 at 105 & 193; *Thesnaar v Die Meester* 1997 (3) SA 169 (C) at 175B–D.

to any beneficiary during the testator's lifetime.[4] In this way, collation preserves the overall scheme devised by the deceased for the devolution of his or her estate amongst his or her descendants.

Collation also applies when the heirs are determined by the rules of intestate succession.[5]

Tandu made a will bequeathing a legacy of R100 000 to his brother, Ravi, and the residue of his estate in equal shares to his three children, Sbu, Jakes, and Melinda, and his granddaughter, Penny (who is Melinda's daughter). Some years later Sbu loses his home as part of a divorce settlement, and Tandu buys Sbu a flat costing R300 000 so Sbu will have a roof over his head. When Tandu dies, the value of his estate for distribution to his heirs is R1 700 000. Without collation, Ravi would take his legacy of R100 000, and Sbu, Jakes, Melinda, and Penny would each inherit R400 000. If either Jakes or Melinda calls for collation to take place, however, the inheritances of each of the heirs who participate in collation will be adjusted to take account of the fact that Sbu benefited substantially during his father's lifetime because his father helped him in a time of personal difficulty.

Only Sbu, Jakes, and Melinda qualify to participate in collation (see pages 193–194) and therefore the adjustment for collation must exclude Penny and Ravi from benefiting. Furthermore, the process of collation does not (normally) increase the value of the assets in the estate, but merely affects the distribution of the estate amongst those heirs who participate in collation. For this reason, the adjustment for collation is made in the distribution account of the estate accounts for Tandu's estate (which shows how the assets are distributed to the beneficiaries) rather than in the liquidation account (which shows the assets in the estate).[6] The features of the liquidation and distribution account are discussed in Chapter 15.

Table 12.1 A collation calculation

		R	R
	Balance for distribution		1 700 000
1	To Ravi legacy		*100 000
2	To Penny $\frac{1}{4}$ of residue ((R1 700 000 – R100 000) ÷ 4)		*400 000
	Balance available to collating heirs (R1 700 000 – R500 000)	1 200 000	
	Add amounts to be collated:		
	By Sbu	300 000	
		1 500 000	

4 *Thesnaar v Die Meester* 1997 (3) SA 169 (C) at 175G–I, see also176D–E.
5 *De Vos v Van der Merwe* [1996] 4 All SA 82 (N) at 86; *Thesnaar v Die Meester* 1997 (3) SA 169 (C) at 174.
6 This method of calculation is in accordance with that discussed in *Abraham v Els* 1964 (2) SA 215 (C) and follows the approach used in Meyerowitz, at para 18.2.5 (the second illustration).

		R	R
3	To Sbu $\frac{1}{3}$ of R1 500 000	500 000	
	Less amount collated	300 000	*200 000
4	To Jakes $\frac{1}{3}$ of R1 500 000		*500 000
5	To Melinda $\frac{1}{3}$ of R1 500 000		*500 000
			1 700 000

Note the following important features of this calculation:

- The inheritances of those beneficiaries who do not qualify to participate in collation (Penny and Ravi respectively) are awarded before the adjustment for collation takes place.
- The flat has been notionally added into the value of the estate for the purpose of calculating the share that each heir who participates in collation is to take out of the estate. Throughout the process, however, Sbu remains the owner of the flat and, therefore, the actual value of the estate does not increase. For this reason, the adjustment for collation takes place in the distribution account, rather than the liquidation account, of the estate accounts.
- The flat has been notionally treated as an advance on Sbu's inheritance by deducting the amount collated in respect of the flat from Sbu's share as heir.
- The amounts marked with an asterisk (*) are the only amounts that are actually paid out to the beneficiaries, and they total R 1 700 000, which is the actual value of the estate. The effect of applying collation was, therefore, that Sbu's inheritance was reduced, and the inheritances of his siblings, who participated in collation, were increased. In this way the fact that Sbu had benefited from Tandu's estate substantially during Tandu's lifetime was brought into account on Tandu's death.
- Although the actual payment that Sbu received on Tandu's death is less than that given to Sbu's siblings, Tandu's children have, if one takes the long-term view, all benefited equally as a result of collation.

12.2 Who participates in collation?

In practice, collation takes place only where one or other person entitled to benefit from collation calls for it because the executor of the estate is often not in a position to be aware of benefits given by the testator during his or her lifetime. However, an executor who is aware of collatable benefits is obliged to give effect to collation in the absence of a waiver by those entitled beneficiaries or the remission of collation by the deceased.[7] The general rule is that only descendants of the testator who are heirs and who would have qualified to inherit had the testator died intestate, can be required to collate. (However, the deceased can during his or her lifetime extend the obligation to collate to further beneficiaries.) Such descendants are also the only persons who can call for and benefit from collation. Thus a descendant who inherits merely as a legatee does not have to collate in respect of the legacy;

7 *Estate Van Noorden v Estate Van Noorden* 1916 AD 175 at 188.

such a descendant is said to inherit under particular title. The question as to whether or not the descendant would have been an heir had the deceased died intestate is used as part of the test for whether or not a beneficiary can call for, or must submit to, collation even if the deceased died testate.

During his or her lifetime, a deceased is entitled to remit (grant exemption from) the duty to collate in favour of heirs,[8] and is also entitled to extend the obligation to collate to persons who would not otherwise be obliged to do so (for example, by stipulating that an heir who is not a descendant must collate).[9] The remission or extension of the duty to collate need not be specified in a will, but can also be deduced from the conduct and statements of the deceased.[10] A beneficiary who would otherwise be entitled to benefit from collation can waive the benefit of collation.

The rules regarding who participates in collation may be illustrated as follows:

- A brother of the deceased cannot be required to collate because he is not descended from the deceased. Similarly, he cannot benefit from collation. Thus Ravi does not participate in collation in Figure 12.1.
- The deceased's grandchildren, the children of the deceased's children, cannot be required to collate if their parents are still living because the grandchildren would then not qualify as heirs in terms of the rules of intestacy. Similarly, the grandchildren cannot benefit from collation. Thus Penny does not participate in collation in Figure 12.1.
- The deceased's children can be required to collate if they inherit as heirs.
- A child of the deceased who only inherits as a legatee cannot be required to collate. In other words, the value of the legacy cannot be reduced through collation. Similarly, he or she cannot benefit from collation.
- A legatee whose legacy is going to be reduced through abatement because there is a shortfall in the estate, cannot require another beneficiary to collate benefits received during the testator's lifetime in order to increase the value of the estate.
- A creditor of the deceased cannot call for collation, for example to increase the value of an estate that is unable to settle its debts fully. Depending on the circumstances, however, the possibility exists that the executor might be able to use the laws of insolvency to reclaim benefits given to a beneficiary by the testator during his or her lifetime.

A grandchild who inherits from a grandparent as an heir in place of his or her predeceased parent (by way of substitution), and who is, therefore, subject to the duty to collate, must collate not merely what he or she personally received from the grandparent, but also what his or her parent received,[11] even if the grandchild is not a beneficiary in his or her parent's estate.[12] Similarly, it seems that an heir who takes his or her co-heir's share by virtue of a right of accrual[13] must collate what his or her co-heir would have been obliged to collate had he or she inherited.

As the object of collation is the equal, or consistent, treatment of children or more remote descendants, there should be no question of a surviving spouse having to participate in collation. The law is clear that a surviving spouse who was married out of community of

8 *Thesnaar v Die Meester* 1997 (3) SA 169 (C) at 175D–E; *De Vos v Van der Merwe* [1996] 4 All SA 82 (N) at 88.

9 *De Vos v Van der Merwe* [1996] 4 All SA 82 (N) at 88.

10 *Thesnaar v Die Meester* 1997 (3) SA 169 (C) at 175C–D; *De Vos v Van der Merwe* [1996] 4 All SA 82 (N) at 88.

11 *Loots v Estate Loots* 1923 CPD 238 at 246.

12 *Estate Van Noorden v Estate Van Noorden* 1916 AD 175 at 187.

13 For a discussion of accrual, see Chapter 10.

property to the deceased does not participate in collation. However, the position of the surviving spouse who was married in community of property to the deceased is problematic. In terms of Roman-Dutch law, collation also operated to benefit a surviving spouse married in community of property to the deceased when division of the joint estate took place.[14] (In other words, collatable assets were brought into account before the value of the survivor's half-share was calculated). The deceased did not have the power to remit (exempt) the heirs from the duty to collate in favour of the surviving spouse. Most academic writers accept that the Roman-Dutch law on collation when the joint estate is divided, is part of South African law.[15] Unlike Roman-Dutch law, however, in modern South African law the surviving spouse takes as an heir if his or her spouse dies intestate. Nevertheless, it seems that a surviving spouse who benefits from collation only does so with respect to the calculation of his or her share of the joint estate but not with respect to the calculation of the surviving spouse's inheritance under the will or on intestacy. The upshot is that the surviving spouse's share of the joint estate is boosted by an amount equivalent to half the value of the collatable benefits and the residue for distribution to all the heirs is reduced accordingly.

COUNTER POINT

Rights of the surviving spouse

Should the surviving spouse benefit from collation in this way in modern South African law? Corbett et al[16] argue that a persuasive case can be made against such a right for the surviving spouse. The basis of their argument is that including the surviving spouse does not accord with the general principle behind collation, there does not appear to be any South African decision enforcing such a right,[17] and the indications are that such a right by the surviving spouse is not being enforced in practice. However, if collation in favour of the joint estate does not take place, then it seems that only half the benefit received by an heir should be collated in favour of the other heirs because effectively half the collatable benefit will have come from the deceased parent and the other half from the surviving parent. When the survivor dies, collation of a half-share of benefits would have to take place again. This issue is not discussed by Corbett.

If a person who is obliged to collate refuses to do so, this amounts to a repudiation of his or her inheritance, and he or she cannot inherit.[18] Since the beneficiary is not required actually to hand over the collatable benefit, or pay any funds into the estate in respect thereof, it would seem that a refusal to collate would take the form of, for example, preventing the extent or value of the collatable benefit from being ascertained, for example when the beneficiary refuses to allow the asset to be inspected for valuation purposes.

14 Political Ordinance of 1580, s 29.

15 Corbett et al at 30.

16 At 24–25.

17 It should be noted, however, that in *J. M. Scheepers v C. F. Scheepers' Executrix* (1873) 3 Buch 1 at 8, the judge was clearly of the view that the surviving spouse had such a right, although on the facts of the case, the survivor had failed to enforce it.

18 *Estate Van Noorden v Estate Van Noorden* 1916 AD 175 at 178 and 184; and *Mosse v Estate Ebden* 1913 CPD 567.

PAUSE FOR REFLECTION

Unequal treatment

Suppose the testatrix is closer to her elder daughter, Anna, and bequeaths her estate to her two daughters, Anna and Beatrix, in the proportion 2:1 with the larger share going to Anna. Does this unequal treatment imply that the testatrix has dispensed with collation? This was the situation in *Thesnaar v Die Meester*,[19] in which the residue of the estate available for distribution to the heirs, who were the testatrix's two daughters, was roughly R112 500 and the elder daughter had received gifts from the testatrix totalling R280 000. The effect of collation would be that the elder daughter would take nothing out of the estate on the death of the testatrix. The elder daughter argued that the presumption that the testatrix intended to treat her children equally was rebutted by the terms of her will, in which she bequeathed a larger share of her estate to her elder daughter. This, it was argued, was proof that the testatrix had dispensed with collation. The Court ruled, however, that collation must take place. It held that where the testatrix chooses to distribute the estate amongst her children in unequal proportions, the rebuttable presumption is that the testatrix intended collation to preserve the proportions she chose.[20] It is interesting to note, however, that according to Voet,[21] if the testator bequeaths all his or her goods amongst his or her children but gives more of his or her estate to those heirs who benefited less during his or her lifetime, this is an indication that he or she has dispensed with collation. Would the same principle apply if the testator gave his or her son a legacy only, thereby insulating him from any duty to collate, and gave the residue of his or her estate to his or her two daughters in the proportion 2:1? Would substantial gifts to one of the daughters be collatable? The reasoning in *Thesnaar v Die Meester*[22] would seem to suggest that collation would still serve the legitimate purpose of preserving the proportions in which the testator appointed his or her two daughters to benefit. However, it is impossible to predict the outcome with any certainty.

If the value of the benefit to be collated is of such a magnitude that it excludes the beneficiary from inheriting, then that beneficiary 'receives nothing and pays nothing, and the distribution of the estate is recalculated as if he or she did not exist'.[23] In such a case, all the remaining heirs, even those who do not participate in collation, benefit from the fact that the balance for distribution is then shared amongst fewer heirs.

12.3 What benefits are collatable?

Whether a benefit received by an heir is collatable is ultimately a question of the deceased's intention.[24] However, the following benefits have been identified as collatable by an heir:[25]

19 1997 (3) SA 169 (C).
20 *Thesnaar v Die Meester* 1997 (3) SA 169 (C) at 175G–I.
21 Voet 37.6.27, third para.
22 1997 (3) SA 169 (C).
23 Corbett et al at 29.
24 *Jooste v Jooste's Executor* (1890–1891) 8 SC 288.
25 See also regarding the presumption of an intention that collation take place *Jooste v Jooste's Executor* (1890–1891) 8 SC 288 at 291 & 292; *Steijn's Executors v Steijn* (1894) 11 SC 55 at 59 & 60.

- money or property given as part of his or her inheritance[26] (in other words, an advance on the inheritance)
- money or property given for advancement in trade, business, or a profession[27] (in other words, to establish or improve the business of the heir)
- money or property given to the heir as a marriage settlement (in other words, a dowry or other wedding gift), excluding expenditure on a child's wedding
- other money or property given to the heir which is a gift of a substantial nature in relation to the donor's means resulting in inequitable treatment so far as the other heirs are concerned
- debts owed by the heir to the deceased, including debts that have been extinguished by prescription or discharged by the heir's insolvency and subsequent rehabilitation, provided that the transaction that gave rise to the indebtedness was one by which something was taken out of the estate, which was thereby diminished in value.[28] Examples of transactions that would not meet this test are promissory notes signed by an heir in favour of the deceased as payment for work done by the deceased, or to satisfy a delictual claim owed by the beneficiary to the deceased. Because the transaction giving rise to the indebtedness in such cases would not have diminished the estate of the deceased, the prescribed debt would not be collatable. Where the debt in question has not prescribed or been discharged by the heir's insolvency (as above), the executor must first attempt to collect payment in the usual way before bringing it into collation.[29]

On the other hand, the following are not collatable unless a contrary intention is shown:

- normal expenditure on maintenance, education, or travel (although expenditure that is totally disproportionate to the benefits enjoyed by other heirs is collatable)[30]
- remuneratory donations, provided the donation is not disproportionately large in relation to the services rendered. A remuneratory donation is one that is not given out of sheer generosity on the part of the donor, but rather is given out of a sense of moral obligation in response to benefits that the donor has received from the donee, for example, where an elderly parent who has been nursed through a long illness by one of her children rewards the child with a holiday overseas.
- a simple and unconditional gift,[31] unless it is disproportionately large in relation to the donor's means and results in unequal treatment so far as the other heirs are concerned. In terms of this approach, gifts given to mark special occasions, such as Christmas gifts or birthday gifts, would not be collatable unless they result in substantial inequality.

---

26 *De Vos v Van der Merwe* [1996] 4 All SA 82 (N) at 86.

27 *Metcalfe v Oates* (1919) 40 NLR at 202.

28 *Estate Van Noorden v Estate Van Noorden* 1916 AD 175 at 186, where it is stated that there must be 'an alienation, advance or payment by the ancestor'.

29 *Estate Van Noorden v Estate Van Noorden* 1916 AD 175 at 185–188.

30 *De Vos v Van der Merwe* [1996] 4 All SA 82 (N) at 86 states that benefits going beyond normal maintenance are collatable where other children do not receive similar benefits.

31 *Jooste v Jooste's Executor* (1890–1891) 8 SC 288 at 292. Although modern writers are in agreement regarding this treatment of simple and unconditional gifts, it seems that amongst the old authorities their correct treatment was seen as problematic.

PAUSE FOR REFLECTION

What is collatable?

The parents of Anna and Bonita pay for the university education of Anna, who wants to become an attorney, and give to Bonita, who is not interested in studying, the sum of R80 000, which is roughly equivalent to what was spent on Anna's education. The parents are middle class, and not wealthy, and this expenditure exhausts their savings. In terms of the general principles discussed above, the education received by Anna is not collatable. But how should the gift received by Bonita be treated? Viewed in isolation, it is a substantial gift in relation to the donor's means and should be collated. But if one takes all the circumstances into account it does not result in inequality. In fact, to require it to be collated in the circumstances would seem to promote inequality!

Wiechers[32] correctly asserts that the rules as to what benefits are collatable can be difficult to apply - leading to uncertainty - and argues that the outcomes can be anomalous, and that collation should, therefore, be abolished.

Is this sufficient reason to abolish collation? Or can it serve a useful purpose? Is it within the power of the courts to bring collation to an end if it has outlived its usefulness? Or is this a task for the legislature? Can difficulties of this nature be resolved by development of the principles governing what is collatable? There are no clear-cut answers to these questions.

12.4 Valuation of collatable benefits

Assets fluctuate in value over time. For example, a house or shares quoted on the stock exchange can be considerably more valuable when the deceased dies than when they were given to a beneficiary. On the other hand, some other gifts, such as a car given by the deceased, will depreciate. This raises the question at what time must the gift be valued for the purposes of collation?

In *De Vos v Van der Merwe*,[33] the following principles regarding valuation were recognised: If the deceased has stipulated how or when the asset is to be valued, then the value is determined accordingly. In the absence of any indication by the deceased as to how or when the asset is to be valued, it must be valued as at date of gift. In either case, if the beneficiary is dissatisfied with the value arrived at, then he or she can elect to surrender the asset itself to the estate.[34] In this way, the loss to the beneficiary is limited to the current value of the asset. In case of surrender, the value of the estate actually increases by the value of the surrendered asset which becomes the property of the estate. It should be borne in mind that surrender of an asset in this way could trigger the obligation to pay transfer duty (in case of immovable property) and donations tax. If the drop in value of the asset is due to neglect by the beneficiary, then he or she is not entitled to avoid the drop in value by surrendering the asset.[35]

32 1974 *De Jure* 150.
33 [1996] 4 All SA 82 (N).
34 *De Vos v Van der Merwe* [1996] 4 All SA 82 (N) at 87–88.
35 Voet 37.6.9.

A deceased's wishes regarding the time or method of valuation need not be expressed in a will, but can be determined by other evidence.[36]

The beneficiary who collates does not actually pay money into the estate, but the relevant sum is notionally added to the value of the estate.[37] The only exception is where the beneficiary elects to surrender the gift to the estate, in which case the value of the assets in the estate increases by the value of the surrendered gift.

The Court in *De Vos v Van der Merwe*[38] appears to have been of the view that if the beneficiary no longer has the asset in his or her possession, then its generic equivalent can be surrendered in its place. An asset would be regarded as one of a genus (generic) if it is completely interchangeable with other assets of the same genus.

> One ordinary share in XYZ Limited (a company whose shares are freely traded on the stock exchange) is the same as any other ordinary share in that company. It makes no difference whether the beneficiary surrenders the particular share that he or she received as a gift from the deceased or whether he or she buys another share in the same company and surrenders that.
>
> On the other hand, the beneficiary would not be permitted to surrender a share in ABC Limited in place of a share in XYZ Limited because it does make a difference which company's shares one owns. Similarly, an asset such as a painting is not generic, because it does make a difference which particular painting one owns, so a beneficiary who received a painting from the deceased and no longer has it in his or her possession would not be permitted to buy and surrender another painting in its place, even if it is by the same artist.

PAUSE FOR REFLECTION

Generic substitution

Suppose the collatable gift comprised a white motor car of a certain make, model, and age with a 1.6 litre engine capacity, that cost R190 000 when new, and that the average used car price for such a vehicle is now R100 000. If the beneficiary has sold the car by the time the testator dies, must the car be collated at R190 000 because the testator has not specified any method of valuation? Or can the beneficiary avoid this unfavourable valuation by buying a second-hand white motor car of the same make, model and age with a 1.6 litre engine capacity and surrendering it to the estate? Is one motor car a generic equivalent of any other of the same make, model, and age? Or is each motor car different because of differences in the kilometres travelled, how carefully it has been driven, the extent to which it has been regularly serviced, whether it has been kept at the coast where rust is more prevalent, and so on? Are there many assets that can be regarded as generic in this sense? There is no case authority on this issue but it seems that a second-hand motor car cannot be regarded as a generic asset because of the differences between motor cars mentioned above. This is not really unfair on the beneficiary because the estate was reduced by the cost price of the asset when the beneficiary received it as a gift and the beneficiary has had the benefit of the asset.

36 *De Vos v Van der Merwe* [1996] 4 All SA 82 (N) at 88.
37 *Abraham v Els* 1964 (2) SA 215 (C).
38 [1996] 4 All SA 82 (N).

In some circumstances, the amount to be collated can be reduced by amounts that the beneficiary has expended on the collatable property. It seems that this applies to necessary or useful expenses to the extent that they exceed the fruits of the property. According to some of the old Roman-Dutch authorities, the amount by which conduct of a beneficiary has substantially increased the value of the deceased's estate can also be deducted so as to reduce the value at which the property is collated.

LEGAL THINKING

To collate or not to collate?

One way to approach the possibility of collation in an estate would be to ask the following questions:

1. Has a beneficiary called for collation of a benefit or is the executor otherwise aware of a benefit conferred by the testator during his or her lifetime?
2. Is the benefit one which the testator intended to be collated, or is presumed to have intended to be collated, in accordance with the applicable principles?
3. Is the recipient of the gift a beneficiary who owes a duty to collate? In particular:
   - Is the beneficiary a descendant of the deceased?
   - Would the beneficiary be entitled to inherit in terms of the rules of intestacy?
   - Is the beneficiary an heir as opposed to a mere legatee?
   - Is the beneficiary someone to whom the deceased has extended the duty to collate, who would not otherwise be obliged to do so?
   - Has the deceased exempted the beneficiary from collation?
4. Is any beneficiary in the estate competent to benefit from collation either because he or she satisfies the test in point 3 above or because the testator has extended to that beneficiary the right to benefit from collation?
5. What value should be attached to the benefit?
   - Did the deceased prescribe a value for the benefit or a method of valuing it?
   - If not, then use the value of the benefit at the time it was given.
   - Are there any deductions that the recipient is entitled to make to reduce the collatable value?
   - If the collatable value exceeds the current market value of the gifted asset, is the recipient willing and able to surrender the asset to the estate? Alternatively, is surrender of a generic equivalent possible?
6. If the recipient thwarts the valuation of the benefit, has the recipient thereby impliedly repudiated his or her inheritance?

12.5 Customary law of succession

Collation is a process unique to the common law of succession and does not currently exist in customary law. Nevertheless, the system of intestate succession applicable in the common law system in terms of the Intestate Succession Act now applies in customary law, pursuant to the decision of the Constitutional Court in *Bhe v Magistrate, Khayelitsha* and the subsequent enactment of the Reform of Customary Law of Succession Act.[39] It is possible

39 Remember that the Act was signed by the President but that it is not yet in operation.

that this may have had the unintended effect of introducing the common law system of collation into customary law.

Customary law allows a family head to dispose of his assets during his lifetime by determining the status of houses, thereby influencing the ranking of succession. If he does so in such a way as to benefit only some descendants, it may be argued that this is a gift during his lifetime that ought to be taken into account when distributing his assets on his death in the same way as collation operates under the common law.

In KwaZulu-Natal, s 71 of the KwaZulu Act on the Code of Zulu Law[40] and the Natal Code of Zulu Law[41] allow a family head to divide his family home into various sections (with a maximum of four sections) consisting of the great house, left-hand house, right-hand house and junior houses of poor relations. In doing so, he usually divides the family property between the houses according to their status, thereby making a gift to those houses during his lifetime.

The family head may also donate family property to a certain house or even a certain child, provided that he does so in an open and transparent manner. For example, it is customary for a family head to assist a son to pay lobolo for his first wife.[42] In all these examples, the family head confers benefits on his descendants during his lifetime.

This conferring of benefits on certain descendants does not entitle those descendants who did not benefit, or who benefited to a lesser extent, to insist that the benefits conferred by the family head during his lifetime be brought into account when his assets are distributed on his death. However, since the Intestate Succession Act now applies to all intestate estates, regardless of whether the deceased lived under a system of customary law or not, there may be room to argue that the system of collation now applies in customary law too, and that dispositions made by a family head during his lifetime are collatable benefits that must be brought into account when the inheritances of the other descendants are calculated. It is, however, impossible to say with any certainty whether the courts will allow the introduction of collation into customary law in this way.

THIS CHAPTER IN ESSENCE

1. The process of collation brings into account significant benefits received by a descendant from the deceased during the deceased's lifetime - over and above the normal costs incurred by the deceased in the maintenance and education of the descendant - and in this way it promotes equal treatment of the deceased's children.
2. Where the deceased chose to appoint his or her descendants as heirs in unequal shares, then collation preserves the proportions chosen by the deceased.
3. The benefits and obligations of collation are, however, limited to a closely defined group, namely those descendants of the deceased who are actually heirs and who would qualify as intestate heirs if the deceased were to (or did) die intestate. (Subject to remission or extension by the testator of the duty to collate.)
4. An heir cannot collate unless he or she received a collatable benefit.
5. The principles determining the benefits that must be collated are not clear cut and their application can be problematic in practice.

40 16 of 1985.
41 Proc R151 of 1987 in *GG* 10966 of 9 October 1987.
42 *Ngcobo v Ngcobo* 1929 AD 233.

6. It has been suggested by one writer that collation should be abolished because of the difficulties that can arise in its practical application. This would, however, be a drastic remedy and would deprive beneficiaries of what can, in appropriate cases, be a valuable tool for ensuring fair treatment.
7. Collation is a process unique to the common law of succession and does not currently exist in customary law, but there are instances where the family head disposes of the family property during his lifetime and only time will tell whether in future those who benefit from such dispositions will be seen as having a duty to collate them by way of a development of customary law.

Chapter 13

Interpretation of wills

What are the rules for the interpretation of wills?

13.1	Introduction	203
13.2	Golden rule	203
13.3	Statutory rules of interpretation	204
13.4	Common law rules of interpretation	207
13.5	Variation of wills	217
13.6	Rectification of wills	219
13.7	Customary law of succession	221
This chapter in essence		221

13.1 Introduction

A will should always be written in clear and unambiguous language. Technical terms or legalistic vocabulary used to describe specialised legal terms of the legal world should be avoided as far as possible. Aside from improving readability, writing in comprehensible language will result in fewer interpretational problems. No matter how carefully a will is written, the possibility of interpretational problems always remains. Sometimes the most carefully drafted provisions can give rise to uncertainty of meaning and the very person who can clear up any ambiguity is no longer available to give evidence as regards his or her intention. For this reason the law of succession has specific rules for interpreting wills.

13.2 Golden rule

The starting point for the interpretation of wills is the so-called golden rule which was stated in *Robertson v Robertson's Executors*[1] as follows:

> *The golden rule for the interpretation of testaments is to ascertain the wishes of the testator from the language used. And when these wishes are ascertained, the Court is bound to give effect to them, unless [it is] prevented by some rule or [of sic] law from doing so.*

1 1914 AD 503 at 507; see also *Greyling v Greyling* 1978 (2) SA 114 (T) at 118.

All the rules for the interpretation of wills are geared towards determining and giving effect to the intention of the testator. As such, it stands to reason that the words that the testator uses in the will must be the primary indication of his or her intention. The courts are, therefore, reluctant to deviate from the ordinary and literal meaning of the words used by the testator, unless it can be shown by clear admissable evidence that the testator:

- had not intended those words to bear their ordinary and literal meaning
- had not intended those words to be used in the first place and had actually intended that other words be used to convey his or her intention.

Whereas the first scenario will require a court to interpret the words used by the testator to give effect to his or her 'true intention', the second scenario is more complicated. If words were inserted in the will which were not intended by the testator to form part of his or her will, one would have to ask the High Court to rectify the will.[2]

The Master of the High Court does not have an adjudicative function. In other words, the Master does not have judicial powers to settle a dispute. The reason for this is that the Master has neither the facilities nor the power to hear evidence. He or she has an administrative function only. Thus, when it comes to the interpretation of wills, the Master interprets a will literally, having regard to the actual words used by the testator. If one wishes to deviate from the ordinary and literal meaning of a will, proceedings must be instituted in the High Court to interpret the will. The lower courts do not have jurisdiction to hear matters involving the validity and interpretation of wills.[3]

13.3 Statutory rules of interpretation

The Wills Act contains certain rules for the interpretation of wills. These rules are referred to as the statutory rules of interpretation and are contained in ss 2B and 2D(1) of the Act.

13.3.1 Ex-spouses

Section 2B applies when a marriage between a testator and his or her former spouse has been dissolved by divorce or has been annulled by a court. The section provides that the testator's will shall be implemented as if the former spouse had predeceased the testator provided that the testator dies within three months of the dissolution of their marriage. Because of the principle of survivorship,[4] treating the former spouse as predeceased effectively deprives him or her of the benefits conferred by will. The former spouse will, however, be entitled to inherit where it appears from the will itself that the testator intended to benefit the former spouse despite the marriage having ended. For this exception to operate, the testator must have made it clear in his or her will that he or she had contemplated the possibility of the marriage being dissolved by divorce or annulment, and expressly or impliedly indicated that his or her spouse was to benefit regardless of whether or not they were still married. Circumstances or statements outside the will indicating such an intention will not be sufficient to save the former spouse's inheritance.

Section 2B only operates to deprive a former spouse of his or her inheritance if the testator dies less than three months after the dissolution of the marriage. If the testator dies more

2 See the discussion on page 220.
3 Section 46(2) of the Magistrates' Courts Act 32 of 1944.
4 No person can inherit unless he or she survives the deceased; see the discussion of the ground rules in Chapter 1.

than three months after the dissolution of the marriage, the former spouse is entitled to all benefits conferred on him or her by the will. In addition, the former spouse is not deprived of his or her inheritance if the will was executed after the divorce or annulment. Section 2B only applies if the testator 'executed a will before the date of such dissolution.'

COUNTER POINT

Why the three-month window period?

Section 2B creates a window period during which the former spouse is excluded and the testator has the opportunity to execute a new will. Notwithstanding the provisions of s 2B, there have been a number of cases in which testators who clearly did not wish their former spouses to inherit, failed to execute new wills during the three-month window period. Hahlo[5] has suggested that statute should provide that on divorce or the annulment of a marriage all provisions in the testator's will in favour of his or her former spouse are automatically revoked and that this should not be dependent on the death occurring less than three months after the divorce or annulment.

PAUSE FOR REFLECTION

Relevance of section 2B for other forms of marriage or partnerships

There can be no doubt that when s 2B was enacted in 1992, it was only intended to apply to persons who had been married in terms of the Marriage Act.

1. What relevance, if any, does s 2B have for persons who were married, for example, in terms of Muslim or Hindu rites, or in terms of the Civil Union Act, and whose former spouse or partner dies less than three months after the dissolution of their marriage or civil union?
2. Does s 2B have relevance for a person who was party to an unformalised same-sex life partnership in which the partners undertook reciprocal duties of support if his or her partner dies less than three months after the termination of their relationship?

Consider these questions in light of the equality clause of the Bill of Rights of the Constitution, the Civil Union Act and the cases concerning the meaning of the term 'spouse' discussed in Chapter 2.

13.3.2 The terms 'child' or 'children'

Section 2D(1) provides as follows:

> *In the interpretation of a will, unless the context otherwise indicates –*
> *(a) an adopted child shall be regarded as being born from his adoptive parent or parents and, in determining his relationship to the testator or another person for the purposes of a will, as the child of his adoptive parent or parents and not as the child of his natural parent or parents or any previous adoptive parent or parents, except in the case of a natural parent who is also the adoptive parent of the child concerned or who was married to the adoptive parent of the child concerned at the time of the adoption;*

5 Hahlo 1964 *SALJ* 381.

(b) *the fact that any person was born out of wedlock shall be ignored in determining his relationship to the testator or another person for the purposes of a will;*

(c) *any benefit allocated to the children of a person, or to the members of a class of persons, mentioned in the will shall vest in the children of that person or those members of the class of persons who are alive at the time of the devolution of the benefit, or who have already been conceived at that time and who are later born alive.*

The preamble to this section, namely 'In the interpretation of a will, unless the context otherwise indicates,' is quite significant. It suggests two things. Firstly, when interpreting a will these rules will apply unless the testator has expressly or impliedly intended that they do not apply. The legislature has, therefore, given the testator freedom to deviate from the statutory interpretation rules contained in this section if he or she so desires. Secondly, these statutory interpretative rules trump common law rules in so far as there is a conflict between the common law and the statutory rules. The use of the word 'shall' in paras (a), (b) and (c) is also indicative that these rules override the common law rules in so far as the common law rules are inconsistent with the statutory rules.

Section 2D(1)(a) deals with adoption and creates a fiction of ascendancy and descendancy. In terms of the section, an adopted child is deemed to be a descendant child of his or her adoptive parents, and all rights and obligations which existed between the child and its biological parents are terminated on adoption, unless the biological parent is the child's adoptive parent, or the biological parent was married to the adoptive parent at the time of the adoption.

PAUSE FOR REFLECTION

Parental rights

The provisos may come as a surprise to many. How is it possible for a biological parent to adopt a child? In terms of the Children's Act some categories of biological parents are not automatically regarded as parents of a child. To acquire parental rights they have to adopt the child concerned. The first proviso in s 2D(1)(a) relates to those people. As regards the second proviso, it is sometimes the case that in a second marriage for example, a spouse may want to adopt his or her spouse's child as his or her own. When this happens, the adoption does not have the effect of terminating the parental rights and obligations that exist between the child and his or her natural parent, who also happens to be the spouse of the adoptive parent.

At a basic level, the effect of s 2D(1)(a) is that when a will is interpreted, any reference to a child in the will includes an adopted child. However, as noted earlier, the adopted child is not only deemed to be a descendant of its adoptive parent(s), but is also deemed to be related to the adoptive parents' relations. The reference to 'or another person for the purposes of a will' means that when interpreting the will, adoption is not only taken into account in relation to the adopted parents, but also the adoptive parents' relations.

A testator provides in his will:

'I bequeath the residue of my estate to my nephews and nieces.'

The reference to nephews and nieces will include any children adopted by the testator's brother or sister.

For all intents and purposes the adopted child is treated as if he or she is a blood relation of the adoptive parents and their relations. A specific exclusion should be inserted in the will to exclude the adopted child from inheriting if the testator does not wish to benefit the child.

The common law also discriminated against extramarital children. When it comes to interpreting a modern will, s 2D(1)(b) provides that the fact that a child was born out of wedlock must be ignored - such a beneficiary will inherit without any discrimination. It is, of course, open to the testator to exclude extramarital children from inheriting, but then the testator has to be specific in this regard.

Section 2D(1)(c) entrenches the *nasciturus* fiction and creates a deeming provision in favour of the *nasciturus*. It is presumed, unless there is a contrary intention in the will, that if the testator leaves an inheritance to his or her children or any other class of persons, he or she would have intended to benefit the *nasciturus* conceived at the time of the devolution of the benefit and subsequently born alive.[6]

13.4 Common law rules of interpretation

13.4.1 Ordinary and plain meaning

When it comes to the interpretation of wills, there are no hard-and-fast rules, just a series of principles which themselves are not unchanging.

As noted earlier, the golden rule of interpretation is to give effect to the wishes of the testator which are to be extracted from the words used by the testator in his or her will. Corbett et al[7] have said that if the words of the testator are unambiguous, the court must give effect thereto even if the testator's dispositions are 'capricious, unreasonable, unfair, inconvenient or even absurd.' Only where the words used by the testator bear two or more possible meanings and there is no other evidence suggesting what the testator had in mind, will the courts lean in favour of a construction that is rational, convenient, and reasonable.

Words should be interpreted according to their usual grammatical (dictionary) meaning and technical terms, such as 'usufruct,' 'fideicommissum' and 'trust,' should be interpreted in terms of their legal-technical meaning. Where words have an ordinary as well as a technical meaning, they must be given their ordinary meaning unless the intention of the testator proves otherwise.[8]

These rules must, however, give way to the real intention of the testator which can be determined by factors such as the context of the will.

PAUSE FOR REFLECTION

The context of the will

The context of the will refers to the construction of the will - in other words, the document itself, or to armchair evidence of the surrounding circumstances. By using the context of the will, the courts have on occasion interpreted the word 'vest' in its loose sense to mean the transfer of possession or ownership, and not in the strict sense of passing a vested interest.[9] Similarly, the courts have, by looking at the construction of a will, inferred that a testator meant to impose a usufruct when he or she had mistakenly used the

6 See Chapter 7 for a detailed discussion of the position of the *nasciturus*.

7 At 453.

8 *Troitz v Trotsky's Executrix* 1924 WLD 53.

9 See *Samaradiwakara v De Saram* 1911 AD 465 at 469; *Jewish Colonial Trust Ltd v Estate Nathan* 1940 AD 163 at 175–176.

word fideicommissum.[10] One must always be careful, however, when construing words and phrases in a will, not to stretch the words or phrases to the point where there is no correlation between the words used by the testator and the meaning given or sought to be given.

It is presumed that every word used by the testator is meaningful. If the same word is used many times in a will, it is presumed that the testator intended the word to convey the same meaning on each occasion that it is used unless the context indicates the contrary.[11] The courts draw a distinction between situations where a person with legal expertise drafts a will as opposed to where a layperson drafts one.[12] In the case of a will drafted by a layperson, the courts are more inclined to deviate from the ordinary and literal meaning of the words used whereas in interpreting a will drafted by a legal expert, it is assumed that the drafter had a specific intent in mind when employing certain words. Of course, if armchair evidence is brought to show that the professional drafter had not followed the instructions of the testator, the court may be inclined either to interpret the will in accordance with the testator's true intention or to order rectification of the will, depending on the extent of the deviation.[13]

The *iusdem generis* (of the same kind or nature) rule which applies in statutory interpretation is also relevant to the interpretation of wills.[14] According to this rule, when a testator lists a series of qualifying words, a meaning is ascribed to each word having regard to the words preceding and following the word.

The testator says in clause 2 of his will:

'I bequeath all the farm property to my son, John,' and in clause 3 of the will 'I bequeath all my rural property to my son, David.'

In this context the farm property and rural property are used as synonyms and there is no ambiguity, which means that the two sons, John and David, will inherit all the farms of the deceased in equal shares.[15]

Attention must also be paid to punctuation and paragraphing when determining the meaning of words and phrases. The interpretational value of the punctuation and order of the paragraphs will depend on the circumstances of each case.[16]

As a general rule, clauses in a will that the testator erased or cancelled, and therefore revoked, may not be considered when interpreting a will.[17] Furthermore, words and phrases must be given the meaning they had at the time the will was made. However, since a will applies from the moment the testator dies, the date of death may have to be considered to determine the meaning of certain words.

10 *Estate Dempers v Estate Dempers* 1912 CPD 779.
11 *Ex Parte Malan* 1951 (3) SA 715 (O).
12 *Campbell v Daly* 1988 (4) SA 714 (T) at 719A–720A.
13 See page 210 para 13.4.3 for a description of armchair evidence.
14 *Estate Levitas v Levitas' Minors* 1962 (4) SA 385 (T).
15 See *Estate Levitas v Levitas' Minors* 1962 (4) SA 385 (T).
16 *Harter v Epstein* 1953 (1) SA 287 (A).
17 *Ex Parte Kops* 1947 (1) SA 155 (O); an opposite viewpoint was taken in *O'Dwyer v Estate Marks* 1957 (1) SA 287 (A).

In *Ex parte Weir's Executors*,[18] the Court construed a bequest of 'my shares' in a company to include shares acquired by the testator after the execution of the will.

Ultimately, the courts are reluctant to strike down wills or provisions in wills just because they seem uncertain. If a testator has taken the time and trouble to draft and execute a will, and has indicated an intention, however obscure, to benefit a particular individual or group of persons, the courts are generally inclined to adopt a construction which makes the bequest effective rather than one which makes it null and void.[19] As Corbett et al[20] note: '... it is only if after every endeavour the court finds it impossible to ascertain what the testator meant that a disposition will be struck down as invalid on grounds of uncertainty.'[21]

Aside from upholding wills or provisions in wills as opposed to striking down ambiguous provisions, the courts have also taken a particularly benevolent approach to charitable bequests. Since charitable bequests are for the public benefit, the courts treat them differently and try to uphold them as opposed to striking them down, even if it means taking a rather strained but workable interpretation.[22]

13.4.2 Construction of the will as a whole

Another important aid that can be used to determine the intention of the testator is the construction of the will when read as a whole. In other words, the words, expressions and clauses should not be read in isolation but against the background of the full will. The physical construction of the will is taken into consideration and things such as division into paragraphs, punctuation, and the place where a stipulation is found in the will in relation to other stipulations, are considered. The will is looked at as a whole and not as isolated words, phrases and paragraphs. All the clauses must be read together and interpreted in relation to each other. If the will contains a dominant clause, the rest of the will must be interpreted in terms of the dominant clause – in other words, secondary clauses must be treated as being subservient to a dominant clause or clauses.[23]

In *Smith v Smith*,[24] the Court relied on the construction of the will as a whole. In this case, a couple made a joint will and appointed the survivor as the sole and universal heir of the first-dying's property. It appeared from the will that the survivor was to have free and undisturbed enjoyment over the property. However, later in the will, they bequeathed all their immovable property to their children. This was an apparent contradiction. The Court resolved the matter by looking at the construction of the will. The Court held that the latter clause had to be read within the context of the general scheme of the will. The Court interpreted the latter clause as imposing a condition which had the effect of entitling the survivor to a life interest in the immovable property and not to unfettered ownership of the property.

18 1939 CPD 340.

19 *Verseput v De Gruchy* 1977 (4) SA 440 (W) at 443C–E; *Ex parte Kock* 1952 (2) SA 502 (C) at 511D–G; *De Villiers v Estate De Villiers* 1929 CPD 106; *Pieters v Van Rensburg* 1926 OPD 94.

20 At 459.

21 See also *Masters v Estate Cooper* 1954 (1) SA 140 (C) at 143H–144A.

22 *Marks v Estate Gluckman* 1946 AD 289 at 297–311; *Ex parte Henderson* 1971 (4) SA 549 (D) at 553A–D; *Ex parte Methodist Church of SA: In re Estate Corderoy* 1965 (4) SA 789 (C); *Ex parte Gibson* 1928 OPD 189 at 193–195.

23 *Estate Cato v Estate Cato* 1915 AD 290 at 301.

24 1913 CPD 869.

Where conflict arises between clauses, one should try to reconcile the clauses by having regard to the scheme of the will. What happens when the conflict cannot be resolved? In that event, the conflicting clauses will cancel each other out and neither will take effect.[25]

13.4.3 Armchair and extrinsic evidence

A court places itself in the position of the testator during the time of the making of his or her will to try to determine the intention of the testator. Evidence gathered in this way is called armchair evidence. Although it has been held that armchair evidence may even be admissible where there is no ambiguity or uncertainty regarding the contents of the will, this submission has been disputed by some courts.[26]

Extrinsic evidence (or evidence *aliunde*) is evidence obtained elsewhere and not from the will itself, and refers to the surrounding circumstances (other than armchair evidence) in which the will was made. If the wording of a will is clear, extrinsic evidence to prove a contra intention of the testator is inadmissible.[27] Extrinsic evidence may only be led when the will or provisions in the will is or are obviously ambiguous or uncertain, and the intention of the testator has to be determined by means other than the wording of the will.[28]

> In *Richter v Bloemfontein Town Council*,[29] Innes CJ set the scene for the admission of armchair evidence for the purpose of interpreting legal documents (which includes wills) when he held that '[e]very document of course should ... be read in the light of the circumstances existing at the time' and that 'evidence may rightly be given of every material fact which will place the Court as near as may be in the situation of the parties to the instrument.'[30]

When interpreting a will, the court projects itself into the armchair of the deceased and considers the provisions of the will in light of all the material facts known or likely to have been known by the deceased at the time when he or she made the will. As noted in *Lello v Dales*:[31]

> *It is in the will [itself] that the indications and pointers must be sought, but it is permissible and sometimes essential to read and interpret the will in the light of the relevant circumstances existing at the time of its making.*

PAUSE FOR REFLECTION

The use of armchair evidence

Whilst the courts can resort to armchair evidence to construe a will, there has been some debate as to when armchair evidence is admissible. Some courts have held that one cannot admit armchair evidence when the words used in the will are clear and unambiguous. In the case of *In re Graumann's Estate*,[32] the Court unequivocally held: '... [I]f the words of the will are clear and unambiguous, then we cannot look even at the surrounding circumstances to interpret their meaning.'

25 *Smith v Smith* 1913 CPD 869 at 878.
26 *Cuming v Cuming* 1945 AD 201.
27 *Campbell v Daly* 1988 (4) SA 714 (T).
28 *Will v The Master* 1991 (1) SA 206 (C).
29 1922 AD 57.
30 1922 AD 57 at 59.
31 1971 (2) SA 330 (A) at 335D–E.
32 1940 CPD 204 at 206.

A similar sentiment was expressed in *Povall v Barclays Bank DCO*[33] where the Court held that a court has to construe a will before considering the surrounding circumstances, with the purpose of ascertaining the intention of the testatrix 'as expressed by the language of the will'. The Court made it clear that the procedure to be followed is as follows:

- Firstly, one has to determine the meaning of the provisions of the will. If the meaning is clear, one cannot use surrounding circumstances to throw doubt on the meaning or to give the provisions another meaning.
- Secondly, if the meaning of the provisions in the will is ambiguous or unclear, surrounding circumstances can be used to determine the intention of the testator.

However, this line of reasoning was questioned by Corbett J in *Allen v Estate Bloch*[34] where the Court held that the correct position regarding armchair evidence has been stated in two decisions of the High Court, namely *Ex parte Froy: In re Estate Brodie*[35] and *Ex parte Eksekuteure Boedel Malherbe.*[36] According to Corbett J (as he then was), the duty of a court is not to ascertain what the testator meant to do when he or she made his or her will, but what the testator's intention is 'as expressed in' his or her will. As a result, if the intention of the testator is clearly ascertained from the words of the will, it will not be permissible to use evidence of surrounding circumstances (extrinsic evidence) to prove that the testator must have had another intention. But Corbett J admits that a will cannot be analysed in isolation and points out that a court is entitled to 'have regard to the material facts and circumstances known to the testator'[37] when he or she made it (in other words, the court puts itself in the testator's armchair). By doing so, the court links the words and surrounding circumstances to find the meaning of the words.

Corbett J's approach of taking armchair evidence into account as part of the overall process of interpretation and not limiting it to situations where there is ambiguous or unclear language in a will is a more pragmatic approach, as it takes a holistic approach to the question of interpretation.

Since the purpose of armchair evidence is to give meaning to the stated words of the testator, it cannot be used to determine what the testator intended to write. Corbett et al[38] note that:

> *... extrinsic evidence may be admitted in order to clarify what is obscure; to render intelligible what at first blush looks unintelligible; to identify the subjects and objects of the testator's dispositions; to resolve ambiguities; and to reconcile apparent inconsistencies. It is not admissible to fill in blanks, or to conjecture which one of two irreconcilable clauses the testator would have considered more important.*

As stated in *Bell v Swan,*[39] one cannot depart from the language of a will 'to give effect to something which the testator may have intended but which he has not expressed at all.'

33 1965 (3) SA 322 (C) at 324E–H.
34 1970 (2) SA 376 (C).
35 1954 (2) SA 366 (C).
36 1957 (4) SA 704 (C).
37 *Allen v Estate Bloch* 1970 (2) SA at 380.
38 At 468–469.
39 1954 (3) SA 543 (W) at 550G–H.

Armchair evidence may be used for both latent and patent ambiguities. A latent ambiguity arises when the testator has identified a subject and an object of the bequest, but the bequest is worded in such a way that it could be equally applicable to another subject or object[40] – 'the so-called equivocation – or where the words do not clearly apply to any subject, as they describe it incompletely or inaccurately.'[41]

If the testator leaves an inheritance to Sam but it later comes to light that the testator knew two people with the name of Sam, one can rely on extrinsic evidence to resolve this. Another example would be where the testator leaves an inheritance to a charitable institution for a particular purpose and it is later discovered that there are two institutions with the same names doing similar work. Extrinsic evidence will be admitted to determine to which institution the testator was more closely affiliated, taking into account the conduct of the testator during his or her lifetime.[42]

13.4.4 Implied provisions

It is sometimes the case that the testator drafts a will or a bequest so inelegantly that it becomes necessary for the court to read words into the will so as to make the will or the bequest stand. South African courts have expressed great caution when reading words into a will. They have stated that reading words into a will is not tantamount to implying bequests into a will as the courts are generally not empowered to imply bequests.[43] To read words into a will, the courts have adopted a rather stringent test, namely:[44]

1. The deduction or implication must be a necessary implication which does not lend itself to a contrary intention.
2. The deduction or implication must be in accordance with the contents of the will.

In *Estate Dempers v Estate Dempers*,[45] the testators had executed a joint and mutual will stipulating that the survivor was to have a life usufruct over their joint estate. The will provided further that on the death of the survivor 'we appoint our children, and by the predeceasing of one or more, the deceased's lawful descendants by substitution, and as such in equal portions.' The problem was that the testators failed to stipulate what the children were appointed as. The Court had no problem finding that, as a necessary implication, the children were the implied ultimate heirs.

In another case, *Aubrey-Smith v Hofmeyr*,[46] the testatrix nominated her husband as the executor of her will and as the guardian of their minor children. She then went on to stipulate what was to happen to her estate in the event of her and her husband dying simultaneously. Strangely, the will did not nominate the husband as her heir in the event of him surviving her. The Court held that the words 'and as the sole and universal heir' of her estate had to be added to the clause appointing the husband as executor of her estate. In so doing, the court implied words into the will because without those words the will would not have made sense.

40 *Ex parte Eksekuteure Boedel Malherbe* 1957 (4) SA 704 (C).
41 Corbett et al at 469.
42 See for a case on similar facts, *Ex parte Eksekuteure Boedel Malherbe* 1957 (4) SA 704 (C).
43 *Morison v Executors of Morison* (1879) 9 Buch 24; *Ex parte Jewish Colonial Trust Ltd: In re Estate Nathan* 1967 (4) SA 397 (N).
44 *Ex parte Jewish Colonial Trust Ltd: In re Estate Nathan* 1967 (4) SA 397 (N) at 411A–C.
45 1912 CPD 779.
46 1973 (1) SA 655 (C).

13.4.5 Legal presumptions

Legal presumptions are another tool the courts have at their disposal for the interpretation of wills.[47] Legal presumptions are common law aids which are employed to determine the meaning of certain words which the testator used in his will. While the law is amenable to the use of presumptions, it must be remembered that they encapsulate a fictional way of reasoning. For this reason, where the words of a will are relatively clear and unambiguous, one should steer away from presumptions to provide definitive answers to questions of interpretation. The relevant presumptions are discussed below.

13.4.5.1 Writing or typing prevails over standard form wills

It is often the case that a testator completes a standard form (do-it-yourself) will. In the blank spaces on the document, necessary words, phrases and paragraphs are added. Additions are either penned by hand on the document or typed. When there is a conflict between the typed or written part and the printed part (the standard form will), there is a presumption that the typed or written part reflects the intention of the testator.[48]

PAUSE FOR REFLECTION

A computer-generated will

It is questionable whether this presumption stands when a testator buys a computer software package containing standard forms of wills. It may be argued that when a testator utilises a software package to draft a will, the standard form document and the testator's subsequent additions should be treated as one composite and seamless document, and that if the testator had intended not to be bound to the standard contents he or she should have deleted them. It must be remembered that it is much easier to delete provisions on an electronic document than it was in the day when people purchased hard-copy standard documents and had to work their way around the contents of the document. The presumption may have assisted testators to get around the inbuilt limitations of using hard-copy standard wills, but with the advent of modern technology, perhaps there is no justification for keeping it.

13.4.5.2 Presumption against intestacy

Despite the principle that a person may die partly testate and partly intestate, if a person has drafted a will, there is a strong presumption that he or she intended to die testate. To this extent, unless it appears clearly from the will that the testator has failed to deal expressly or impliedly with a portion of his or her estate, it is presumed that the testator had intended the will to govern his or her entire estate and not just a portion of it.[49]

13.4.5.3 Ambulatory nature of a will

Ambulatory means something that can be changed, altered, or revoked. A will speaks from when the testator dies; this is when it takes effect and has legal consequences. It is presumed, unless there is a contrary intention in the will, that vesting takes place, beneficiaries are to be ascertained, and the capacity of beneficiaries to inherit is to be determined only when the

47 *Havemann's Assignee v Havemann's Executor* 1927 AD 473.
48 *Snyders v Snyders* 1923 CPD 204.
49 *Havemann's Assignee v Havemann's Executor* 1927 AD 473 at 476.

testator dies as the testator has the power to amend or revoke the will until his or her death. There are, however, circumstances when the date the will was executed is the determining date, rather than death. Examples include where testamentary capacity has to be determined, where the provisions of a will have to be interpreted, or where armchair evidence has to be utilised.

13.4.5.4 Immediate vesting, acceleration of benefits, finality of institution, maximum benefit and minimum burden

There is a presumption that a testator intended vesting of an inheritance to occur on his or her death and did not intend it to be postponed. Of course, if there is a clear intention to create a conditional bequest, the presumption falls away. In light of the presumption in favour of immediate vesting, it is also presumed that he or she did not intend to create a fideicommissum and would have intended an unconditional bequest.[50] This also explains why there is a presumption in favour of direct substitution as opposed to fideicommissary substitution.[51] Where there is uncertainty as to whether the testator intended to create a fiduciary or usufructuary interest, there is a presumption in favour of a fiduciary interest.[52]

If a usufruct is bequeathed to an intermediate beneficiary, but the will fails to state who is to be the ultimate beneficiary, the presumption is that it was intended for the intermediate beneficiary also to be the ultimate beneficiary unless it is clear that the testator had not intended to give the intermediate beneficiary anything more than a life interest in the property.[53]

Where a testator postpones vesting of an inheritance on an ultimate beneficiary until an intermediate beneficiary has died, the courts will, unless there is an indication to the contrary, presume that the testator intended an acceleration of benefits in favour of the ultimate beneficiary if the intermediate beneficiary refuses to adiate, or waives or renounces the intermediate interest.[54]

A bequest left to the children of the deceased, subject to the condition that in the event of their death their children will succeed, shall be presumed to mean that the testator intended representation to take place in respect of his or her children who died during his or her (the testator's) lifetime and not after his or her death.[55] Furthermore, where in a mutual will there is a bequest to children and on the death of one or more of them to the descendants of those children, the presumption will be that the clause refers to the contingency of the children dying either before the death of the first-dying of the testators and not after the death of the first-dying testator or after the death of the surivor.[56]

A bequest subject to a restraint of ownership or enjoyment will, in the absence of clarity, be construed so as to limit the rights of the beneficiary as little as possible. In conformity with this principle, a restraint of alienation will be presumed to be personal rather than real in effect.[57]

In the absence of clarity of intent, conditions will be interpreted restrictively so as to impose the least burdensome result on the beneficiaries, for there is a presumption in

---

50 *Webb v Davis* 1998 (2) SA 975 (SCA) at 983B–C.
51 *Van Zyl v Van Zyl* 1951 (3) SA 288 (A).
52 *Schaumberg v Stark* 1956 (4) SA 462 (A).
53 *Havemann's Assignee v Havemann's Executor* 1927 AD 473 at 478.
54 *Ex parte Marais* 1953 (4) SA 620 (T).
55 *Whiting v Estate Whiting* 1922 CPD 82.
56 *De Wet v De Villiers* 1914 CPD 285 at 291.
57 *Ex parte Dell* 1957 (3) SA 416 (C).

favour of freedom as opposed to restraint, convenience as opposed to inconvenience and reasonableness as opposed to unreasonableness.[58] In the face of doubt as to whether a restriction attached to a bequest is a condition or a modus, there is a presumption in favour of a modus.[59]

13.4.5.5 Presumption against disinheritson

A parent is presumed to have equal affection for each of his or her children and to place their claims above those of collaterals and strangers. There is, therefore, a strong presumption against disinherison and in favour of equal treatment of children.[60] If the testator wants to exclude his or her children, he or she needs to be quite specific in this regard. It is an open question whether the presumption extends to grandchildren.

The following case study is a good illustration of the application of the rules of interpretation. What makes this case really interesting and worthy of detailed study is the manner in which the court integrated all the principles relating to the interpretation of wills to arrive at a well-considered conclusion. (This case is also of relevance for the discussion of vesting of rights in Chapters 1 and 3.)

In *Webb v Davis*,[61] the Supreme Court of Appeal was required to interpret a will. The facts of the case were as follows:

The testator executed his will in 1976. In 1978 he suffered a severe stroke that left him incapacitated and he died in 1990. He was survived by his sons, Gary and Rodney. Rodney died in 1993. His widow was the executrix in his estate and also the sole beneficiary under his will.

During his lifetime, the testator owned a trading station in Transkei which Rodney helped to run. In 1976, the day after the testator executed his will, he gave Rodney a power of attorney which, in effect, authorised Rodney to conduct the business on his behalf. After the testator's incapacitation on account of the stroke, a *curator bonis* was appointed to take charge of his property, but Rodney remained in effective control of the trading store until his own death in 1993. The legal dispute in question concerned the proper interpretation to be given to clauses 2 and 3 of the testator's will. These clauses stipulated as follows:

The testator bequeathed his trading station to Rodney and as a condition to this inheritance, Rodney had to pay his brother, Gary, R70 000, subject to the conditions:

1. That the R70 000 was to be paid, free of interest, in equal annual instalments of R10 000; the first instalment within one year of the testator's death and thereafter R10 000 per annum until the full sum had been paid. In the event of any one instalment not being paid by the stipulated date, the full balance owing would immediately become due and payable.
2. That Rodney would register a mortgage bond over the trading station, as security for his indebtedness, in favour of Gary. The mortgage bond had to be registered on transfer of the property into Rodney's name.
3. That should Rodney fail to accept the inheritance as set out above, in writing within thirty days of the date of the testator's death, or fail to comply with the terms and conditions of the inheritance, or should he not wish to inherit subject to the conditions, then the bequest would

58 *Holley v Commissioner for Inland Revenue* 1947 (3) SA 119 (A).
59 *Webb v Davis* 1998 (2) SA 975 (SCA) at 983B–C.
60 *Executor of A. Neveling v Executor of P. Neveling* (1909) 26 SC 196.
61 1998 (2) SA 975 (SCA).

'fall away' and Rodney and Gary would be appointed as the sole and universal heirs, in equal shares, of all the testator's estate and effects, including the trading station.

Rodney accepted the inheritance in writing within 30 days of the testator's death, but he never registered the mortgage bond over the property. (It would appear that the reason why the mortgage was never registered was because of certain restrictions in Transkeian law which prevented a non-Transkeian citizen from acquiring ownership of immovable property in Transkei.)

The first three instalments of the R70 000 were paid each year after the testator's death. Shortly after the third instalment, Rodney died. Following Rodney's death Rodney's wife, who was also his executrix and sole beneficiary, offered to pay Gary the outstanding balance on the R70 000. This offer was rejected.

The issue was whether, on a proper construction of the will, the bequest of the trading station vested in Rodney's estate and was thus transmissible to his heirs. Gary's counsel argued that the words 'fall away' in clause 3, together with the phrases 'subject to the conditions' and 'terms and conditions' in clauses 2 and 3, respectively, clearly indicated that the testator had imposed suspensive conditions that had to be fulfilled before Rodney could acquire a vested interest in the testator's estate. Since Rodney had neither paid the full amount of R70 000 nor registered the mortgage bond, his estate could not have acquired a vested interest that could be transmitted to his heirs.

To determine whether Rodney had acquired a vested right to the testator's estate, the Court turned to the terms of the testator's will to ascertain his intention. The Court found that the isolated words and phrases used by the testator were not suggestive of a clear intention. Consequently, the Court turned to 'the general scheme of the will' and the 'material facts and circumstances known to [the testator] when he made [the will].'[62]

The Court held that the fact that Rodney had to register a mortgage bond simultaneously with taking transfer of the property was a clear indication that the testator intended Rodney to acquire a vested right to the property even before completing payment of the R70 000.[63]

As part of the armchair evidence, the Court noted that since the testator had already given Rodney power of attorney authorising him to run the business and since the business was Rodney's only source of income from which he could pay Gary, the testator intended that Rodney acquire a vested right to the property. It was unlikely that the testator would have wanted Rodney to have a mere *spes* (a hope) and no vested right over the property for seven years while he paid his brother. Surely, the testator must have also known that in this time Rodney also would have had to make and implement important decisions pertaining to the business?[64]

Following the assessment of the scheme of the will and armchair evidence, the Court turned to various presumptions in support of its finding on the facts. To this extent, the Court relied on 'the presumption in favour of an immediate as opposed to a postponed vesting; the presumption in favour of an unconditional bequest; and the presumption that a provision attached to a bequest is a modus rather than a condition.'[65]

62 *Webb v Davis* 1998 (2) SA 975 (SCA) at 982D.
63 At 982E–G.
64 At 982H–983A.
65 At 983B–C.

Applying a combination of interpretive tools, the Court eventually held that the bequest in favour of Rodney was not contingent on the fulfilment of a suspensive condition, and the inheritance was subject to a modus which did not have the effect of delaying vesting. Gary acquired a personal right against Rodney to claim the balance of the R70 000. The Court held that the effect of the words 'fall away' was to attach a resolutive condition to the modus which allowed for a divesting in the event that Rodney failed to comply with his obligations. However, the fact that he could be divested had no bearing on the question of vesting, or, for that matter, on the transmissibility of the inheritance.

On the question of whether or not the bequest in favour of Rodney was transmissible to his heirs, the Court, after exploring the theoretical link between the concept of vesting and the transmissibility of rights, concluded that the result turned on the intention of the testator as expressed in his will. The Court held that the intention may be gathered from the nature of the right and whether it was intended to endure only for the lifetime of the beneficiary. On the facts of the case, the Court held that the vested interest was a right to acquire ownership. It was not limited in time. Although the testator provided for the possibility of divesting, his intention was not to prevent the right from being transmissible. Therefore, the interest vested in Rodney was transmissible to his heirs, namely his wife.[66]

This case illustrates how the beginning point of any interpretation enquiry lies in the golden rule, namely to determine the intention of the testator. If the words in a testator's will are ambiguous, the intention of the testator can be deduced from the general scheme of the will, armchair evidence and presumptions of law.

PAUSE FOR REFLECTION

Hierarchy of interpretive rules

One of the interesting questions that arises from *Webb v Davis*[67] is whether or not there is a hierarchy of interpretive tools. In other words, should a court discount the scheme of the will, armchair evidence and presumptions if the words of a will are clear. Or should a court, faced with a question of interpretation, rather take a holistic approach and not see each leg of the enquiry as being mutually exclusive or exhaustive. There seems to be merit in an argument that a court should, in its endeavour to find the 'true intention' of the testator, be willing to employ the full range of interpretive tools as opposed to taking a restrictive approach.

13.5 Variation of wills

The general rule is that the courts will not vary a will which is capable of being carried out unless it is contrary to law or public policy. Applications for variation have frequently been made to South African courts by beneficiaries who are unhappy with stipulations in a will as to how the property of the deceased is to be realised or invested. The argument is sometimes made that there are more profitable ways of distribution. The courts have, however, not

66 At 983F–984B.
67 1998 (2) SA 975 (SCA).

agreed with such arguments. They have taken the view that if the stipulation is clear, effect must be given to it, even if it results in a loss of profit.[68]

In *Jewish Colonial Trust Ltd v Estate Nathan*,[69] the testator executed a will in which he created a testamentary trust. He stipulated, amongst other things, that the trust income be paid in the form of annuities to certain individuals, charitable societies and institutions. These annuities were to be paid for a period of 50 years whereupon the trust was to be wound up and the residue paid to the Jewish Colonial Trust for the purpose of creating a fund to be named The Solomon Nathan Family Fund. This fund was to be 'used for the restoration of the Jews to their ancient home in Palestine, either by acquisition of lands, financial assistance or otherwise in such manner as may be found most expedient.' A few years after the testator died, the Jewish Colonial Trust instituted an action in which they claimed payment of so much of the residue as was not needed for the payment of the annuities. They claimed that the trust had sufficient surplus funds, that the money was immediately needed and that there was no need to defer payment for 50 years. In this regard, the Court held that the Jewish Colonial Trust was asking it to do more than enforce its legal rights by asking it (the Court) to supplement the legal rights of the Trust. The Court made it clear that this could only be done if a power or discretion was conferred on it (the Court) by law. However, although the Court had 'certain powers of dealing with immovable property contrary to the will of the testator', it has 'no general discretionary power to modify or supplement rights given under a will or to authorise the property of a testator to be dealt with otherwise than in terms of his will'.[70]

When the Jewish Colonial Trust tried again in 1967 to avoid the fifty-year period by securing releases and waivers from the annuitants, the Natal Provincial Division also denied the request. On this occasion it stated that the Court will interpret a will in order to ascertain who the beneficiaries are and the extent of their benefits, and it will give consideration to what may be properly implied into the will in order to do this. It cannot, however, vary the will and change the devolution of the estate, nor add to or subtract from the benefits conferred. The beneficiaries must, the Court said, be content to take what they are given, in accordance with the terms on which it is given. Furthermore, the Court held that there is no principle which justifies a departure from the will just because circumstances have changed since the testator made his or her will. For a departure, the testator must have envisaged a departure in the event of changed circumstances, or it must have become impossible or impractical to carry out the provisions of the will. The Court held that it was not so in this case.

The position expressed in *Jewish Colonial Trust Ltd v Estate Nathan* reflects the general attitude of South African courts in these matters. The courts are, however, prepared to permit variation of the terms of a will in certain circumstances. It is not possible to provide an exhaustive list of such circumstances. However, as Corbett et al[71] note, upon a survey of cases, certain defined principles may be extracted. They list the following occasions when the courts will permit a variation:

- where the circumstances of a case make it practically impossible or utterly unreasonable to fulfil the testator's intentions

68 *In re Crosbie's Estate* (1910) 27 SC 50 at 52.
69 1940 AD 163.
70 *Jewish Colonial Trust Ltd v Estate Nathan* 1940 AD 163 at 182–183.
71 At 491–492.

- where the strict enforcements of the testator's directions would result in a failure of the testator's bequests or would result in the testator's intentions being frustrated
- where the testamentary mechanisms mentioned in the will are unable to realise the intentions of the testator and/or would result in severe loss to the estate
- where the circumstances of a case demand a departure from the will
- where the testator makes dispositions but the dispositions are based on mistaken assumptions about the testator's assets or liabilities.

To justify variation, an applicant would have to show a change of circumstance, not contemplated by the deceased, causing prejudice to the estate and/or the beneficiaries.

In *Ex parte Estate Marks*,[72] the testator prohibited the sale of any immovable property until the death of his children and directed that the cash in his estate be invested in approved stocks. Some of the property had to be sold to meet the liabilities of the estate, and some was expropriated. The Court permitted a variation of the terms of the will to permit the proceeds of the expropriated property to be invested in new property or in shares in property-owning companies. The Court held that since the testator had intended to preserve a property portfolio for future inheritance, the proceeds of the unforeseen expropriation could be invested in entities which would approximate his general intention. It was thus not necessary to invest the proceeds of the expropriation in the stocks identified by him in the will. However, as regards the proceeds of the sale of the properties to meet the estate liabilities, the Court was unwilling to permit these proceeds to be invested in stocks other than those identified by the testator. The Court was of the opinion that the sale of the properties to meet liabilities was not indicative of changed circumstances.

In *Ex parte Sidelsky*,[73] the testator executed a will in 1944. In it he provided for an amount of £75 to be paid to his daughter for her upkeep. This amount was increased by the Court to R1 500 with provision for an inflation linked annual increase based on changes in the consumer price index. This was to take into account the intention of the deceased to provide a reasonable amount of money for his daughter to maintain herself.

The law reports are peppered with instances where the courts have permitted variation of wills on account of unforeseen changed circumstances.

The courts do not have discretion to vary a will to rectify an illegality. Thus where a testator makes a stipulation that is invalid because it is illegal (either in terms of statute or the common law), the court cannot vary the terms of the will to make it legal. The consequence is that the stipulation will fall away without affecting the rights of the beneficiary to the inheritance in question.

When it comes to charitable bequests, the courts are more inclined to vary the terms of the will to meet the general objectives of the testator, as it is in the public interest for such bequests to yield the best possible results as opposed to being hamstrung by conditions which are difficult to carry out.

13.6 Rectification of wills

The rectification of a will must be distinguished from its variation or amendment. A testator may amend or vary his or her will at any time before his or her death as long as he or she

72 1970 (3) SA 539 (T).
73 1983 (4) SA 598 (C).

complies with the relevant formalities.[74] A court, on the other hand, will rarely vary or amend a testator's will, but may do so in a few limited cases where it is authorised to do so by legislation. An example of such a variation is the removal of restrictions, such as fideicommissa, in terms of the Immovable Property (Removal or Modification of Restrictions) Act.[75] In terms of this Act, the court may vary a testator's will in order to yield a better result where circumstances have changed, having regard to the general intention of the testator. Rectification, on the other hand, entails correcting clerical errors or adding or deleting words that were omitted or inserted by mistake (perpetrated either by the testator or a third party who drafts the will), or as a result of duress or undue influence. To perform a rectification, the court would have to be satisfied on a balance of probabilities that a will does not reflect the true intentions of the testator. Furthermore, evidence would have to be presented as to what his or her intention was.[76]

A typing error favouring a beneficiary with the sum of R100 when the testator intended to bequeath R1 000 can be rectified. If the incorrect erf number is used to describe a property or address, or the testator makes reference to Johan when he or she meant to benefit John, these situations may also be rectified.

Whenever a mistake is made, rectification will turn on the reliability of the evidence brought to court. The courts are loath to interfere with the provisions of a will just because someone alleges a mistake has been made. One of the contentious issues in the realm of rectification is whether the courts can add words into a will. It is beyond doubt that the courts can delete words once a mistake has been proved.

In *Aubrey-Smith v Hofmeyr*,[77] the Court held that South African courts are generally reluctant to rectify wills by inserting words. The insertion of words would amount to remaking the testator's will and it would not comply with the necessary testamentary formalities laid down in the Wills Act. Corbett J (as he then was) went on to hold that there is an important difference between excising words from a will because they crept in inadvertently and without *animus testandi*, and adding words to a will simply because there is extrinsic evidence to suggest that the testator inadvertently omitted words.

Subsequent to *Aubrey-Smith v Hofmeyr*,[78] the courts have adopted the view that rectification by insertion is indeed an option. In *Botha v The Master*,[79] the Court questioned whether it is logically justifiable to distinguish between rectification by deletion and rectification by insertion. The Court held that in both instances the phrase and provision in the will is defective as it fails to reflect what the testator intended. Insertion of words in error is no less of a mistake than the omission of words by a testator, and rectification, whether by deletion or insertion, has an equally far-reaching result. It therefore seems strange to allow a rectification by deletion and not to allow a rectification by insertion.

74 See Chapter 5.
75 Another example is the variation of trust provisions in terms of s 13 of the Trust Property Control Act.
76 Du Bois and Bradfield (eds) *Wille's Principles* (2007) at 688–689.
77 1973 (1) SA 655 (C) at 662H–663H.
78 1973 (1) SA 655 (C).
79 1976 (3) SA 597 (E).

13.7 Customary law of succession

If a testator living under a system of customary law executes a will, the same rules or principles of interpretation will apply to his or her will as to any other. However, the legal situation might be somewhat more difficult as certain words may have different meanings.

For instance, in terms of the common law of succession the word 'descendant' refers to the lineal descendants of the deceased in a direct line, whilst in terms of the customary law of succession, it includes other persons such as a person accepted by the deceased as his or her own child in terms of customary law, and also women involved in substitute and woman to woman marriages in order to bear children for a deceased male. The same argument can be followed with regard to the variations in meaning of the word 'spouse' which may vary according to the common and customary law understanding of the word.

There is no way to predict how the courts are going to deal with these conflicting situations between the common and customary law of succession if and when they arise. Therefore, testators, and especially their legal advisors, should ensure that there is no possibility of ambiguity whenever drawing up a will. It would be wise to add a list of concepts with their definitions to the will to ensure that the intention of the testator appears clear and unambiguous from his or her will when the time comes to interpret the will.

THIS CHAPTER IN ESSENCE

1. The principles relating to the interpretation of wills presuppose that there is a valid will to begin with. If the testator has not made a will, one cannot make up a will for the testator on the basis of armchair or extrinsic evidence of how he or she would have wanted his or her estate to devolve.
2. After the testator's death, it may become necessary to interpret the will if there is something in the will that is not clear.
3. The purpose of interpretation is to determine the intentions of the testator and it may be necessary for a court (the High Court) to apply the principles or rules of interpretation.
4. Generally, there are statutory and common law rules or principles of interpretation. The golden rule for the interpretation of wills is to ascertain the wishes of the testator from the language used. When these wishes are ascertained the court is bound to give effect to them unless it is prevented by some rule of law from doing so.
5. The different aids that can be used to determine the intention of the testator include:
   - the ordinary and plain meaning of words
   - the construction of the will as a whole
   - armchair evidence
   - implied provisions
   - presumptions.
6. In the process of interpretation, the courts are generally inclined to use armchair evidence.
7. The general rule is that the courts will not vary a will which is capable of being carried out unless the will is contrary to law or public policy.
8. A court will rectify a will if an applicant can prove that a mistake occurred and what the testator's true intentions really were.

Chapter 14

Succession by contract (*pactum successorium*)

Can a testator regulate the devolution of his estate by means of a contract?

14.1 Introduction 223

14.2 Origin of the prohibition of the *pactum successorium* 224

14.3 What is a *pactum successorium*? 225

14.4 Customary law of succession 231

This chapter in essence 231

14.1 Introduction

In South Africa succession normally takes place either in accordance with the provisions of a will or according to the rules of the law of intestate succession. There are occasions, however, when testators try to regulate the devolution of their estates by means of a bilateral juridical act inter vivos, in other words by contract. These agreements are generally seen as *pacta successoria* and, since earliest law, have not been tolerated.

PAUSE FOR REFLECTION

What is a *pactum successorium*?

Parties sometimes attempt to regulate the devolution of the entire estate (or part of the assets) of one or both parties by means of a contract,[1] for example, 'I promise that I will bequeath my antique clock to you when I die'. A promise would normally be a binding contract when the promissee accepts the offer. In this example, however, it is linked to the devolution of property which is supposed to fall into the estate of the promissor who has freedom of testation over all of his property. It is therefore invalid. The reason for the aversion against the *pactum successorium* will be discussed hereafter.

Two exceptions to this general rule exist, namely a succession contract embodied in an antenuptial contract and a *donatio mortis causa* executed in compliance with the formalities of a will. In South Africa these two forms of *pacta successoria* are regarded as valid.[2]

1 See also the explanation on page 225 (at para 14.3).

2 See page 229 (at para 14.3.2).

14.2 Origin of the prohibition of the *pactum successorium*

The prohibition of *pacta successoria* originates in common law. The earliest Roman sources of law only mention two methods of succession, namely by means of a valid will (*successio ex testamento*) and through intestate succession (*successio ab intestato*). Besides a few exceptions, succession by means of a *pactum successorium* was unknown or not permitted. The fact that the *pactum successorium* was avoided, is not entirely strange - the right of private ownership and the right to have command of one's private assets by means of a will was practised very early in Rome. The Romans considered it a disgrace to die intestate. Consequently, it was a non-debatable principle that a will was revocable until the death of the testator. Most juridical acts that could restrict the freedom of testation of the testator inter vivos were treated with suspicion and seen as *contra bonos mores*.

PAUSE FOR REFLECTION

Other reasons for the prohibition of the *pactum successorium*

Apart from the principle of freedom of testation, the *pactum successorium* was also prohibited because it was feared that such an agreement could cause the desire to bring about the death of the testator who was a contractual party. It is generally accepted that this objection no longer applies in modern South African law.

In Western Europe, the general prohibition of the *pactum successorium* was systematically received from Roman law. However, the influence of Germanic law brought about an important development - in their antenuptial contracts, prospective spouses could bindingly have command over the devolution of their respective assets.

Roman-Dutch law is the basis of South African law and this explains the aversion to the *pactum successorium* in this country. Since 1919 there has been a series of rulings in which the courts have unanimously decided that a *pactum successorium* which is not embodied in an antenuptial contract is invalid. The position of the Appellate Division (as it was then known) was confirmed in 1976 in *Borman en De Vos v Potgietersrusse Tabakkorporasie*[3] and later again in 1997 in *McAlpine v McAlpine*.[4]

COUNTER POINT

Objections in modern South African law

Objections to the *pactum successorium* are not limited to those raised by the common law writers. Further objections are that:

- The *pactum successorium* results in the evasion of the formalities that are normally required for the execution of wills. In the light of s 2(3) of the Wills Act, this objection is rather diluted. This section grants the court a mandate, in spite of non-compliance with the formality requirements regarding a will, to order the Master to accept the document invoked as a will.[5]
- The *pactum successorium* denies the court the opportunity to hear oral evidence from the alleged contracting party when deciding on a dispute regarding the *pactum successorium* because such party will be deceased. The courts are burdened with the same problem in the case of a dispute regarding a deceased testator's will. This objection, therefore, is not unique to the law of testate succession.

3 1976 (3) SA 488 (A).
4 1997 (1) SA 736 (A).
5 See Chapter 5.

- The *pactum successorium* creates an easy method of evading the provisions of the Estate Duty Act.[6] As a result of such a *pactum* (contract), the Receiver of Revenue can forfeit its income from estate duty because the assets are no longer a part of the deceased's taxable estate. This argument is not that strong given the provisions of ss 55 and 58 of the Income Tax Act[7] and the capacity of the Commissioner for the South African Revenue Service to levy donations taxes in appropriate cases.

The fact that the *pactum successorium* restricts the freedom of testation of the testator is presently still the predominant reason why the *pactum successorium* is considered *contra bonos mores* and invalid.

14.3 What is a *pactum successorium*?

Translated literally, *pactum successorium* means 'an agreement of succession'. A *pactum successorium* is a bilateral juridical act that operates succession law consequences inter vivos. In other words, the testator commits himself or herself during his or her lifetime to give someone else a share of his or her estate (or part of it) *mortis causa*. In *Borman en De Vos v Potgietersrusse Tabakkorporasie*,[8] the *pactum successorium* was defined as an agreement in which the parties arrange the succession to the estate (or part of it) of one or more of the parties after the death (*mortis causa*) of the party or parties involved.

Practical examples of *pacta successoria* are:

- 'We, Anton and Ben, hereby agree that the survivor will be the first-dying person's only heir.'

According to this *pactum successorium*, Anton and Ben agree to appoint each other as heirs.

- 'I, Jacobus, hereby agree that I will leave the residue of my estate to Maria.'

In this agreement, Jacobus agrees with Maria that he will leave his estate (or part of it) to Maria.

- 'I, Axel, hereby undertake to Rose that I will leave half my estate to my stepson, Carl.'

In this agreement, Axel agrees with Rose that he will leave his estate (or part of it) to Carl.

14.3.1 Identifying the *pactum successorium*

In practice, the general prohibition of the *pactum successorium* has caused the law to become unnecessarily technical and complicated. In an attempt to allow freedom of testation to take its important position in the South African law of succession, the courts have developed several tests that they apply to differentiate between a *pactum successorium* and other similar

6 45 of 1955.
7 58 of 1962.
8 1976 (3) SA 488 (A) at 501A–D.

but valid agreements. The application of these tests is not without problems and, as a result, there is considerable legal uncertainty.

PAUSE FOR REFLECTION

Partnership agreements and *pacta successoria*

Some judges declared partnership agreements valid in an attempt to help the wronged party to the contract.[9] For example, in *Van der Merwe v Sekretaris van Binnelandse Inkomste*[10] the Court had to interpret a partnership agreement which had, amongst others, the following clause:

In the event of the death of any of the partners, the following provisions shall apply: The widow of the deceased, or the nominated beneficiary under his will, as the case may be, shall continue to draw profits which would otherwise have accrued to the deceased partner ...

Normally a partnership agreement dissolves when one of the partners dies and, consequently, the assets of the deceased partner fall into his or her estate to be distributed amongst his or her beneficiaries. The clause in the partnership agreement in *Van der Merwe v Sekretaris van Binnelandse Inkomste* restricts the deceased partner's freedom of testation because he cannot bequeath his partnership profits to anyone apart from his widow or his nominated beneficiaries. This clause in the partnership agreement seems to be an invalid *pactum successorium*, but the Court decided the case without dealing with the validity of the clause. According to the Court, the clause merely regulated payment of the profits to the widow of the deceased partner and thus it was not necessary to decide whether it was indeed a *pactum successorium*. However, when one considers the principles applied in *Borman en De Vos v Potgietersrusse Tabakkorporasie*,[11] it is clear that the clause restricts the deceased partner's freedom of testation and, consequently, the clause should have been held to be invalid.

The tests used by the courts are the following:

Absence of a counterperformance

In *Schauer v Schauer*,[12] the Court ruled that an agreement is an invalid *pactum successorium* unless proof can be provided that a counterperformance has been given to the promissor. This judgment has been criticised and it is generally accepted that giving a counterperformance is not the criterion to establish whether or not an agreement is a *pactum successorium*.[13]

Revocability test

One of the fundamental principles in the law of testate succession is that the testator must be able to revoke a will at any stage during his or her lifetime. Barring a few exceptions, a testator cannot sign away his or her capacity to revoke. However, the revocability test has

9 See in general *Costain and Partners v Godden* 1960 (4) SA 456 (SR); *D'Angelo v Bona* 1976 (1) SA 463 (A); *Erasmus v Havenga* 1979 (3) SA 1253 (T); *Jubelius v Griesel* 1988 (2) SA 610 (K).

10 1977 (1) SA 462 (A).

11 1976 (3) SA 488 (A); see page 227.

12 1967 (3) SA 615 (W) at 616H–617A.

13 For example, see *Jubelius v Griesel* 1988 (2) SA 610 (K) at 622H.

caused some confusion in its application. In *Costain and Partners v Godden,*[14] it was decided that an option is a straightforward commercial contract which becomes irrevocable the moment it is entered into. It was further held that if it is irrevocable, it escapes the stigma of a *pactum successorium* and it is enforceable. It is evident that the revocability test was applied incorrectly in *Costain and Partners v Godden*[15] – no agreement that is revocable can curtail or restrict the promissor. A more satisfactory application of the revocability test is found in *Varkevisser v Varkevisser*[16] and *Ex Parte Calderwood: In Re Estate Wixley.*[17] In both judgments it was decided that the fundamental principle of a *pactum successorium* lies in the fact that the promissor has committed himself or herself irrevocably to the agreement. He or she does not reserve the right to revoke his or her offer. Should the promissor reserve the right to revoke his or her offer, the agreement will not be contrary to the general rule that succession may only take place *ex testamento* or *ab intestato*. However, the revocability of an agreement cannot always satisfactorily be used as the only criterion to differentiate between the *pactum successorium* and other agreements.

Restriction of freedom of testation

It is a basic principle of the South African law of succession that a testator has complete freedom of testation over his or her assets and, with a few exceptions, any agreement that restricts this freedom is null and void. In practice, the courts have used freedom of testation as a test for determining whether or not an agreement is a *pactum successorium.* It is clear from *Borman en De Vos v Potgietersrusse Tabakkorporasie*[18] that the principle of freedom of testation in South African law enjoys high priority.

COUNTER POINT

Freedom of testation versus freedom of contract

The fact that such a high premium is placed on the principle of freedom of testation is not one that has unanimous support. In principle, all alienations inter vivos or *mortis causa* restrict the freedom of testation of the testator. The reason why the *pactum successorium* is prohibited is the fact that the *pactum successorium* vests rights irrevocably in the beneficiary after the death of the promissor. The result is that the freedom of testation of the testator is restricted because he or she cannot bequeath the promised property to anyone else. To determine whether or not a person's freedom of testation is being restricted, the revocability and vesting tests are applied. Strictly speaking, the restriction of the testator's freedom of testation is not a test that determines whether or not an agreement is an invalid *pactum successorium*, but it is rather the result if an agreement is not recognised as an invalid *pactum successorium*.

By placing a prohibition on the *pactum successorium*, another freedom is encroached on, namely freedom of contract. Both freedom of testation and freedom of contract are based on private possession and private autonomy, and both freedoms are important principles in a capitalist system. The question consequently arises as to whether it is defensible to protect one freedom, namely freedom of testation, at the expense of another freedom, namely freedom of contract. It can be argued that a person should

14 1960 (4) SA 456 (SR) at 459C–D.
15 1960 (4) SA 456 (SR).
16 1959 (4) SA 196 (SR).
17 1981 (3) SA 727 (Z).
18 1976 (3) SA 488 (A).

have a free choice to decide for himself or herself which one of the two freedoms comes first. Preventing a testator by means of the prohibition of the *pactum successorium* from exercising his or her freedom of contract seems to be an anachronism. It creates unnecessary tension between the two freedoms from which the testator should be allowed to choose for himself or herself.

Vesting test

The courts have ruled in several cases that rights are already vested in the beneficiary as soon as an agreement is concluded and that such an agreement is consequently not a *pactum successorium.*[19] In other words, if rights are vested in the beneficiary inter vivos, even if the execution thereof is postponed until after death, the agreement is not a *pactum successorium.* Alternatively, the *pactum successorium* is an agreement inter vivos, but the vesting of rights only takes place after death. Application of this test does not always yield satisfactory results. For instance, the nature of the vested rights is not always clear.[20]

Intention test

A more satisfactory criterion to determine whether an agreement is an invalid *pactum successorium* or not is the intention of the parties. This test came under discussion for the first time in the minority judgment in *McAlpine v McAlpine*[21] and therefore deserves special mention.

In *McAlpine v McAlpine*,[22] two brothers agreed, amongst other things, that '[i]n the event of either parties death, the other party will get 100% of the shares in the company ...–in other words, the deceased parties (sic) shareholding will go to the one remaining alive'.[23]

A few years later, Ian (one of the brothers) died and the appellant (the surviving brother) instituted a claim against Ian's widow, in her capacity as executor of his estate, for transfer of the 50% of the shares. She opposed the claim based on the fact that the agreement amounted to an invalid *pactum successorium*. The Court *a quo* upheld this plea and an appeal against this decision failed. However, according to the minority judgment of Nienaber J, the intention of the parties to the contract and not the nature of the right (namely a vested or contingent right) is the dominant feature of an agreement. The intention of the parties to the contract is a factual question and different considerations can be taken into account, including the revocability of the agreement and the vesting of rights in terms of the agreement, in order to determine the intention of the parties to the contract.

Seen in this light, vesting and revocability tests are nothing more than aids to establish the parties' intentions. This approach also explains why ordinary commercial agreements, such as pension schemes, partnership agreements, life insurance policies (that are not necessarily related to the content of the will but can nevertheless bind a party to the *mortis causa* bequest of his property) cannot be considered *pacta successoria*. Such agreements are concluded without *animus testandi* and can therefore not be regarded as invalid *pacta successoria*.

19 See for example, *Keeve and Keeve* 1952 (1) SA 619 (O) at 623F–G.
20 See Chapter 9.
21 1997 (1) SA 736 (A).
22 1997 (1) SA 736 (A).
23 *McAlpine v McAlpine* 1997 (1) SA 736 (A) at 267H.

Yet another important principle in considering the intention of the parties to a contract is that if it is not clear what the intention of the parties is, the agreement should rather be recognised than rejected. From *McAlpine v McAlpine* it is clear that the parties did not have the intention of making a will. The agreement did not interfere with the freedom of testation of the two brothers and it was also not an attempt to evade the formalities for a will. Consequently, it was an:

> *... ordinary although comprehensive commercial agreement between two brothers who, through the medium of a company of which they were the sole shareholders, sought to provide contractually for various foreseeable eventualities relating to their co-ownership; more particularly, to ensure that each party would be protected should the other mortgage or sell his shares or predecease him.*[24]

This approach of Nienaber J is illustrative of the practical problems that arise from commercial agreements as a result of the prohibition of *pacta successoria*. Because South African law follows the doctrine of *stare decisis*, the verdict of the Appeal Court in *Borman en De Vos v Potgietersrusse Tabakkorporasie*[25] and the majority judgment in *McAlpine v McAlpine*[26] is the prevailing law. In other words, if the succession agreement restricts the freedom of testation of the testator, it is an invalid *pactum successorium*.

14.3.2 Valid forms of the *pactum successorium*

Whilst most agreements that regulate succession between parties are generally invalid, there are two forms of the *pactum successorium* that are permitted, namely the *donatio mortis causa* and succession agreements in an antenuptial contract.

14.3.2.1 *Donatio mortis causa*

A *donatio mortis causa* is a donation aimed at the death of the donor and must comply with the formalities laid down for a will. For example, in *Meyer v Rudolph's Estate*[27] the deceased wrote a letter to the plaintiff in which she said, amongst others, the following:

> *... I feel very weak and it is quite possible that I will not see you again, for that reason I write you this. You ask me how it goes with your cattle; do not worry about them; you are entitled to them, therefore I have thought fit to give you all my cattle and also Boschberg; after my death it belongs to you. ...*

The Court found the contents of this letter to be a *donatio mortis causa* which has to comply with the formalities of a will.

The characteristics of a *donatio mortis causa* include:

- the death of the donor must be contemplated
- the governing motive for the gift must be pure benevolence
- the gift may be revoked at any time.

In practice, differentiating between the *pactum successorium* and the *donatio mortis causa* can be problematic. Like the *pactum successorium,* the *donatio mortis causa* is an agreement

24 *McAlpine v McAlpine* 1997 (1) SA 736 (A) at 757G.
25 1976 (3) SA 488 (A).
26 1997 (1) SA 736 (A).
27 1918 AD 70 at 83.

with testamentary characteristics. There is also a handing over of assets to the beneficiary *mortis causa* but the ground for the invalidity of the agreement, namely irrevocability, is missing. Since the *donatio mortis causa* is revocable, the freedom of testation of the testator is not restricted. For this reason, it is not *contra bonos mores* and is not invalid. Because a *donatio mortis causa* has to comply with testamentary formalities, it can be stated that a *donatio mortis causa* and a will are essentially one and the same thing.

14.3.2.2 Antenuptial contract

A *pactum successorium* in an antenuptial contract is not a will. Although it has succession implications, it does not have to comply with testamentary formalities. As far back as 1896, it was decided in *In re Intestate Estate of JF Manistry*[28] that '... the parties had power to enter into an antenuptial contract making provision for the devolution of the property as they did.' A *pactum successorium* in an antenuptial contract can take various forms:

1. The spouses benefit each other mutually or the one benefits the other. In this case, the agreement can only expressly or by means of inevitable implication be revoked or amended by the spouses' joint will. If the joint will is revoked, the *pactum successorium* revives. Unilateral revoking by one of the spouses by making a new will is not possible.

In *Ex Parte Executors Estate Everard*[29] the following *pactum successorium* was taken up in the antenuptial agreement of the spouses:

For and in consideration of the said intended marriage the said Horace Nathaniel Everard, herewith nominates and appoints the said Frances Getrude Milne, major spinster, to be the sole heiress of one half of his estate, movable and immovable, wherever situate, at the time of his death.

In a later will the testator effected a disposition of his estate in conflict with the *pactum successorium*. The Court held that such an agreement (the *pactum successorium*) cannot be revoked by means of a will without the permission of the other party.

2. The spouses agree to benefit a third party. In this case, there are two possibilities of revocation. If the third party is a party to the agreement, revoking is only possible with his or her permission. If the third party is not a party to the agreement, the rules that ordinarily apply to agreements in favour of a third party are applicable:
   - If the spouses agree to a revoking capacity or where the third party has not yet accepted the benefit, the agreement can be modified by means of a joint will.
   - If the third party has already accepted the benefit, revoking is only possible with his or her permission.

In *Ex Parte Basillie et Uxor*[30] a husband and wife executed an antenuptial contract in which the husband donated a life policy to his wife 'together with any children which may be born from this marriage'. The Court held that the husband and wife had stipulated for a benefit in favour of their unborn children. When the children are in existence and if they accept the benefit in terms of the life policy, their rights cannot be taken away by means of a later will. In other words, the husband

28 17 NLR 149 at 151.
29 1938 TPD 190 at 192.
30 1928 CPD 218 at 219.

and wife cannot have a stipulation in their will that excludes the children from the benefits of the life policy.

14.4 Customary law of succession

In customary law, it is normal for a family head (usually a male) to make his wishes known on his deathbed as to how his property should be dealt with. A family head may even make the declaration when he is still in good health but, in both cases, it is with his probable death in mind and therefore it may be compared with the common law concept *donatio mortis causa*. Nevertheless, a *donatio mortis causa* has to comply with the testamentary formalities whilst the deathbed wishes of a family head do not.

PAUSE FOR REFLECTION

The deathbed wishes of a family head

In making his final disposition, a family head may not discard customary law. In other words, the principle of male primogeniture may not be disregarded, heirs who are entitled to inheritance may not be disinherited, and the status of the houses may not be altered. His disposition must be made known to several persons, normally the family council and ideally those who would be disadvantaged by the disposition. A family head's deathbed wishes are normally respected, but a disgruntled heir may protest immediately or even approach a court.

THIS CHAPTER IN ESSENCE

1. South African law does not generally permit a testator to bequeath his or her estate by means of a contract (*pactum successorium*). This rule is derived from the general rule that originated in Roman law that an estate must devolve either by will or in terms of the law governing intestate succession. Two exceptions to this general rule exist:
   - A *pactum successorium* embodied in an antenuptial contract is valid.
   - A *donatio mortis causa* executed in compliance with the formalities of a will is valid.
2. Despite the prohibition against succession contracts, numerous attempts have been made by contracting parties to regulate succession of their estates by means of contract. Such contracts are commonly called *pacta successoria*, and have been invalid and unenforceable since early law.
3. There are a number of reasons for maintaining the prohibition of *pacta successoria*, including the following:
   - They might evoke a desire for the death of a contracting party.
   - They interfere with the testator's freedom of testation.
   - They evade the prescribed formalities for the execution of a will.
   - They deprive the courts of the opportunity to hear the evidence of the alleged promissor in a dispute with regard to a *pactum successorium*.
   - They might establish an easy method to evade the provisions of the Estate Duty Act[31] and the Receiver of Revenue might lose its income from estate duty.

31 45 of 1955.

4. The idea that a *pactum successorium* is dangerous has long been rejected by authors and the courts. However, our courts still uphold a testator's freedom of succession and as such, the prohibition of the *pactum successorium*.
5. A study of the case law reveals that great difficulty has been experienced in defining the distinctive nature of the *pactum successorium* and determining when a contract is a *pactum successorium*. A variety of tests to identify the *pactum successorium* has been suggested.
6. A *pactum successorium* displays the following characteristics:
   - It purports to effect a *mortis causa* disposition of an asset(s) in the estate of the testator by providing for *mortis causa* vesting of a right to that asset(s) in the beneficiary.
   - It seeks to prevent the testator from revoking the disposition *mortis causa* or inter vivos.
   - The first characteristic gives the *pactum successorium* its testamentary nature and the second gives the grounds for its illegality by infringing on the testator's freedom of testation.
7. Although the *pactum successorium* is a concept unique to the common law, the customary law of succession makes provision for a family head to dispose of his assets during his lifetime by means of a final disposition or according to traditional customs.

Chapter 15

Administration of estates

What are the rules for the administration or winding-up of estates?

15.1	**Introduction**	**233**
15.2	**Legal reform of the administration of intestate estates of black persons**	**234**
15.3	**Uniform rules for the administration of deceased estates**	**241**
This chapter in essence		**255**

15.1 Introduction

In South Africa, the administration of a deceased estate is regulated by legislation and the estate is distributed in accordance with the rules of testate succession, the Intestate Succession Act (intestate succession), or a combination of the rules of both. Besides the Administration of Estates Act and the regulations[1] that deal directly with the administration process, there are a number of other acts dealing with related issues such as income tax, estate duty, insurance, maintenance and donations tax that should be kept in mind. These acts include the following:

- The Black Administration Act deals with various issues pertaining to black persons in South Africa. The Act has been severely criticised over the years and although most parts of it have been repealed, some of its provisions still apply.
- The Deeds Registries Act[2] provides for the order in which immovable property in a deceased estate must be transferred to certain beneficiaries or buyers of immovable property from the deceased estate.
- The Estate Duty Act[3] provides for the levy and payment of tax on a deceased estate when it exceeds a certain net value.
- The Immovable Property (Removal or Modification of Restrictions) Act is important with regard to immovable property and certain restrictions applicable to it, for example a fideicommissum attached to certain immovable property.
- The Intestate Succession Act prescribes the rules applicable to the assets of a testator who dies intestate.
- The Long-term Insurance Act[4] deals with long-term insurance policies and the rules applicable to them.

1 Issued in terms of s 103 of the Administration of Estates Act.
2 47 of 1937.
3 45 of 1955.
4 52 of 1998.

- The Maintenance of Surviving Spouses Act[5] prescribes the conditions under which a surviving spouse may claim maintenance from the deceased estate of a first-dying spouse.
- The Matrimonial Property Act[6] deals with matrimonial property law issues.
- The Recognition of Customary Marriages Act prescribes the requirements for polygynous customary marriages.
- The Subdivision of Agricultural Land Act[7] prohibits the subdivision of agricultural land.
- The Trust Property Control Act regulates the control of trust property in the case of *mortis causa* and inter vivos trusts.
- The Wills Act provides for the formalities for and interpretation of a valid will.

The process of the administration or winding-up of estates starts the day the testator dies. Depending on the circumstances, the estate of the deceased testator must be liquidated and distributed amongst his or her beneficiaries according to the rules of the common or customary law of intestate or testate succession. In other words, the administration of an estate is the process by which a deceased estate is liquidated by an executor under the supervision of the Master of the High Court and then divided amongst the beneficiaries, whether heirs or legatees, as well as all administrative actions aimed at initiating and completing the administration process.

The process of administration is conducted according to a set of rules, most of which can be found in legislation. Before December 2000, different sets of rules which depended on the race of a deceased, especially if it was a black person who died intestate, applied. In terms of the repealed s 35 of the Black Administration Act, the term 'black' includes 'any person who is a member of any aboriginal race or tribe of South Africa'. For the purposes of this chapter, the term 'black persons' will accordingly be used in explanations of how the winding-up and administration of certain estates of black persons developed in post-apartheid South Africa.

Since 2000, the process of administration of estates has changed considerably. Although the rules for the administration of estates are mostly uniform, the amending legislation is generally not retroactive and there might be circumstances where it is important to know what the legal position used to be.

15.2 Legal reform of the administration of intestate estates of black persons

Legal reform of the administration of intestate estates of black persons may roughly be divided into three stages:

- that pertaining to the estates of black persons who died intestate before 6 December 2000
- that pertaining to those who died between 6 December 2000 and 15 October 2004
- that pertaining to those who died after 15 October 2004.

5 27 of 1990.

6 88 of 1984.

7 70 of 1970. The whole of this Act has been repealed by s 1 of the Subdivision of Agricultural Land Act Repeal Act 64 of 1998, a provision which will come into operation on a date to be proclaimed by the President by proclamation in the *Government Gazette*.

15.2.1 Black persons who died before 6 December 2000

Before 6 December 2000, there was a different set of rules for the administration of deceased estates for different racial groups in South Africa. A magistrate had jurisdiction over the intestate estates of black persons, whilst the Master of the High Court had jurisdiction over all other remaining intestate and testate estates.

The powers of the Master regarding the administration of the intestate estates of black persons were expressly excluded by s 23(7)(a) of the Black Administration Act[8] which reads as follows:

> *Letters of administration from the Master of the Supreme Court shall not be necessary in, nor shall the Master or any executor appointed by the Master have any powers in connection with, the administration and distribution of –*
> *(a) the estate of any Black who has died leaving no valid will;*
> *(b) any portion of the estate of a deceased Black which falls under subsection (1)[9] or (2).[10]*

Regulation 3(1) of the Regulations for the Administration and Distribution of the Estates of Deceased Blacks (hereinafter referred to as the Black Estates Regulations)[11] had a similar provision that confined the power to administer an intestate estate of a black person to a magistrate. It provided as follows:[12]

> *All the property in any estate falling within the purview of paragraphs (a),[13] (b),[14] (c),[15] and (d)[16] of regulation 2 of these regulations shall be administered under the supervision of the magistrate in whose area of jurisdiction the deceased ordinarily resided and such magistrate shall give such directions in regard to the distribution thereof as shall seem to him fit and shall take all steps necessary to ensure that the provisions of the Act and of these regulations are complied with.*

In order to provide for the administration of the intestate estates of black persons, the Black Estates Regulations described how the estate of a deceased black person had to devolve if s 23 of the Black Administration Act[17] was not applicable and if the deceased died without a valid will. The process of administration of the intestate estate of black persons depended largely on how a relevant estate was classified. Three categories could be distinguished:

1. **Intestate estates of black persons that devolved under the common law and the Intestate Succession Act:** This could happen in two instances, namely when the

8 This provision was repealed by the Administration of Estates Amendment Act 47 of 2002 which commenced on 5 December 2002.
9 Movable property allocated to a house or wife in a customary marriage.
10 Quitrent land.
11 Published in *GG* 10601 of 6 February 1987. These regulations were issued in terms of s 23(1) of the Black Administration Act. They were amended by the Black Administration Act, 1927: Amendment of the Regulations for the Administration and Distribution of Estates published in *GG* 24120 of 3 December 2002 (hereinafter referred to as GN R1501 of 2002).
12 This regulation was amended by regulation 3 of GN R1501 of 2002 to exclude the jurisdiction of the Master only in the case where customary law is applicable.
13 Movable assets of the deceased ordinarily resident in any territory outside South Africa.
14 Property of a deceased who was in possession of a letter of exemption in terms of s 31 of the Black Administration Act.
15 Property of a deceased who was involved in a valid civil marriage.
16 Property declared to be from a marriage out of community of property under the direction of the Minister.
17 See Chapter 2 for a discussion of the repealed s 23.

deceased indicated during his or her lifetime that he or she preferred not to live according to customary law,[18] or when the Minister of Justice and Constitutional Development was of the opinion that it would be inequitable or inappropriate to devolve the deceased estate under customary law.[19] A representative appointed by the magistrate in whose jurisdiction the deceased normally resided, would wind up these estates under the magistrate's supervision.[20] A representative was usually appointed at a meeting attended by the deceased's family and he or she had more or less the same duties and responsibilities as an executor appointed in terms of the Administration of Estates Act.

If there was immovable property in an estate, the magistrate was obliged to issue a certificate of appointment to the representative in which the representative was directed to represent the estate and to assume responsibility for the payment of debts, the collection of assets and the general administration of the estate's property.[21] In *Moseneke v The Master,*[22] the Court gave the family members of a deceased a choice to have these estates administered by a Master or a magistrate. The window period for the family members to make their choice was two years from 6 December 2000. Since 5 December 2002, the administration of these types of estates is regulated in terms of new legislation which commenced on 5 December 2002.[23]

2. **Intestate estates of black persons that devolved under customary law in which there was no immovable property:** These estates had to devolve according to customary law rules[24] which did not require any official formalities. Normally the heir, who was instituted according to custom, took control of the estate upon the death of the deceased. After the period of mourning had lapsed, the property of the deceased was formally distributed at a family meeting in accordance with the rules of customary law of succession. Although the magistrate had no power to appoint an executor in the estate,[25] he could conduct an enquiry in an administrative capacity whenever necessary to determine the beneficiaries of the estate. The magistrate could then give such directions with regard to the distribution of the estate as he deemed fit.[26] The winding-up and administration of these estates was also greatly affected by *Bhe v Magistrate, Khayelitsha.*[27]
3. **Intestate estates of black persons that devolved under customary law in which there was immovable property:** These estates were wound up under the supervision of a magistrate. The magistrate had to appoint a representative to represent the estate and to assume responsibility for the payment of debts, the collection of assets and the general administration and distribution of the estate.[28] The appointment of a representative did not affect the rights of the customary heirs and the estate of the deceased had to devolve in terms of the customary rules of succession. The administration of these estates was

18 In other words, when the deceased applied for a letter of exemption in terms of s 31 of the KwaZulu-Natal Act on the Code of Zulu Law 16 of 1985, and when the deceased entered into a civil marriage without entering into a customary marriage.
19 In terms of the repealed regulation 2(d) of the Black Estates Regulations.
20 In terms of reg 3(1) of the Black Estates Regulations. Regulation 3(1) was amended by the Amendment of the Regulations for the Administration and Distribution of Estates GN R1501 of 2002.
21 Repealed reg 4(1) of the Black Estates Regulations.
22 2001 (2) SA 18 (CC). Hereinafter referred to as *Moseneke v The Master.*
23 See para 15.2.2.
24 Repealed s 23(1) of the Black Administration Act.
25 Repealed reg 4(1) of the Black Estates Regulations.
26 Repealed reg 3(2) of the Black Estates Regulations.
27 See discussion in Chapter 2.
28 Repealed reg 4(1) of the Black Estates Regulations.

not affected by *Moseneke v The Master* and the ensuing legislative amendments, but it was affected finally by *Bhe v Magistrate, Khayelitsha* as of 15 October 2004.[29]

15.2.2 Black persons who died between 6 December 2000 and 15 October 2004

On 6 December 2000, the Constitutional Court in *Moseneke v The Master* considerably amended the legal position regarding the administration of the intestate estates of black testators.

Mr Moseneke (hereinafter referred to as the deceased) died intestate in October 1999. He was survived by his wife and four sons (hereinafter referred to as 'the appellants'). The deceased and the appellants led a so-called urban lifestyle. The estate of the deceased had to be administered by a magistrate in terms of reg 3(1) of the Black Estates Regulations. The appellants were dissatisfied with the situation and expressed their concern to the Master on the basis that the differential treatment amounted to unfair discrimination on the grounds of race. Following their letter to the Master, the appellants referred the matter to the High Court for an order declaring that reg 3(1) of the Black Estates Regulations was unconstitutional and that the Master be instructed to administer the estate of the deceased. The Court decided that both reg 3(1) of the Black Estates Regulations and s 23(7) of the Black Administration Act distinguished between people on the grounds of race, ethnicity and colour and, in terms of s 9 of the Constitution, this amounted to unfair discrimination. However, Sachs J realised that an immediate annulment of both s 23(7)(a) of the Black Administration Act and reg 3(1) of the Black Estates Regulations could cause socio-economic problems and ordered the following:

- that the status quo with regard to estates already submitted in terms of s 23(7)(a) and reg 3(1) had to be maintained
- that black families should have a choice as to whether they wished to report the deceased estate to the Master or the magistrate.[30]

In order to give black families this choice, s 23(7)(a) was declared invalid with immediate effect but the invalidation of reg 3(1) was postponed for a period of two years. To enable the Master to administer the estates of black testators, the word 'shall' in reg 3(1) was replaced by the word 'may' for a period of two years. The Court further ordered that any interested person could approach the Court to amend the order if serious administrative or practical problems were experienced. The Master of the High Court was ordered to administer the estate of the deceased in accordance with the Administration of Estates Act and the Minister of Justice and Constitutional Development was ordered to bring the order of the Constitutional Court to the attention of all Masters and magistrates who administer estates in terms of the Black Administration Act and the regulations of the Black Estates Regulations.

Although the Court declared any legislation that prescribes different systems of administration on the ground of race to be unconstitutional, it did not change the circumstances pertaining to the administration of estates that had to devolve in accordance with the customary law. These estates still had to be administered by the magistrate.

---

29 See para 15.2.3.

30 This order only applies with regard to the estates of black testators that did not have to devolve in terms of customary law.

After two years, the verdict of the Constitutional Court was embodied in legislation which amended the legal position even further. The first statutory amendments in the field of intestate estates of black testators were brought about by the Administration of Estates Amendment Act[31] which amended the Administration of Estates Act and the Black Administration Act to provide for the administration of deceased estates which had to be regulated in terms of the principles of customary law. The law came into operation on 5 December 2002 and amended the legal position as follows:

1. Section 2A was added to the Administration of Estates Act to provide for the setting up of service points at magistrates' offices. The wording of s 2A is important and reads as follows:

   (1) *The Minister may designate posts in, or additional to, the fixed establishment of the Department of Justice and Constitutional Development for the purpose of this section.*

   (2) *Persons appointed to, or acting in, posts which have been designated by the Minister, must exercise the powers and perform the duties delegated to them on behalf of, and under the direction of, the Master.*

   (3) *The Minister may designate places within the area of jurisdiction of a Master as service points where the powers are exercised and the duties are performed on behalf of the Master in terms of subsection (2).*

   (4) *The Minister may delegate any power conferred on him or her in terms of this section to the Director-General: Justice and Constitutional Development or to a person in the Department holding the rank of a deputy Director-General.*

In other words, a service point is an office at a magistrates' court where appointed persons have to perform similar functions to that of the Master.

2. Section 4(1) of the Administration of Estates Act was amended by adding sub-section (1A) in order to extend the jurisdiction of the Master to all testate and intestate estates, with the exception of intestate estates which should devolve in terms of customary law. Section 4(1A) has not yet been repealed and reads as follows:

   The Master shall not have jurisdiction in respect of any property if the devolution of the property is governed by the principles of customary law, or of the estate of a person if the devolution of all the property of the person is governed by the principles of customary law, and no documents in respect of such property or estate shall be lodged with the Master, except a will or a document purporting to be a will.

3. Section 23(7) of the Black Administration Act was amended by deleting para (a) which excluded the jurisdiction of the Master over the estates of all black testators.

Further amendments to the legal position of black intestate testators were brought about by GN R1501 of 2002. This legislation amended regulations 2 and 3 as contained in the Black Estates Regulations considerably to provide for the possibility that the Master could administer the estates of black testators. However, the jurisdiction of the Master regarding estates which had to devolve in terms of customary law was still excluded.

---

31 47 of 2002.

15.2.3 Black persons who died on or after 15 October 2004

On 15 October 2004, the Constitutional Court amended the legal position even further.

In *Bhe v Magistrate, Khayelitsha*, the Court investigated the constitutionality of section 23 of the Black Administration Act and the Black Estates Regulations, and declared them unconstitutional in their entirety. The Court found that there should be no distinction in the administration of estates in South African law and ordered that all estates (testate or intestate and irrespective of the race of the deceased) should be administered under supervision of the Master. This ruling includes intestate estates of black testators that had to devolve in terms of customary law.

Bhe v Magistrate, Khayelitsha has the following important consequences for the law of succession:

- Section 23 of the Black Administration Act was invalidated with retrospective effect to 27 April 1994.
- Magistrates no longer have the authority to administer the intestate estates of black persons.
- All estates, irrespective of race, colour or creed have to be administered by the Master of the High Court in terms of the Administration of Estates Act.
- The order of the Court in respect of the administration of estates was not made retrospective. Estates that are currently being administered by magistrates in terms of s 23 of the Black Administration Act will continue to be administered by those magistrates. However, these estates must not be administered in terms of the customary rules of intestate succession but in terms of the provisions of the Intestate Succession Act.
- Although the declaration of invalidity of s 23 was made retrospective to 27 April 1994, the retrospectivity does not apply to any completed transfer of ownership to an heir who had no notice of a challenge to the legal validity of the statutory provisions and the customary law rule in question.
- Anything done pursuant to the winding-up of an estate in terms of the Act, other than the identification of heirs in a manner inconsistent with the judgment, would not be invalidated by the order of invalidity in respect of s 23 of the Act and its regulations.

Bhe v Magistrate, Khayelitsha required the Department of Justice and Constitutional Development (under which the office of the Master falls) to design and implement a new system for the supervision and administration of deceased estates that complies with the values embedded in the Constitution. The new system followed by the office of the Master is posted on their website[32] and involves the following changes:

- Only the Master of the High Court has the power to supervise all deceased estates.
- All deceased estates have to be administered in terms of the Administration of Estates Act.
- All intestate estates have to be administered in terms of the Intestate Succession Act.
- The Intestate Succession Act is supplemented by *Bhe v Magistrate, Khayelitsha* to accommodate cases where the deceased was married in terms of customary law.
- Magistrates no longer have jurisdiction to supervise and administer deceased estates, irrespective of the race of the deceased. They are, however, required to finalise matters reported to them on or before 15 October 2004, but these estates must be finalised in terms of the Intestate Succession Act.

32 At http://www.doj.gov.za/Master/m_docs/2004_BHE%20Ruling%20Notice.htm.

- Magistrates' offices shall remain designated service points of the Master, but with limited jurisdiction. However, they have to transfer the following types of deceased estates to the Master's office:
  - estates with wills
  - estates with a value of more than R50 000
  - insolvent estates
  - estates where one or more of the beneficiaries are minors who are not assisted by a legal guardian, and the cash assets in the estate are worth more than R20 000.

Since the handing down of *Bhe v Magistrate, Khayelitsha,* the Repeal of the Black Administration Act and Amendment of Certain Laws Act[33] came into operation. This Act repealed, amongst other things, s 23 of the Black Administration Act. Apart from this, the Reform of Customary Law of Succession and Regulation of Related Matters Bill was passed into law and confirms the above-mentioned judicial changes made to the customary law of succession.[34] The date of commencement of the Act still has to be published.

PAUSE FOR REFLECTION

Service points

To facilitate a uniform process for the administration of estates at magistrates' offices, Justice College[35] compiled a policy and procedure manual which had to be followed at every service point as from 5 December 2002.[36] The rules indicating which administration process has to be followed in the case of black deceased can be summarised as follows:

- If the deceased died intestate before 27 April 1994, his or her estate must be referred to the Master and must be administered according to the regulations promulgated in terms of the Black Administration Act.
- If the deceased died intestate after 27 April 1994, his or her estate must be administered by the Master in terms of the Administration of Estates Act and the Intestate Succession Act.
- If the deceased died intestate after 27 April 1994, but before 15 October 2004, and his or her estate was reported to a magistrate in terms of the Black Administration Act, that magistrate must finalise the estate in terms of the Intestate Succession Act, read in conjunction with *Bhe v Magistrate, Khayelitsha*. However, where the estate has already been wound up in terms of the regulations promulgated in terms of the Black Administration Act, the devolution of the estate should be finalised in terms of the latter unless there is a dispute by an heir.
- If the deceased died intestate after 15 October 2004, his or her estate must be administered in terms of the Administration of Estates Act and the Intestate Succession Act.

33 28 of 2005.

34 Reform of Customary Law of Succession and Regulation of Related Matters Act 11 of 2009 (RCLSA).

35 The Justice College is a department of government involved with the training of government officials, especially those involved in justice such as magistrates and prosecutors.

36 Meyer and Rudolph *Interim policy and procedure manual: administration of intestate deceased estates at service points* (Master's Training Note 49) (2002) 1 *et seq.*

A service point has jurisdiction over the estate of a deceased person who was, prior to his or her death, ordinarily resident within the area of jurisdiction of the magistrate's office where the service point is situated. The service point has to determine whether it or the Master has jurisdiction in the matter and then proceeds to deal with the administration of the estate according to the practice manual compiled for the Master's representatives at the magistrates' offices. The Deputy Director-General of the Department of Justice and Constitutional Development decided, as an interim measure, to appoint all magistrates' offices as service points to manage any estates to a maximum value of R50 000. At least one official - not necessarily a magistrate - at each office was appointed to deal with such estates. The business unit of the Master's office and the Department of Justice agreed internally that the Master's representatives will deliver the same services as the Master with regard to estates administered in terms of common law. Several of these arrangements are not contained in public documents and consequently are not readily accessible to legal practitioners and estate administrators.

15.3 Uniform rules for the administration of deceased estates

The process of administering deceased estates starts the day the testator dies. The process is conducted according to a certain set of legislated rules and has to be conducted under the supervision of the Master of the High Court. The Administration of Estates Act and various regulations issued in terms of the Act make up the principal legislation that regulates the administration of all deceased estates in South Africa.[37] Other important legislation that deals with aspects of the administrative process was listed above.

15.3.1 Basic concepts of administration of estates

15.3.1.1 Estate

A deceased estate consists of a collection of all the patrimonial rights vested in a natural person at the time of his or her death as well as all the claims against him or her at the time of death. Should the assets exceed the liabilities, the deceased estate is solvent and should it be vice versa, the estate is insolvent and has to be executed as prescribed in the Administration of Estates Act.[38]

PAUSE FOR REFLECTION

Meaning of 'estate' for purposes of estate tax

What constitutes an estate for the purposes of estate duty is, in many cases, different from what constitutes an estate for the purposes of a liquidation and distribution account[39] governed by the Administration of Estates Act. According to the Estate Duty Act,[40] an estate has a broader meaning and includes the property of a deceased at his death and all property that is deemed to be property of that person at that date.[41] Estate duty is levied in respect of the estate of every person who dies and deemed property

37 The authorisation for the promulgation of the regulations is s 103 of the Administration of Estates Act.
38 See s 34.
39 The contents of the liquidation and distribution account is discussed on page 249.
40 45 of 1955; section 2(1).
41 Section 3 of the Estate Duty Act.

includes the property of a deceased which, according to the rules of jurisprudence, is not strictly speaking property, for example a life insurance policy ceded to a third person. It is vital that these different concepts are not equated or confused with each other.

15.3.1.2 Executor

The Administration of Estates Act[42] defines an executor as the 'person who is authorized to act under letters of executorship granted or signed and sealed by a Master ... .' One of two situations may prevail.

Firstly, the testator might have nominated an executor in a valid will, in which case the Master will appoint the nominated person as executor after he or she has completed an acceptance of executorship. Such an executor is known as an executor testamentary.

Secondly, if the deceased died without a valid will and did not nominate an executor, the Master will appoint an executor who has completed an acceptance of executorship. Such an executor is known as an executor dative.

If the gross value of the estate is less than R125 000,[43] it is possible to appoint someone who is not an executor to administer the estate. This kind of appointment is referred to as a s 18(3) appointment. Section 18(3) of the Administration of Estates Act reads as follows:

> *If the value of any estate does not exceed the amount determined by the Minister by notice in the Gazette, the Master may dispense with the appointment of an executor and give directions as to the manner in which any such estate shall be liquidated and distributed.*

The advantages of this procedure are that because no executor is appointed, no executor's fee is payable and there is no need for a liquidation and distribution account. This is a great benefit to smaller deceased estates. In addition, the winding-up of the estate is much faster than when an executor is nominated by the deceased.

The executor is in a position of trust in relation to the deceased estate. He or she receives remuneration for his or her activities and should administer the estate with due care and diligence. The testator may give the nominated executor the power of assumption which means that the appointed executor has the power to appoint a co-executor or agent to assist with the winding-up of the estate. Certain persons, for example minors, are not qualified to be appointed as executors.

Under normal circumstances, an executor must provide security regarding the proper performance of his or her duties, but a testator may exempt the executor from this obligation. The Master determines the amount of security which must be provided - it is usually the value of the assets in the deceased estate. Certain persons are automatically exempted from giving security, for example a parent, spouse or child of the deceased.[44]

> A typical clause in a will nominating an executor with the power of assumption and exempting him or her from giving security, may be worded as follows: 'We nominate as executor the survivor of us with the power of assumption. In the event of our

42 Section 1.
43 The amount was fixed in GN R1318 in *GG* 25456 of 19 September 2003.
44 Section 23 of the Administration of Estates Act.

simultaneous death or should the survivor not be able to accept the appointment, we appoint a senior partner of the attorney's firm Lubbe & Schoeman, practising at Potchefstroom, to be the executor of our estates with the power of assumption. We direct that neither the survivor nor any partner from the attorney's firm Lubbe & Schoeman shall be called upon to furnish security for acting as such in this capacity.'

PAUSE FOR REFLECTION

Executors' fees

The business of administration of estates has become quite lucrative, especially in light of the executor's fee which is payable to each and every executor or assumed executor. In terms of s 51 of the Administration of Estates Act and its regulations, the executor's fee may be stipulated in a will. If it is not stipulated in a will, the following rules apply: The executor is entitled to 3,5% on the gross value of the estate plus 6% on any income obtained after the death of the deceased. A minimum fee of R350 is applicable. For example, the executor's fee on an estate with a gross value of R1 million, would be R35 000. The deceased estate has to pay the executor's fee and paying it could have a negative effect on the value of the bequests that have to devolve on the beneficiaries.

15.3.1.3 Master

The Administration of Estates Act[45] defines the Master 'in relation to any matter, property or estate, [to] mean the Master, Deputy Master or Assistant Master of a High Court appointed under s 2, who has jurisdiction in respect of that matter, property or estate and who is subject to the control, direction and supervision of the Chief Master'. The Master of the High Court is thus a statutory institution appointed for every provincial division of the High Court of South Africa. Masters' Offices are situated in Bloemfontein, Cape Town, Grahamstown, Kimberley, Mmabatho (or Mafikeng), Pietermaritzburg, Pretoria, Mthatha, Bisho, Thohoyandou, Johannesburg, Polokwane, Durban, and Port Elizabeth. A Master normally has jurisdiction over the estate of a deceased who was ordinarily resident within the area of jurisdiction of that particular Master's Office, but it is also possible for a Master to assume jurisdiction of a particular estate if so requested by a person who has an interest in the deceased estate and with the consent of the Master who has jurisdiction.[46]

A fee[47] is payable to the Master. The fee is calculated on the gross value of the estate as follows: R42 on the first R17 000 and R6 for every completed R2 000 thereafter. No Master's fee is payable on estates of less than R15 000. A maximum fee of R600 is payable.

COUNTER POINT

An exception to the jurisdiction of the Master

Although the customary law of intestate succession has, to a great extent, been replaced with an adapted Intestate Succession Act,[48] there is no guarantee that all estates normally governed by the principles of customary law will now devolve according to the rules of the Intestate Succession Act. It would be difficult, if not impossible, to determine whether it is indeed happening in the traditional communities or whether

45 Section 1.
46 Section 4.
47 Section 103(1)(d) and reg 16.
48 See the discussion in Chapter 2.

a deceased's estate is devolved as always, namely within the privacy of the family according to customary principles. If a testator stipulates in his or her will that his or her estate has to devolve in terms of the customary law of succession, there is a will which, under normal circumstances, has to be reported to the Master. However, s 4(1) and 4(1A) of the Administration of Estates Act still says that the Master does not have jurisdiction in the case of deceased estates governed by the principles of customary law. It seems that the wording of s 4 could create an anomaly if interpreted literally and it should be altered in the near future.

The Master's Office consists of the Master, Deputy and Assistant Masters and trained examiners who supervise the administration process. For example, they supervise the designated service points at magistrates' offices, inspect the liquidation and distribution accounts, and make sure that the correct procedures are followed by executors. However, the functions of the Master are more than mere supervision of the administration process. The Master's Office also fulfils judicial functions such as making a pronouncement on issues of jurisdiction,[49] and quasi-judicial functions such as pronouncing on objections lodged against liquidation and distribution accounts. The Master's Office also fulfils administrative functions such as the handling and filing of documents, and discretionary functions such as the acceptance or rejection of wills. Finally, they perform an advisory function, for example by advising executors with regard to the winding-up of estates.

15.3.2 The administration process

The administration process can broadly be divided into three phases. The first phase starts on the death of the deceased and involves the steps which have to be taken until an executor is appointed. Strictly speaking, the executor is only allowed to begin with the winding-up of the estate when he or she is appointed by the Master but, in reality, certain preliminary tasks can be performed during this phase. The second phase is the actual process of administration that culminates in the submission of a liquidation and distribution account to the Master of the High Court. The third phase begins when the account has been approved and certain final requirements are met.

15.3.2.1 Phase 1

The administration process starts when someone dies leaving any assets or any document purporting to be a will.[50] The first step is to report the death of the testator to the Master by completing a document referred to as the death notice. This has to be done by the surviving spouse, nearest relative or the person in control of the place where the death occurred. Usually the executor (to be appointed) will do this task. The executor will conduct an interview with the family of the deceased as soon as possible to obtain the necessary information and documents. In order to report the deceased estate to the Master, he or she has to complete the following documents to send to the Master, together with the original will (if there was one):[51]

49 Section 4.
50 Section 7.
51 Section 8.

- death notice[52]
- inventory of estimated values[53]
- acceptance of executorship.

While the executor awaits his or her letter of executorship, he or she may continue with certain tasks, such as obtaining valuations for the assets and establishing the liabilities of the deceased estate.

15.3.2.2 Phase 2

This phase begins when the letter of executorship has been issued. This letter entitles the executor to administer the deceased estate, in other words to continue with the winding-up process. The duties of the executor are fully set out in the Administration of Estates Act and its regulations. These duties are essentially aimed at preserving the estate during the administration process and eventually liquidating it. Basically the rules entail that the executor must:

- take control of the assets of the estate[54]
- advertise for creditors and debtors to submit claims within 30 days after the last date of publication[55]
- determine whether the estate is solvent[56]
- open an account in the name of the estate if there is more than R1 000 in the executor's possession[57]
- choose a method of liquidation in consultation with relatives and beneficiaries
- prepare a liquidation and distribution account which must be submitted to the Master together with other documents.[58]

The distribution of assets in an estate occasionally causes conflict between the beneficiaries. In many cases, it leads to bitter disputes between family members who then resort to legal action. Because this can delay the winding-up of an estate, executors usually choose a method of liquidation in consultation with the beneficiaries and next of kin. It is also important to have knowledge of the nature of the assets in the estate, the debts of the estate, the provisions of the will (if there is one), and how practical it is to carry out the estate plan. There are five methods of liquidation:

15.3.2.2.1 Awarding and handing over of specific assets

In this method, the beneficiaries receive their benefits in a specific form and not in an alternative form such as cash.

> A testator bequeaths his or her farm to his or her son. The son will receive the farm and not the proceeds of the farm after it has been sold by the executor. This form of liquidation is preferable, especially if it was instructed in the will and there is enough cash on hand to pay the liabilities of the estate.

52 Sections 14–18.
53 Section 9.
54 Section 26.
55 Section 29.
56 Section 34.
57 Section 28.
58 Section 35.

15.3.2.2.2 Partial sale

When applying this method, the executor sells some of the assets in order to meet the liabilities of the estate. This form of liquidation is applied in circumstances that make it necessary, for example:

- a shortage of cash to pay the liabilities of the estate
- instructions in the will that certain assets have to be sold
- the nature of an asset is such that it cannot be divided between multiple beneficiaries and it would be easier to sell the asset and divide the proceeds.

A testator bequeaths his farm to his three sons but, in terms of the Subdivision of Agricultural Land Act,[59] subdivision of agricultural land is prohibited. In such a case it would be better for the executor to sell the farm and distribute the cash evenly amongst the three sons unless the sons themselves reach a different agreement which can be reflected in a redistribution agreement (also a method of liquidation).

15.3.2.2.3 Total sale

When using this method, the executor sells all the assets in the estate. This method should only be applied in exceptional circumstances.

This method applies when a testator instructs a total sale in his or her will or if circumstances, such as a cash deficiency, necessitate it. In both cases the executor is normally under an obligation to sell all the assets in the estate.

A total sale could also be done at the request of all the beneficiaries, for example when they prefer to receive cash instead of assets.

15.3.2.2.4 Taking over by surviving spouse[60]

When this method is used, it is not necessary for the surviving spouse to be a beneficiary in terms of the will. Under certain exceptional circumstances, the surviving spouse may take the estate over at an amount determined by an appraiser. This method is subject to the discretion of the Master who will only consider such an application under the following circumstances:

- The application has been submitted in the prescribed way.
- There is no provision in the will prohibiting the taking over.
- All the beneficiaries and creditors have agreed.
- There is no disadvantage for any interested parties.

The Master will only give consent to the taking over once the required security has been provided. This method could ensure that the continuity of the estate is maintained and could also ensure the finalisation of an estate where it is difficult to divide it.

15.3.2.2.5 Redistribution agreement

It is possible for the beneficiaries of an estate to conclude an agreement with regard to the redistribution of the assets in the estate. This form of liquidation is especially popular when the beneficiaries want to divide the property in a different way than determined in the will or where the beneficiaries of an intestate estate want to renounce co-ownership of property

---

59 70 of 1970; note that this Act stands to be repealed.
60 Section 38.

in favour of individual ownership of specific assets. A redistribution agreement could also be considered if a family living under a system of customary law wants to give effect to the rules of customary law of succession. The agreement must be submitted to the Master for approval and special requirements must be met in the case of minor beneficiaries. The formalities for these contracts are that they must be in writing, signed by the parties, and dated.

> Assume that a testator bequeathed the whole of his estate to his son, Jan Botma, subject to the condition that his son must pay R100 000 to the deceased's sister, Jasmina Daniels. Instead of paying the R100 000 to Jasmina, the parties can agree to divide the assets as follows: (1) to Jan Botma all the immovable assets; and (2) to Jasmina Daniels (née Meyer) all the movable assets. The heirs hereby acknowledge that they understand and accept the contents of this agreement, and that they shall have no further claims to the assets of the Estate, other than agreed above.'

The final liquidation and distribution account has to be submitted within six months after the letter of executorship has been issued by the Master.[61] If the executor is unable to submit the account in time, he or she must apply in writing (with reasons) to the Master for an extension of the date. In this application the executor must state the following:

- the reasons why the account cannot be submitted on time
- the steps taken to expedite the submission of the account and what progress has been made
- what progress has been made with the liquidation of the estate
- what the financial position of the estate is (in other words, the status of the bank account)
- whether or not the estate is solvent.

Regulation 5 of the Administration of Estates Act prescribes the formalities of the account. In short, it must contain:[62]

- a heading
- a liquidation account
- a recapitulation statement
- a distribution account
- an income and expenditure account
- a fiduciary assets account
- an estate duty addendum.

The executor must certify at the end of the account that it is a true and proper reflection of the liquidation and distribution of the estate. The account is then submitted to the Master for approval and must lie open for public inspection (at the Master's Office as well as the magistrate's office of the district where the deceased was resident before his or her death) for a certain period of time. The fact that the account is lying open for inspection has to be advertised in the *Government Gazette* and a local newspaper.[63]

---

61 Section 35.

62 See para 15.3.3 for an overview of each account.

63 Section 35(5).

15.3.2.3 Phase 3

This phase begins when the final liquidation and distribution account has been approved. The executor has to fulfil the so-called final requirements of the liquidation of the estate including:

- proof of advertisement
- certificate of magistrate
- proof of payment of Master's fee
- proof of payment to creditors and cash legacies
- proof of delivery of legacies and inheritances
- obtaining the final bank statement with a zero balance.

After the executor has done the final tasks, he or she is entitled to his or her discharge.[64]

PAUSE FOR REFLECTION

Executors' duties

Wiechers and Vorster[65] supply a handy checklist for executors or administrators to use in the performance of their duties. In summary:

1. Report the estate to the Master by forwarding the following information to the Master's office:
   - the death notice
   - the death certificate
   - an inventory
   - the will
   - the acceptance of executorship form.
2. Ascertain value of all assets in estate.
3. Ascertain liabilities.
4. Open an estate banking account.
5. Determine a suitable method of liquidation of the estate.
6. Establish a suitable procedure for administration of the estate and consult heirs if there is a cash deficit.
7. Pay all liabilities after ensuring that there is no cash deficit and that the estate is solvent.
8. If the estate is insolvent, act in terms of s 34 of the Administration of Estates Act.
9. Draw a liquidation and distribution account and submit to the Master.
10. Obtain permission from the Master to advertise the account for inspection.
11. Pay all creditors, legacies and inheritances.
12. Pay Master's fees.
13. Pay estate duty.
14. Attend to the Master's final requirements.
15. Obtain the Master's release (filing slip).

64 Section 56 of the Administration of Estates Act.
65 Annexure A1.

15.3.3 Liquidation and distribution account

A liquidation and distribution account (which has to comply with the formalities in reg 5) must be submitted to the Master within six months after the letters of executorship have been issued. There are a number of formal requirements for this account that are discussed below.

15.3.3.1 Heading

The heading of the account must contain the number of the account, the full name, surname and identity number of the deceased, and the date he or she died.[66] The marital status of the deceased, details of the surviving spouse, and the Master's reference number are also required.

> First and final Liquidation and distribution account in the estate of deceased Amanda Little with identity number 4301305167 088 and married in community of property to James Little with identity number 4402180007 080, ordinarily residing at 10 Blom Street, Potchefstroom and deceased on 28 May 2005.
> Master's Reference Number: 712/05

15.3.3.2 Money column

The executor must provide for a money column.[67] In practice, most executors make provision for a double column on the right-hand side of the account, one for subtotals and the other for grand totals. See Table 15.1 and Table 15.3 later in this chapter.

15.3.3.3 Liquidation account

The liquidation account contains the assets and liabilities of the deceased.[68] It is the most important part of the account and must be drawn up with caution. In the assets column, a distinction is made between immovable property, movable property and claims in favour of the estate. The total sum of these assets reflects the gross value of the estate. The value of the assets must be reflected in the money column. The value that must be reflected depends to a large extent on the mode of liquidation that has been chosen. If the assets were, for example, a specific asset awarded and handed over, the value of the assets must be reflected. If the executor sells the property, the proceeds must be reflected in the money column. The liabilities column contains administration costs, claims against the estate and estate duty (if any) payable by the estate. Administration costs include costs of advertisements, the Master's and executor's fee, bank costs, funeral expenses and transfer costs.

Each exhibit (voucher, receipt or quittance) that forms part of the liquidation account must be numbered. The number must be reflected in the liquidation account next to the particular asset. The exhibits in support of the account need not be sent to the Master; they must remain on file as the Master may require them at any time. The executor must also indicate how he or she intends dealing with all the assets that have not been realised. This indication is known as a divestment note. The balance (assets minus liabilities) is the amount to be distributed.

---

66 Regulation 5(1)(a).
67 Regulation 5(1)(b).
68 Regulation 5(1)(c).

Table 15.1 A simple example of a liquidation account

DESCRIPTION	EXHIBIT NUMBER	MONEY COLUMN	MONEY COLUMN
ASSETS			
Immovable property (allotted and transferred to the surviving spouse as heir in terms of the joint will)	1	500 000	
Movable property (allotted and transferred to the surviving spouse as heir in terms of the joint will)	2	50 000	
TOTAL ASSETS			550 000
LIABILITIES			
Funeral costs	3	10 000	
Master's fee	4	600	
LESS TOTAL LIABILITIES			10 600
LESS ESTATE TAX			Nil
BALANCE FOR DISTRIBUTION			539 400
GROSS TOTAL		550 000	550 000

15.3.3.4 Recapitulation statement

The purpose of the recapitulation statement is to reflect the cash position of the estate.[69] If there is a cash deficit, it must be met by applying the right method of liquidation. If there is a cash surplus, it must be divided amongst the residuary heirs.

15.3.3.5 Distribution account

The distribution account reflects the balance available for distribution amongst the beneficiaries and details of how it must be distributed amongst the beneficiaries.[70] If the testator died testate, his or her estate must be divided according to the stipulations of the will. If he or she died intestate, the estate must be divided according to the rules of intestate succession. If there is a redistribution agreement, it must be attached to the distribution account.

69 Regulation 5(1)(d).
70 Regulation 5(1)(e).

Table 15.2 A simple example of a distribution account

BALANCE FOR DISTRIBUTION	**550 000**	
To the Surviving Spouse James Little in terms of the joint will		550 000

15.3.3.6 Income and expenditure account

The income and expenditure account reflects the income and expenditure incurred after the death of the testator.[71] Deductions, such as the executor's fee, must be reflected here. If there is a balance, it must be distributed amongst the beneficiaries.

15.3.3.7 Fiduciary assets account

If the testator enjoyed a fideicommissum during his or her life, such a fiduciary right must be reflected in the fiduciary assets account.[72] This account is actually an account within an account. The executor must give a description of the fiduciary asset, and must reflect all the income and expenditure relating to the asset. The balance must be distributed amongst the fiduciary heirs.

15.3.3.8 Estate duty addendum

The estate duty addendum reflects the calculation that determines the amount of estate duty payable.[73] The calculations regarding estate duty form an integral part of the liquidation and distribution account and must be done in terms of the Estate Duty Act. Estate duty is a complex and difficult subject. If a testator's estate was not properly planned during his or her lifetime, it can create numerous complications for an executor when he or she has to calculate the estate duty.

15.3.3.9 Certificate

This is the last section of the liquidation and distribution account and consists of a statement by the executor that the account is a true and proper account of the administration of the estate.[74]

> I, the undersigned, James Little, do hereby declare that the above is to the best of my knowledge and belief, a true and proper account of the liquidation and distribution account of the estate of the late Amanda Little and that, to the best of my knowledge and belief, all the assets and income collected subsequent to the death of the deceased to the date of the account have been disclosed therein.
> Signed at Potchefstroom on 20 October 2000

15.3.3.10 Example of a simple liquidation and distribution account

> Anny Leighton died in a motor car accident on 28 May 2009. She is survived by her husband, James Leighton (to whom she was married out of community of property

71 Regulation 5(1)(f).
72 Regulation 5(1)(g).
73 Regulation 5(1)(h).
74 Regulation 5(1)(i).

with the exclusion of the accrual system), her major daughters from a previous marriage, Debby Bush and Kelly Bush, and George Meyer, a major son adopted by James and Anny. Kelly and George are both minors.

Anny and James had a mutual will (in which they declared that the estate of the first-dying had to devolve upon the survivor in their will).

The surviving spouse, James Leighton, is appointed as executor. The following information is available to the executor:

1 **Assets**

1.1 Fixed deposit at the New South Africa Bank, account number 295-307: R300 000,00.

1.2 Savings account at the New South Africa Bank, account number 195-620: R24 576,00.

1.3 5 000 Iscor Ltd shares. The shares were sold by International Brokers @ 1 146 cents per share. The broker's commission amounts to 5% of the proceeds of the shares.

1.4 Proceeds of an Old Mutual life insurance policy: R65 000,00.

1.5 STAND 240, POTCHEFSTROOM, Registration Section IQ, NORTHWEST Big 200 square metres. Held by the deceased in terms of deed of transfer T70471/88. The municipal valuation of the property is R500 000,00.

1.6 Furniture and household goods to the value of R160 000,00.

2 **Liabilities**

2.1 Edgars – outstanding balance on clothing account as at date of death: R1 750,00.

3 **Administration expenses**

3.1 Bank charges – once-off fee R100,00.

3.2 Commission on the sale of the shares (Calculate amount).

3.3 Dove & Allen – funeral expenses R3 450,00.

3.4 Advertisement costs – section 29: *Citizen* R42,00 and *Government Gazette* R14,00. The same amounts for the section 35 advertisement were paid.

3.5 Postages and petties – maximum allowed by the Master: R30,00.

3.6 All statutory fees which must/may be levied.

4 **Other information**

4.1 There was no income or expenditure after death.

4.2 There are no fiduciary assets that need to be dealt with.

Proposed liquidation and distribution account

Table 15.3 The proposed final liquidation and distribution account

FIRST AND FINAL LIQUIDATION AND DISTRIBUTION ACCOUNT IN THE ESTATE OF DECEASED ANNIE LEIGHTON WITH IDENTITY NUMBER 430130 5167 08 8 AND MARRIED OUT OF COMMUNITY OF PROPERTY (WITH EXCLUSION OF THE ACCRUAL SYSTEM) TO JAMES LEIGHTON WITH IDENTITY NUMBER 440218 0007 08 0, ORDINARILY RESIDING AT 10 BLOM STREET, POTCHEFSTROOM AND DECEASED ON 28 MAY 2009.

MASTER'S REFERENCE NUMBER: 712/04

LIQUIDATION ACCOUNT			
Assets		**R**	**R**
IMMOVABLE PROPERTY			
1. STAND 240, POTCHEFSTROOM, Registration Section IQ, NORTHWEST Big 200 square metres. Held by the deceased Deed of Transfer T70471/88 Per municipal valuation Item 1 transferred to the surviving spouse in terms of the will.	(1)	500 000,00	
MOVABLE PROPERTY			
2. Furniture and household goods Per valuation Item 2 transferred to the surviving spouse in terms of the will.	(2)	160 000,00	
CLAIMS IN FAVOUR OF THE ESTATE			
3. Fixed deposit at New South Africa Bank, account number 295-307 Proceeds to the estate account	(3)	300 000,00	
4. Savings account at New South Africa Bank, account number 195-620 Proceeds to the estate account	(4)	24 576,00	
SHARES			
5. 5 000 (five thousand) Iscor Ltd shares @ 1 146 cents per share as per certificate number 4007 Transferred to surviving spouse in terms of the will (5 000 × 1 146 = 57 300)	(5)	57 300,00	

LIFE POLICY			
6. Old Mutual life policy no. 789756484X Proceeds to the estate account	(6)	65 000,00	
Total assets: Gross estate		1 106 876,00	
LIABILITIES			
ADMINISTRATION COSTS			
7. Debtors and creditors account:			
Citizen	(7)		42,00
Government Gazette	(8)		14,00
8. Estate account for inspection:			
Citizen	(9)		42,00
Government Gazette	(10)		14,00
9. Master's fee: maximum fee	(11)		600,00
10. Executor's remuneration (1 106 876 × 3.5%)			38 740,66
OTHER COSTS			
11. Funeral expenses: Dove & Allen	(12)		3 450,00
12. Bank costs	(13)		100,00
13. Edgars	(14)		1 750,00
14. Commission on shares (57 300 × 5% = 2 865)			2 865,00
15. Postage and petties			30,00
16. No estate duty payable			
Total liabilities			47 647,66
Net estate (balance for distribution)		1 059 228,34	
RECAPITULATION STATEMENT			
Cash on hand (items 3, 4, 6)			389 576,00
Less total liabilities		47 647,66	
Cash available for distribution		341 928,34	
DISTRIBUTION ACCOUNT			
Balance for distribution			1 059 228,34
To: Surviving spouse James Leighton		1 059 228,34	

INCOME AND EXPENDITURE ACCOUNT FROM DATE OF DEATH TO DATE OF ESTATE ACCOUNT			
None			
FIDUCIARY ACCOUNT			
None			
ESTATE TAX			
Property in terms of liquidation account - s 3(2)			1 106 876,00
Less Old Mutual policy			65 000,00
			1 041 876,00
plus			
Property i.t.o. sec 3(3) Old Mutual policy			65 000,00
Gross taxable estate			1 041 876,00
less			
S 4 deductions: liabilities			47 647,66
S 4q deduction: bequest to surviving spouse			1 059 228,34
Net tax estate			0
Tax payable			Nil

CERTIFICATE

I, the undersigned, James Leighton, do hereby declare that the above is, to the best of my knowledge and belief, a true and proper account of the liquidation and distribution account of the estate of the late Annie Leighton and that, to the best of my knowledge and belief, all the assets and income collected subsequent to the death of the deceased to the date of the account have been disclosed therein.

Signed at Potchefstroom on 4 November 2009.

____

James Leighton

THIS CHAPTER IN ESSENCE

1. The process of administration or winding-up of estates commences the day the testator dies.
2. The estate of the deceased testator must be liquidated and distributed in terms of the Administration of Estates Act and the regulations promulgated in terms of s 103 of the Act.

3. Besides the Administration of Estates Act and its regulations dealing directly with the administration process, numerous other acts dealing with related issues such as income tax, estate duty, insurance, donations tax, and the maintenance of a surviving spouse may be applicable.
4. Before 6 December 2000, different sets of rules for the winding-up and administration of deceased estates existed for the various racial groups in South Africa. A magistrate had jurisdiction over the intestate estates of black persons, whilst the Master of the High Court had jurisdiction over all other remaining intestate and testate estates.
5. Since 6 December 2000, there have been various legal developments in this area of law as a result of a number of legislative changes and the judgments delivered in *Moseneke v The Master* and *Bhe v Magistrate, Khayelitsha*.
6. The judicial and legislative changes required an entirely new system for the supervision and administration of deceased estates, irrespective of the race of a deceased.
7. The result of all the developments is that there is now a uniform process for all deceased estates in South Africa.
8. The administration process can be divided into three phases:
    - The first phase entails the preliminary steps which have to be taken when a testator dies.
    - The second phase begins when the letter of executorship has been issued and the executor can continue with the winding-up process.
    - The third and final phase is when the final liquidation and distribution account has been approved and the executor has to comply with the final requirements of the estate. Once this has been done, he or she is entitled to his or her discharge and the winding-up process is over.

Appendix A

WILLS ACT
NO. 7 OF 1953

[ASSENTED TO 25 FEBRUARY, 1953]
[DATE OF COMMENCEMENT: 1 JANUARY, 1954]
(English text signed by the Governor-General)

This Act has been updated to *Government Gazette* 17477 dated 4 October, 1996.

as amended by
Wills Amendment Act, No. 48 of 1958
General Law Amendment Act, No. 80 of 1964
[with effect from 24 June 1964, unless otherwise indicated]
Wills Amendment Act, No. 41 of 1965
Law of Succession Amendment Act, No. 43 of 1992
General Law Amendment Act, No. 49 of 1996
[with effect from 4 October 1996]

ACT

To consolidate and amend the law relating to the execution of wills.

ARRANGEMENT OF SECTIONS

1.	Definitions
2.	Formalities required in the execution of a will
2A.	Power of court to declare a will to be revoked
2B.	Effect of divorce or annulment of marriage on will
2C.	Surviving spouse and descendants of certain persons entitled to benefits in terms of will
2D.	Interpretation of wills
3.	. . . . . .
3*bis*.	Validity of certain wills executed in accordance with the internal law of certain other states
4.	Competency to make a will
4A.	Competency of persons involved in execution of will
5.	. . . . . .
6.	. . . . . .
7.	Repeal of laws

8.	......
9.	Short title and date of commencement
Schedule 1	Certificate in terms of section 2 (1) (*a*) (v)
Schedule 2	Certificate in terms of section 2 (1) (*b*) (iv)
Schedule 3	Laws repealed

1. Definitions. — In this Act, unless the context otherwise indicates—
"amendment" means a deletion, addition, alteration or interlineation;

[Definition of "amendment" inserted by s. 2 (*a*) of Act No. 43 of 1992.]

"competent witness" means a person of the age of fourteen years or over who at the time he witnesses a will is not incompetent to give evidence in a court of law;

"Court" means a provincial or local division of the Supreme Court of South Africa or any judge thereof;

[Definition of "Court" amended by s. 1 of Act No. 49 of 1996.]

"deletion" means a deletion, cancellation or obliteration in whatever manner effected, excluding a deletion, cancellation or obliteration that contemplates the revocation of the entire will;

[Definition of "deletion" inserted by s. 2 (*b*) of Act No. 43 of 1992.]

"internal law" means the law of a state or territory, excluding the rules of the international private law of that state or territory;

[Definition of "internal law" inserted by s. 2 (*c*) of Act No. 43 of 1992.]

"Master" means a Master, Deputy Master or Assistant Master of the Supreme Court appointed under section 2 of the Administration of Estates Act, 1965 (Act No. 66 of 1965);

[Definition of "Master" substituted by s. 2 (*d*) of Act No. 43 of 1992.]

"sign" includes the making of initials and, only in the case of a testator, the making of a mark and **"signature"** has a corresponding meaning;

[Definition of "sign" substituted by s. 2 (*e*) of Act No. 43 of 1992.]

"will" includes a codicil and any other testamentary writing.

2. **Formalities required in the execution of a will.** — (1) Subject to the provisions of section 3*bis*—

(*a*) no will executed on or after the first day of January, 1954, shall be valid unless—

(i) the will is signed at the end thereof by the testator or by some other person in his presence and by his direction; and

(ii) such signature is made by the testator or by such other person or is acknowledged by the testator and, if made by such other person, also by such other person, in the presence of two or more competent witnesses present at the same time; and

(iii) such witnesses attest and sign the will in the presence of the testator and of each other and, if the will is signed by such other person, in the presence also of such other person; and

(iv) if the will consists of more than one page, each page other than the page on which it ends, is also signed by the testator or by such other person anywhere on the page; and

[Sub-para. (iv) amended by s. 20 (*a*) of Act No. 80 of 1964 and substituted by s. 3 (*b*) of Act No. 43 of 1992.]

(v) if the will is signed by the testator by the making of a mark or by some other person in the presence and by the direction of the testator, a commissioner of oaths certifies that he has satisfied himself as to the identity of the testator and that the will so signed is the will of the testator, and each page of the will, excluding the page on which his certificate appears, is also signed, anywhere on the page, by the commissioner of oaths who so certifies: Provided that—

(*aa*) the will is signed in the presence of the commissioner of oaths in terms of subparagraphs (i), (iii) and (iv) and the certificate concerned is made as soon as possible after the will has been so signed; and

(*bb*) if the testator dies after the will has been signed in terms of subparagraphs (i), (iii) and (iv) but before the commissioner of oaths has made the certificate concerned, the commissioner of oaths shall as soon as possible thereafter make or complete his certificate, and sign each page of the will, excluding the page on which his certificate appears;

[Sub-para. (v) amended by s. 1 (*a*) of Act No. 48 of 1958 and substituted by s. 20 (*b*) of Act No. 80 of 1964 and by s. 3 (*c*) of Act No. 43 of 1992.]

(*b*) no amendment made in a will executed on or after the said date and made after the execution thereof shall be valid unless—

(i) the amendment is identified by the signature of the testator or by the signature of some other person made in his presence and by his direction; and

(ii) such signature is made by the testator or by such other person or is acknowledged by the testator and, if made by such other person, also by some other person, in the presence of two or more competent witnesses present at the same time; and

(iii) the amendment is further identified by the signatures of such witnesses made in the presence of the testator and of each other and, if the amendment has been identified by the signature of such other person, in the presence also of such other person; and

(iv) if the amendment is identified by the mark of the testator or the signature of some other person made in his presence and by his direction, a commissioner of oaths certifies on the will that he has satisfied himself as to the identity of the testator and that the amendment has been made by or at the request of the testator: Provided that—

(*aa*) the amendment is identified in the presence of the commissioner of oaths in terms of subparagraphs (i) and (iii) and the certificate concerned is made as soon as possible after the amendment has been so identified; and

(*bb*) if the testator dies after the amendment has been identified in terms of subparagraphs (i) and (iii) but before the commissioner of oaths has made the certificate concerned, the commissioner of oaths shall as soon as possible thereafter make or complete his certificate.

[Sub-s. (1) amended by s. 1 of Act No. 41 of 1965 and by s. 3 (*a*) of Act No. 43 of 1992. Para. (*b*) amended by s. 3 (*d*) of Act No. 43 of 1992. Sub-para. (iv) amended by s. 1 (*b*) of Act No. 48 of 1958 and substituted by s. 3 (*e*) of Act No. 43 of 1992.]

(2) Any amendment made in a will executed after the said date shall for the purposes of subsection (1) be presumed, unless the contrary is proved, to have been made after the will was executed.

[Sub-s. (2) substituted by s. 3 (*f*) of Act No. 43 of 1992.]

(3) If a court is satisfied that a document or the amendment of a document drafted or executed by a person who has died since the drafting or execution thereof, was intended to be his will or an amendment of his will, the court shall order the Master to accept that document, or that document as amended, for the purposes of the Administration of Estates Act, 1965 (Act No. 66 of 1965), as a will, although it does not comply with all the formalities for the execution or amendment of wills referred to in subsection (1).

[Sub-s. (3) added by s. 3 (*g*) of Act No. 43 of 1992.]

(4) The certificate of a commissioner of oaths referred to in subsection (1) (*a*) (v) or (*b*) (iv) may be in the form set out in Schedule 1 or 2, as the case may be.

[Sub-s. (4) added by s. 3 (*g*) of Act No. 43 of 1992.]

2A. Power of court to declare a will to be revoked.—If a court is satisfied that a testator has—

(*a*) made a written indication on his will or before his death caused such indication to be made;

(*b*) performed any other act with regard to his will or before his death caused such act to be performed which is apparent from the face of the will; or

(*c*) drafted another document or before his death caused such document to be drafted,

by which he intended to revoke his will or a part of his will, the court shall declare the will or the part concerned, as the case may be, to be revoked.

[S. 2A inserted by s. 4 of Act No. 43 of 1992.]

2B. Effect of divorce or annulment of marriage on will.—If any person dies within three months after his marriage was dissolved by a divorce or annulment by a competent court and that person executed a will before the date of such dissolution, that will shall be implemented in the same manner as it would have been implemented if his previous spouse had died before the date of the dissolution concerned, unless it appears from the will that the testator intended to benefit his previous spouse notwithstanding the dissolution of his marriage.

[S. 2B inserted by s. 4 of Act No. 43 of 1992.]

2C. Surviving spouse and descendants of certain persons entitled to benefits in terms of will.— (1) If any descendants of a testator, excluding a minor or a mentally ill descendant, who, together with the surviving spouse of the testator, is entitled to a benefit in terms of a will renounces his right to receive such benefit, such benefit shall vest in the surviving spouse.

(2) If a descendant of the testator, whether as a member of a class or otherwise, would have been entitled to a benefit in terms of the provisions of a will if he had been alive at the time of death of the testator, or had not been disqualified from inheriting, or had not after the testator's death renounced his right to receive such a benefit, the descendants of that descendant shall, subject to the provisions of subsection (1), *per stirpes* be entitled to the benefit, unless the context of the will otherwise indicates.

[S. 2C inserted by s. 4 of Act No. 43 of 1992.]

2D. Interpretation of wills.—(1) In the interpretation of a will, unless the context otherwise indicates—

(*a*) an adopted child shall be regarded as being born from his adoptive parent or parents and, in determining his relationship to the testator or another person for the purposes of a will, as the child of his adoptive parent or parents and not as the child of his natural parent or parents or any previous adoptive parent or parents, except in the case of a natural parent who is also the adoptive parent of the child concerned or who was married to the adoptive parent of the child concerned at the time of the adoption;

(*b*) the fact that any person was born out of wedlock shall be ignored in determining his relationship to the testator or another person for the purposes of a will;

(*c*) any benefit allocated to the children of a person, or to the members of a class of persons, mentioned in the will shall vest in the children of that person or those members of the class of persons who are alive at the time of the devolution of the benefit, or who have already been conceived at that time and who are later born alive.

(2) In the application of this section "will" means any writing by a person whereby he disposes of his property or any part thereof after his death.

[S. 2D inserted by s. 4 of Act No. 43 of 1992.]

3. ......

[S. 3 repealed by s. 5 of Act No. 43 of 1992.]

3*bis*. Validity of certain wills executed in accordance with the internal law of certain other states.— (1) A will, whether executed before or after the commencement of this section, shall—

(*a*) not be invalid merely by reason of the form thereof, if such form complies with the internal law of the state or territory—

(i) in which the will was executed;

(ii) in which the testator was, at the time of the execution of the will or at the time of his death, domiciled or habitually resident; or

(iii) of which the testator was, at the time of the execution of the will or at the time of his death, a citizen;

(*b*) so far as immovable property is disposed of therein, not be invalid merely by reason of the form thereof, if such form complies with the internal law of the state or territory in which that property is situate;

(*c*) so far as therein a power conferred by any instrument is exercised or a duty imposed by any instrument is performed, not be invalid merely by reason of the form thereof, if such form complies with the internal law of the state or territory in which such instrument was executed;

(*d*) so far as it revokes a will or a portion of a will which by virtue of the provisions of paragraph (*a*), (*b*) or (*c*) is not invalid, not be invalid merely by reason of the form thereof, if such form complies with the internal law referred to in the paragraph in terms of which the revoked will or portion is not invalid;

(*e*) not be invalid merely by reason of the form thereof, if it was executed on board a vessel or aircraft and such form complies with the internal law of the state or territory in which such vessel or aircraft was registered at the time of such execution, or with which it was otherwise most closely connected at that time.

(2) Any requirement of the internal law of any other state or territory in terms of which a testator of a particular age or nationality or having any other personal qualification is to observe special formalities in the execution of a will, or a witness to a will is to possess certain qualifications, shall be construed as a requirement relating to form only.

(3) If there are in force in any state or territory two or more systems of internal law relating to the form of wills, the internal law to be applied for the purposes of this section shall be the internal law determined in accordance with any relevant rule in force in the state or territory in question or, if there is no such rule in force therein, the internal law with which the testator was most closely connected at the time of his death, if the matter is to be determined by reference to the circumstances prevailing at his death, or at the time of the execution of the will in any other case.

(4) The provisions of this section shall not apply in respect of—

(*a*) a will made by a South African citizen otherwise than in writing; and

(*b*) a will made by a person who died before the commencement of this section.

(5) The provisions of this section shall not affect the validity of a will which but for such provisions would be valid.

[S. 3*bis* inserted by s. 2 of Act No. 41 of 1965 and amended by s. 6 of Act No. 43 of 1992.]

4. Competency to make a will.—Every person of the age of sixteen years or more may make a will unless at the time of making the will he is mentally incapable of appreciating the nature and effect of his act, and the burden of proof that he was mentally incapable at that time shall rest on the person alleging the same.

4A Competency of persons involved in execution of will.—(1) Any person who attests and signs a will as a witness, or who signs a will in the presence and by direction of the testator, or who writes out the will or any part thereof in his own handwriting, and the person who is the spouse of such person at the time of the execution of the will, shall be disqualified from receiving any benefit from that will.

(2) Notwithstanding the provisions of subsection (1)—

(*a*) a court may declare a person or his spouse referred to in subsection (1) to be competent to receive a benefit from a will if the court is satisfied that that person or his spouse did not defraud or unduly influence the testator in the execution of the will;

(*b*) a person or his spouse who in terms of the law relating to intestate succession would have been entitled to inherit from the testator if that testator has died intestate shall not be thus disqualified to receive a benefit from that will: Provided that the value of the benefit which the person concerned or his spouse receives, shall not exceed the value of the share to which that person or his spouse would have been entitled in terms of the law relating to intestate succession;

(*c*) a person or his spouse who attested and signed a will as a witness shall not be thus disqualified from receiving a benefit from that will if the will concerned has been attested and signed by at least two other competent witnesses who will not receive any benefit from the will concerned.

(3) For the purposes of subsections (1), and (2) (*a*) and (*c*), the nomination in a will of a person as executor, trustee or guardian shall be regarded as a benefit to be received by such person from that will.

[S. 4A inserted by s. 7 of Act No. 43 of 1992.]

5. ......

[S. 5 repealed by s. 8 of Act No. 43 of 1992.]

6. ......

[S. 6 repealed by s. 8 of Act No. 43 of 1992.]

7. Repeal of laws.—The laws specified in Schedule 3 are hereby repealed to the extent set forth in the fourth column of the Schedule: Provided that the laws so repealed shall continue to apply in respect of any will executed before the first day of January, 1954.

[S. 7 substituted by s. 9 of Act No. 43 of 1992.]

8. ......

[S. 8 substituted by s. 21 of Act No. 80 of 1964 with effect from 1 January, 1954 and repealed by s. 10 of Act No. 43 of 1992.]

9. Short title and date of commencement.—This Act shall be called the Wills Act, 1953, and shall come into operation on the first day of January, 1954.

Schedule 1

Certificate in terms of section 2 (1) (*a*) (v)

I, (full name)
of (full address)

in my capacity as commissioner of oaths certify that I have satisfied myself as to the identity of the testator (full name)

and that the accompanying will is the will of the testator.

Signature
Commissioner of Oaths
Capacity

Place Date

Schedule 2

Certificate in terms of section 2 (1) (*b*) (iv)

I, (full names)
of (full address)

in my capacity as commissioner of oaths certify that I have satisfied myself as to the identity of the testator (full name)

and that the alterations(s) to this will was/were made by/at the request of the testator.

Signature
Commissioner of Oaths
Capacity

Place Date

Schedule 3
LAWS REPEALED

Province or Union	*No. and Year of Law*	*Title or Subject of Law*	*Extent of Repeal*
Cape of Good Hope	Ordinance No. 15 of 1845	Execution of Wills	So much as is unrepealed
"	Act No. 22 of 1876	Attesting Witnesses Act, 1876	The whole, excepting section two in so far as it applies to powers of attorney
"	Act No. 3 of 1878	Wills Attestation Amendment Act, 1878	The whole
Natal	Ordinance No. 1 of 1856	Testamentary dispositions of Natal-born subjects of Great Britain and Ireland	The whole
"	Law No. 2 of 1868	Execution of Wills and Codicils	The whole
Orange Free State	Ordinance No. 11 of 1904	Execution of Wills and other Testamentary Instruments Ordinance, 1904	Sections one to five inclusive and sections seven and ten in so far as the two last mentioned sections apply to wills
South-West Africa	Proclamation No. 23 of 1920	Wills Proclamation, 1920	The whole
Transvaal	Ordinance No. 14 of 1903	Wills Ordinance, 1903	The whole
Union	Act No. 14 of 1920	Wills Ordinance, 1903 (Transvaal) Amendment Act, 1920	The whole

Appendix B

INTESTATE SUCCESSION ACT NO. 81 OF 1987

[ASSENTED TO 30 SEPTEMBER, 1987]
[DATE OF COMMENCEMENT: 18 MARCH, 1988]
(*English text signed by the State President*)

This Act has been updated to *Government Gazette* 32147 dated 21 April, 2009.

as amended by
Law of Succession Amendment Act, No. 43 of 1992

proposed amendment by
Reform of Customary Law of Succession and Regulation of Related Matters Act, No. 11 of 2009
(provisions not yet proclaimed)

Reform of Customary Law of Succession and Regulation of Related Matters Act, No. 11 of 2009 (provisions not yet proclaimed)	
Proposed amendment by	*Sections to be amended*
S. 8 of Act No. 11 of 2009	S. 1 of Act No. 81 of 1987

ACT

To regulate anew the law relating to intestate succession; and to provide for matters connected therewith.

ARRANGEMENT OF SECTIONS

1. Intestate succession
2. Repeal of laws
3. Short title and commencement
Schedule Laws repealed

1. Intestate succession.— (1) If after the commencement of this Act a person (hereinafter referred to as the "deceased") dies intestate, either wholly or in part, and—

(*a*) is survived by a spouse, but not by a descendant, such spouse shall inherit the intestate estate;

(*b*) is survived by a descendant, but not by a spouse, such descendant shall inherit the intestate estate;

(*c*) is survived by a spouse as well as a descendant—

(i) such spouse shall inherit a child's share of the intestate estate or so much of the intestate estate as does not exceed in value the amount fixed from time to time by the Minister of Justice by notice in the *Gazette*, whichever is the greater; and

(ii) such descendant shall inherit the residue (if any) of the intestate estate;

(*d*) is not survived by a spouse or descendant, but is survived—

(i) by both his parents, his parents shall inherit the intestate estate in equal shares; or

(ii) by one of his parents, the surviving parent shall inherit one half of the intestate estate and the descendants of the deceased parent the other half, and if there are no such descendants who have survived the deceased, the surviving parent shall inherit the intestate estate; or

(*e*) is not survived by a spouse or descendant or parent, but is survived—

(i) by—

(*aa*) descendants of his deceased mother who are related to the deceased through her only, as well as by descendants of his deceased father who are related to the deceased through him only; or

(*bb*) descendants of his deceased parents who are related to the deceased through both such parents; or

(*cc*) any of the descendants mentioned in subparagraph (*aa*), as well as by any of the descendants mentioned in subparagraph (*bb*),

the intestate estate shall be divided into two equal shares and the descendants related to the deceased through the deceased mother shall inherit one half of the estate and the descendants related to the deceased through the deceased father shall inherit the other half of the estate; or

(ii) only by descendants of one of the deceased parents of the deceased who are related to the deceased through such parent alone, such descendants shall inherit the intestate estate;

(*f*) is not survived by a spouse, descendant, parent, or a descendant of a parent, the other blood relation or blood relations of the deceased who are related to him nearest in degree shall inherit the intestate estate in equal shares.

(2) Notwithstanding the provisions of any law or the common law, but subject to the provisions of this Act and section 5 (2) of the Children's Status Act, 1987, illegitimacy shall not affect the capacity of one blood relation to inherit the intestate estate of another blood relation.

(3) A notice mentioned in subsection (1) (*c*) (i) shall not apply in respect of the intestate estate of a person who died before the date of that notice.

(4) In the application of this section—

(*a*) in relation to descendants of the deceased and descendants of a parent of the deceased, division of the estate shall take place *per stirpes*, and representation shall be allowed;

(*b*) "intestate estate" includes any part of an estate which does not devolve by virtue of a will or in respect of which section 23 of the Black Administration Act, 1927 (Act No. 38 of 1927), does not apply;

(*c*) ......

[Para. (*c*) deleted by s. 14 (*a*) of Act No. 43 of 1992.]

(*d*) the degree of relationship between blood relations of the deceased and the deceased—

(i) in the direct line, shall be equal to the number of generations between the ancestor and the deceased or the descendant and the deceased (as the case may be);

(ii) in the collateral line, shall be equal to the number of generations between the blood relations and the nearest common ancestor, plus the number of generations between such ancestor and the deceased;

(*e*) an adopted child shall be deemed—

(i) to be a descendant of his adoptive parent or parents;

(ii) not to be a descendant of his natural parent or parents, except in the case of a natural parent who is also the adoptive parent of that child or was, at the time of the adoption, married to the adoptive parent of the child; and

(*f*) a child's portion, in relation to the intestate estate of the deceased, shall be calculated by dividing the monetary value of the estate by a number equal to the number of children of the deceased who have either survived him or have died before him but are survived by their descendants, plus one.

(5) If an adopted child in terms of subsection (4) (*e*) is deemed to be a descendant of his adoptive parent, or is deemed not to be a descendant of his natural parent, the adoptive parent concerned shall be deemed to be an ancestor of the child, or shall be deemed not to be an ancestor of the child, as the case may be.

(6) If a descendant of a deceased, excluding a minor or mentally ill descendant, who, together with the surviving spouse of the deceased, is entitled to a benefit from an intestate estate renounces his right to receive such a benefit, such benefit shall vest in the surviving spouse.

[Sub-s. (6) added by s. 14 (*b*) of Act No. 43 of 1992.]

(7) If a person is disqualified from being an heir of the intestate estate of the deceased, or renounces his right to be such an heir, any benefit which he would have received if he had not been so disqualified or had not so renounced his right shall, subject to

the provisions of subsection (6), devolve as if he had died immediately before the death of the deceased and, if applicable, as if he was not so disqualified.

[Sub-s. (7) added by s. 14 (*b*) of Act No. 43 of 1992.]

2. **Repeal of laws.**—The laws specified in the Schedule are hereby repealed to the extent set out in the third column of the Schedule.

3. **Short title and commencement.**—This Act shall be called the Intestate Succession Act, 1987, and shall come into operation on a date to be fixed by the State President by proclamation in the *Gazette*.

Schedule
LAWS REPEALED

No. and year of law	*Title, subject or heading*	*Extent of repeal*
The Political Ordinance of 1 April 1580 ("Groot Placaet-Boek", Part 1)	"Ordonnantie van die Policien binnen Hollandt."	Sections 19 to 28, inclusive
Interpretation of 13 May 1594 ("Groot Placaet-Boek", Part 1)	"Verklaringe van de Heeren Staten van Hollandt en de Wes-Vrieslandt op de Ordonnantie van de Successien."	The whole
Octrooi of 10 January 1661 ("Groot Placaet-Boek", Part 2)	"Octroy, by haer Hoogh Mog: Verleent aende Oost-Indische Compagnie deser Landen op 't recht van de Successien ab intestato in Oost-Indien, ende op de reyse gints ende herwaerts."	The whole
Act No. 13 of 1934	Succession Act, 1934	The whole
Act No. 93 of 1962	General Law Further Amendment Act, 1962	Section 15
Act No. 44 of 1982	Succession Amendment Act, 1982	The whole
Act No. 88 of 1984	Matrimonial Property Act, 1984	Section 27

REFORM OF CUSTOMARY LAW OF SUCCESSION AND REGULATION OF RELATED MATTERS ACT, NO. 11 OF 2009

[ASSENTED TO 19 APRIL, 2009]
[DATE OF COMMENCEMENT TO BE PROCLAIMED]

(*English text signed by the President*)

This Act was published in *Government Gazette* 32147 dated 21 April, 2009.

ACT

To modify the customary law of succession so as to provide for the devolution of certain property in terms of the law of intestate succession; to clarify certain matters relating to the law of succession and the law of property in relation to persons subject to customary law; and to amend certain laws in this regard; and to provide for matters connected therewith.

PREAMBLE

SINCE a widow in a customary marriage whose husband dies intestate does not enjoy adequate protection and benefit under the customary law of succession;

AND SINCE certain children born out of a customary marriage do not enjoy adequate protection under customary law;

AND SINCE section 9 of the Constitution provides that everyone has the right to equal protection and benefit of the law;

AND SINCE social circumstances have so changed that the customary law of succession no longer provides adequately for the welfare of family members;

AND SINCE the Constitutional Court has declared that the principle of male primogeniture, as applied in the customary law of succession, cannot be reconciled with the current notions of equality and human dignity as contained in the Bill of Rights,

ARRANGEMENT OF SECTIONS

1. Definitions
2. Modification of customary law of succession
3. Interpretation of certain provisions of Intestate Succession Act
4. Disposition of property allotted or accruing to woman in customary marriage
5. Dispute or uncertainty in consequence of nature of customary law
6. Disposal of property held by traditional leader in official capacity

7. Property rights in relation to certain customary marriages
8. Amendment of laws
9. Short title and commencement
Schedule

Parliament of the Republic of South Africa therefore enacts as follows:—

1. Definitions.—In this Act, unless the context indicates otherwise—

"customary law" means the customs and practices observed among the indigenous African people of South Africa which form part of the culture of those people;

"descendant" means a person who is a descendant in terms of the Intestate Succession Act, and includes—

(*a*) a person who is not a descendant in terms of the Intestate Succession Act, but who, during the lifetime of the deceased person, was accepted by the deceased person in accordance with customary law as his or her own child; and

(*b*) a woman referred to in section 2 (2) (*b*) or (*c*);

"house" means the family, property, rights and status which arise out of the customary marriage of a woman;

"Intestate Succession Act" means the Intestate Succession Act, 1987 (Act No. 81 of 1987);

"spouse" includes a partner in a customary marriage that is recognised in terms of section 2 of the Recognition of Customary Marriages Act, 1998 (Act No. 120 of 1998);

"traditional leader" means a traditional leader as defined in section 1 of the Traditional Leadership and Governance Framework Act, 2004 (Act No. 41 of 2004);

"this Act" includes any regulation made under section 5; and

"will" means a will to which the provisions of the Wills Act, 1953 (Act No. 7 of 1953), apply.

2. Modification of customary law of succession.—(1) The estate or part of the estate of any person who is subject to customary law who dies after the commencement of this Act and whose estate does not devolve in terms of that person's will, must devolve in accordance with the law of intestate succession as regulated by the Intestate Succession Act, subject to subsection (2).

(2) In the application of the Intestate Succession Act—

(*a*) where the person referred to in subsection (1) is survived by a spouse, as well as a descendant, such a spouse must inherit a child's portion of the intestate estate or so much of the intestate estate as does not exceed in value the amount fixed from time to time by the Cabinet member responsible for the administration of justice by notice in the *Gazette*, whichever is the greater;

(*b*) a woman, other than the spouse of the deceased, with whom he had entered into a union in accordance with customary law for the purpose of providing children for his spouse's house must, if she survives him, be regarded as a descendant of the deceased;

(*c*) if the deceased was a woman who was married to another woman under customary law for the purpose of providing children for the deceased's house, that other woman must, if she survives the deceased, be regarded as a descendant of the deceased.

3. **Interpretation of certain provisions of Intestate Succession Act.**—(1) For the purposes of this Act, any reference in section 1 of the Intestate Succession Act to a spouse who survived the deceased must be construed as including every spouse and every woman referred to in paragraphs (*a*), (*b*) and (*c*) of section 2 (2).

(2) For the purposes of this Act and in the application of section 1 (1) (*c*) of the Intestate Succession Act, the following subparagraph must be regarded as having been added to that section—

"(iii) where the intestate estate is not sufficient to provide each surviving spouse and woman referred to in paragraphs (*a*), (*b*) and (*c*) of section 2 (2) of the Reform of Customary Law of Succession and Regulation of Related Matters Act, 2008, with the amount fixed by the Minister, the estate shall be divided equally between such spouses;".

(3) In the determination of a child's portion for the purposes of dividing the estate of a deceased in terms of the Intestate Succession Act, paragraph (*f*) of section 1 (4) of that Act must be regarded to read as follows—

"(*f*) a child's portion, in relation to the intestate estate of the deceased, shall be calculated by dividing the monetary value of the estate by a number equal to the number of children of the deceased who have either survived the deceased or have died before the deceased but are survived by their descendants, plus the number of spouses and women referred to in paragraphs (*a*), (*b*) and (*c*) of section 2 (2) of the Reform of Customary Law of Succession and Regulation of Related Matters Act, 2008.".

4. **Disposition of property allotted or accruing to woman in customary marriage.**—

(1) Property allotted or accruing to a woman or her house under customary law by virtue of her customary marriage may be disposed of in terms of a will of such a woman.

(2) Any reference in the will of a woman referred to in subsection (1) to her child or children and any reference in section 1 of the Intestate Succession Act to a descendant, in relation to such a woman, must be construed as including any child—

(*a*) born of a union between the husband of such a woman and another woman entered into in accordance with customary law for the purpose of providing children for the first-mentioned woman's house; or

(*b*) born to a woman to whom the first-mentioned woman was married under customary law for the purpose of providing children for the first-mentioned woman's house.

(3) Nothing in this section is to be construed as preventing any person subject to customary law, other than the woman referred to in subsection (1), from disposing assets in terms of a will.

5. **Dispute or uncertainty in consequence of nature of customary law.**—(1) If any dispute or uncertainty arises in connection with—

(*a*) the status of or any claim by any person in relation to a person whose estate or part thereof must, in terms of this Act, devolve in terms of the Intestate Succession Act;

(*b*) the nature or content of any asset in such estate; or

(*c*) the devolution of family property involved in such estate,

the Master of the High Court having jurisdiction under the Administration of Estates Act, 1965 (Act No. 66 of 1965), may, subject to subsection (2), make such a determination as may be just and equitable in order to resolve the dispute or remove the uncertainty.

(2) Before making a determination under subsection (1), the Master may direct that an inquiry into the matter be held by a magistrate or a traditional leader in the area in which the Master has jurisdiction.

(3) After the inquiry referred to in subsection (2), the magistrate or a traditional leader, as the case may be, must make a recommendation to the Master who directed that an inquiry be held.

(4) The Master, in making a determination, or the magistrate or a traditional leader, as the case may be, in making a recommendation referred to in this section, must have due regard to the best interests of the deceased's family members and the equality of spouses in customary and civil marriages.

(5) The Cabinet member responsible for the administration of justice may make regulations regarding any aspect of the inquiry referred to in this section.

6. **Disposal of property held by traditional leader in official capacity.**—Nothing in this Act is to be construed as amending any rule of customary law which regulates the disposal of the property which a traditional leader who has died held in his or her official capacity on behalf of a traditional community referred to in the Traditional Leadership and Governance Framework Act, 2003 (Act No. 41 of 2003).

7. **Property rights in relation to certain customary marriages.**—(1) A marriage under the Marriage Act, 1961 (Act No. 25 of 1961), does not affect the proprietary rights of any spouse of a customary marriage or any issue thereof if the marriage under the Marriage Act, 1961, was entered into—

(*a*) on or after 1 January 1929 (the date of commencement of sections 22 and 23 of the Black Administration Act, 1927 (Act No. 38 of 1927)), but before 2 December 1988 (the date of commencement of the Marriage and Matrimonial Property Law Amendment Act, 1988 (Act No. 3 of 1988)); and

(*b*) during the subsistence of any customary marriage between the husband and any woman other than the spouse of the marriage under the Marriage Act, 1961 (Act No. 25 of 1961).

(2) The widow of the marriage under the Marriage Act, 1961, referred to in subsection (1), and the issue thereof have no greater rights in respect of the estate of the deceased spouse than she or they would have had if the marriage under the Marriage Act, 1961, had been a customary marriage.

8. Amendment of laws.—The laws mentioned in the Schedule are hereby amended to the extent indicated in the third column of that Schedule.

9. Short title and commencement.—This Act is called the Reform of Customary Law of Succession and Regulation of Related Matters Act, 2009, and comes into operation on a date fixed by the President by proclamation in the *Gazette.*

Schedule
AMENDMENT OF LAWS

(Section 8)

No. and year of law	*Short title*	*Extent of amendment*
Act 66 of 1965	Administration of Estates Act, 1965	1. The amendment of section 4— (*a*) by the substitution in subsection (1) for the words preceding paragraph (*a*) of the following words: "In respect of the estate of a deceased person, or of any portion thereof, jurisdiction shall lie—"; and (*b*) by the deletion of subsection (1A). 2. The amendment of section 7 by the substitution in subsection (1) for paragraph (*a*) of the following paragraph: "(*a*) the surviving spouse of such person or more than one surviving spouse jointly, or if there is no surviving spouse, his or her nearest relative or connection residing in the district in which the death has taken place, shall within fourteen days thereafter give a notice of death substantially in the prescribed form, or cause such a notice to be given to the Master; and". 3. The amendment of section 9 by the substitution in subsection (1) for the words preceding paragraph (*a*) of the following words: "(1) If any person dies within the Republic or if any person ordinarily resident in the Republic at the time of his or her death dies outside the Republic leaving any property therein, the surviving spouse of such person or more than one surviving spouse jointly, or if there is no surviving spouse, his or her nearest relative or connection residing in the district in which such person was ordinarily resident at the time of his or her death, shall, within fourteen days after the death or within such further period as the Master may allow—".

No. and year of law	*Short title*	*Extent of amendment*
Act 81 of 1987	Intestate Succession Act, 1987	1. The amendment of section 1— (*a*) by the substitution for subsection (2) of the following subsection: "(2) Notwithstanding the provisions of any law or the common or customary law, but subject to the provisions of this Act and sections 40 (3) and 297 (1) (*f*) of the Children's Act, 2005 (Act No. 38 of 2005), having been born out of wedlock shall not affect the capacity of one blood relation to inherit the intestate estate of another blood relation."; (*b*) by the substitution in subsection (4) for paragraph (*b*) of the following paragraph: "(*b*) **'intestate estate'** includes any part of an estate which does not devolve by virtue of a will;" and (*c*) by the insertion in subsection (4), after paragraph (*e*), of the following paragraph: "(*e*A) a person referred to in paragraph (*a*) of the definition of 'descendant' contained in section 1 of the Reform of Customary Law of Succession and Regulation of Related Matters Act, 2009, shall be deemed— (i) to be a descendant of the deceased person referred to in that paragraph; (ii) not to be a descendant of his or her natural parent or parents, except in the case of a natural parent who is also the parent who accepted that person in accordance with customary law as his or her own child, as envisaged in the said definition, or was, at the time when the child was accepted, married to the parent who so accepted the child; and"; and (*d*) by the insertion after subsection (5) of the following subsection: "(5A) If a person referred to in paragraph (*a*) of the definition of 'descendant' contained in section 1 of the Reform of Customary Law of Succession and Regulation of Related Matters Act, 2009, is deemed to be a descendant of the deceased person referred to in that paragraph, or is deemed not to be a descendant of his or her natural parent, the deceased person shall be deemed to be an ancestor of the person referred to in that paragraph, or shall be deemed not to be an ancestor of that person, as the case may be."

No. and year of law	*Short title*	*Extent of amendment*
Act 27 of 1990	Maintenance of Surviving Spouses Act, 1990	1. The amendment of section 1 by the substitution for the definition of "survivor" of the following definition " **'survivor'** means the surviving spouse in a marriage dissolved by death, and includes a spouse of a customary marriage which was dissolved by a civil marriage contracted by her husband in the customary marriage to another woman on or after 1 January 1929 (the date of commencement of sections 22 and 23 of the Black Administration Act, 1927 (Act No. 38 of 1927)), but before 2 December 1988 (the date of commencement of the Marriage and Matrimonial Property Law Amendment Act, 1988 (Act No. 3 of 1988));".

BIBLIOGRAPHY

Abrie, W, Graham, CR & Van der Linde, A. 2003. *Estate and financial planning,* fifth edition. Pretoria: Pro Plus Publishers.

Banda, T. 2005. 'The Constitutional Court's Approach to Customary Law in *Bhe v Magistrate, Khayelitsha*: Has the Baby been Thrown out with the Bath Water?'. *Responsa Meridiana*: 5.

Barker, HJ. 1997. 'To vest or not to vest, that is the question'. *De Rebus*: 351.

Beinart, B. 1953. 'Testamentary form and capacity and the Wills Act'. *SALJ*: 159 and 280.

Beinart, B. 1958. 'Liability of a deceased estate for maintenance'. *Acta Juridica*: 92.

Beinart, B. 1959. 'Some aspects of priviliged wills'. *Acta Juridica*: 200.

Beinart B. 1966. 'The forgotten widow: Provision by a deceased estate for dependants'. *Acta Juridica*: 285.

Bekker, JC. 1989. *Seymour's customary law,* fifth edition. Cape Town: Juta.

Bekker, JC & Coertze, JJJ. 1982. *Seymour's customary law in Southern Africa,* fourth edition. Cape Town: Juta.

Bekker, JC & Maithufi, IP. 1992. 'The dichotomy between "official customary law" and "non-official" customary law'. *TRW*: 47.

Bekker, JC, Rautenbach, C & Goolam, NMI (eds). 2006. *Introduction to legal pluralism in South Africa,* second edition. Durban: LexisNexis Butterworths.

Bennett, TW. 1985. *Application of customary law in Southern Africa: The conflict of personal laws.* Cape Town: Juta.

Bennett, TW. 2004. *Customary law in South Africa.* Cape Town: Juta.

Boonzaaier, CC. 1990. 'Die familie-, erf- en opvolgingsreg van die Nkuna van Ritavi met verwysing na ander aspekte van die privaatreg'. University of Pretoria: LLD thesis.

Burge,W. 1838. *Commentaries on colonial and foreign laws generally and in their conflict with each other and with the law of England.* London: Saunders & Benning.

Cameron, E, De Waal, MJ, Wunsch, B, Solomon, P & Khan, E. 2002. *Honore: The South African Law of Trusts,* fifth edition. Cape Town: Juta.

Caney, LR. 1930. 'Minor's contracts'. *SALJ*: 180.

Christie, RH. 2006. *The law of contract,* fifth edition. Durban: Butterworths.

Clark, JB. 1982. *Theobald on Wills,* fourteenth edition. London: Stevens & Sons.

Clark, JB. 1988. *Parry and Clark: The law of succession,* ninth edition. London: Sweet & Maxwell.

Coertze, RD. 1990. *Bafokeng family law and law of succession,* revised edition. Pretoria: Sabra.

Corbett, MM. 1983. 'Discretionary Trusts, Powers of Appointment and the Rule regarding the Delegation of Testamentary Power' in Kahn, E, *Fiat Iustitia*: 188–210.

Corbett, MM, Hofmeyr, G, & Kahn, E. 2001. *The law of succession in South Africa,* second edition. Cape Town: Juta.

Cornelius S. 2003. 'Condonation of electronic documents in terms of section 2(3) of the Wills Act 7 of 1953'. *TSAR*: 208.

Cowen, DV. 1949. 'Vested and Contingent Rights'. *SALJ*: 404.

Cronjé, DSP. 1983. '*Kidwell v The Master* 1983 1 SA 509 (OK): Ondertekening aan die end van 'n testament'. *THRHR*: 345.

Cronjé, DSP & Roos, A. 1997. *Casebook on the law of succession/Erfreg vonnisbundel,* third edition. Pretoria: Unisa Press.

Cronjé, DSP & Roos, A. 2002. *Casebook on the law of succession/Erfreg vonnisbundel*, fourth edition. Pretoria: Unisa Press.

Davis, DM, Beneke, C & Jooste, RD. 2009. *Estate planning*, service issue 24. Durban: Lexis Nexis Butterworths.

De Clercq, B, Evans, RG, Abrie, E & Graham, CR. 2006. *Deceased estates*, sixth edition. Pretoria: Pro Plus.

De Clercq, JLW. 1975. 'Die familie-, erf- en opvolgingsreg van die abakwaMzimela, met verwysing na prosesregtelike aspekte'. University of Pretoria, LLD thesis.

De Waal, MJ. 1993. 'Anomalieë in die Suid-Afrikaanse trustreg'. *THRHR*: 1.

De Waal, MJ. 1999. 'Die strekwydte van trustees se beleggingsbevoegdheid'. *TSAR*: 376.

De Waal, MJ. 2000. 'The core elements of the trust: Aspects of the English, Scottish and South African trusts compared'. *SALJ*: 548.

De Waal, MJ. 2004. 'The Courts' power of condonation in respect of the execution and revocation of wills: Unfortunate new elements of uncertainty'. *SALJ*: 529.

De Waal, MJ. 2005. 'The law of succession and the Bill of Rights' in *Bill of Rights Compendium*. Durban: LexisNexis Butterworths.

De Waal, MJ & Schoeman-Malan, MC. 2003. *Introduction to the law of succession*, third edition. Cape Town: Juta.

De Waal, MJ & Schoeman-Malan, MC. 2008. *Law of succession*, fourth edition. Cape Town: Juta.

Du Bois, F (ed). 2007. *Wille's principles of South African law*, ninth edition. Cape Town: Juta.

Du Toit, F. 1999. 'The impact of social and economic factors on freedom of testation in Roman and Roman-Dutch law'. *Stell LR*: 232.

Du Toit, F. 2000. 'The limits imposed upon freedom of testation by the *boni mores*: Lessons from common law and civil law (continental) legal systems'. *Stell LR*: 358.

Du Toit, F. 2001. 'The constitutionally bound dead hand? The impact of constitutional rights and principles on freedom of testation in South African law'. *Stell LR*, (2): 222.

Du Toit, F. 2005. 'Mental capacity as an element of testamentary capacity'. *SALJ*: 661.

Du Toit, F. 2007. *South African trust law – principles and practice*, second edition. Durban: Lexis Nexis Butterworths.

Erasmus, HJ & De Waal, MJ. 1989. *The South African law of succession*. Durban: Butterworths.

Faber, JT & Rabie, PJ. 2005. 'Van tikmasjien tot rekenaar: 'n ondersoek na die ontwikkeling van die Suid-Afrikaanse erfreg in die tegnologiese era'. *TSAR*: 767.

Gane, P (translator). 1956. *The selective Voet being the commentary on the pandects [Paris edition of 1829] by Johannes Voet*, Volumes 4 and 5. Durban: Butterworths.

Greeff, M. 1991. 'Probleme voortvloeiend uit die weglating van die datum van verlyding van 'n testament'. *De Jure*: 127.

Grobbelaar, P (ed). 1987. *Reader's Digest Afrikaans – Engelse Woordeboek English – Afrikaans Dictionary*. Cape Town: The Reader's Digest Association of South Africa.

Hahlo, HR. 1950. 'Jewish faith and race clauses in wills. A note on *Aronson v Estate Hart*'. *SALJ*: 231.

Hahlo, HR. 1952. 'De bloedige hand erft niet'. *SALJ*, 69: 136.

Hahlo, HR. 1958. '*Aronson v Estate Hart* revisited'. *SALJ*: 152.

Hahlo, HR. 1959. 'The case against freedom of testation'. *SALJ*: 435.

Hahlo, HR. 1962. 'Widow's claim to maintenance out of deceased husband's estate'. *SALJ*: 361.

Hahlo, HR. 1964. 'Revocation of wills by divorce'. *SALJ*, 81: 381.

Hall, CG. 1968. *Maasdorp's institutes of Cape Law*, ninth edition. Cape Town: Juta.

Hutchison, D. 1983. 'Isolating the *pactum successorium*'. *SALJ*: 221.

Isaacs, I & Horwitz, M. 1979. *The South African law of testate succession*. Durban: Butterworths.

Isakow, LE. 1982. 'Some problem areas in the Law of Succession'. *SALJ*: 300.

Isakow, LE. 1985. *The law of succession through the cases*. Cape Town: Juta.

Jacobs, PP. 1974. 'Die judisiële stelsel en die familie-, erf- en opvolgingsreg van die imiDushane'. University of Pretoria: LLD thesis.

Jamneck, J. 1991. 'Die sertifikaat ingevolge artikel 2(1)(a)(v) van die Wet op Testamente 7 van 1953 *Jeffrey v The Master* 1990 4 SA 759 (N)'. *THRHR*: 669.

Jamneck, J. 1998. 'Herroeping en wysiging van testamente'. *THRHR*: 600.

Jamneck. J. 2008. 'Testeerbevoegdheid, *animus testandi*, testeervryheid, bedoeling en die "bedoeling" ingevolge artikel 2(3) van die Wet op Testamente'. *THRHR*: 603.

Jamneck. J. 2009. 'Testeerbevoegdheid, *animus testandi*, testeervryheid, bedoeling en die "bedoeling" ingevolge artikel 2(3) van die Wet op Testamente'. *THRHR*: 113.

Jennings, R & Harper, JC. 1986. *Jarman on wills*, eighth edition. London: Sweet & Maxwell.

Joubert, CP. 1952. 'Die fideicommis, die trust en die stigting'. *THRHR*: 181.

Joubert, CP. 1957. 'Die Kodisil'. *THRHR*: 159.

Joubert, CP 1961. '*Pactum successorium*'. *THRHR*: 18, 106, 177 and 250.

Joubert, CP. 1968. 'Jewish faith and race clauses in Roman-Dutch law'. *SALJ*: 402.

Joubert, CP. 1970. 'Some aspects of *metus reverentialis*'. *SALJ*: 94.

Joubert, WA (ed). 1995. *The law of South Africa*. Volume 8, Part 1, Donations. Durban: LexisNexis Butterworths.

Joubert, WA (ed). 2001. *The law of South Africa*. Volume 31, Wills and succession, Administration of deceased estates and trusts. Durban: LexisNexis Butterworths.

Joubert, WA (ed). 2004. *The law of South Africa*. Volume 32, Indigenous law. Durban: LexisNexis Butterworths.

Kahn, E. 1984. 'The will that won't – formalities gone bananas' in Van der Westhuizen, J (editorial chair), *Huldigingsbundel Paul Van Warmelo*. Pretoria: Unisa.

Kernick, LA. 1998. *Administration of estates and drafting of wills*, third edition. Cape Town: Juta.

Kernick, LA. 2007. *De Rebus*: 29.

Knoetze, E. 2004. 'End of the Road for the Customary Law of Succession?' *THRHR*: 515.

Kotze L & Rautenbach C. 2007. 'Bereddering van intestate boedels van swart persone: van toeka tot nou' . *THRHR*: 43.

Koyana, DS. 1980. *Customary law in a changing society*. Cape Town: Juta.

Lee, RW. 1953. *An introduction to Roman-Dutch Law*, fifth edition, London: Clarendon Press.

Lee, RW, Honoré, AM & Price, TW. 1954. *The South African law of property, family relations and succession*. Durban: Butterworths.

Maithufi, IP & Moloi, GMB. 2004. 'Customary Law of Succession: *Bhe v. Magistrate, Khayelitsha* Case No 9489/02 (C)'. *THRHR*: 507.

Mellows, AR. 1977. *The law of succession*, third edition, London: Butterworths.

Meyerowitz, D. 1989. *The law and practice of administration of estates and estate duty*, sixth edition. Cape Town: The Taxpayer CC (looseleaf publication).

Meyers, EM. 1939. 'Inbreng van schulden en gedwongen verrekening'. *THRHR*: 130.

Mqeke, RB. 2003. *Customary law and the new millennium*. Alice: Lovedale Press.

Murray, IB. 1962. 'Law of succession (including administration of estates)'.

Annual Survey of South African Law: 273.

Murray, IB. 1963. 'Law of succession (including administration of estates)'. *Annual Survey of South African Law*: 335.

Murray, IB. 1983. 'Law of Succession (including administration of estates)'. *Annual Survey of South African Law*: 254.

Myburgh, AC. 1985. *Papers on indigenous law in Southern Africa*. Pretoria: Van Schaik.

Nortjé, M. 1998. 'Partial validity of a substitution – *Olivier v Die Meester en andere: In re Boedel Wyle Olivier*.' *SALJ*: 1.

Odendaal, FF (chief ed), Schoonees, PC, Swanepoel, CJ, Du Toit, SJ, Booysen, CM. 1981. *HAT: Verklarende handwoordeboek van die Afrikaanse taal*, second edition. Johannesburg: Perskor.

Olivier NJJ, Olivier NJJ & Olivier, WH. 1989. *Die privaatreg van die Suid-Afrikaanse Bantoetaalsprekendes*, third edition. Durban: Butterworths.

Olivier, PA, Strydom, S & Van den Berg, GPJ. 2006. *Trustreg en praktyk*, second edition. Durban: LexisNexis Butterworths.

Pace, RP & Van der Westhuizen, WM. 2008. *Wills and trusts, s*ervice issue II. Durban: LexisNexis Butterworths.

Paleker, M. 2004. '*Bekker v Naude*: The Supreme Court of Appeal settles the meaning of "drafted" in section 2(3) of the Wills Act, but creates a potential constitutional problem'. *SALJ*: 27.

Pretorius, C-J. 2004. 'The basis of contractual liability in South African law'. *THRHR*: 179.

Radesich, GAM & Roos, A. 1988. 'The effect of a resolutive condition on the formation of a *pactum successorium*'. *TRW*: 572.

Rautenbach, C. 1994. Die *pactum successorium* in die Suid-Afrikaanse reg. University of the North West: LLM dissertation.

Rautenbach, C. 1995. 'Die praktiese implikasies van die verbod op die *pactum successorium* met betrekking tot vennootskapsooreenkomste'. *De Jure*: 98.

Rautenbach, C. 1997. 'Die *pactum successorium* in die Duitse reg'. *THRHR*: 131.

Rautenbach, C. 1998. 'Die bedoeling van die kontrakspartye as maatstaf by die *pactum successorium*'. *THRHR*: 651.

Rautenbach, C. 1999. 'Die *pactum successorium*: stiefkind van die Suid-Afrikaanse reg'. *Koers*: 357.

Rautenbach, C. 2001. 'The legal position of South African women under the law of succession'. University of the North West: LLD thesis.

Rautenbach, C. 2003. 'Male primogeniture unconstitutional: a legal victory for SA women'. *Afla Quarterly*: 30.

Rautenbach, C. 2004. 'Modern day impact of customary succession laws in South Africa'. *International Journal of the Humanities*, 2: 673.

Rautenbach, C. 2004. 'The administration of black estates: life before and after 5 December 2002'. *THRHR*: 1.

Rautenbach, C. 2007. 'Rethinking South African customary succession laws in a global society' in Calera, NL (ed). *Archiv für Rechts- und Sozialphilosophie*, volume 4: Globalization, Law and Economy: 69.

Rautenbach, C. 2008. 'South African common and customary law of intestate succession: a question of harmonisation, integration or abolition'. *The Journal of Comparative Law*: 119.

Rautenbach, C & Du Plessis, W. 2003. 'South African Law Commission's proposals for customary law of succession: retrogression or progression?' *De Jure*: 20.

Rautenbach, C & Du Plessis, W. 2004. 'Customary law of succession and inheritance' in WA Joubert (ed), 'Indigenous Law' (volume 32), *The law of South Africa*. Durban: LexisNexis Butterworths.

Rautenbach, C, Du Plessis, W & Pienaar, G. 2006. 'Is primogeniture extinct like the dodo, or is there any prospect of it rising from the ashes? Comments on the evolution of customary succession laws in South Africa'. *SAJHR*: 99.

Roos, A. 2002. '*Theron v Master of the High Court* [2001] 3 All SA 507 (NC)'. *De Jure*: 372.

Schoeman, L. 1988. 'Enkele opmerkings oor die regskommissie se verslag insake die wysiging en herroeping van testamente'. *De Jure*: 141.

Schoeman, MC. 1990. 'Herroeping van 'n testament deur vernietiging of informele handeling'. *De Jure*: 216.

Schoeman, MC. 1991. 'Outomatiese verval van 'n testament weens veranderde omstandighede'. *De Jure*: 44 and 268.

Schoeman, MC. 1996. 'Is daar 'n verskil tussen wysiging en gedeeltelike herroeping van 'n testament?'. *De Jure*: 336.

Schoeman-Malan, MC. 2001. 'Die inbringverpligtiging - bestaan dit nog?'. *De Jure*: 171.

Schoeman-Malan, MC. 2002. 'Onbehoorlike beïnvloeding: Testeerbevoegdheid v Testeervryheid'. *De Jure*: 333.

Schoeman-Malan, MC. 2007. 'Recent developments regarding South African common and customary law of succession'. (1) *PER* at http://www.puk.ac.za/opencms/export/PUK/html/fakulteite/regte/per/issues/2007x1x Schoeman_Malan_art.pdf.

Schoeman, MC & Van der Linde, A. 1995. 'Artikel 2(3) en 2A van die Wet op Testamente - Kondonasiebevoegdheid van die Hof - verlyding en herroeping van testamente: *Logue v The Master* 1995 1 SA 199 (N); *Horn v Horn* 1995 SA 48 (W)'. *THRHR*: 517.

Scholtens, JE. 1960. 'Undue influence'. *Acta Juridica*: 276.

Shrand, D. 1973. *The administration of deceased estates in South Africa*, third edition. Cape Town: Legal & Financial Publishing.

Sonnekus, JC. 1982. 'Vereistes vir testamentsherroeping'. *TSAR*: 110 and 230.

Sonnekus, JC. 1983. '*Kidwell v The Master* 1983 1 SA 509 (OK)'. *TSAR*: 188.

Sonnekus, JC. 1993. 'Erkenning van ondertekening van testament'. *TSAR*: 169.

Sonnekus, JC. 1995. 'Kondonerings-bevoegdheid van Hof by vormgebrekkige testament'. *TSAR*: 359.

Sonnekus, JC. 1996. 'Adiasie, insolvensie en historiese perke aan die logiese'. *TSAR*: 240.

Sonnekus, JC. 2001. 'Testamentsvervalsing en wilsonderskuiwing van verswakte bejaardes'. *TSAR*: 357.

Sonnekus, JC. 2003. 'Kondonering van vormgebrekkige testamente? Vergeet dit!'. *Stellenbosch Law Review*: 337.

South Africa. 1956. *Pension Funds Act 24 of 1956*. Pretoria: Government Printer [Laws].

South Africa. 1965. *Administration of Estates Act 66 of 1965*. Pretoria: Government Printer [Laws].

South Africa. 1965. *Immovable Property (Removal or Modification of Restrictions) Act 94 of 1965*. Pretoria: Government Printer [Laws].

South Africa. 1970. *Subdivision of Agricultural Land Act 70 of 1970*. Pretoria: Government Printer [Laws].

South Africa. 1984. *Close Corporations Act 69 of 1984*. Pretoria: Government Printer [Laws].

South Africa. 1990. *Maintenance of Surviving Spouses Act 27 of 1990*. Pretoria: Government Printer [Laws].

South Africa. 1998. *Recognition of Customary Marriages Act 120 of 1998*. Pretoria: Government Printer [Laws].

South Africa. 2002. *Mineral and Petroleum Resources Development Act 28 of 2002*. Pretoria: Government Printer [Laws].

South Africa. 2005. *Children's Act 38 of 2005*. Pretoria: Government Printer [Laws].

South African Law Commission. 1991. *Project 22 review of the law of succession*. Report. Pretoria: South African Law Commission.

South African Law Reform Commission. 1998. *Project 90: Harmonisation of the common law and indigenous law (succession in customary law)*. Issue paper 12. Pretoria: South African Law Reform Commission.

South African Law Reform Commission. 2000. *Project 90: Customary law – succession*. Discussion paper 93. Pretoria: South African Law Reform Commission.

South African Law Reform Commission. 2004. *Project 90: Customary law of succession*. Report. Pretoria: South African Law Reform Commission.

Spiro, E. 1951. 'Liability of parents for contracts of their minor children'. *SALJ*: 172.

Steyn, G. 1948. *The law of wills in South Africa*, second edition, Cape Town: Juta.

Tennant, H. 1877. *The notary's manual*, fourth edition, Cape Town: Juta.

Tennant, H. 1902. *The notary's manual*, seventh edition. Cape Town: Juta.

Van der Merwe, NJ. 1965. *'Spes fideicommissi* of *ius in personam*?' *THRHR*: 138.

Van der Merwe, NJ & Rowland, CJ. 1974. *Die Suid-Afrikaanse erfreg*, second edition. Pretoria: Van der Walt.

Van der Merwe, NJ, Rowland, CJ & Cronjé, MB. 1990. *Die Suid-Afrikaanse erfreg*, sixth edition. Pretoria: Van der Walt.

Van der Walt, JC & Sonnekus, JC. 1981. 'Die nalatige bloedige hand – neem dit "erfenis"?'. *TSAR*, 1: 30.

Van der Walt, JC & Sonnekus, JC. 1992. 'Die nalatige bloedige hand – voor die hof en die wetgewer'. *TSAR*, 1: 147.

Van Warmelo, P. 1971. *'n Inleiding tot die studie van die Romeinse Reg*. Pretoria: Van Schaik.

Vorster, LP. 2000. 'Succession to bukHosi among the Swazi of Mpumalanga Province, South Africa'. *South African Journal of Ethnology*: 143.

Watney, MM. 1993. 'Beginsels van die opvolgingsreg van die Bapedi van Sekwati en Noord-Sothosprekendes in Vosloorus'. University of Pretoria: LLD thesis.

Weimar, P. 1994. 'Inheritance contracts and public policy'. *TRW*: 787.

Wiechers, NJ. 1973. '*Contra bonos mores*'. *De Jure*: 54.

Wiechers, NJ. 1974. 'Inbring: uitgedien of nie?' *De Jure*: 147.

Wiechers, NJ & Vorster, I. 2008. *Administration of estates*. Durban: LexisNexis Butterworths (looseleaf service).

Williams, RC . 1969. *'Pacta successoria'*. *Responsa Meridiana*: 45.

Wood-Bodley, MC. 1998, 'The coup de grâce provision – judicial revocation of wills in terms of section 2A of the Wills Act 1953'. *SALJ*: 202.

Wood-Bodley, MC. 2004. 'Did you say "asinine" Milord? *Bekker v Naude* 2003 5 SA 173 (SCA)'. *Obiter*: 222.

Wood-Bodley, MC. 2004. '*Macdonald v The Master*: Computer files and the "rescue" provision of the Wills Act'. *SALJ*: 34.

Wood-Bodley, MC. 2004. 'Wills, data messages, and the Electronic Communications and Transactions Act'. *SALJ*: 526.

Wood-Bodley, MC. 2005. 'Tertius Bosch's final over: *Van Wetten v Bosch*'. *SALJ*: 52.

Wood-Bodley, MC. 2006. 'Revocation of a will by the presumed destruction of a copy: *Sansole NO v Ncube*' *SALJ*: 3.

Table of cases

A

Abraham v Els 1964 (2) SA 215 (C) 191, 192, 199
Administrators, Estate Richards v Nichol 1996 (4) SA 253 (C) 126, 176, 178, 180, 184, 189
Alexkor Ltd v Richtersveld Community 2003 (12) BCLR 1301 (CC) 3, 18
Allen v Estate Bloch 1970 (2) SA 376 (C) 211
Anderson and Wagner v The Master 1996 (3) SA 779 (C) 82
Arkell v Carter 1971 (3) SA 243 (R) 127
Aronson v Estate Hart 1950 (1) SA 539 (A) 118, 120, 139
Attridge v Lambert 1977 (2) SA 90 (D) 137
Aubrey-Smith v Hofmeyr 1973 (1) SA 655 (C) 212, 220

B

Back v Master of the Supreme Court [1996] 2 All SA 161 (C) 79, 80
Bagnall v Colonial Government (1907) 24 SC 470 143
Bank v Sussman 1968 (2) SA 15 (O) 122
Barclays Bank DC v Anderson 1959 (2) SA 478 (T) 119, 120
Barnett v Estate Schereschewske 1957 (3) SA 679 (C) 119
Barnhoorn v Duvenage 1964 (2) SA 486 (A) 160, 161
Barrow v The Master 1960 (3) SA 253 (E) 89, 137
Battan Singh v Amirchand [1948] 1 All ER 152 84
Bekker v Naude 2003 (5) SA 173 (SCA) 80, 81, 82
Bell v Swan 1954 (3) SA 543 (W) 212
Benoni Town Council v Minister of Agricultural Credit and Land Tenure 1978 (1) SA 978 (T) 142
Bhe v Magistrate, Khayelitsha (Commission for Gender Equality as *Amicus Curiae*); Shibi v Sithole; South African Human Rights Commission v President of the Republic of South Africa 2005 (1) SA 580 (CC) 5, 6, 16, 17, 23, 24, 25, 26, 27, 29, 31, 40, 64, 84, 129, 167, 200, 236, 237, 239, 240, 256
Bielovich v The Master 1992 (4) SA 736 (N) 55
BOE Bank Bpk v Van Zyl 1999 (3) SA 813 (C) 50
Borman en De Vos v Potgietersrusse Tabakkorporasie 1976 (3) SA 488 (A) 224, 225, 226, 227, 229
Botha v The Master 1976 (3) SA 597 (E) 220
Boyce v Bloem 1960 (3) SA 855 (T) 182
Bradfield v Bradfield's Executors 1914 CPD 147 133
Braun v Blann and Botha 1984 (2) SA 850 (A) 126, 127, 173, 174, 176, 177, 178, 180, 185
Bredenkamp v The Master and Bredenkamp 1947 (1) SA 388 (T) 88
British South Africa Company v Bulawayo Municipality 1919 AD 84 141
Brown v Rickard (1883-1884) 2 SC 314 158
Brummund v Brummund's Estate 1993 (2) SA 494 (Nm) 146
Burton-Moore v The Master 1983 (4) SA 419 (N) 49, 50, 72
Bydawell v Chapman 1953 (3) SA 514 (A) 115

C

Caldwell v Erasmus 1952 (4) SA 43 (T) 105, 106
Campbell v Daly 1988 (4) SA 714 (T) 208, 210

Carelse v Estate De Vries (1906) 23 SC 532 ... 122
Casey v The Master 1992 (4) SA 505 (N) ... 105, 106
Cohen v Roetz 1992 (1) SA 629 (A) ... 136
Coll v Murray (1917) 38 NLR 222 ... 158
Colonial Treasurer v Rand Water Board 1907 TS 479 ... 54
Commissioner for Inland Revenue v Lukin's Estate 1956 (1) SA 617 (A) ... 128
Commissioner for Inland Revenue v MacNeillie's Estate 1961 (3) SA 833 (A) ... 175
Commissioner for Inland Revenue v Sive's Estate 1955 (1) SA 249 (A) ... 140
Costain and Partners v Godden 1960 (4) SA 456 (SR) ... 226, 227
Craig v Lamoureux 1920 AC 349 (PC) ... 50
Crookes v Watson 1956 (1) SA 277 (A) ... 54
Cuming v Cuming 1945 AD 201 ... 210

D

Dalrymple v Colonial Treasurer 1910 TPD 372 ... 143
D'Angelo v Bona 1976 (1) SA 463 (A) ... 226
Daniels v Campbell 2004 (5) SA 331 (CC) ... 18, 25, 124
Davis v Steel and Eriksen 1949 (3) SA 177 (W) ... 90, 91
Davis' Tutor v Estate Davis 1925 WLD 168 ... 122, 123
Dawood v Minister of Home Affairs; Shalabi v Minister of Home Affairs; Thomas v Minister of Home Affairs [2000] (8) BCLR 837 (CC); 2000 (3) SA 936 (CC) ... 125
De Klerk v De Witt 1973 (3) SA 865 (NC) ... 139
De Reszke v Maras 2006 (2) SA 297 (SCA) ... 83
De Villiers v Estate De Villiers 1929 CPD 106 ... 209
De Vos v Van der Merwe [1996] 4 All SA 82 (N) ... 192, 194, 197, 198, 199
De Wayer v SPCA Johannesburg 1963 (1) SA 71 (T) ... 118
De Wet v De Villiers 1914 CPD 285 ... 214
Deedat v The Master 1995 (2) SA 377 (A) ... 177
Dempers v The Master (1) 1977 (4) SA 44 (SWA) ... 137
Donaghy v Estate Hablutzel (1905) 22 SC 162 ... 143
D'Oyly-John v Lousada 1957 (1) SA 368 (N) ... 146
Du Plessis v Strauss 1988 (2) SA 105 (A) ... 158, 159
Durandt v Pienaar 2000 (4) SA 869 (C) ... 132, 133
Du Toit v Minister for Welfare and Population Development [2002] (10) BCLR 1006 (CC) ... 125

E

Els v Els 1993 (2) SA 436 (E) ... 136
Erasmus v Havenga 1979 (3) SA 1253 (T) ... 226
Essop v Mustapha and Essop 1988 (4) SA 213 (D) ... 60, 61, 62
Estate Cato v Estate Cato 1915 AD 290 ... 132, 209
Estate Dempers v Estate Dempers 1912 CPD 779 ... 208, 212
Estate Freedman v Freedman 1962 (3) SA 79 (W) ... 141, 143
Estate Gonsalves v Pataca 1957 (4) SA 585 (T) ... 54
Estate Kemp v McDonald's Trustee 1915 AD 491 ... 174
Estate Koopmans v Estate De Wet 1912 CPD 1961 ... 53, 143
Estate Levitas v Levitas' Minors 1962 (4) SA 385 (T) ... 208
Estate McIntyre v Burne 1957 (4) SA 488 (N) ... 54

Estate Orpen v Estate Atkinson 1966 (2) SA 639 (C) 126, 128
Estate Orpen v Estate Atkinson 1966 (4) SA 589 (A) 13
Estate Smith v Estate Follett 1942 AD 364 54
Estate Van Noorden v Estate Van Noorden 1916 AD 175 191, 193, 194, 195, 197
Estate Watkins-Pitchford v Commissioner for Inland Revenue 1955 (2) SA 437 (A) 126
Ex parte Administrator Estate Sandler 1976 (4) SA 930 (C) 120
Ex parte Administrators Estate Asmall 1954 (1) PH G4 (N) 101
Ex parte Administrators Estate Lesser 1940 TPD 11 119, 120
Ex Parte Basillie et Uxor 1928 CPD 218 230
Ex parte Berrange 1938 WLD 39 158
Ex parte Blomerus 1936 CPD 368 101
Ex parte BOE Trust Ltd, case no 211/09 of 27 May 2009 179, 189
Ex parte Boedel Steenkamp 1962 (3) SA 954 (O) 28, 101
Ex parte Burstein 1941 CPD 87 122
Ex Parte Calderwood: In Re Estate Wixley 1981 (3) SA 727 (Z) 227
Ex parte Davies 1957 (3) SA 471 (N) 52
Ex parte De Swardt 1998 (2) SA 204 (C) 82
Ex parte Dell 1957 (3) SA 416 (C) 215
Ex parte Dessels 1976 (1) SA 851 (D) 139
Ex parte Dodds 1949 (2) SA 311 (T) 121
Ex parte Eksekuteure Boedel Malherbe 1957 (4) SA 704 (C) 211, 212
Ex parte Engelbrecht 1956 (1) SA 408 (E) 14
Ex parte Estate Edwards 1964 (2) SA 144 (C) 121
Ex parte Estate Hack 1945 TPD 414 120
Ex parte Estate Marks 1970 (3) SA 539 (T) 219
Ex parte Estate Pitt-Kennedy 1946 (NPD) 776 123
Ex parte Estate Van Rensburg 1965 (3) SA 251 (C) 55, 56
Ex parte Esterhuyse 1971 (4) SA 261 (O) 141
Ex Parte Executors Estate Everard 1938 TPD 190 230
Ex parte F 1914 WLD 27 62
Ex parte Fleishman 1983 (4) SA 866 (E) 139
Ex parte Fourie's Estate 1927 EDL 185 70
Ex parte Froy: In re Estate Brodie 1954 (2) SA 366 (C) 211
Ex parte Gardner 1940 EDL 175 142
Ex parte Gibson 1928 OPD 189 209
Ex parte Gitelson 1949 (2) SA 881 (O) 119, 142
Ex parte Gouws 1952 (3) SA 793 (O) 144
Ex parte Govender 1993 (3) SA 721 (D) 14
Ex parte Henderson 1971 (4) SA 549 (D) 126, 127, 177, 179, 209
Ex parte Higgs: In re Estate Rangasami 1969 (1) SA 56 (D) 119 121
Ex parte Insel 1952 (1) SA 71 (T) 122
Ex parte Isaacs 1964 (4) SA 606 (GW) 119
Ex parte Jacobs 1982 (2) SA 276 (O) 122, 123
Ex parte Jeffrey 1922 CPD 260 101
Ex Parte Jewish Colonial Trust Ltd: In re Estate Nathan 1967 (4) SA 397 (N) 115, 212
Ex parte Kock 1952 (2) SA 502 (C) 121, 209
Ex Parte Kops 1947 (1) SA 155 (O) 208
Ex parte Kruger 1976 (1) SA 609 (O) 115

Ex parte Laxton 1998 (3) SA 238 (N) 80
Ex parte Lutchman 1951 (1) SA 125 (T) 88
Ex parte Macdonald 1947 (2) SA 150 (C) 136
Ex parte Malan 1951 (3) SA 715 (O) 144, 208
Ex parte Marais 1953 (4) SA 620 (T) 214
Ex parte Marks' Executors 1921 TPD 284 ..... 119, 120
Ex parte Marriott 1960 (1) SA 814 (D) 179
Ex parte Maurice 1995 (2) SA 713 (C) 54, 83
Ex parte Methodist Church of South Africa: In re Estate Corderoy 1965 (4) SA 789 (C) 209
Ex parte Mostert: In re Estate late Mostert 1795 (3) SA 312 (T) 121
Ex parte Mouton 1955 (4) SA 460 (A) 141
Ex parte Muller 1949 (4) SA 429 (O) 158
Ex parte Olfsen 1976 (1) SA 205 (W) 88
Ex parte Perel 1948 (3) SA 195 (GW) 120
Ex parte Pieters 1993 (3) SA 379 (D) 14
Ex parte President of the Conference of the Methodist Church of Southern Africa: In re William Marsh Will Trust 1993 (2) SA 697 (C) 117, 189
Ex parte Reay: In re McGregor's Estate 1982 (4) SA 27 (C) 128
Ex parte Roads 1978 (4) SA 649 (O) 140, 141
Ex parte Rungsamy 1958 (4) SA 688 (N) 14
Ex parte Saunders 1927 SWA 122 ..... 49, 50
Ex parte Schnehage 1972 (1) SA 300 (O) 116, 159
Ex parte Sidelsky 1983 (4) SA 598 (C) 219
Ex parte Sieberhagen 1946 CPD 83 121
Ex parte St Clair Lynn 1980 (3) SA 163 (W) 119
Ex parte Steenkamp and Steenkamp 1952 (1) SA 744 (T) 105, 107, 108
Ex Parte Stoter 1996 (4) SA 1299 (E) 14
Ex parte Stranack 1974 (2) SA 692 (D) 116
Ex parte Strümpfer 1945 OPD 268 ..... 141, 143
Ex parte Suknanan 1959 (2) SA 189 (N) 71
Ex parte Swanevelder 1949 (1) SA 733 (O) 119
Ex parte The Dutch Reformed Church of Dewetsdorp 1938 OPD 136 142
Ex parte Trustees Estate Loewenthal 1939 TPD 250 115
Ex parte Visagie 1940 CPD 42 101
Ex parte Vonzell 1953 (1) SA 122 (C) 106, 109
Ex parte Warren 1955 (4) SA 326 (W) 89, 90
Ex parte Watling 1982 (1) SA 936 (C) 115
Ex parte Weir's Executors 1939 CPD 340 209
Ex parte Wessels 1946 OPD 123 ..... 133, 142
Ex parte Williams: In re Williams' Estate 2000 (4) SA 168 (T) 80, 83
Executor of A. Neveling v Executor of P. Neveling (1909) 26 SC 196 215
Executors of Cerfonteyn v O'Haire (1873) 3 Buch 47 51

F

Ferreira v Die Bybelgenootskap van Suid-Afrika 1994 (2) Juta's Supreme Court Digest 9 (CPD 15 October 1993 Case 1652/93 (unreported) 85
Ferreira v Die Meester 2001 (3) SA 365 (O) 105
Ferreira v Otto (1883-1884) 3 SC 193 55

Ferreira v Smit 1981 (3) SA 1264 (A) 128
Finucane v MacDonald 1942 CPD 19 50
Fram v Fram 1943 TPD 362 119, 210
Fram v Fram's Executrix 1947 (1) 787 (W) 86, 89

G

Galant v Mahonga 1922 EDL 69 55
Galliers v Rycroft (1900) 17 SC 569 133
Geft v Gelbart 1984 (4) SA 515 (C) 166
Geldenhuys v Borman 1990 (1) SA 161 (E) 62
Glazer v Glazer 1963 (4) SA 694 (A) 122
Goldman v Executor Estate Goldman 1937 WLD 64 123
Gory v Kolver 2007 (4) SA 97 (CC) 18, 25, 26, 124
Govender v Ragavayah [2009] 1 All SA 371 (D) 18, 25
Greenberg v Estate Greenberg 1955 (3) SA 361 (A) 54 132, 146
Greyling v Greyling 1978 (2) SA 114 (T) 14, 203
Griessel v Bankorp Trust Bpk 1990 (2) SA 328 (O) 166
Grusd v Grusd 1946 AD 465 139, 160
Gumede v President of the Republic of South Africa 2008 ZACC 23 148

H

Harksen v Lane 1998 (1) SA 300 (CC) 179
Harlow v Becker 1998 (4) SA 639 (D) 78, 83, 84
Harpur v Govindamall 1993 (4) SA 751 (A) 68
Harris v Assumed Administrator, Estate MacGregor 1987 (3) SA 563 (A) 20, 21, 101
Harter v Epstein 1953 (1) SA 287 (A) 126, 208
Harvey v Estate Harvey 1914 CPD 892 144
Hassam v Jacobs unreported case CCT 83/08 [2009] ZACC 19 25, 27, 31, 124
Hassam v Jacobs [2008] 4 All SA 350 (C) 18, 25, 29, 124
Havemann's Assignee v Havemann's Executor 1927 AD 473 213, 214
Henwick v The Master 1997 (2) SA 326 (C) 94
Heymans v Van Tonder 1983 (2) SA 242 (O) 161
Hoffmann v Herdan 1982 (2) SA 274 (T) 122
Holley v Commissioner for Inland Revenue 1947 (3) SA 119 (A) 141, 215
Hoosen v Deedat 1999 (4) SA 425 (SCA) 182
Hoppen v Shub 1987 (3) SA 201 (C) 182
Hughes v The Master 1960 (4) SA 936 (C) 100

I

In re Crosbie's Estate (1910) 27 SC 50 218
In re Denton's Estate 1951 (4) SA 582 (N) 179
In re Estate of W.R. Shaw (1905) 26 NLR 3 71
In re Estate Visser 1948 (3) SA 1129 (C) 123
In re Graumann's Estate 1940 CPD 204 210
In re Intestate Estate of JF Manistry 17 NLR 149 230
In re Kemp (1844) 2 Menzies 435 62
In re Leedham (1901) 18 SC 450 49
In re Murray's Estate: Ex parte Mulhearn (1901) 18 SC 213 53, 143
In re Nortje 1956 (4) SA 180 (C) 86

In re Winter (1894) 15 NLR 287 49, 50
In the estate of Cook (deceased) Murison v Cook [1960] 1 All ER 689 (PDA) 68

J

J. M. Scheepers v C. F. Scheepers' Executrix (1873) 3 Buch 1 195
James v James's Estate 1941 EDL 67 85
Jeffrey v The Master 1990 (4) SA 759 (N) 74
Jewish Colonial Trust Ltd v Estate Nathan 1940 AD 163 115, 132, 140, 141, 207, 218
Jhajbhai v The Master 1971 (2) SA 370 (D) 68
Jooste v Jooste's Executor (1890-1891) 8 SC 288 196, 197
Joubert v Ruddock 1968 (1) SA 95 (E) 85
Jowell v Bramwell-Jones 1998 (1) SA 836 (W) 137
Jubelius v Griesel 1988 (2) SA 610 (K) 226

K

Katz v Katz [2004] All SA (4) 545 (C) 60, 61
Keeve and Keeve 1952 (1) SA 619 (O) 228
Kellerman v Van Vuren 1994 (4) SA 336 (T) 54
Kerkraad van die Nederduitse Gereformeerde Kerk, Douglas v Loots 1990 (3) SA 451 (NK) 141
Kidwell v The Master 1983 (1) SA 509 (E) 69
King v Nel 1922 CPD 520 71
Kinloch v Kinloch 1980 (2) SA 449 (N) 161
Kirsten v Bailey 1976 (4) SA 108 (C) 50, 51, 60, 61
Kohlberg v Burnett 1986 (3) SA 12 (A) 53, 175
Konyn v Viedge Bros (Pty) Ltd 1961 (2) SA 816 (E) 132
Kruger v Terblanche 1978 (2) SA 198 (T) 146, 161

L

L. Taylor v A.E. Pim (1903) 24 NLR 484 105
Land and Agricultural Bank v Parker 2005 (2) SA 77 (SCA) 183
Le Roux v Le Roux 1963 (4) SA 273 (C) 86, 89, 91, 92
Leeb v Leeb [1999] 2 All SA 588 (N) 106, 109
Lello v Dales 1971 (2) SA 330 (A) 164, 166, 210
Letsekga v The Master 1995 (4) SA 731 (W) 83, 94
Levy v Schwartz 1948 (4) SA 930 (W) 119
Lewin v Lewin 1949 (4) SA 241 (T) 62
Liebenberg v MGK Bedryfsmaatskappy (Edms) Bpk [2002] 4 All SA 322 (SCA) 71, 183
Liebenberg v The Master 1992 (3) SA 57 (D) 71
Loock v Steyn 1968 (1) SA 602 (A) 121, 122
Loots v Estate Loots 1923 CPD 238 194
Louw v Engelbrecht 1979 (4) SA 841 (O) 85, 88

M

Macdonald v The Master 2002 (5) SA 64 (O) 82
Makhanya v Minister of Finance 2001 (2) SA 1251 (D) 108
Marais v The Master 1984 (4) SA 288 (D) 85, 86, 87, 88, 95
Marks v Estate Gluckman 1946 AD 289 126, 209
Masters v Estate Cooper 1954 (1) SA 140 (C) 209

McAlpine v McAlpine 1997 (1) SA 736 (A) 224, 228, 229
McEwan's Estate v McEwan's Estate 1933 CPD 489 132
Mdlulu v Delarey [1998] 1 All SA 434 (W) 81, 85, 86, 94, 95
Metcalfe v Oates (1919) 40 NLR 202 197
Meyer v Rudolph's Estate 1918 AD 70 229
Mhlonhlo v Mhlonhlo 3 NAC 114 (1913) 113
Mijiet's Executors v Ava (1897) 14 SC 511 133
Millward v Glaser 1949 (4) SA 931 (A) 50
Minister of Education v Syfrets Trust Ltd 2006 (4) SA 205 (C) 117, 118, 122, 178, 179, 189
Morison v Executors of Morison (1879) 9 Buch 24 212
Morley v Standard Bank Trustees Department 1970 (4) SA 299 (W) 141
Moseneke v The Master 2001 (2) SA 18 (CC) 6, 236, 237, 256
Moses v Abinader 1951 (4) SA 537 (A) 92
Mosse v Estate Ebden 1913 CPD 567 195
Moyce v Estate Taylor 1948 (3) SA 822 (A) 55

N

Narshi v Ranchod 1984 (3) SA 926 (C) 88
Nel v The Master 1975 (3) SA 271 (T) 155
Nell v Nell 1976 (3) SA 700 (T) 109
Ngcobo v Ngcobo 1929 AD 233 201

O

O'Connor v The Master of the High Court [1999] 3 All SA 652 (NC) 68, 73
O'Dwyer v Estate Marks 1957 (1) SA 287 (A) 208
Olivier v Die Meester: In re Boedel Wyle Olivier 1997 (1) SA 836 (T) 79, 96, 97, 98
Oosthuizen v Bank Windhoek 1991 (1) SA 849 (Nm) 119
Oosthuizen v Die Weesheer 1974 (2) SA 434 (EC) 53
Oosthuizen v Sharp 1935 WLD 22 70
Oxenham v Oxenham's Executor 1945 WLD 57 55

P

Pieters v Van Rensburg 1926 OPD 94 209
Pillay v Nagan 2001 (1) SA 410 (D) 110, 111
Povall v Barclays Bank DCO 1965 (3) SA 322 (C) 211
Preller v Jordaan 1956 (1) SA 483 (A) 50
Price v The Master 1982 (3) SA 301 (N) 88, 89
Prinsloo v The Master of the Supreme Court (OFS) 1960 (3) SA 882 (O) 90, 91
Pritchard's Trustee v Estate Pritchard 1912 CPD 87 126, 141

R

Raabe v The Master 1971 (1) SA 780 (T) 86, 91
Radley v Stopforth 1977 (2) SA 516 (A) 73, 74, 75
Rampathy v Krumm 1978 (4) SA 935 (D) 147
Ramsumer v The Master (NPD) 1978 (4) SA 877 (N) 132
Rapson v Putterill 1913 AD 417 62
Re Beaglehole 1908 TS 49 14
Re Gibson (deceased) [1949] 2 All ER 90 70
Reek v Registrateur van Aktes, Transvaal 1969 (1) SA 589 (T) 161

Rhode v Stubbs 2005 (5) SA 104 (SCA) 143, 144, 145, 146, 147
Richter v Bloemfontein Town Council 1922 AD 57 210
Ritchken's Executors v Ritchken 1924 WLD 17 123
Robertson v Robertson's Executors 1914 AD 503 203
Robinson v Volks 2004 (6) BCLR 671 (C) 125
Rosenberg v Dry's Executors 1911 AD 679 146
Rubin v Altschul 1961 (4) SA 251 (W) 119
Ruskin v Sapire 1966 (2) SA 306 (W) 140

S

Samaradiwakara v De Saram 1911 AD 465 207
Schauer v Schauer 1967 (3) SA 615 (W) 226
Schaumberg v Stark 1956 (4) SA 462 (A) 162, 163, 214
Schnetler v Die Meester 1999 (4) SA 1250 (C) 115
Scott v Estate Scott 1943 (NPD) 7 119, 120
Secretary for Inland Revenue v Estate Roadknight 1974 (1) SA 253 (A) 54
Secretary SA Association v Mostert (1869) 2 Buch 231 146
Secretary SA Association v Mostert (1873) 3 Buch 31 53
Senekal v Meyer 1975 (3) SA 372 (T) 86, 87, 90
Sim v The Master 1913 CPD 187 49, 50
Smit v Du Toit 1981 (3) SA 1249 (A) 128, 141
Smith v Smith 1913 CPD 869 209, 210
Smith v Strydom 1953 (2) SA 799 (T) 62
Snyders v Snyders 1923 CPD 204 213
Sorge v Estate Preuss 1933 CPD 61 137
Spies v Smith 1957 (1) SA 539 (A) 50, 51, 60, 61,62
Standard Bank of SA Ltd v Betts Brown 1958 (3) SA 713 (N) 120
Standard Bank of SA Ltd v Estate C.J. van Rooyen 1927 (NPD) 300 146
Steenkamp v De Villiers (1892-1893) 10 SC 56 133
Steijn's Executors v Steijn (1894) 11 SC 55 196
Sterban v Dixon 1968 (1) SA 322 (C) 71, 72
Stevenson v Greenberg 1960 (2) SA 276 (W) 119
Stock v Keren Hayesod, Israel 1978 (4) SA 92 (WLD) 166
Swift v Pichanick 1982 (1) SA 904 (ZS) 55

T

Taylor v Pim (1903) 24 NLR 484 109, 110, 111
The Leprosy Mission v The Master of the Supreme Court 1972 (4) SA 173 (C) 71
The Receiver of Revenue Pretoria v Hancke 1915 AD 64 144, 146, 147
The Town Council of Bloemfontein v Bloemfontein Licensing Board and John Duff 1917 OPD 34 143
Theron v The Master of the High Court [2001] 3 All SA 507 (NC) 54
Thesnaar v Die Meester 1997 (3) SA 169 (C) 191, 192, 194, 196
Thienhaus v The Master 1938 CPD 69 54
Thirion v Die Meester 2001 (4) SA 1078 (T) 50, 51, 62, 83
Tijmstra v Blunt-MacKenzie 2002 (1) SA 459 (T) 181, 184
Tregea v Godart 1939 AD 16 60
Troitz v Trotsky's Executrix 1924 WLD 53 207
Tshabalala v Tshabalala 1980 (1) SA 134 (O) 69

U

Union Government (Minister of Finance) v Olivier 1916 AD 74 128

V

Van der Merwe v Registrateur van Aktes 1975 (4) SA 636 (T) 160
Van der Merwe v Sekretaris van Binnelandse Inkomste 1977 (1) SA 462 (A) 226
Van der Merwe v Van der Merwe's Executrix 1921 TPD 9 147
Van Huyssteen v Die Meester 1975 (4) SA 449 (W) 70
Van Jaarsveld v Van Jaarsveld's Estate 1938 TPD 85
Van Rensburg v Van Rensburg 1963 (1) SA 505 (A) 54
Van Soelen v Van Soelen 1964 (4) SA 24 (O) 140
Van Staden v Van Staden 1984 (4) SA 507 (T) 163
Van Wetten v Bosch 2004 (1) SA 348 (SCA) 82, 83
Van Wyk v Van Wyk's Executor (1887-1888) 5 SC 1 .... 49, 50
Van Zyl v Van Zyl 1951 (3) SA 288 (A) 153, 162, 214
Varkevisser v Varkevisser 1959 (4) SA 196 (SR) 227
Verseput v De Gruchy 1977 (4) SA 440 (W) 155, 209
Vickers' Trustees v Cloete 1914 CPD 575 141
Vimpany v Attridge 1927 CPD 113 88
Volks v Robinson 2005 (5) BCLR 446 (CC) 18, 26, 124, 125
Vorster v Steyn 1981 (2) SA 831 (O) 141

W

Wasserman v Sackstein 1980 (2) SA 536 (O) 132, 140, 161
Wasserzug v Administrators of Estate Nathanson 1944 TPD 369 120
Watson v Burchell (1891-1892) 9 SC 2 .... 55, 147
Webb v Davis 1998 (2) SA 975 (SCA) 132, 214, 215, 216, 217
Webster v The Master 1996 (1) SA 34 (D) 79, 84, 95
Weiner v The Master (1) 1976 (2) SA 830 (T) 54
Wepener v Estate Henning 1921 CPD 814 55
Wessels v DA Wessels en Seuns (Edms) Bpk 1987 (3) SA 530 (T) 141
Wessels v De Jager 2000 (4) SA 924 (SCA) 104
Wessels v Die Meester [2007] SCA 17 (RSA) 92, 93
Westminster Bank v Zinn 1938 AD 57 128
Whiting v Estate Whiting 1922 CPD 82 214
Will v The Master 1991 (1) SA 206 (C) 210
Winstanley v Barrow 1937 AD 75 166

Table of legislation

A

Administration of Estates Act 66 of 1965 ... 1, 6, 12, 79, 100, 101, 103, 145–147, 149, 175, 233, 236, 238–245, 247, 248, 255, 256
- Section 1 ... 242, 243
- Section 2A ... 238
- Section 3(2)–(3) ... 255
- Section 4 ... 243, 244, 255
- Section 4(1)–(1A) ... 238, 244
- Section 7–8 ... 244
- Section 9 ... 245
- Sections 14–8 ... 245
- Section 18(3) ... 242
- Section 23 ... 242
- Section 26 ... 245
- Section 28 ... 245
- Section 29 ... 245, 252
- Section 34 ... 241, 245, 248
- Section 35 ... 245, 247, 252
- Section 35(5) ... 247
- Section 37 ... 145–147, 149
- Section 38 ... 246
- Section 39 ... 101, 147
- Section 40 ... 175
- Section 43 ... 101, 103
- Section 43(1)–(2) ... 100
- Section 51 ... 243
- Section 56 ... 248
- Section 76 ... 101
- Section 80(2)(a)–(b) ... 101
- Section 90 ... 100
- Section 90(1) ... 100
- Section 103 ... 241, 255
- Section 103(1)(d) ... 243

Administration of Estates Amendment Act 47 of 2002 ... 235, 238

B

Black Administration Act 38 of 1927 ... 1, 2, 4, 5, 17, 23, 24, 27, 40, 45, 63, 84, 129, 233–240
- Section 1(4)(b) ... 4
- Section 22 ... 40
- Section 23 ... 4, 5, 23, 24, 40, 64, 84, 129, 235, 239, 240
- Section 23(1) ... 63, 129, 235, 236
- Section 23(2)–(3) ... 63
- Section 23(7) ... 237, 238
- Section 23(7)(a) ... 235, 237
- Section 31 ... 235
- Section 35 ... 2, 234

C

Children's Act 38 of 2005 ... 1, 22, 45, 59, 100
- Chapter 19 ... 22
- Section 17 ... 100
- Section 40 ... 22
- Section 297(2) ... 22

Children's Status Act 82 of 1987 ... 1, 22
- Section 5(2) ... 22

Civil Union Act 17 of 2006 ... 2, 11, 25, 26, 126, 205
- Section 1 ... 126
- Section 13(1) ... 126

Close Corporations Act 69 of 1984 ... 116

Constitution of the Republic of South Africa 200 of 1993 (Interim Constitution) ... 2, 24

Constitution of the Republic of South Africa, 1996 (Constitution) ... 2, 3, 16, 24, 26, 116, 117, 122, 125, 130, 178, 237
- Bill of Rights ... 125
- Section 9 ... 26, 117, 178, 237
- Section 9(3) ... 24, 122
- Section 9(4) ... 122
- Section 9(5) ... 118
- Section 10 ... 24, 26
- Section 15(3)(a)(i) ... 125
- Section 18 ... 122
- Section 21 ... 122
- Section 25 ... 178
- Section 211 ... 3

Criminal Procedure Act 51 of 1977 ... 72
- Section 1 ... 72

D

Deeds Registries Act 47 of 1937 ... 101, 175, 233

Section 25 101
Section 102 175

E

Electronic Communications and Transactions Act 25 of 2002 67
Estate Duty Act 45 of 1955 225, 231, 233, 241, 251
Section 2(1) 241
Section 3 241

G

General Law Amendment Act 62 of 1955 117
Section 33(1) 117
Government Service Pension Act 57 of 1973 108

I

Immovable Property (Removal or Modification of Restrictions) Act 94 of 1965 2, 116, 156, 159, 160, 170, 175, 220, 233
Section 2 116
Section 2(1) 160
Section 3 116
Section 6 116, 159, 170
Section 7 116, 159
Section 8 116
Income Tax Act 58 of 1962 175, 225
Section 55 225
Section 58 225
Insolvency Act 24 of 1936 103, 175
Section 2 175
Section 20 103
Sections 96–103 103
Intestate Succession Act 81 of 1987 2, 4–6, 8, 16–9, 22–28, 35–38, 45, 46, 103, 104, 112, 113, 124, 126, 201, 233, 235, 239, 240, 243, 266–269
Section 1 25
Section 1(1) 26
Section 1(1)(a) 27
Section 1(1)(b) 28-29
Section 1(1)(c) 29-32
Section 1(1)(d)(i)-(ii) 32-33
Section 1(1)(e)(i) 33-34
Section 1(1)(e)(i)(aa)-(cc) 33-34
Section 1(1)(e)(ii) 34
Section 1(1)(f) 35
Section 1(2) 22, 103, 113
Section 1(4)(a) 28, 32, 33
Section 1(4)(b) 5
Section 1(4)(d) 19
Section 1(4)(e) 23
Section 1(4)(f) 28, 29
Section 1(5) 23
Section 1(6) 28, 35, 36, 37
Section 1(7) 35, 112
Section 2 6
Section 2(2)(b)-(c) 38
Section 5 6

J

Justices of the Peace and Commissioners of Oaths Act 16 of 1963 72

K

KwaZulu-Natal Act on the Code of Zulu Law 16 of 1985 40, 148, 201, 236

L

Law of Evidence Amendment Act 45 of 1988 2, 3
Section 1(3) 3
Section 1(4) 2
Law of Succession Amendment Act 43 of 1992 17, 47, 77
Section 15 47
Long-term Insurance Act 52 of 1998 233

M

Magistrates' Courts Act 32 of 1944 204
Section 46(2) 204
Maintenance of Surviving Spouses Act 27 of 1990 2, 25, 26, 109, 116, 123–126, 130, 234
Section 2(1) 123
Section 2(3)(b)–(d) 123
Section 3(a)–(c) 123
Marriage Act 25 of 1961 2, 11, 45, 124, 126, 205
Marriage and Matrimonial Property Law Amendment Act 3 of 1988 40
Matrimonial Property Act 88 of 1984 29, 234

Mineral and Petroleum Resources Development Act 28 of 2002 116

P

Pension Funds Act 24 of 1956 116

R

Recognition of Customary Marriages Act 120 of 1998 2, 11, 147, 148, 234
- Section 1 2
- Section 7(1)-(2) 148

Reform of Customary Law of Succession and Regulation of Related Matters Act 11 of 2009 (RCLSA) 2, 6, 8, 11, 17, 27, 29, 31, 37-40, 46, 200, 240, 270-276
- Section 1 8, 38
- Section 2 11, 37, 39
- Section 3 39
- Section 3(3) 31
- Section 4-5 39
- Section 7 39
- Section 7(1) 39
- Section 7(2) 40

Repeal of the Black Administration Act and Amendment of Certain Laws Act 28 of 2005 64, 129, 240

S

Subdivision of Agricultural Land Act 70 of 1970 234, 246

Subdivision of Agricultural Land Act Repeal Act 64 of 1998 116, 234
- Section 1 234

T

Traditional Leadership and Governance Framework Act 41 of 2003 39

Trust Property Control Act 57 of 1988 2, 117, 171, 172, 174, 176, 179, 180, 183, 189, 190, 220, 234
- Section 1 171-174, 176, 190
- Section 4 180
- Section 4(1) 181
- Section 5 181
- Section 6 180
- Section 6(1) 180
- Section 6(4) 180
- Section 7 180
- Section 7(1) 180
- Section 9(1)-(2) 181
- Section 10 181
- Section 11-12 179, 181
- Section 13 117, 180, 189, 220
- Section 16 180, 181
- Section 17 182
- Section 19 186
- Section 20 180
- Section 20(1)-(2) 184
- Section 22 171

W

Wills Act 7 of 1953 2, 15, 20, 21, 47-49, 51, 52, 57, 59-68, 70-79, 84, 86, 93, 98, 102, 103, 111-113, 138, 152, 153, 164, 167, 176, 180, 204, 220, 224, 234, 257-265
- Schedules 1 and 2 73
- Section 1 48, 51, 68, 70, 78
- Section 2 49, 52
- Section 2(1) 48, 84
- Section 2(1)(a) 47, 65, 66, 176
- Sections 2(1)(a)(i) 66, 70, 72
- Section 2(1)(a)(ii) 66, 71, 72, 112
- Section 2(1)(a)(iii) 66, 71, 72
- Section 2(1)(a)(iv) 66, 69, 70, 72
- Section 2(1)(a)(v) 66, 67, 72, 73, 74, 75
- Section 2(1)(a)(v)(aa) 72, 75
- Section 2(1)(a)(v)(bb) 75
- Section 2(1)(b) 77
- Section 2(2) 77
- Section 2(3) 20, 21, 65, 74-76, 78-84, 91, 93, 96-98, 224
- Section 2A 79, 80, 85-88, 93-98
- Section 2A(a)-(c) 94, 95
- Section 2B 204, 205
- Section 2C 112, 138, 152, 153, 164, 167
- Section 2C(1) 152-155
- Section 2C(2) 152-155, 164
- Section 2D(1) 204, 205
- Section 2D(1)(a) 206
- Section 2D(1)(b) 103, 113, 206, 207
- Section 2D(1)(c) 15, 102, 206, 207
- Section 4 59-64, 180
- Section 4A 71, 111
- Section 4A(1)-(2) 111, 112
- Section 4A(2)(a)-(c) 111, 112
- Section 4A(3) 111

Bills

Reform of Customary Law of Succession and Regulation of Related Matters Bill 10B-2008 ..... 37, 240

Codes

Code of Zulu Law (KwaZulu Act on the Code of Zulu Law 16 of 1985 and the Natal Code of Zulu Law, Proc R151 of 1987, *GG* 10966 of 9 October 1987) 40, 148, 201, 236

Government notices and proclamations

GN R200 in *GG* 10601 of 6 February 1987 ..... 40, 235
Proc R151 in *GG* 10966 of 9 October 1987 ..... 40, 148, 201
GN 483 in *GG* 11188 of 18 March 1988 29
GN R609 of 31 March 1989 181
GN 903 in *GG* 19033 of 10 July 1998 72
GN R1501 in *GG* 24120 of 3 December 2002 ..... 235, 236, 238
GN R1318 in *GG* 25456 of 19 September 2003 ..... 100, 242

Ordinances

Political Ordinance of 1580 (section 29) 195

Regulations and rules

Administration of Estates
  Regulations 233, 245, 255, 256
  Regulation 5 ..... 247, 249
  Regulation 5(1)(a)-(c) 249
  Regulation 5(1)(d)-(e) 250
  Regulation 5(1)(f) -(i) 251
Black Administration Act
  Regulations 5, 45
Black Estates Regulations 40, 235-239
  Regulation 2 238
  Regulation 3 238
  Regulation 2(d) 236
  Regulation 3(1) 235-237
  Regulation 3(2) 236
  Regulation 4(1) 236
Intestate Succession .....
  Rule 1 27
  Rule 2 28-29
  Rule 3 29-32
  Rule 4 32
  Rule 5 32-33
  Rule 6 33-34
  Rule 7 34
  Rule 8 35
Trust Property Control Act Regulations
  Regulation 2 181
Uniform Rules of Courts,
  Rule 57(10), (12) 103

Index

Page numbers in **bold** refer to figures and tables.

A

absolute bequest **7**, **134**, 135–136, 138
accrual *(ius accrescendi)* **7**, 29, 30, 31, 36, 55, **55**, 109, 133, 138, 151, 152, 153, 163–166, 194, 252
  intention of testator 164–165
  statutory 153
  where intention not clear 165–166
ademption **7**, 89, 137
  revocation by 89
adiation **7**, 54–56, **55**, 56, 57, 144, 145, 146, 153, 214
  certificate 56
  consequences of 146
administration of estates 6, **7**, 39, 233–255
  administration process 244
  awarding/handing over of specific assets 245
  basic concepts of 241–244
  certificate 251
  estate duty addendum 251
  estate tax 241
  executor 242–243
  executor's duties 243
  executor's fees 243
  fiduciary assets account 251
  income and expenditure account 251
  jurisdiction of Master 243–244
  Master *see* the main entry for Master of the High Court
  meaning of 'estate' 241–242
  legal reform relating to black persons 234–241
  liquidation and distribution account 249–255, **250**, **251**
  partial sale 246
  recapitulation statement 247, 250, **254**
  redistribution agreement 246–247, 250
  service points 238, 240, 241, 244
  taking over by surviving spouse 246
  three phases 244–248
  total sale 246
  uniform rules for 241–255
Administration of Estates Act 66 of 1965 6, 12, **79**, 100, 101, 103, 145, 146, 147, 175, 233, 236, 237, 238, 239, 240, 241, 242, 243, 244, 245, 247, 248, 258, 260, 273, 274
Administration of Estates Amendment Act 47 of 2002 235, 238
animus testandi **7**, 48, 49–50, 51, **51**, 63, 220, 228
'armchair evidence' 5, **7**, 207, 208, 210, 211, 212, 214, 216, 217
ascendants **7**, 18, 27, 41, **154**, 191
attestation clause **7**, 69, 72

B

beneficiary(ies) **7–12**, 13, 14, 15–16, 20, 42, 45, 52, 53, 54, 55, **55**, 56, 61, 71, 77, 84, 89, 99, 100, 101, 102, 103, 104, 105, 106, 107, 108, 110, 11, 112, **112**, 113, 115, 116, 118, 120, 121, 122, 126, 127, 128, 129, 131, 132, 133, 134, 135, 136, 138, 139, 140, 141, 142, 143, 144, 145, 146, 147, 151, **152**, 152, 153, 154, **154**, 156, 157, 158, 159, 162, 163, 164, 165, 166, 169, 170, 171, **172**, 172, 173, 174, **174**, 175, 176, 177, 178, 179, 180, 181, 182, 183, 184, 185–188, 189, 192, 193, 194, 195, 196, 197, 198, 199, 200, 207, 214, 215, 216, 217, 218, 219, 220, 226, 227, 228, 230, 233, 234, 236, 240, 243, 245, 246, 247, 250, 251
  capital 145, 169, 173, 176, 177, 180, 181, 185, **186**, 187–188, 189
  income 13, 20, 145, 166, 169, 170, 173, 177, 180, 185, **186**, 186–187, 189
  nomination of 185
  qualifications of 185
  rights of 185–186, **186**
  types of **186**
beneficiaries (of a trust) 185–188
  bewind trusts 187

capital 187
discretionary trusts 186, 188
income 186–187
nomination of 185
non-discretionary trusts 186, 187–188
ownership trusts 187
qualifications of 185
rights of 185–186, **186**
types of **186**
bequeath **7**
bequest
absolute **7**, **134**, 135–136, 138
conditional **7**, 134, **134**, 139–140, 157, 214
Bill of Rights 81, 125, 205, 270
Black Administration Act 38 of 1927 1, 2, 4, 5, 17, 23, 24, 27, 40, 63, 84, 129, 233, 234, 235, 236, 237, 238, 239, 240, 268, 273, 276
section 23 declared unconstitutional 5, 64, 239

C

capacity to inherit 99–113
beneficiary causing death of deceased 105
bloedige hand maxim 105–106, 108–109
causation 107–108
consequences of disqualification 112
customary law of succession 113
forgery of a will 110
illegitimate children 103
indignus (unworthy person) 109–111
insolvents 103–104
juristic persons 104
major beneficiary 100
minor beneficiary 100–101
nasciturus (unborn) 101–103
(*see also* the main entry for *nasciturus* fiction)
natural persons may inherit 99
onus and evidence 106
persons disqualified from inheriting 105–112, **112**
persons involved in execution 111–112
persons of unsound mind 103
capacity to inherit intestate 22–23
adopted children 22
adulterine children 22
artificial fertilisation 22
extramarital children 22
incestuous children 22
natural persons may inherit 22
surrogacy 22
unborn children 22
Children's Act 38 of 2005 1, 22, 59, 100, 206, 275
Children's Status Act 82 of 1987 1, 22, 267
Civil Union Act 17 of 2006 2, **11**, 25, 26, 36, 126, 205
Close Corporations Act 69 of 1984 116
codicils 48, 51–52, 77, 82, 83, 93, 94, 96, 117, 258
collateral 18, 32, 37, 41, **154**, 215
definition 18
line 37, 268
collation *(collatio bonorum)* **7**, 136, 191–202
calculation 192–193, **192–193**
collatable benefits 196–198
definition 191
generic substitution 199
participants in 193–196
rationale behind 191
rights of surviving spouse 195
unequal treatment 196
valuation of benefits 198–200
whether or not to collate 200
colonialism 2
common law 2, 3, 5, 6, 21, 22, 38, 40, 47, 57, 61, 62, 86, 94, 95, 98, 103, 104, 105, 107, 108, 109, 111, 112, 117, 118, 119, 120, 121, 122, 126, 129, 130, 132, 145, 146, 162, 164, 167, 171, **172**, 180, 183, 188, 200, 201, 206, 207–217, 219, 221, 224, 231, 235, 241, 267
rules of interpretation (wills) 207–217
common law of succession 3, 4, 5, 12, 15, 17, 27, 37, 221
freedom of disposal of property 3
regulation of transfer of wealth of the deceased 3
commorientes **7**, 14
competent witness **7**, 66, 70, 71, 72, 76, 112, 258, 259, 263
compos mentis **7**, 51, 60
conditional bequest **7**, 134, **134**, 139–140, 157, 214

resolutive conditions 139
suspensive conditions 139–140
terminative conditions 139
conflict of laws 4–6
administration of estates 6
'armchair evidence' rule 5
changes to rules 5
conflicting rights and obligations
freedom of testation 4, 5
intestate law of succession 5–6
testate law of succession 4–5
vagueness in will 5
coniunctissimi **7**, 105, 106, 108, 109
Constitution of the Republic of South Africa, Act 200 of 1993 ('Interim Constitution') 2, 24, 26
Constitution of the Republic of South Africa, 1996 2, 3, 5, 24, 26, 116, 117, 121, 122, 125, 178, 205, 237, 239, 270
Bill of Rights 81, 125, 205, 270
Constitutional Court 5, 6, 16, 18, 23, 24, 25, 26, 64, 84, 124, 125, 129, 148, 167, 200, 237, 238, 239, 270
constitutional values 117, 122
equality 117
human dignity 117
non-racialism 117
non-sexism 117
constitutionality 23, 24, 239
contents of wills 131–148
(*see also* accrual (*ius accrescendi*); direct substitution; fideicommissary substitution; trusts; usufruct)
absolute bequests **134**, 135–136, 138
accrual 133
bequests 134–140, **134**
conditional bequests 134, **134**, 139–140
customary law of succession 147–148, 167, 190
estate massing 143–147, 148
modus/condition (obligation) 141–143
nudum praeceptum (nude prohibition) 140–141
time clauses 138–139
vesting of rights 132–134
contrary to public policy *(contra bonos mores)* 22, 104, 116, 117, 118, 119, 120, 122, 179, 218
Criminal Procedure Act 51 of 1977 72
curator **8**, **9**, **12**, 1001, 101, 103, 108, **172**
curator ad litem 108
curator bonis 103, 215
curatorship 62
customary house **8**, 271
customary law 2, 3, 4, 5, 6, **8**, **10**, **11**, 12, 17
living **10**, 17, 18
official **10**
property **8**
customary law of succession 3, 4, 5, 6, **11**, 12, 15, 16, 17, 24, 27, 37, 39, 40, 57, 63–64, 84, 98, 113, 129, 147–148, 167, 190, 200–201, 221, 231, 236, 240, 244, 247
application of choice of law rules 3
conflict between various customary laws 3
devolution of estates 6
may be amended by legislation 3
must be compatible with Constitution 3
modification of 271
preservation of family and community 3
customary law property **8**, 57
customary marriage 4, **8**, **10**, **11**, 24, 39, 40, 147, 148, 234, 235, 236, 270, 271, 272, 273, 276
definition of 'spouse' 271
disposition of property accruing to woman in 272
property rights 273

D

deceased estate 3, 5, **7**, **8**, 9, 13, 19, 31, 40, 123, 125, 129, **160**, 187, 233–252
administration of 233–252
Deeds Registries Act 47 of 1937 101, 175, 233
descendant(s) 5, **7**, **8**, **10**, **11**, 18, **19**, 19, 23, 27–35, **27**, **28**, **30**, **32**, **33**, **34**, **35**, 36, 37, 38, 41, 43–45, **43**, **44**, **45**, 113, 119, 120, 121, 127, 153, **154–155**, 155, 158, 159, 164, 188, 191, 192, 193, 194, 200, 201, 206, 212, 214, 221, 261, 266, 267, 268, 271, 272, 275
definition of 38, 271
development of law in South Africa 2
colonialism 2
common law 2

indigenous law 2
Roman-Dutch law 2
dies cedit **8**, 14, 15, 132, 133, 134, 135, 138, 139, 140, **160**, 162–163, 173
dies venit **9**, 15, 132, 133, 134, 135, 138, 139, 140, **160**, 162–163, 173, 187
direct substitution **9**, 11, 55, 138, 151, **152**, 152–156, 162, 187, 188, 214
ambiguous clauses 153
express 152–153
implied by law *(ex lege)* 153–156, **154–155**
doctrine of dependent relative revocation 91
doctrine of election 56–57, 144
donatio mortis causa 223, 229–230

E
Electronic Communications and Transactions Act 25 of 2002 67
English common law *see* common law
Estate Duty Act 45 of 1955 225, 233, 241, 251
estate massing **9**, 14, 57, 85, 143–147, 148, 170
adiation 144, 145, 146
consequences of 146–147
effecting of 144–145
later will 88–89
regulation of 145–146
repudiation 148
execution (of will) **9**, 49, 51, 61, 65, 75, 77, 78, 79, 80, 87, 92, 96, 209, 224
ademption 89
amendment of will 75, 77, 78
certification of 73, 75
defective 75
electronic 67
formalities 66–67, **66,** 75
persons involved in 111–112
signature 66, 75
executor **9**, **12**, 13, 47, 48, 54, 110, 111, 120, 123, 125, 127, 129, 133, 136, 137, 142, 143, 147, **172**, 187, 193, 194, 197, 200, 212, 213, 228, 234, 235, 236, 242–243, 244, 245, 246, 247, 248, 249, 263
duties of 24, 2515, 248
fees 243, 251
executorship 245
acceptance 245
letter of 245, 247, 249, 256
extrinsic evidence **9**, 210–212, 220

F
fideicommissary substitution **9**, **11**, 151, **152**, 153, 156–159, 162, 214
fideicommissum **9**, 52, 116, 119, 127, 128, 140, 141, 144, 145, 151, **152**, 156–159, **156**, 163, 167, 170, 171, 174, **174**–175, 207, 208, 214, 233, 251
conditional 157
difference between usufruct and 163
expressly created 157–158
forms of 157–159
impliedly created (tacit) 158–159
in diem 157
legal restriction on parties to 159, **160–161**
presumption against 162
residui 157–158
si sine liberis decesserit clause 158–159
special power of appointment 157
statutory restriction on 159
formalities **9**, **12**, 20
adiation 54
codicils 52
customary law 236
liquidation and distribution account 247, 249–255, **250**, **251**, **253–255**
redistribution agreement 247
succession 113
wills 20, 21, 47, 48, 49, 51, 52, 53, 59, 61, 62, 65–84, 86, 87, 88, 91, 92, 96, 97, 176, 220, 223, 224, 229, 230, 231, 234, 258–259, 262
formalities (wills) **9**, **12**, 20, 21, 47, 48, 49, 51, 52, 53, 59, 61, 62, 65–84, 86, 87, 88, 91, 92, 96, 97, 176, 220, 223, 224, 229, 230, 231, 234, 258–259, 262
acknowledgement of signature 72
additional 72–76
amendment of wills 77–78
attestation clause 72
certification 73–74, **73**
commissioner of oaths 73, 74, 75
concept of 'mark' 67–68
customary law of succession 84
dating of will 72

- defective execution 75
- definition of 'sign' and 'signature' 67
- electronic communication 67
- electronic format not permitted 66–67
- end of will 68–70
- execution of will 81–82
- flexible approach to interpretation 79
- guarding against fraud 75
- intention requirement 82–84
- interpretation of provisions 78–81
- meaning of witnessing 71
- method of execution 66, **66**
- oral will not possible 66
- order directing acceptance of will 78–79
- place where will should be signed 68–70
- proper execution 76
- signature by amanuensis 70
- signature/mark 66, 67–68
- strict approach to interpretation 79
- unfair discrimination 81
- witnesses 70–71
- written document 66–67

freedom of testation 4, 5, **9**, 39, 57, 63, 64, 115–130, 141, 223, 224, 225, 230
- bequests for charitable purposes 127
- common law limitations 117–118
- conditions interfering with marital relationship 118–121
- conditions limiting freedom of movement 121–122
- Constitution and 178–179
- constitutional limitations 122
- customary law of succession and 129–130
- delegation of power of appointment 127
- delegation to bearer of interim right 127–128
- exceptions to delegation rule 127–128
- fairness of limiting conditions 121
- faith clauses 120–121
- indirect limitations 122–126
- infringement of 146
- limitations on 116–126
- loss of 144
- maintenance of children 122–123
- maintenance of surviving spouse 123–126
- measure of 146
- power of appointment 126–128
- restriction of 224–225, 226, 227–229
- statutory limitations 116–117

G

General Law Amendment Act 62 of 1955 117

Government Service Pension Act 57 of 1973 108

ground rules of succession 12–16
- beneficiary must be alive or have been conceived 15
- beneficiary must be competent to inherit 16
- *commorientes* 14
- disappearance 13
- estate massing 14
- no presumption of simultaneous death 14
- person must have died 12–14
- presence of body 13
- presumption of death 13–14
- transfer of rights and duties 15

Guardian's Fund 100
- administration of, by Master 100
- disadvantage of 100

H

heir(s) 3, 4, **7**, **9**, **10**, 14, 15, 16, 19, 24, 104, 110, 113, 123, 133, 135, 136, 151, 163, 164, 170, 193, 194, 195, 196, 197, 200, 225, 234, 236, 239, 240
- disqualification of 35
- disqualified 35
- intestate 19, 21, 25, 35, 111, **112**
- repudiation 35, 55–56
- residual 55, **55**
- succession by representation 19

High Court 6, 78, 100, 101, 105, 108, 111, **112**, 115, 116, 117, 125, 148, **160**, **172**, 204, 211
- (*see also* Master of the High Court)
- Cape 124, 125

I

Immovable Property (Removal or Modification of Restrictions) Act 94 of 1965 2, 116, 159, 160, 170, **175**, 220, 233

Income Tax Act 58 of 1962 175, 225

indigenous law 2, 3

Insolvency Act 24 of 1936 103, 175

inter vivos **9**, 223, 224, 225, 227, 228
disposal of property 158
trusts 53, 169, 171, **172**, 175, 177, 183, 190, 234
interpretation of wills 203-221
acceleration of benefits 214-215
ambulatory nature of wills 214
'armchair evidence' *see* the main entry for 'armchair evidence'
'child'/'children' 205-207
common law rules of 207-217
computer-generated will 213
construction of will as a whole 209
context of will 207-208
customary law of succession 221
ex-spouses 204-205
finality of institution 214-215
golden rule 203-204
hierarchy of rules of interpretation 217
immediate vesting 214-215
implied provisions 212
iusdem generis rule 208
legal presumptions 213-217
maximum benefit 214-215
minimum burden 214-215
ordinary and plain meaning 207-209
presumption against disinherison 215-217
presumption against intestacy 213
rectification of wills 220
statutory rules of 204-207
three-month window period 205
variation of wills 218-219
writing/typing prevails over standard form wills 213
intestate succession 1, 4, 5-6, 16, 17-45, 54, 57, 102, 103, 111, 124, 132, 200, 224, 233, 243, 263, 266-269, 270, 271
ascendants **7**, 18, 27, 41
basic concepts 18
capacity to inherit intestate 22-23
collateral 18, 32, 37, 41
constitutional challenges 23-27
customary law of succession, reform of 37-45
(*see also* Reform of Customary Law of Succession and Regulation of Related Matters Act 11 of 2009)
descendant(s) 5, **7**, **8**, **10**, **11**, 18, **19**, 19, 23, 27-35, **27**, **28**, **30**, **32**, **33**, **34**, **35**, 36, 37, 38, 41, 43-45, **43**, **44**, **45**
disqualification 35-37
dying intestate 20
inheritance by representation 19
inheritance *per capita* 19
living customary law **10**, 17-18
official customary law **10**, 17-18
order of succession 27-35, **27**, **28**, **30**, **32**, **33**, **34**, **35**, 40-41
per capita succession 19
repudiation 35-37
rules of 54, 55, 111, 152, 192, 223, 239, 250
stirps/*stirpes* **11**, 18-19, **19**, **20**, 29, 30
succession by representation *(per stirpes)* 19
surviving spouse 37
(*see also* the main entry for surviving spouse (partner)/survivor)
vesting of intestate in heritance 20-21
Intestate Succession Act 81 of 1987 2, 4, 5, 6, **8**, 17, 18, 19, 21, 22, 23, 24, 25, 26, 27, 28, 35, 36, 37, 38, 39, 103, 104, 112, 113, 124, 126, 200, 201, 233, 235, 239, 240, 243, 266-269, 270, 271, 272, 273, 275

J

joint wills **9**, **10**, 13, 14, 53-54, 83, 85, 146, 170, 209, 230, **250**, **251**
juristic act **9**, **12**, 71
Justices of the Peace and Commissioners of Oaths Act 16 of 1963 72

K

KwaZulu Act on the Code of Zulu Law 16 of 1985 (KwaZulu) 40, 148, 201

L

Law of Evidence Amendment Act 45 of 1988 2, 3
law of succession
common 3, 4, 5, 12, 15, 17, 27, 37, 221
customary 3, 4, 5, 6, **11**, 12, 15, 16, 17, 24, 27, 37, 39, 40, 57, 63-64, 84, 98, 113, 129, 147-148, 167, 190, 200-201, 221, 231, 236, 240, 244, 247
dual character of 2-3
in the legal system 2

Law of Succession Amendment Act 43 of 1992 17, 47, 77

Law Reform Commission, South African 2

legacy **7**, **10**, 55, 77, 84, 88, 89, 96, 97, 135, 138, 192, 193, 194, 196

lapse of 137-138

pre- 136

legal capacity **10**, **12**, 59, 99, 104

limited 104

legatee(s) **9**, **10**, 16, 110, 123, 135, 136, 137, 138, 151, 152, 163, 164, 165, 193, 194, 200, 234

death prior to inheriting 138

destruction of bequeathed object 138

incapacity 138

insolvency of testator's estate 138

repudiation of legacy 138

letter of executorship 245, 247, 249, 256

letters of administration 235

liquidation and distribution account 21, 133, 192, 241, 242, 244, 245, 247, 248, 249–255, **250**, **251**, **253–255**

living customary law **10**, 17, 18

lobolo **8**, **10**, 201

Long-term Insurance Act 52 of 1998 233

M

magistrate(s) 6, 39, 72, 235, 236, 237, 239, 240, 247, 248, 256

(*see also* Master of the High Court)

service points 238, 240, 241, 244

Magistrates' Courts Act 32 of 1944 204

Maintenance of Surviving Spouses Act 27 of 1990 2, 25, 26, 109, 116, 123, 124, 125, 126, 234, 276

section 1 declared unconstitutional 125

male primogeniture, rule of **10**, 15, 16, 23, 24, 40, 41, 129, 167, 231, 270

declared unconstitutional 16, 167

Marriage Act 25 of 1961 2, **11**, 124, 126, 205, 273

Marriage and Matrimonial Property Law Amendment Act 3 of 1988 40, 273, 276

Master of the High Court 6, **7**, 21, 25, 39, 47, 54, 56, 78, 100, 101, 105, 107, 111, 112, **112**, 123, 124, 142, 143, 171, **172**, **175**, 180, 181, 183, 184, 204, 224, 234, 235, 237, 238, 239, 240, 241, 242, 243-244, 245, 246, 247, 248, 249, 273

adiation certificate 56

administration of estates 6, **7**, 39, 233–252

administration of Guardian's Fund 100

appointment of executors 242, 244

appointment of trustees 180

authorisation of mortgage or alienation 101

authorisation of trustees **172**

consent to alienate or mortgage property 101

Court's power of condonation 78

deferral of claim for maintenance 123

determination re: disqualification 111, 112, **112**

disputes 39, 273

fees 181, 243, 248, 249, 250, 254

functions of 238, 244

Guardian's Fund 100

interpretation of wills 204

jurisdiction of 39, 235, 238, 244, 273

letter of executorship 245, 247, 249, 256

letters of administration 235

liquidation and distribution account 21, 133, 192, 241, 242, 244, 245, 247, 248, 249–255, **250**, **251**, **253–255**

magistrates' offices subject to 240

order directing acceptance of will 78–79, 224, 260

referral to magistrate 6

removal of trustees 184

repudiation certificate 56

service points 238, 240, 241, 244

submission of will to 47

supervision of administration of estates by 6, 171, 234, 239, 241

supervision of execution of trusts **175**, 180, 181, 184

supervision of minors by 100

Matrimonial Property Act 88 of 1984 29, 234, 269

Mineral and Petroleum Resources Development Act 28 of 2002 116

modus/condition (obligation) **10**, 56, 141–143, 215, 217

difference between modus and condition 143

presumption in favour of modus 215, 217

types of 141–143

mortis causa **10**, 225, 227, 228
donatio 223, 229–230, 231
trusts 171, **172**, 174, 190, 234
mutual wills **10**, 53–54, 85, 143, 144, 145, 146, 147, 148, 212, 214, 252

N

nasciturus fiction 15, 101–103, 207
application of 102
Natal Code of Zulu Law, 1987 (Natal) (Proc R151 of 1987) 40, 148, 201
nudum praeceptum (nude prohibition) 140–141

O

official customary law **10**, 17
order directing acceptance of will 78–79

P

pactum successorium (succession by contract) 1, **7**, **9**, 223–232
absence of counterperformance 226
antenuptial contract 230
customary law of succession 231
definition 223
donatio mortis causa 223, 229–230
identification of 225–231
intention test 228–229
objections to 224–225
origin of prohibition of 224–225
restriction of freedom of testation 227–228
revocability test 226–227
tests used by courts 226
valid forms of 229
vesting test 228
Pension Funds Act 24 of 1956 116
per capita succession 19
Political Ordinance of 1580 ('Groot Placaet') 195, 269
polygyny **10**
polygamy **10**
polygynous family 44, **45**
polygynous marriage **10**, 24, 25, 37, 41, 42, 113, 124, 147, 234
succession in polygynous households 42
posthumous **10**
child 28
power of appointment **10**, 13, 116, 126–128, 176, 177
bequests for charitable purposes 127
conferment of 128, **152**, 177
delegation of 127, 129
delegation to bearer of interim right 127–128
fideicommissum *residui* 157–158
invalid 127
may not be delegated 127
special 127, 157
power of condonation 78
prodigal/prodigality **10**, 62, 99, 103
public policy 106, 108, 109, 121, 122, 123, 125, 126
contrary to *(contra bonos mores)* 22, 104, 116, 117, 118, 119, 120, 122, 179, 218
prevailing values of 111

Q

quid pro quo **10**
quitrent land *(erfpag)* 4, **10**, 63, 64, 235

R

recapitulation statement 247, 250, **254**
Recognition of Customary Marriages Act 120 of 1998 2, **11**, 31, 147, 148, 234, 271
customary law, definition 2
section 7(1) and (2) declared unconstitutional 148
rectification (of wills) **7**, **10**, 115, 208, 220
redistribution agreement 246–247, 250
Reform of Customary Law of Succession and Regulation of Related Matters Act 11 of 2009 (RCLSA) 2, 6, **8**, **11**, 27, 29, 31, 37–45, 200, 240, 266, 270–276
application of customary succession rules 42–45
contents of Act 37
definitions 38, 271
disposal of property held by traditional leader 273
disposition of property 272
disputes 39, 273
freedom of testation 39
interpretation 39, 272
modification of customary law of succession 271–272

order of succession in customary law 40–41
property rights 39–40, 273
succession in monogamous households 41–42, **43**, **44**
succession in polygynous households 42, **45**
traditional leaders 39, 273
Reform of Customary Law of Succession and Regulation of Related Matters Bill (B10B-2008) 37, 240
Regulations for the Administration and Distribution of the Estates of Deceased Blacks (GN R200 in *GG* 10601 of 6 February 1987) 40, 235, 236, 237, 238, 239
declared unconstitutional 5, 23, 40, 237, 239
Regulations for the Administration and Distribution of the Estates of Deceased Blacks, Amendment of (GN R1501 in *GG* 24120 of 3 December 2002) 235, 236, 238
Repeal of the Black Administration Act and Amendment of Certain Laws Act 28 of 2005 64, 129, 240
repudiation **10**, 35–37, 54–56, **55**, 56, 104, 134, 146–147, 195
certificate 56
consequences of 147
devolution of benefit 55–56
resolutive conditions **11**, 139, 140, **160**, 161, 163, 217
resolutive terms **11**, 163
resolutive time clauses **11**, **134**, 138, 163
revival of wills 92–93
not possible if will physically destroyed 93
revocation of wills 85-92, 93–98, 258, 260, 262
ademption 89
by court 93–98, 260
cancellation of will 95
customary law of succession 98
destruction of part of will 87
destruction of whole will 86–87
doctrine of dependent relative revocation 91
duplicate of original will 90
execution of later, conflicting will 88
express 87–88
freedom to revoke 85
implied 88–89
informal 87–88
legal issues 97–98
methods of revoking 86–89
presumptions concerning 89–90
Roman law 51, 101, 191, 224
Roman-Dutch law 2, 14, 17, 47, 51, 101, 105, 191, 195, 200, 224
authorities 200

S

service points 238, 240, 241, 244
si sine liberis decesserit clause **11**, **152**, 158–159
South African Law Reform Commission 2
spes (hope) **11**, 161, 216
stipulatio alteri (third person contract) **11**
stipulation(s)/provision(s) **11**, 13, 64, 128, 129, 131, 132, 166, 209, 218, 219, 231, 250
Subdivision of Agricultural Land Act 70 of 1970 116, 234, 246
Subdivision of Agricultural Land Act Repeal Act 64 of 1998 234
substitution **9**, **11**, 55, 96, 97, 112, 138, 151, **152**, 153, 155, 164, 173, **186**, 188, 194, 212
(*see also* direct substitution; fideicommissary substitution)
ex lege 15
generic 199
no provision for 187–188
successio ab intestato (intestate succession) 1, **9**, 224
(*see also* the main entry for intestate succession)
successio ex contractu (succession by contract) 1
(*see also pactum successorium* (succession by contract))
successio ex testamento (succession by testament) 1, **12**, 224
successio legitima (legitimate succession) 1
succession by contract *see pactum successorium* (succession by contract)
succession by representation *(per stirpes)* 19
succession to status **11**, 15, 40
surviving child/children 18, **19**, 20, 164
surviving *nasciturus* 15

surviving spouse (partner)/survivor 11, 13, 14, 18, 25, 26, 27-35, **27**, **28**, **30**, **32**, **33**, **34**, **35**, 36, 37, 85, 109, 116, 119, 125, 143, 144, 145, 146, 147, 148, 153, **154**, 170, 194, 195, 204, 209, 212, 215, 225, 234, 243, 244, 246, 249, **250**, 252, **253**
  maintenance of 123-126
  rights of 195
  taking over by 246
suspensive conditions **11**, **134**, 139-140, 141, 143, 161, 164, 216, 217
  fulfilment of 217
suspensive terms **11**
suspensive time clauses **11**, **134**, 138

T

terminative conditions **11**, **134**, 139, 140, **160**, 161, 163, 217
terminative time clauses **11**, **134**, 138
terminology 6, **7–12**
testamentary capacity **12**, 49, 50, 51, 59-64, 83, 84, 99, 110, 214
  animus testandi **51**, 63
  customary law of succession 63-65
  definition 59
  freedom of testation 63
  mental capabilities 60-63
  prescribed age 59-60
  volition 63
testamentary trusts *see* trusts
testamentary writing **12**, 48-53, 88
  codicils and 51-53
testate succession 1, 21, 47-57, 102, 103, 111, 132, 169, 224, 226, 233, 234
  (*see also* adiation; codicils; joint wills; mutual wills; repudiation; testamentary writing; wills)
  customary law of succession 57
  doctrine of election 56
Traditional Leadership and Governance Framework Act 41 of 2003 39, 271, 273
Trust Property Control Act 57 of 1988 2, 117, 171, **172**, 174, 176, 179, 180, 181, 183, 189, 220, 234
  inter vivos trusts 53, 169, 171, **172**, 175, 177, 183, 190, 234
  mortis causa trusts 171, **172**, 174, 190, 234
trustees 174, 180-185
  appointment 180
  authorisation 180
  breach of fiduciary duty 182
  duties of 180-182
  position of trust 183
  powers of 183-184
  termination of trusteeship 184-185
  voidable transactions 182
trusts 169-190
  amendment of provisions 188-189
  beneficiaries 185-188
  (*see also* the main entry for beneficiaries (of a trust))
  bewind **172**, 173
  clear trust object 177-178
  core elements of 179-180
  creation of binding obligation 176
  customary law of succession 190
  definition of 171
  delegation 177-178
  determined or determinable trust property 176-177
  discretionary 173
  fideicommissum 170-171
  fiduciary 174
  fiduciary position of trustee 179
  formalities 176
  history 171
  intention of creating 176
  inter vivos 169, 171, **172**, 175, 177, 183, 190
  lawful trust object 178-
  legal nature of 174-175
  legal persons 175
  mortis causa (testamentary) 171, **172**, 174, 190
  non-discretionary 173
  ownership **172**, 173
  ownership of assets 174
  principle of real subrogation 179
  requirements for creation of valid 176
  separate estates 179
  termination of 189
  testamentary 170-171, **172**, 174, 190
  trustees 174, 180-185
  (*see also* the main entry for trustees)

trusteeship as office 180
types of **172**
usufruct 170–171

U

unconditional bequest **7**, 134, 214, 217
usufruct 12, 13, 52, 99, 127, 128, 144, 145, 147, 148, 151, 162–163, 170, 171, 207, 212
difference between fideicommissum and 163
influence on *dies cedit* and *dies venit* 162–163
usufructuary 145, 163, 214

V

volition 50–51, **51**, 60, 63

W

ways in which succession takes place 1
absence of a valid will (intestate succession) 1
contract or agreement 1
valid will (testamentary succession) 1
wills 48–54
(*see also* the main entries for adiation; codicils; contents of wills; doctrine of election; formalities (wills); interpretation of wills; joint wills; mutual wills; repudiation; revival of wills; revocation of wills; testamentary writing; volition)
adiation 54–56, **55**, 56, 57
animus testandi 48, 49, **51**, 63
basic requirements for valid 49–51
codicils 48, 51–52
customary law of succession 57
definition of 48, **48**
doctrine of election 56–57
duress 50
force 50
formalities **9**, **12**, 20, 21, 47, 48, 49, 51, 52, 53, 59, 61, 62, 65–84, 86, 87, 88, 91, 92, 96, 97, 176, 220, 223, 224, 229, 230, 231, 234, 258–259, 262
freedom and capacity 50
joint 53–54, 83, 85, 146, 170, 209, 230, **250**, **251**
mistake 50
mutual wills 53–54
rectification of **7**, **10**, 115, 208, 220
repudiation 54–56, **55**, 56
testamentary writing 48–53
variation of 218–219
volition 50–51, **51**, 60, 63
Wills Act 7 of 1953 2, 15, 20, 21, 47, 48, 49, 51, 52, 57, 59, 60, 61, 62, 63, 65, 66, 67, 68, 71, 72, 73, 77, 78, 86, 93, 98, 102, 103, 111, 112, 113, 138, **152**, 152, 153, 164, 176, 180, 204, 220, 224, 234, 257–265, 271